Canadian Politics

CONCISE SECOND EDITION

Rand Dyck

Laurentian University

THOMSON

NELSON

Australia   Canada   Mexico   Singapore   Spain   United Kingdom   United States

To Joan,
the love of my life

THOMSON
NELSON

**Canadian Politics,
Concise Second Edition**

Rand Dyck

Editorial Director and Publisher:
Evelyn Veitch

Executive Editor:
Chris Carson

Marketing Manager:
Murray Moman

Developmental Editor:
Rebecca Rea

Production Editor:
Natalia Denesiuk

Production Coordinator:
Helen Jager Locsin

Copy Editor:
Karen Rolfe

Creative Director:
Angela Cluer

Cover and Interior Design:
Peter Papayanakis

Cover Photos:
CP Picture Archive (Fred Chartrand) (townhall meeting); PhotoDisc (leaf)

Compositor:
Nelson Gonzalez

Printer:
Webcom

**National Library of Canada
Cataloguing in Publication Data**

Dyck, Rand, 1943–
Canadian politics

Concise 2nd ed.
Includes bibliographical references and index.
ISBN 0-17-616928-8

1. Canada—Politics and government. I. Title.

JL75.D93 2002   320.971
C2002-900347-4

Contents in Brief

Preface   iv
1   Introduction   1

Part 1 The Societal Context   14
2   Regional Economic and Class Cleavages   15
3   French Canada and the Quebec Question   41
4   Aboriginal Peoples, Other Ethnic Groups, and Gender Issues   63
5   The Global Context of Canadian Politics   91

Part 2 Linking People to Government   116
6   Political Culture, Socialization, and Participation   117
7   The Mass Media and Public Opinion Polls   137
8   Elections and the Electoral System   155
9   Political Parties   179
10   Pressure Groups and Lobbying   203

Part 3 The Constitutional Context   224
11   The Canadian Constitution and the Charter of Rights and Freedoms   225
12   The Provinces and the Federal System   249

Part 4 Governing   267
13   The Executive   269
14   The Bureaucracy   293
15   Parliament   317
16   The Courts and the Administration of Justice   343

Glossary   363
Index   381

Contents

Preface   iv

1 Introduction   1
Chapter Objectives   1
The Political System   2
    Linking People to Government   4
    Government   5
    Completing the System   6
Foundations of Canadian Government Institutions   8
    The Parliamentary System   8
    Federalism   11
    Fusing the Parliamentary System with Federalism   12
Discussion Questions   13

Part 1 The Societal Context   14

2 Regional Economic and Class Cleavages   15
Chapter Objectives   15
Regional Economic Cleavages   16
    Distance and Division   16
    Regions, Provinces, and Territories   18
    Regional Economic Differences   20
    Regional Economic Conflicts   22
    Regional Economic Disparities   28
Class Cleavages   30
    Defining and Measuring Class   30
    The Upper Class   31
    The Middle Class   33
    The Working Class   34
    The Poor   36
Discussion Questions   38

3 French Canada and the Quebec Question   41
Chapter Objectives   41
Historical Overview of French–English Relations   42
    Pre-Confederation Developments   42
    Post-Confederation Conflicts   43

Quebec Nationalism 45
The French-English Cleavage, 1960–82 46
    The Quiet Revolution: Quebec in the 1960s 46
    Quebec-Canada Relations, 1970–82 49
French–English Relations in the Other Provinces 50
Quebec-Canada Relations since 1982 52
    The Meech Lake Accord 52
    The Charlottetown Accord 55
    The Chrétien Government Record and the 1995 Referendum 58
The Future of French–English Relations 60
Discussion Questions 61

4 Aboriginal Peoples, Other Ethnic Groups, and Gender Issues 63
Chapter Objectives 63
Canada's Aboriginal Peoples 64
    History and Numbers 64
    The Condition of Aboriginal Peoples 65
    Aboriginal Political Issues since 1970 66
Other Ethnic Groups and Multiculturalism 74
    Canadian Immigration Patterns 74
    Multiculturalism and Related Policies 77
    Reaction against Multiculturalism and Immigration 79
The Women's Movement and Other Gender Issues 80
    Evolution of Women's Rights to 1970 80
    The Women's Movement since 1970 82
    Gay and Lesbian Issues 86
Discussion Questions 87

5 The Global Context of Canadian Politics 91
Chapter Objectives 91
The Road to Canadian Sovereignty from Britain 92
The American Sphere of Influence 93
    Defence and Foreign Policy 94
    Economic Policy 95
    American Influence on Canadian Culture 102
Globalization 106
    Foreign Governments 107
    International Organizations 107

International Agreements   109
Transnational Corporations   111
Discussion Questions   112

Part 2 Linking People to Government   116

6 Political Culture, Socialization, and Participation   117
Chapter Objectives   117
Political Culture   118
Democracy   118
Distinguishing between Canadian and American Values   120
The Changing Canadian Political Culture   124
Political Socialization   125
Agents of Socialization   126
Political Participation   130
Electoral Participation   131
Nonelectoral Participation   133
Discussion Questions   135

7 The Mass Media and Public Opinion Polls   137
Chapter Objectives   137
The Mass Media   138
The State of the Media   138
The Changing Media World: Convergence in Canadian Media
Ownership   142
The Media and the Public   143
The Media and the Politicians   145
Public Opinion Polls   147
Measuring Public Opinion   148
Impact of Polls on the Public   149
Impact of Polls on the Authorities   151
Discussion Questions   152

8 Elections and the Electoral System   155
Chapter Objectives   155
The Election Organization   156
Drawing the Electoral Map   156
The Official Election Organization   157

The National Party Campaign   161
The Local Candidate Campaign   164
Evaluating the Electoral System   165
Financing Elections   170
Third-Party Advertising   172
Electoral Behaviour and Party Support   173
Electoral Behaviour   173
Party Support   175
Discussion Questions   176

9 Political Parties   179
Chapter Objectives   179
The Functions of Political Parties   180
Historical Evolution of Canadian Political Parties   181
1867–1921   181
1921–93   182
1993–Present   185
The Number and Kinds of Parties   186
Broker Parties   186
Class-Based and Ideological Parties   187
One-Party Dominance   189
Minor Parties   189
The Decline of Parties?   190
Party Organization   191
Party Membership   191
Party Leadership   192
Party Policymaking   193
Party Conventions   194
Federal–Provincial Party Links   194
Party Ideology   195
Discussion Questions   199

10 Pressure Groups and Lobbying   203
Chapter Objectives   203
The Functions of Pressure Groups and Lobbying   204
The Array of Canadian Pressure Groups   204
Business Groups   204
Nonbusiness Groups   205

Other Categorizations of Pressure Groups   207
Pressure Group Structures   208
Targets and Methods of Pressure Group Activity   210
The Bureaucracy   211
The Cabinet   212
Parliament   213
Other Targets   214
Group Resources and Determinants of Success   216
Lobbying in Canada   218
Registration of Lobbyists   218
Discussion Questions   222

Part 3 The Constitutional Context   224

11 The Canadian Constitution and the Charter of Rights and Freedoms   225

Chapter Objectives   225
Early Political institutions   226
The Road to Confederation   228
Components and Principles of the Canadian Constitution   229
The Constitution Act, 1867, and its Amendments   229
British and Canadian Statutes   230
The Constitution Act, 1982   231
Judicial Decisions   232
Constitutional Conventions   232
Principles of the Constitution   232
The Charter of Rights and Freedoms   233
Guaranteed Rights and Freedoms   235
Limitations on Rights and Freedoms   243
Implications of the Charter for the Political System   244
Discussion Questions   246

12 The Provinces and the Federal System   249

Chapter Objectives   249
The Confederation Settlement   250
Division of Powers   253
Federal–Provincial Finance   254
Federal Controls   260
Canadian Federalism Today   261

Cooperative Federalism   261
The Decline of Cooperative Federalism   262
Discussion Questions   265

Part 4 Governing   267

13 The Executive   269
Chapter Objectives   269
The Policymaking Process   270
The Crown   273
The Prime Minister and Cabinet   275
Powers of the Prime Minister and Cabinet   275
The Prime Minister   278
Composition of the Cabinet   281
Operation of the Cabinet   284
Cabinet Support Agencies   287
Discussion Questions   289

14 The Bureaucracy   293
Chapter Objectives   293
Functions and Powers of the Bureaucracy   294
Government Departments   295
Relations with Other Departments and Central Agencies   299
Staffing the Bureaucracy   300
The Estimates System   301
Interaction with Provinces and Pressure Groups   303
Crown Corporations   303
Administrative Agencies and Regulatory Tribunals   305
Controlling the Bureaucracy   307
Reform of the Bureaucracy: The New Public Management   310
Discussion Questions   314

15 Parliament   317
Chapter Objectives   317
Functions and Powers of the House of Commons   318
Composition of the House of Commons   319
The Parliamentary Timetable   320
The Typical Session   320
The Typical Week   321

Party Discipline and the Caucus   323
Stages and Kinds of Legislation   326
Officers and Procedure of the Commons   328
    The Speaker   328
    House Leaders, Party Whips, and Clerks   328
    Procedure in the Commons   329
The Committee System   330
Members' Roles and Services   332
The Government–Opposition Balance and Parliamentary Reform   334
The Senate   335
    Purposes and Powers   335
    Composition of the Senate   336
    Operation of the Senate   338
    Senate Reform   339
Discussion Questions   340

16 The Courts and the Administration of Justice   343
Chapter Objectives   343
Functions and Powers of the Courts   344
    Access to and Costs of Justice   345
Categories of Laws   346
Structure of the Courts   348
    Provincial Courts   349
    The Superior Trial Court   350
    Provincial Courts of Appeal   350
    The Federal Court of Canada   351
The Supreme Court of Canada   352
The Appointment of Judges   353
Retirement, Removal, and the Independence of Judges   356
Policing and the Correctional System in Canada   358
    Policing in Canada   358
    The Canadian Correctional System   359
Discussion Questions   360

Glossary   363

Index   381

Preface

This is the second edition of the concise version of *Canadian Politics*, which was first published in 1998 for those who wanted a briefer and less detailed version of *Canadian Politics: Critical Approaches*. As in the case of the original edition, this book is most appropriate for first-year university courses and community college use.

This book addresses Canadian government and politics in two separate but equal parts, either of which can be studied first. Chapters 2 through 10 could be classified as "politics," and chapters 11 to 16 could be called "government." In this way, the book remains a comprehensive treatment of the whole subject, although it is more factual and less analytical than *Critical Approaches*.

This edition continues to emphasize the societal setting in which most political activity originates, including regional–economic and class cleavages; the French and Quebec questions; Aboriginal, other ethnic, and gender issues; and external forces. Part Two turns to linking people to government, including political culture, socialization, and participation; the mass media and public opinion polls; elections and the electoral system; political parties; and pressure groups and lobbying. Part Three deals with the constitutional context, including the Constitution, the Charter of Rights and Freedoms, and federalism. Part Four, "Governing," comprises chapters on the executive, the bureaucracy, Parliament, and the courts.

Apart from updating and refining the material covered in the first edition, the book is distinctive in that it is accompanied by its own Web site, which is intended to be used as an integral part of studying the book. On the Web site you will find the following items:

1. regular updates of material in the book that has changed
2. constitutional documents, such as parts of the Constitution Act, 1967, the Constitution Act, 1982 (including the Charter of Rights and Freedoms), and the 1987 Meech Lake Accord.
3. relevant Web links for each chapter
4. additional discussion questions
5. detailed citations for important Supreme Court decisions

It should be added that Nelson Thomson Learning also maintains a more general political science Web site at polisci.nelson.com, which supplements the one for this specific book.

Nelson Thomson Learning also offers a new 90-minute videotape featuring two- and three-minute television news clips, compiled from the CTV network archives, that correspond to each chapter of the book. The segments were chosen to amplify some of the concepts found in the book and provide topical discussion material. More detailed information on these news items, including discussion questions, is provided in the Instructor's Manual. Instructors can also avail themselves of a test bank and overhead transparency masters. In addition, Nelson Thomson Learning has prepared a student workbook to accompany this book.

I hasten to extend my thanks to everyone who helped me in the preparation of this book. Many individuals and organizations were generous in providing information, and I have a particular affection for the cartoonists who permitted their work to be used. Glen Milne deserves special appreciation for allowing me to use his humorous depiction of the policy marketplace from his book, *Making Policy*. I am very grateful for the many constructive suggestions contributed by reviewers of the manuscript: Sheila Bell, Durham College; Mike Burke, Ryerson Polytechnic University; Sandra Burt, University of Waterloo; Anne Charles, Conestoga College; David Close, Memorial University; Lee Farnworth, Algonquin College; James B. Haaland, Kwantlen University College; Robert Keaton, Dawson College; Randy Knapp, Sir Sandford Fleming College; Miriam Lapp, University of Western Ontario; Ronald J. MacDonald, Lethbridge Community College; David Model, Seneca College; Robert Schwab, University of Saskatchewan; Richard Sigurdson, University of New Brunswick; and Martin W. Westmacott, University of Western Ontario.

These suggestions have greatly improved the final product. I would also like to thank my colleagues at Laurentian University for their answers to my queries and general support.

As usual, it was a delight to work with the staff of Nelson Thomson Learning. I personally interacted most regularly with Rebecca Rea, Kelly Torrance, Chris Carson, Natalia Denesiuk, and Murray Moman, but there were many others behind the scenes who also contributed their magical talents to this production. I thank them all most warmly. Finally, as usual, my wife Joan provided the most supportive home environment imaginable.

Rand Dyck

Chapter 1

Introduction

Politics and government are often seen in a negative light, although anyone reading this book is probably already open to the excitement and importance of the subject. How a whole society makes collective, public decisions is a fascinating question. Political personalities are often as interesting as movie stars, and the conflicts between them and their respective teams are as hard-fought as any hockey game. Politics often brings out the worst in human nature—ambition, selfishness, greed, and the will to control—but it is sometimes characterized by the best—an altruistic desire to serve the public interest and to improve the lives of those less fortunate. Politics and government may be the only way to solve many societal problems, and may well be the best way to solve some of your own!

Chapter Objectives

After you have completed this chapter, you should be able to:

Identify the many ways in which government action does or could affect your life

Understand how politics and government can be encompassed into the concept of a political system and be able to draw a model of that system

Explain the basic function of each of the major institutions of Canadian government, including the prime minister and cabinet, House of Commons, Senate, bureaucracy, and judiciary

Appreciate the concentration of power in the executive branch of the government of Canada

Compare the basic differences between the Canadian and American systems of government regarding the separation of powers, party discipline, and the framework of federalism

....

The Political System

Perhaps it is best to begin with the 31 million residents of Canada. All these individuals have an array of needs that they attempt to satisfy, ranging from water, food, and shelter through security and friendship to self-esteem and self-fulfillment. Some of these needs will be felt personally and individually, although others are concerns that we share with people of similar position, in small or large groups. Most of us spend much of our time trying to satisfy such needs.

In the first instance, we do so by our own efforts, in pairs, in families, in organizations of all kinds, at work and at play. We do not automatically call for government help. At some point, however, we may begin to feel that the satisfaction of such needs is beyond such personal, interpersonal, family, or group capacity, and come to the conclusion that the government should step in to help us. When we express the opinion that the government should take some action, we are converting a "need" into a "demand" and crossing the threshold between the **private sector** and the **public sector.** We can therefore say that a demand is the expression of opinion that government take some action (or desist from an action that it is already taking).

The first fundamental question that arises in politics and government is therefore whether people should "solve their own problems" or whether they should ask the government or the state to intervene. Almost everyone agrees that the government should provide certain security measures, such as police services and armed forces. Most also support public highways and a public education system. People are more divided, however, on the extent to which the government should provide such programs as social assistance, social housing, public pensions, and universal health care. One of the main reasons for such divisions of opinion is that government intervention normally costs money, and usually relies on taxes of one kind or another. People also disagree on which areas of life the state should regulate, and how much regulation is appropriate.

The largest group of people reading this book will be young students, some of whom have probably not yet given too much attention to the role of government in their lives. But if they do, they will find many interesting questions come to mind. To what extent should I be expected to pay for my postsecondary education, and to what extent should it be financed by the state? Why do tuition fees keep increasing, and what form and level of student assistance is most appropriate? In travelling to school or work, should the state (provincial or municipal) provide a transit system and/or subsidize bus or subway fares? Should the state (federal or provincial) intervene to regulate the price of gasoline? If living away from home, should students' housing needs be negotiated with a private landlord, should the province regulate the rental market, or should the municipality, university, or college provide public housing? Should there be a minimum wage, and if so, what is an appropriate rate? Should all colleges and universities be public institutions, or is private postsecondary education a good idea?

Many of these and other questions go beyond one's status as a student. For example, should affluent people be able to get quicker medical attention because they can pay for such health care, or should Canada's be a universal system where no one can "jump the queue"? Should the public health care system be extended to pharmaceuticals and dental care?

Should the state put more restrictions on gasoline exhaust and other environmental hazards, or should companies be unrestricted in pollution emissions because of the need to provide jobs? What about municipal antismoking bylaws? How far should the state go in prohibiting discrimination in the workplace? Should it engage in employment equity programs to enhance the employment prospects of those discriminated against in the past? Should the federal government enact a national daycare program? Should people be able to enjoy pornographic materials, or should these be censored by the state? Such a list barely scratches the surface of questions involving potential government action, but serves to demonstrate the relevance of government to our daily lives. Of course, it is generally true that the more we rely on government, the more money it will have to raise through taxation.

Figure 1.1   A Model of the Political System

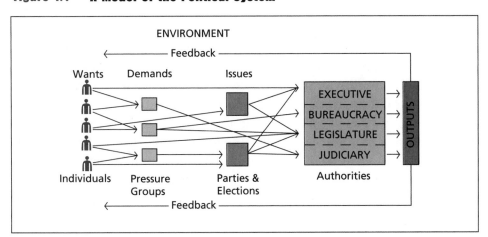

Linking People to Government

Both those who have the knowledge and other resources to seek state intervention, which may well exclude a large proportion of those on the margins of society, and those who prefer to tell the authorities to leave them alone must transmit their demands to the government. Figure 1.1 (see page 3) shows the different ways for individuals to transmit a demand to the government. This can be done on a personal basis, by means of a letter, fax, telephone call, e-mail, or face-to-face encounter. Sometimes such directly transmitted demands will achieve their desired result, but very often they will not. When they do not, it may be time to consider some kind of group action. Canadian society contains many groups, and it is quite likely that a group already exists to articulate the demand that any individual decides to transmit to the government. If such a group is not already in existence, it may be worthwhile to create one since, as a general rule, the authorities are more likely to respond to a demand coming from a group than from a single individual. Such groups are usually called **interest groups** or **pressure groups** and constitute an important part of Canadian political activity. The Canadian Chamber of Commerce, the Canadian Labour Congress, and the Canadian Federation of Students are prominent examples. Corporations and other institutions also make demands, either individually or in groups.

A special kind of group that is even more overtly political is the **political party,** and it can also be used to transmit demands to the government. People join a political party or support it financially, and try to get it to recognize their concerns in its platform or policies. If the party comes to power, it can incorporate the demand into government policy; if the party is in opposition, it may be able to use the media to bring the problem to national attention. Parties are particularly responsive to such demands during an election campaign, as they appeal for the support of large numbers of individuals and groups by promising them the action they seek. Those dissatisfied with the manner in which existing parties are responding to their demands can create new parties, such as the Reform Party (now the Canadian Alliance) and the Bloc Québécois.

Another means of transmitting the demand to the government is, as suggested earlier, via the **mass media** of communication. The media are usually eager to publicize controversial issues and often delight in pointing out problems that the government has failed to resolve. Although there is a potential problem of media bias, they give attention to individual and interest group concerns on a regular basis, cover political party activities, and are especially active in election campaigns, all of which helps to bring demands to the attention of the government. On the other hand, the media also provide the electorate with most of its information about politics, and in doing so, serve to shape the whole nature of political discourse in Canada. All of these aspects of linking people to government are covered in Chapters 6 to 10.

Despite the various avenues that can be used to transmit demands to the government, relatively few have any impact. The authorities are likely to ignore demands that do not concern very many people or that are contrary to their own values. Since the number of demands under serious consideration at any given time is such a small proportion of the total number being made, it is sometimes useful to distinguish between demands and "issues," the latter including only those demands that the government has taken under serious consideration. It should be added that the authorities can make their own demands, which sometimes carry more weight than those arising from the wider society.

Government authorities are thus bombarded by demands from all directions, but what is even more striking than the vast quantity of demands is that there is usually intense conflict among them. The essence of politics and government, therefore, is choosing among competing demands, trying to resolve conflict, or making social choices in the midst of social conflict. **Politics** involves that activity in which conflicting interests struggle for advantage or dominance in the making and execution of public policies.

Government

Having repeatedly mentioned **government,** we may now define it as the set of institutions that make and enforce collective, public decisions for a society. We must also deal with the concept of **power,** which is often defined as the ability of one actor to impose its will on another, to get its own way, to do or get what it wants. Government, backed up by armed forces, police, and punishments, if necessary, possesses a particular kind of power called **coercion.** That is, the government has the ability to impose its will upon us by means of sanctions or penalties. Indeed, as a general rule, only the government, as an agent of the state, is allowed to use force or coercive power in society. But if we (or our ancestors) had a hand in the creation of such a government apparatus, as well as in the selection of the current governors, then we have in a sense agreed to be bound by its decisions, and we have cloaked it with legitimacy. Legitimacy can be defined as "being accepted as morally binding." Such legitimate power is often called authority, and a synonym for government is "the authorities." To some extent we obey the government because of the threat or expectation of penalties if we do not, but we also obey because we accept government decisions to be binding upon us and necessary for the general good. Think of stopping at a red light or paying income taxes, for example.

Who are these government authorities? As can be seen in the diagram in Figure 1.1, we usually divide them into four branches: the **legislature,** the **executive,** the **bureaucracy,** and the **judiciary.** The authoritative decision that a demand seeks can sometimes be made by a single branch of government. The legislature or Parliament passes laws, so if the demand requires the passage of a law, then action of the legislative branch will be necessary. The executive, consisting of the prime minister and cabinet, has a wide variety of powers. These include deciding where the government will spend money and appointing people to public positions. Thus, if the demand can be satisfied by an appointment or large monetary grant, it should be addressed to the executive. The bureaucracy is made up of public servants who work for the government, providing services and advising the politicians. If the demand is for the provision of routine government services or for changes in regulations, then bureaucratic action will probably suffice. Finally, the judiciary comprises the courts, which interpret the laws and make other decisions in case of dispute, and if the demand can be settled only by a judicial decision, it should be transmitted in that direction.

In many instances, however, the demand will require the combined actions of any two of the executive, legislative, and bureaucratic branches, or even all three working together, such as in the formulation, passage, and implementation of a new law. The courts normally stand somewhat apart from the other three organs of government. Judicial decisions usually follow authoritative actions in other branches of government, such as when the Supreme Court threw out the abortion provisions of the Criminal Code as being a violation of the Charter of Rights and Freedoms. But judicial decisions may also lead to subsequent legislative action: when the Supreme Court ruled that a total ban on tobacco advertising was unconstitutional, the government introduced a revised law with fewer restrictions on tobacco advertising.

Government decisions take many forms—laws, regulations, appointments, grants, contracts, services, and judgments—and can be collectively referred to as the "outputs" of the political system. Authoritative decisions are also made in the provinces and in an assortment of regional and local councils and boards, and often require the agreement of two or more levels of government.

Completing the System

Whatever the type of output, it usually sparks a reaction in the rest of the system. This leads us to the concept of "feedback"—that is, a communication of the out-

The Parliament Buildings, Ottawa—the seat of the Government of Canada
(Peter Bregg/CP Picture Archive)

puts back into the system. If an output satisfies a particular demand, that demand will no longer have to be articulated. Take the federal Official Languages Act as an example, where many French-speaking Canadians demanded that their language be regarded as equal to English in government operations. The Pearson and Trudeau governments, who grasped at the opportunity to counter nationalism in Quebec, enacted the Official Languages Act as a result. But that was not the end of it: there was feedback or reaction to such a decision. On the one hand, some francophones then demanded French-language services at the provincial as well as the federal level. On the other, many anglophones protested that the act (as well as Quebec language legislation favouring French) went too far. Thus, the reaction to one demand created a new pattern of demands, and especially in Quebec, the language issue is still very much alive. The political system is thus a dynamic, circular process in which the authorities react to demands, convert some of them into outputs, and then respond in turn to whatever changes in the pattern of demands have resulted from the feedback from such outputs.

Individuals and groups raise conflicting demands, but because there is a widespread consensus on the legitimacy of the government, people generally abide by its authoritative decisions, even when they disagree with them. (A current exception includes dissenters on gun registration). It is sometimes said, therefore, that politics and government are characterized by both conflict and consensus. The daily conflict normally operates within an underlying consensus about the decision-making apparatus and about remaining together as part of a united political community. Moreover, the authorities usually seek to develop some kind of consensus out of the conflicting demands.

Many of these demands arise from deep, persistent divisions within society that are sometimes called "cleavages." The cleavages in Canadian society that generally have the greatest political significance are those between the geographic regions; between English, French, Aboriginal, and other ethnic and linguistic groups; and between various socioeconomic classes. Other common cleavages are related to gender, religion, and age. The relative importance and nature of these cleavages changes over time, and they are the subject of Chapters 2, 3, and 4.

The modern world is composed of some 200 states such as Canada, and each has a government that makes its public decisions. With only a few exceptions, each state claims its own **sovereignty,** that is, to be self-governing; it has the final say over its own territory and people. But today's world is characterized by a tremendous amount of interplay among such states as well as cross-border inter-action and movement in terms of individuals, corporations, other organizations, and information. States often join international organizations and sign interna-tional agreements, and transnational corporations operate around the world. These developments comprise the concept of **globalization.** Beyond the internal demands discussed above, such external actions increasingly serve as the source of demands on national political systems and as constraints upon domestic policy-making. As noted in Chapter 5, external pressures often lead government into actions that it otherwise would not take, and no state is as sovereign as it would like to be. The terrorist attacks on the United States in September 2001 remind us that terrorism is another external force in the modern world.

Foundations of Canadian Government Institutions
The Parliamentary System

Before going any farther, it would be useful to outline more specifically the basic institutions of government in Canada, which are dealt with in detail in Chapters 11 to 16. Within the central or national government in Ottawa (often called the "federal government"), the British parliamentary system provides the foundations of these governmental institutions. This system is based on the popular election of the members of the House of Commons. Parliament also has a second or "upper" chamber, the Senate, whose members are appointed by the prime min-ister. Such a two-chamber legislature is labeled "bicameral." The third part of Parliament is the monarch or the Crown. Because it was a British colony at the time the Constitution was adopted in 1867, Canada automatically shared the

British monarch. The current monarch, Queen Elizabeth II, still resides in Britain, so on a practical daily basis, her representative, the governor general, exercises the functions of the Crown.

Although the British system is called **parliamentary government,** such a label is somewhat misleading. The core of the parliamentary system, even in 1867, was the executive branch—the prime minister and the cabinet. Although they must be members of Parliament, they are such an important part of Parliament that they often relegate both the monarch and other members of the House of Commons and Senate to a position of insignificance. Like the executive of any organization, the prime minister and cabinet are given the powers to lead and make the most important decisions. But the principle of **responsible government** holds that they retain their position and powers only as long as they are supported by a majority in the House of Commons. If the House of Commons declares a lack of confidence in the prime minister and cabinet, they must either resign, making way for another group to take their place, or call an election. Because the prime minister and cabinet ministers have seats in the legislative branch, mostly the House of Commons, the system is often termed a "fusion of powers"—that is, it involves a combination of legislative and executive powers.

Evidence that the parliamentary system is executive-dominated can be seen in that the prime minister and cabinet ministers are given the power to introduce most legislation and the right to control most of the agenda of the legislature. They have the exclusive power to introduce legislation of a financial nature— laws either to raise or to spend money. They have other wide powers: of appoint- ment, to draft subordinate legislation under the authority of laws, and in

Figure 1.2   An Outline of Canadian Political Institutions

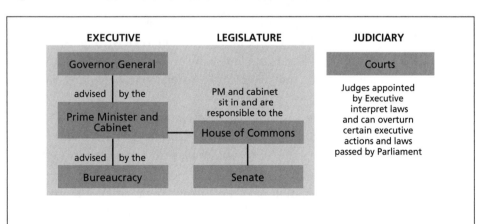

international affairs—essentially all powers necessary to provide effective political leadership for the country. Other members of Parliament may criticize, delay, and propose amendments, but the prime minister and cabinet almost always get their way. This is so because a majority of the members of Parliament normally belong to the same political party as the prime minister and cabinet, and together they constitute a **majority government.** In this situation, prime ministers impose rigid party discipline on their MPs to support their every move.

The significance of the Senate has declined since Confederation because arriving there by appointment rather than election diminishes its members' legitimacy in a democratic age. The powers of the Senate have remained virtually equal to those of the House of Commons, but senators have rarely felt it proper to exercise them. Moreover, independent behaviour has been discouraged by the fact that the same party has usually held a majority both in the Senate and in the Commons. If for any reason the Senate should ultimately defeat a government bill, it does not affect the constitutional standing of the prime minister and cabinet. The model outlined here is also operational in each of the provinces, except that they all possess one-chamber (unicameral) legislatures.

Government was small and simple at the time of Confederation, but it has gradually developed another important branch, the bureaucracy or public service. The bureaucracy essentially advises the prime minister and cabinet on their decisions and then carries out whatever government programs have been authorized. The current Canadian bureaucracy consists of over 350 000 public servants who make a vast array of government decisions.

The British parliamentary system also incorporates the principle of **judicial independence.** Although courts are established by acts of Parliament, and judges are appointed by the prime minister and cabinet, the whole judicial system is expected to operate independently of the executive and legislative branches of government. In the case of Britain itself, judges have considerable discretion in interpreting laws but lack the power of **judicial review,** that is, the power to declare them invalid. The Canadian judiciary soon appropriated to itself the power to invalidate laws that violated the federal–provincial division of powers, but was otherwise quite restrained.

Since the Canadian institutional structure was established in 1867, the only major change has been the adoption of the **Charter of Rights and Freedoms** in 1982. It expanded the scope of judicial review to include the new task of protecting individual rights and freedoms. Henceforth, the courts could disallow federal or provincial legislation or other government actions that violated the Constitution in terms of either the division of powers or the Charter of Rights and Freedoms.

The British parliamentary system is distinct in many ways from the presidential-congressional system of the United States. There, the president and the two houses of the legislature are independently elected, and no one is permitted to sit in more than one branch of government. The "separation of powers" means that executive, legislative, and judicial powers are distributed to three separate branches of government: president, Congress, and the courts respectively. Moreover, as indicated in Figure 1.3, the U.S. system is also characterized by a maze of "checks and balances" designed to ensure that the actions of any one branch of government are subject to veto by another. Members of the House of Representatives and the Senate have much more legislative power than their counterparts in the parliamentary system, in terms of both initiating bills themselves and amending or vetoing those emanating from the executive. Party discipline is also much looser, so that even if a majority of the members of Congress belong to the same party as the president, there is no guarantee that the legislature will pass the president's initiatives. The Supreme Court also has the power of judicial review and can overturn any legislation that it feels is in violation of the Constitution.

Figure 1.3   U.S. System of Separation of Powers and Checks and Balances

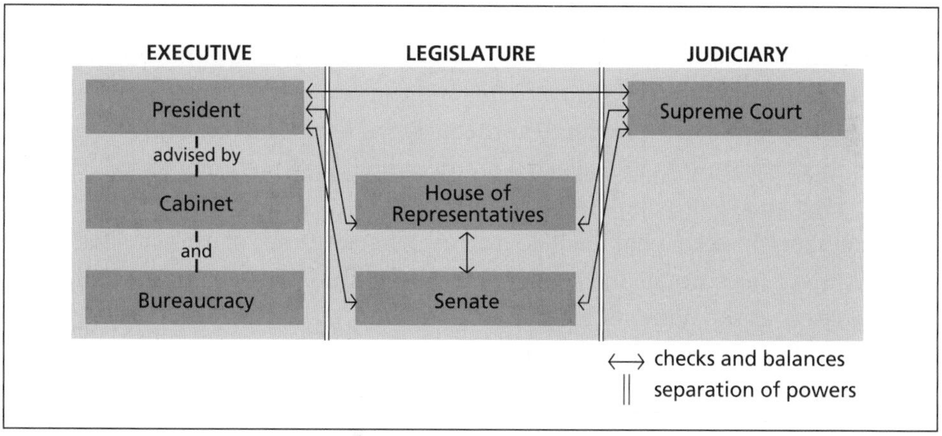

Federalism

The Fathers of Confederation were dealing with a large piece of territory, and were contending with colonies that had separate identities and a previous semi-autonomous existence. In this respect, the new country would have to be a **federation** of some kind, with a division of powers between the central and provincial governments.

Confederation was to a large extent the work of Sir John A. Macdonald, who went on to become the first Canadian prime minister. Macdonald preferred a unitary state or legislative union in which the new central government would have almost all the powers, and the provinces would be little more than municipalities. But Quebec and the Maritimes were not prepared to join such a system. Quebec demanded an autonomous provincial government so that its cultural concerns, such as education and civil law, would be placed in the hands of a French-speaking majority. Hence, the logical compromise was a system that contained a central government to deal with common purposes and provincial governments to look after local concerns.

Macdonald accepted a federal form of government, allowing the former colonies to retain some of their political and economic independence, but he intended the new country to be a highly centralized federation. He felt that its economic and defensive objectives required a strong central government, a conviction reinforced by the conclusion among most of the other Fathers of Confederation that the American Civil War (which was ending just as they began their deliberations) had been the result of too much power at the state level. Thus, at their creation, the Canadian and American federations were quite different. The U.S. deliberately established a weak central government and strong states, while Canada preferred a strong central government along with weak provinces.

Besides dividing powers between the two levels of government, constitutional architects in both the United States and Canada had to decide how the provinces or states would be represented at the national level. In both cases, the lower house of the legislature would be based on the principle of representation by population, so that the most populous provinces or states would have the largest number of members in that chamber. To protect the interests of the smaller states, the United States decided that each state, regardless of population, would have two senators at the national level. Some Fathers of Confederation also preferred this idea, but others wanted representation by population in both houses of Parliament. The Canadian compromise was to base the Senate on the principle of equal regional representation rather than equal provincial representation.

Fusing the Parliamentary System with Federalism

The basic governmental institutions established in 1867 thus combined the parliamentary system from Britain with a more centralized form of federalism than that found in the United States. But the whole ethos underlying the Canadian and U.S. systems was different. In the parliamentary system, everything is designed to *facilitate* government action by concentrating power in the hands of the executive, both in terms of its relationship with other institutions of government such as Parliament and the courts, and with territorial units such as local and regional governments. In the American system, everything is designed to *inhibit* government action by preventing the concentration of power in the hands of any government. The individual institutions of the national government are able to veto each other and are collectively kept in line by a division of powers that gives most authority to the states. It is largely because the British system is designed to facilitate government action whereas the American system is designed to inhibit it that the fusion of the two systems in Canadian Confederation was such a distinctive creation. Macdonald saw the contradiction and therefore tried to establish a federal system that was much more centralized than that next door. He would turn over in his grave if he saw how powerful Canadian provinces have become and how much of a constraint they are on the actions of the national government!

As well, all provinces in Canada have found it convenient to delegate certain powers to local municipal governments. These are often headed by a mayor and council, usually include a separate school board, and sometimes incorporate other local elected or appointed authorities. Their responsibilities vary from province to province, and sometimes within a province, but municipal governments are often very significant. Unlike the federal–provincial division of powers, which is laid out in the Constitution, municipal governments are subordinate to provincial governments, and their responsibilities and taxing powers can be expanded or contracted at the province's whim. Municipalities typically have more responsibilities than their taxation powers can support, leading them to plead for increased provincial (or federal) funding.

This book concentrates on the federal or national system of government in Canada, but does not deny the significance of the provinces and municipalities.

DISCUSSION QUESTIONS

1. What do you think are the most pressing issues facing Canada as it enters the 21st century?
2. What can or should the government do about each of these issues?
3. Do you feel you are part of the political process? What could you do to be more involved?

PART 1

The Societal Context

The next four chapters deal with the main elements of the societal or socioeconomic context of the Canadian political system. The aspects of Canadian society most relevant to politics are its regional economic, ethnic, and class features, primarily because they represent deep, persistent divisions called cleavages. In modern times, gender issues have also become a prominent feature of Canadian politics. Many of the demands with which the authorities have to contend originate from such cleavages.

Beyond the four factors mentioned are the external forces that also affect the Canadian political system. The world has become a "global village," and international, multinational, transnational, and supranational—that is, "global"—factors are important elements of any national political system. This is especially true of Canada, which has always been open to such external influences.

Chapter 2

Regional Economic and Class Cleavages

Canada's deep-seated geographic and economic divisions are some of its most obvious characteristics. Such regional economic cleavages are a daily fact of Canadian political life, and many government decisions are direct responses to them. These cleavages can be most usefully discussed in terms of distance and division, regional economic differences, regional economic conflicts, and regional economic disparities. But economic divisions also exist in nongeographic class terms; that is, disparities and conflicts among individuals with different levels of income and varied degrees of economic power. Governments must also deal with such class conflicts on a regular basis.

Chapter Objectives

After you have completed this chapter, you should be able to:

Discuss how distance and division and the distribution of population affect the operation of the Canadian political system

Identify the principal regions in Canada and the relationship between regions and provinces

Identify the key economic factors that distinguish one region from another

Enumerate the principal historic regional economic conflicts in Canada, especially those that give rise to a feeling of western alienation

Discuss different means of measuring regional economic disparities and measures that have been adopted to reduce them

Define the concept of class

Identify the traditional demands made by the upper class, middle class, and working class

Discuss the causes, extent, and implications of poverty in Canada

Regional Economic Cleavages
Distance and Division

Canada's tremendous distances have always had a crucial influence on its political system, especially in generating regional economic demands. The difficulties of dealing with such distances are immensely complicated by divisions caused by natural physical barriers running essentially in a north–south direction. Canada is usually divided into seven geographic regions, as shown in Figure 2.1.

The Great Lakes–St. Lawrence water route is an important means of linking several such regions to each other, rather than to neighbouring states to the south. Otherwise, however, transportation and communications linkages in Canada had to be constructed across natural barriers. Demands to overcome distances and divisions have featured prominently in Canadian politics, and the establishment of some of these great transportation and communications projects has dominated whole eras of Canadian history. Governments have responded primarily by giving assistance to private corporations, establishing their own Crown corporations, and creating regulatory agencies in these fields.[1]

Figure 2.1   Canada's Geographic Regions

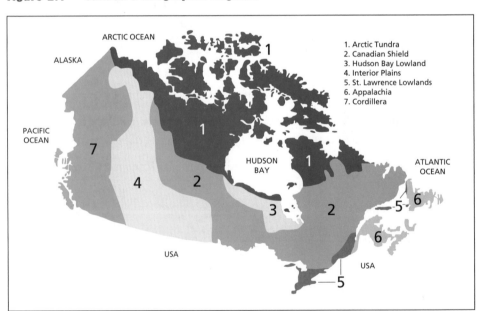

The major transportation and communications links and agencies with which the federal government has been associated are as follows:

- Canadian Pacific Railway
- Canadian National Railway
- VIA Rail
- Trans-Canada Highway
- Trans-Canada Airlines/Air Canada
- Trans-Canada Pipeline
- Canadian Broadcasting Corporation (CBC)
- Canadian Radio-television and Telecommunications Commission (CRTC)
- Telesat
- Teleglobe

In short, in order to create and hold together a nation, Canadians built east-west institutions that ran counter to the natural north-south geographic features of the continent and the perpetual pull of the United States. These ultimately included satellite services linking Canadians domestically (Telesat) and to the rest of the world (Teleglobe). In recent years, however, successive federal governments have deregulated, privatized, or reduced financial support for a number of these government operations.

Since people are not spread uniformly throughout this gigantic territory, the distribution of population also complicates the distances involved in Canada. The overall density of the Canadian population is one of the lowest in the world, but it is really more significant that there is no permanent settlement in nearly 90 percent of the country and that 75 percent of the population is huddled together within 150 kilometres of the U.S. border. The population of the various provinces in the 1996 census and in 2000 can be seen in Table 2.1. Provincial population disparities affect the allocation of seats in the House of Commons—indeed, the whole power structure in Ottawa—and the calculation of federal transfer payments. Quebec is sensitive to the fact that in recent years its proportion of the total Canadian population has fallen below a symbolic 25 percent.

Ontario and Quebec combined contain about 62 percent of the population, and the Toronto–Ottawa–Montreal triangle obviously constitutes the "core" or "heartland" of Canada. While central Canada forms the political core of the country, it is also the economic heartland, with more large corporate head offices, especially in the Toronto area, than anywhere else in the country. Moreover, it is the communications and cultural core, containing the headquarters of English and French CBC, CTV, CanWest Global, and private French television, the

TABLE 2.1 POPULATION OF PROVINCES AND TERRITORIES

	1996 Census		July 1, 2001	
Ontario	10 753 573	(37.3%)	11 874 400	(38.2%)
Quebec	7 138 795	(24.7%)	7 410 500	(23.8%)
British Columbia	3 724 500	(12.9%)	4 095 900	(13.2%)
Alberta	2 696 826	(9.3%)	3 064 200	(9.9%)
Manitoba	1 113 898	(3.9%)	1 150 000	(3.7%)
Saskatchewan	990 237	(3.4%)	1 015 800	(3.3%)
Nova Scotia	909 282	(3.2%)	952 700	(3.0%)
New Brunswick	783 133	(2.7%)	757 100	(2.4%)
Newfoundland	551 792	(1.9%)	533 800	(1.7%)
Prince Edward Island	134 557	(0.5%)	138 500	(0.4%)
Northwest Territories	64 402	(0.2%)	40 900	(0.1%)
Yukon	30 766	(0.1%)	29 900	(0.1%)
Nunavut	—		28 200	(0.1%)
Canada	28 846 761		31 081 900	

Source: "Population of Provinces and Territories," adapted from the Statistics Canada Web site: www.statcan.ca/english/Pgdb/ People/population/demo02.htm (Retrieved 16 Nov. 2001)

national newspapers, many other Canadian cultural institutions, and much of the Canadian computer industry. The rest of the country, the "periphery" or "hinterland," regularly complains that it is overlooked by both public and private decisionmakers, given such a concentration of population at the centre.

Regions, Provinces, and Territories

In speaking of **regionalism** in Canada, then, we begin with great distances complicated by geographic barriers and concentrations of population that cause variations in political and economic power. In addition, it is partly because of such distances and divisions that provinces and territories were created. The constitutional basis of such units is somewhat different from the natural, geographic basis of regions, however, and the fit between regionalism and provincialism is not perfect. Feelings of regionalism can exist within a province, such as in the northern parts of many provinces; regional sentiment can cut across provinces, as in the

Figure 2.2 Canada's Provinces, Territories, and Capitals

case of people in northwestern Ontario feeling psychologically closer to Manitoba than to southern Ontario; and provinces can be lumped together into regions, such as the Maritimes or the Prairies. Nevertheless, as the 1979 Task Force on Canadian Unity pointed out, "the provinces ... are the basic building blocks of Canadian society and the logical units on which to focus a discussion of Canadian regionalism, even though they may not be the most 'natural' regions from an economic point of view."[2] It could be added that the creation of such provinces served to enhance regional sentiment, as provincial politicians became exponents of regional problems and protectors of provincial interests.

In the 1990s, Quebec came closer than ever before to separating from the rest of Canada. If it were to leave with its existing borders intact (a somewhat debatable issue), Quebec would take with it almost one-quarter of the Canadian population, about 16 percent of the territory, and nearly 22 percent of Canada's gross domestic product. From a strictly geographic point of view, the separation of Quebec would raise the question of continuing transportation links between Atlantic Canada and Ontario, border-crossing impediments, and jurisdiction over the St. Lawrence Seaway.

Regional Economic Differences

A discussion of the economies of the Canadian regions and provinces reveals striking regional economic differences that serve to reinforce their geographic distinctiveness and create another pattern of demands facing the Canadian political system.

Regional economic differences begin with primary industries or the natural resource base of the various provinces. The importance of natural resources to the national economy has been a central tenet of Canadian political economy for generations, usually termed the **staples theory** and identified with economic historian Harold Innis.[3] It postulates that Canadian economic development has relied on a succession of resource exports—furs, fish, timber, wheat, minerals, and energy—rather than manufacturing; Canadians are mere "hewers of wood and drawers of water."

Secondary industry consists of manufacturing, construction, and utilities. Manufacturing includes the initial processing and refining of primary products as well as the making of finished goods. Generally speaking, it produces more revenue and more jobs than primary industry, is less seasonal, and commands higher wages. Primary and secondary industries are often combined as "goods-producing" industries.

Economists put transportation and communications, trade, finance, insurance and real estate, private services, and public administration into the "tertiary" or "services-producing" category. Manufacturing was never an important factor in the Canadian economy, and much political attention in this postindustrial era is focused on the services sector. The tertiary sector now furnishes about three-quarters of the employment in the country.

THE ATLANTIC PROVINCES

The Atlantic provinces have a distinctive and heavy reliance on fishing. This industry fell into deep trouble in the 1990s, primarily due to a dramatic reduction in cod stocks, but the abundance of shellfish has led to a partial recovery. The three Maritime provinces have a substantial agricultural base, while New Brunswick, Newfoundland, and Nova Scotia also engage in forestry and mining, and Newfoundland possesses great quantities of hydroelectric power in Labrador. Some processing and refining of natural resources takes place in the region, but the small local market and the distance from major population centres have left the region in a state of underdevelopment. Led by New Brunswick, however, a new emphasis on communications technology has revitalized the Atlantic provinces' economies to some extent, for in the modern technological world, physical distance is not the hindrance it was in the past. The Hibernia offshore oil project has already had an economic impact on Newfoundland, as has the Sable Island offshore gas project on Nova Scotia, and when the nickel mine is developed at Voisey's Bay in Labrador, it will also provide badly needed income and employment.

QUEBEC

The Quebec economy is more diversified than that of the Atlantic region and somewhat more prosperous. Quebec's outstanding primary industries include farming in the St. Lawrence Lowlands, and mining and forestry in the Canadian Shield. The Shield is also traversed by numerous powerful rivers, making hydro-electricity Quebec's most valuable resource. Huge dams have been built on many of its rivers, including the controversial James Bay hydroelectric project. Hydro is the basis of Quebec's aluminum industry, as well as many other secondary industries. Quebec also stands out in the production of pulp and paper, especially newsprint, and is much stronger than the Atlantic region in the more sophisticated aspects of manufacturing, including aeronautics and pharmaceuticals. It also houses a large financial sector. The fact that economic power in Quebec used to rest largely in Anglo-Canadian and foreign hands fuelled the nationalist debate in that province. But since 1960 a major transformation has occurred, and both the public and francophone private sectors in Quebec have repatriated a great deal of industrial ownership.

ONTARIO

Ontario has always had the most diversified and strongest economy of any region. The province has an abundance of natural resources, including a great expanse of prime agricultural land in the south, and vast stretches of trees and almost every conceivable mineral in the Canadian Shield. Ontario's early development of hydroelectricity and of a steel industry gave it a head start over other regions. A skilled labour force, a large domestic market, proximity to the United States, and the advantage of federal tariff and banking policies also helped to make it the manufacturing heartland of the country. Sparked by the auto industry, it now produces over half of the Canadian manufacturing total. In addition, Ontario leads the country in the tertiary sector, such as finance, trade, and other services.

THE PRAIRIE PROVINCES

The Prairie provinces are historically associated with agriculture, especially wheat, other grain, and livestock. Alberta doubles as Canada's petroleum province and has become the richest part of the country by almost any measure. Petroleum is also of increasing significance in Saskatchewan, in concert with that province's other mineral resources, potash and uranium. Forestry is of some importance in Manitoba and Alberta, while Manitoba's hydroelectricity complements the petroleum of the other two Prairie provinces. The Prairies are also engaged in an increasing amount of manufacturing, and especially since 1960, the finance, trade, and service industries have expanded rapidly.

BRITISH COLUMBIA

Mountainous British Columbia is the leading forestry province and also specializes in mining, including natural gas, copper, and coal. Several fertile river and lake valleys provide for farming, and B.C. also possesses a significant fishing industry. The mountains are the source of several large rivers that have been dammed for the production of hydroelectricity. Manufacturing is primarily related to the forestry, mining, and agricultural bases of the B.C. economy, while recent Asian immigration has expanded the services sector, especially finance.

THE NORTH

In the North, the inhospitable climate, isolation, small and transient labour force, and poor transportation facilities conspire to retard economic development. It is primarily mining that has inspired many southerners to venture north over the years. Northern Aboriginal peoples used to be self-sufficient in hunting, fishing, and trapping, activities that continue to occupy them to some extent, but their lives have been disrupted by the arrival of newcomers. Settlement of many Aboriginal land claims and increased autonomy from Ottawa should better allow the Northern territories to respond to local needs in the future. Tourism is on the increase, and several petroleum pipeline proposals are under consideration.

Regional Economic Conflicts

As a result of such regional economic differences, the national government regularly faces demands to assist the economy of a single province, region, or industry. Such demands do not necessarily involve conflict between one region and another, and sometimes benefit them all. More often than not, however, demands from one region do conflict with those from another. The most common expression of such regional economic conflict has undoubtedly been between the Prairie and central regions. Since central Canada's regional interests have historically been persuasive with the federal government, the analysis is usually put in terms of the economic complaints of the West against the central core of the country.[4]

OWNERSHIP, TAXATION, AND REGULATION OF NATURAL RESOURCES

While the eastern provinces and British Columbia have always had jurisdiction over their own natural resources, Ottawa decided to retain such control when Manitoba was created in 1870, as well as with Saskatchewan and Alberta in 1905. The logic of this discrimination was that the federal government (i.e., central Canada) should control such resources in the national interest, allowing Ottawa to guide the development of the West. The Prairie provinces fought vehemently against this discrimination and were finally successful in gaining control of their natural resources in 1930.

The conflict over natural resources re-emerged in the 1970s and 1980s, especially with respect to petroleum pricing. National energy policy in the 1950s and 1960s had actually favoured the West, for Alberta was guaranteed a market for its oil and natural gas as far east as Ontario. But after the OPEC (Organization of Petroleum Exporting Countries) cartel agreed on an artificial rise in the international price of oil in 1973, federal policy began to favour the consumer/manufacturing interest of central Canada at the expense of the producer interest of the West. The height of the regional economic conflict occurred in 1980 with the Trudeau government's **National Energy Program,** which imposed new federal taxes, kept the national price below the world level, encouraged frontier development, and promoted Canadianization of the industry, all objectives opposed by most westerners. Eventually, a partial compromise between central and western interests was reached in 1981, and the Mulroney government later scrapped the NEP entirely. Nevertheless, the NEP had a profound effect on the western Canadian psyche, especially when combined with the West's simultaneous opposition to Ottawa's constitutional initiatives and official bilingualism policy.

TARIFFS

The West complained for generations that Canadian tariff policy was designed in the interest of Ontario at the expense of the Prairies. As early as the 1879

National Policy, John A. Macdonald saw the tariff as a means of promoting and protecting the industrial heartland of central Canada. Adding a tariff (an import tax) to the price of imported manufactured goods would raise their price above that of goods manufactured in Canada, and allow domestic goods to be sold more cheaply than imports. Ontario thus gained employment in producing tractors, for example, but western Canadians felt that this was contrary to their interests. In the absence of such a tariff, they would have been able to buy cheaper tractors from abroad. The West demanded lower tariffs at every opportunity, and in the 1920s sent its own farmer representatives—the Progressive Party—to the House of Commons to fight on this front. Tariffs among all countries have gradually come down since 1945, but the issue took on a new life in the 1980s with the western demand for a free trade agreement between Canada and the United States. By this time, business interests in central Canada also supported such a measure, and it was adopted to their mutual satisfaction.

TRANSPORTATION

Another aspect of Macdonald's National Policy that displeased the West was railway freight rates. Living so far from the central core of the country, westerners expected to pay additional transportation costs, although they demanded that freight rates be subsidized by Ottawa. Indeed, the Crow's Nest Pass Act (or Crow Rate) of 1897 was an attempt to do just that, and provided a low rate for transporting Prairie grain to eastern ports. Westerners successfully fought to retain the Crow Rate in the 1920s, but were greatly upset by the Trudeau government's decision to increase these rates, as well as by the Chrétien government's decision to abolish the subsidy entirely in 1995. A related complaint centres on peculiar inequities within the freight rate structure, including higher rates for finished goods than for raw materials, which discouraged the development of manufacturing in the West.

BANKING

Canada deliberately developed a centralized branch banking system in an attempt to construct a sound, stable banking community that would avoid frequent local collapses. The result was a handful of large national banks, with headquarters in Toronto or Montreal and with local branches spread across the country. From a hinterland perspective, money deposited in the local branch of a national bank did not remain in the community to be lent out for local purposes, but was sent to headquarters in central Canada to be used in the economic development of

Ontario or Quebec. This was another reason for the farmers' revolt of the 1920s, and displeasure with the Canadian banking system had much to do with the rise of the Social Credit party in Alberta in the 1930s. In the 1970s, when the West became stronger in spite of this policy, the federal government finally allowed regional banks to be established. Several of these new western financial institutions faltered in the 1980s, however, largely because of a downturn in the western economy that westerners blamed on Trudeau's National Energy Program.

WESTERN ALIENATION

These four policy areas—tariffs, transportation, banking, and resources—can be put in a broader context. The metropolitan–hinterland thesis suggests that the West was created as a colony of central Canada and was intended to be held in a subordinate and dependent relationship.[5] The flavour of this relationship is captured in the cartoon at the bottom of the page. Dissatisfaction with the Liberal party's focus on Quebec issues in the 1970s and 1980s and again in the early 1990s led to a new outburst of **Western alienation,** defined as follows:

> *A regionally distinct political culture through and within which are expressed economic discontent, the rejection of a semi-colonial status within the Canadian state, antipathy towards Quebec and French-Canadian influence within the national government, the irritation of*

Source: "The Milch Cow," by Arch. Dale (1882–1962), from the *Grain Growers Guide*, 15 December 1915, NA.3055.24. Reproduced courtesy of the Glenbow Archives, Calgary, Alberta.

the West's partisan weakness within a succession of Liberal national governments, and the demand from provincial political elites for greater jurisdictional autonomy.[6]

The fact that after 1984 the Mulroney Conservative government continued to put priority on Quebec led to the formation of the Reform Party, whose initial slogan was "The West Wants In." The Reform Party won the majority of seats west of Ontario in the 1993 and 1997 elections, and almost all of them in British Columbia and Alberta. In 2000, however, the party changed its leader and name (to the Canadian Alliance) in an effort to become more appealing to the rest of the country. Table 2.2, illustrating the regional support of the various political parties in the 2000 federal election, shows that the Alliance was only marginally successful.

TABLE 2.2 REGIONAL DISTRIBUTION OF POPULAR VOTE BY PARTY, 2000 ELECTION (PERCENTAGES)

	Liberal	Alliance	PC	NDP	Bloc
Atlantic	41.2	10.2	31.3	16.6	—
Quebec	44.2	6.2	5.6	1.9	40.0
Ontario	51.4	23.6	14.5	8.3	—
West	25.2	50.0	10.0	12.3	—

Source: Data compiled from Elections Canada Web site: www.elections.ca/gen/rep/37g/table8_e.html (Retrieved 15 Nov. 2001). Extrapolation and analysis rests with the author. Used with permission.

The majority of westerners remain extremely sensitive to any federal government interest in the petroleum industry; they share with Quebec an inclination for decentralization of the federal system; they remain suspicious of Ottawa's apparent preference toward Quebec and the Atlantic provinces in its policies and finances; and, given their relative prosperity, they tend to prefer individual self-reliance over collective, public solutions to demands being made. Despite Alberta's prosperity at the turn of the new century, it experienced a new bout of western alienation after the 2000 federal election, pleading for respect, for appreciation of its views, and for assurances of being heard.

OTHER ASPECTS OF REGIONAL CONFLICTS

Many of the western economic conflicts with central Canada have been echoed by the Atlantic provinces. Nova Scotia and New Brunswick entered Confederation in 1867 as proud and prosperous colonies, but their economies quickly declined. While changes in marine technology (from wooden sailing ships to steel steamships) were probably the principal factor responsible, Maritimers blamed federal economic policy for much of their difficulty. Post-Confederation tariff policy appeared to do the Maritimes more harm than good; the Atlantic provinces shared the West's concerns about freight rates, although they received subsidization in this area, too; and they fought for provincial ownership of off-shore petroleum in the 1990s. They also complained of an insufficiently aggressive federal government when it came to protecting Atlantic fish stocks from foreign overfishing.

Smaller-scale regional economic disputes are also a routine occurrence in Canadian politics. Attempts to support the steel plant in Sydney, Nova Scotia, aroused opposition in Sault Ste. Marie, Ontario; awarding the CF-18 maintenance contract to Canadair of Montreal infuriated supporters of Bristol Aerospace of Winnipeg; extending drug patent protection for multinational pharmaceutical firms in Quebec offended Canadian generic drug producers in Ontario; and promoting frontier petroleum exploration (including federal assistance to Newfoundland's Hibernia project) upset conventional oil and gas producers in Alberta. In recent years, Ontario Premier Mike Harris complained that employment insurance premiums are too high, especially when Ontarians pay a large part of the premiums and residents of the five Eastern provinces collect a disproportionate amount of the payments.

Case Study: The CF-18 Maintenance Contract

In 1986, the Mulroney government had to choose between two bids for the contract to maintain Canada's new, sophisticated CF-18 fighter aircraft. The bid from Winnipeg's Bristol Aerospace was cheaper and technically superior to that of Montreal's Canadair. Yet the government gave the contract to Quebec for political reasons: Quebec had more seats in the House of Commons than Manitoba; the PC party was already strong in the West and needed to deepen its newfound roots in Quebec; Quebec felt that it was owed this contract because it considered itself the aerospace centre of Canada and because of previous preferential treatment of Ontario; and, of course, Quebec separatism was always an option. The move outraged Manitoba and all of western Canada, and inflamed feelings of western alienation.

Regional-Economic Disparities

Conflicts between regions are exacerbated in Canada because of regional economic inequalities or disparities. Whatever the fault of federal policies, Canada's primary resources are not evenly distributed, the regions have different sizes and populations, and they are located at variable distances from key export markets.

Among the available ways to measure regional economic disparity are provincial gross domestic product, that is, the total value of all goods and services produced. Because of such differences in the size of provincial populations, it is more useful to divide each province's GDP by its population, giving the GDP per capita. A third measure of provincial disparities is provincial unemployment rates. These measures are provided in Table 2.3, which generally indicates three categories of provinces: three rich ones, Ontario, Alberta, and British Columbia; four poor ones, the Atlantic provinces; and three intermediate provinces, Quebec, Manitoba, and Saskatchewan.

TABLE 2.3 PROVINCIAL GROSS DOMESTIC PRODUCT, GDP PER CAPITA, AND UNEMPLOYMENT RATE

	1999 GDP (millions)	1999 GDP per capita	Unemployment Rate 2000
Newfoundland	$ 12 110	$22 393	16.7%
Prince Edward Island	2 994	21 759	12.0%
Nova Scotia	22 407	23 858	9.1%
New Brunswick	18 390	24 380	10.0%
Quebec	204 062	27 767	8.4%
Ontario	396 775	34 450	5.7%
Manitoba	30 995	27 127	4.9%
Saskatchewan	30 143	29 388	5.2%
Alberta	116 990	39 532	5.0%
British Columbia	118 783	29 489	7.2%
Canada	957 627	31 404	6.8%

Source: "Provincial Gross Domestic Product, GDP per Capita, and Unemployment Rate," adapted from the Statistics Canada Web sites, www.statcan.ca/english/Pgdb/Economy/Economic/econ15htm and www.statcan.ca/english/Pgdb/People/Labour/labor07a.htm (Retrieved 15 Sept. 2001).

EQUALIZATION PAYMENTS

In addition to developing national social programs and assisting various industries in a uniform national policy, successive governments have focused on two principal means to deal with the specific question of regional economic disparities. One is to give federal funding to have-not provincial governments, and the other is to provide grants to individual firms in designated have-not regions of the country.

In 1957 Ottawa finally responded to repeated demands and began to make **equalization payments,** payments that are funded by various federal taxes levied in all provinces. These annual cash grants to the have-not provinces are designed to allow them to raise their services to an acceptable national level but can be spent for any purpose. In other words, they are unconditional grants, with no strings attached. The sums involved are quite impressive, as Table 2.4 reveals. Atlantic provinces often complain, however, that when they take in additional natural resource revenues, they experience a proportional decrease in their equalization payments.

TABLE 2.4 EQUALIZATION PAYMENTS, 2001–02

Quebec	$5 152 000 000
Nova Scotia	1 298 000 000
Manitoba	1 185 000 000
Newfoundland	1 098 000 000
New Brunswick	1 224 000 000
Saskatchewan	240 000 000
P.E.I.	251 000 000
Total	10 448 000 000

Source: "Federal Transfers to Provinces and Territories," www.fin.gc.ca/fedprov/mtpe.html (Retrieved 15 Nov. 2001). Reproduced with the permission of the Minister of Public Works and Government Services Canada, 2001.

REGIONAL ECONOMIC DEVELOPMENT PROGRAMS

The second means of trying to reduce regional economic disparities is to establish federal regional economic development programs. The basic thrust of these programs is to designate those parts of the country in need of economic assistance, and then to provide grants to firms that would locate or expand existing operations in such areas. Some grants also go to provinces or municipalities in order to provide the basic infrastructure that might attract industry, such as highways, water and sewage systems, and industrial parks. Several separate regional economic development agencies now exist, principally the Atlantic Canada Opportunities Agency (ACOA), Federal Economic Development in Northern Ontario (FEDNOR), Western Economic Diversification (WED), and the

Canadian Economic Development for Quebec Regions. Many observers are increasingly dubious about the effectiveness of these programs and agencies.

....

Class Cleavages

Turning from economic disparities based on geography to inequalities in individual incomes and power, we come to class cleavages. The concept of class is not as clear-cut as that of region, and Canadians are generally more aware of their regional and ethnic identities. In fact, because of such other divisions, class may not be as important a generator of political activity in Canada as it is in most countries. We do have significant class cleavages, but lack a strong consciousness of class and class conflict. This part of the chapter will begin by discussing various definitions and measurements of class and then examine the political role of the different classes.

Defining and Measuring Class

When dealing with the concept of class, it is customary to start with Karl Marx, who predicted that every capitalist economy would produce a class system consisting primarily of the bourgeoisie, the owners of the means of production, and the proletariat, the workers. The proletariat would sell their labour for a price; the bourgeoisie would pay them as little as possible (and less than they were worth), thereby accumulating profit or surplus value. While religion and the prospect of a pleasant afterlife might keep them content for a while, the workers would eventually come to resent their low wages and state of exploitation, and finally engage in a violent revolt.

Other social scientists divide individuals and families into the upper, middle, and working classes, based on such interrelated factors as income, occupation, and education. Using these measures, the divisions between the classes are less clear-cut than in the neo-Marxist analysis. Income is the simplest measure to employ in discussing this subject.

One means of measuring income inequality is to divide the population into five equal groups, or quintiles, from highest to lowest income and to indicate the share of total income received by each group. Table 2.5 presents such proportions for the 1997; it also shows that the income shares before social program transfers (such as employment insurance and social assistance) were dramatically inequitable, and how the tax system takes a little away from the rich to redistribute to the poor. Thus, even after taxes and transfers, the highest 20 percent of

TABLE 2.5 INCOME SHARES BY QUINTILES BEFORE AND AFTER TRANSFERS, AND AFTER TAX, 1997

Income before Transfers	Total Money Income	Income after Tax
0.6	4.6	5.5
7.3	10.1	11.4
16.1	16.4	17.1
26.5	24.8	24.6
49.5	44.3	41.4

Source: Statistics Canada, Income Shares by Quintiles before and after Transfers, and after Tax, 1997, adapted from the Statistics Canada publication *Income after Tax, Distributions by Size in Canada*, cat. no. 13-210, July 1999, p. 23.

the population still receive over 41 percent of the total income, while the lowest 20 percent receive just 5.5 percent.

Another problem in using the concept of class is the distinction between "objective" and "subjective" class. Objective class refers to the class into which analysts place a person, according to criteria such as type of work or level of income, while subjective class means the class to which people think or feel they belong, even if it contradicts objective standards. Many people who consider themselves to be middle class would be categorized as working class by social scientists. Behaving as if they belonged to a different class than they really do, such people could be said to be lacking in **class consciousness,** something that Marx also foresaw and called "false consciousness." This factor reduces the significance of class in motivating political activity.

The Upper Class

Canada is home to many fabulously rich entrepreneurs and some of the wealthiest families on earth. In 2001, the *National Post* counted 31 Canadian billionaires; at the top of the list were Ken Thomson at $29 billion, Galen Weston at $8 billion, the Bombardier family at $6.5 billion, and the Irving family at $3.3 billion.[7] Thomson owns a large number of firms in the information and publishing fields, especially online databases. Galen Weston is the proprietor of Loblaws, Holt Renfrew, and Weston Bakeries, and the Bombardiers produce a wide range of transportation equipment, especially aircraft and railroad equipment. The Irving family owns most of New Brunswick, including large tracts of woodlands, pulp mills, all the English-language daily newspapers in the province, oil refineries, gas stations, ship-building companies, trucking firms, bus lines, railways, and potato operations. Other Canadian billionaires include Terry Matthews, who became rich in the telecommunications industry; Barry Sherman, in pharmaceuticals; Jimmy Pattison, in a variety of enterprises; Paul Desmarais (Power Corp, Investors Group, and Great-West Life); Ted Rogers (Rogers Communications); Jean Coutu (drugstores); Harrison and Wallace McCain (McCain Foods and Maple Leaf Foods, respectively); André Chagnon (cable television); and Izzy Asper (CanWest Global).

Another category of wealthy Canadians comprises the corporate chief executive officers who do not own their firms. The annual remuneration packages of bank presidents and other top CEOs, including the value of salary, bonus, incentives, shares, and other benefits, now routinely exceed $5 million.[8]

The general lines of the public policy demands of the economic elite are easily drawn. Essentially, they want to be left alone: minimize the role of government in society and rely more extensively on private market forces. They want both to cut government spending on social programs so that their taxes can be minimized and reduce the annual government deficit and the accumulated national debt. If taxes are necessary, avoid corporate and progressive individual taxes as much as possible, and provide generous loopholes, write-offs, and tax shelters. Their goal is to minimize government regulation, labour and environmental protection, and anti-combines laws and other restrictions on corporate takeovers.

Governments have normally responded to such demands with alacrity. The Canadian state gives priority to big business demands in the first place because it depends on the private sector to create jobs. Politicians are especially sensitive to a corporate threat to move to a country with more favourable policies. Second, corporate executives and the politicians often come from the same ranks, including prime ministers and ministers of Finance. Brian Mulroney and Paul Martin provide ideal examples. Third, companies have many avenues of influence available: making a direct, personal pitch, using professional lobby firms to help them make contact with public decisionmakers for a fee, and taking advantage of their membership in pressure groups. Among the hundreds of business pressure groups in existence, the **Business Council on National Issues** is probably most powerful, representing chief executive officers of the 150 largest firms in the country. Fourth, the corporate elite also control the mass media to a large extent. Finally, throughout their history, both the Conservative and Liberal parties have been financed primarily by large corporate contributions. Such donations guarantee access to decisionmakers, and it is not difficult to establish a link between corporate contributions and general public policy, if not to specific corporate favours. The Canadian Alliance is also increasingly beholden to the generosity of large corporations.

Thus, the progressive nature of the personal income tax was reduced when 10 tax brackets were reduced to 3, and capital gains continue to be taxed at a lower rate than other forms of income. In her book *Behind Closed Doors*, Linda McQuaig shows how the rich use their political influence to obtain tax breaks that are paid for by those with lesser incomes.[9] Personal and corporate income taxes are riddled with loopholes, and Canada is one of the few countries in the world without a tax on wealth or inheritance. Beyond the recent moves toward deregulation, the various free trade agreements represent a commitment on the part of the Canadian government not to restrict the operations of corporations. Moreover, for a fee of $500 000, a corporation could send its CEO to address the national leaders at the Summit of the Americas in Quebec City in April 2001, while antiglobalization protesters were kept outside by a high fence and tear gas.

Three principal exceptions to this corporate pressure to minimize the role of government must be noted. First, while the economic elite demands that government minimize spending on others, it often expects sizable chunks of public funds for itself, such as in government contracts and grants. A second exception is the rare occasion on which the economic elite has actually favoured new social programs. Such programs would increase the purchasing power of lower-income people, reduce the amounts that companies themselves have to pay in employee benefits, and ensure the basic stability of society so that upper classes do not have to worry about violent protests from the poor or unemployed. Third, business leaders expect government to provide such basics as roads, railways, and electricity that will decrease their costs or increase their profits. Despite the overwhelming tendency of governments to respond to demands from the corporate elite, however, it should not be forgotten that politicians ultimately get elected by voters, the great majority of whom belong to other classes. Thus, other classes can influence events to some extent, but only if they act as a class.[10]

The Middle Class

On a subjective basis, probably a majority of Canadians think that they belong to the middle class. Academic analysts, however, challenge this assumption, although they do allow a large middle class in a modern society. They often divide their smaller version of the middle class between the upper middle class, made up of small business people, self-employed professionals (e.g., lawyers and doctors), and affluent farmers, and the **new middle class**—middle managers (who take orders from the corporate elite and give them to the working class), civil servants, teachers, nurses, and other salaried professionals. While the middle class is far from being a unified force, its members are normally well educated and receive above-average levels of income. Their main asset is their home, but they usually own cars and have assorted other material possessions. While members enjoy such tax shelters as RRSPs, the middle class often claims that it pays a disproportionate amount of the taxes to finance government programs of all kinds. With the many tax changes of recent years, however, this claim is difficult to document. On the other hand, such groups as teachers and nurses increasingly feel they are being treated by governments as if they were working class.

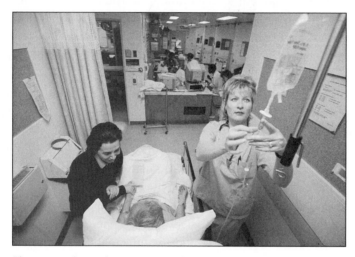

The nursing profession is becoming increasingly active politically and increasingly class conscious (Phill Snel/CP Picture Archive)

The Working Class

The working class is generally identified as doing manual or routine work. The typical member of the working class is engaged in resource exploitation, assembly line production, secretarial and clerical work, sales, and a variety of crafts and trades. Less-affluent farmers could also be included. Academic analysts would put the bulk of the population into this category, even though many so labelled identify subjectively with the middle class. Normally lacking postsecondary education, members of the working class usually receive less income than those in the middle class.

Karl Marx's predictions of a violent proletarian revolt were dealt a blow when governments unexpectedly legalized trade unions and extended the franchise to the working class. Nevertheless, most governments and companies have been somewhat hostile toward the formation of labour unions, and Canada has experienced a large number of violent strikes, either over the formation of a union or over its subsequent demands. Among the key labour struggles in Canadian history were the 1919 Winnipeg General Strike, the 1937 General Motors Strike in Oshawa, the 1945 Ford Strike in Windsor, the 1949 Asbestos Strike in Quebec, and the woodworkers' strike in Newfoundland in 1959.[11] While legislation dealing with conciliation, mediation, arbitration, picketing, labour standards, occupational health and safety, and compensation for injury on the job is ostensibly passed to protect the working class, governments usually avoid offending their own corporate supporters in the design or implementation of labour laws. Some, like the Mike Harris government in Ontario, systematically undermine existing labour standards in the province.

Others things being equal, it is in the interests of members of the working class to belong to a trade union. Unionized employees usually have higher wages, more adequate benefits, better working conditions, and more protection against dismissal than those who do not engage in collective bargaining. Many more unionized workers have private pension coverage, for example, than those who are not unionized. In spite of these advantages, the rate of unionization among "paid workers" in Canada is very low (except in comparison to the United States!). Total union membership in 1998 was 3 938 000 or 32.5 percent of the 12 117 000 paid workers in the country.[12]

Moreover, the number of blue-collar jobs is declining in such areas as resource industries, construction, and manufacturing, where unionization used to be most common. New jobs in the postindustrial society are found largely in sales and services, especially in the private sector, where workers are traditionally part-time, poorly paid, and hard to organize. Lacking a union, and given the nature of their job, those in sales and service occupations are not as likely to be class conscious or to develop social democratic values as those who produce goods.

The composition of the unionized workforce is also changing in other ways. Once comprising primarily private sector, male, manual workers, it is increasingly composed of public sector unions, and women constitute nearly 45 percent of union members. Public sector unions now make up three of the six largest unions in the country: the Canadian Union of Public Employees, 389 300 members; National Union of Public and General Employees, 309 000; Canadian Auto Workers, 222 500; United Food and Commercial Workers, 200 000; United Steelworkers, 180 000; and Public Service Alliance, 143 300.

As far as labour legislation is concerned, the principal federal interest is in the Unemployment Insurance program, now called "Employment Insurance." This program was introduced in 1941 to tide workers over between jobs, but given the high national unemployment rates in many years since, and the even higher rates in certain regions in every year, it is relied upon much more heavily than was originally anticipated. With such large numbers of workers drawing on the fund, it became a vital source of both individual and regional income, although governments repeatedly restricted its coverage in the 1980s and 1990s. The Chrétien government siphoned off the significant surplus in the EI account to pay down the national debt and then loosened up the program, especially for Atlantic Canada, just prior to the 2000 election.

The **Canadian Labour Congress** is the main lobbying body for over 2.6 million workers. The CLC is thus one of the largest pressure groups in the country and represents a significant number of voters. Its influence is diminished, however, by its outsider status in Ottawa, as well as by the fact that not all unions belong to it. The historic factionalism within the Canadian union movement is another factor that has not helped the cause of the working class.[13] Governments are often justified in assuming that a gap exists between labour leaders and rank and file members with respect to policy positions and party support. Union leaders often support the NDP, while large numbers of rank and file members vote for each of the other parties.

The Poor

The poor can be defined as those living below the **poverty line.** The most widely accepted definition of poverty in Canada is the low-income cutoff provided annually by Statistics Canada. It is calculated as follows: any individual or family that spends more than 54.7 percent of its income on food, clothing, and shelter is living in poverty (given that the average family spends 34.7 percent of its income on these three necessities). Table 2.6 shows the proportion of the population below the Statistics Canada poverty line in selected years.

TABLE 2.6 NUMBER OF PEOPLE AND PERCENT OF POPULATION BELOW THE POVERTY LINE

	1973		1981		1989		1997	
Families	701 000	13.4	721 000	11.3	786 000	11.0	1 175 000	14.0
Unattached Individuals	767 000	40.2	940 000	37.5	1 101 000	34.4	1 633 000	39.6
All Households	1 468 000	20.6	1 661 000	18.7	1 887 000	18.3	2 808 000	224
Total Persons	3 269 000	16.2	3 339 000	14.0	3 489 000	13.5	5 222 000	17.5

Source: Canadian Council on Social Development, *The Canadian Fact Book on Poverty—2000*, 47. Reproduced with permission.

Thus, Canada had over 5 000 000 residents living in poverty at the turn of the new century. Even more disturbing, a large proportion of these people lived far below the poverty line, and these figures do not include the large group of near-poor that exists just above it.

Probably the most heartbreaking and most intractable aspect of poverty is that it includes 20 percent of Canadian children. While a majority of the poor children live in two-parent families, over 40 percent live with lone-parent mothers; indeed, 56 percent of such mothers exist in a state of poverty. The high-school dropout rate among children from poor families is much higher than that of others, and the tie between low income and low education is self-perpetuating. *The Canadian Fact Book on Poverty* documents how children from low-income families stand out from their better-off peers:

> *They are less healthy, have less access to skill-building activities, have more destructive habits and behaviours, live more stressful lives, and are subject to more humiliation. In short, they have less stable and less secure existences and as a result they are likely to be less secure as adults.*[14]

Many poor people work full-time, and others part-time; in fact, the poor can be about equally divided between those who work and those who are unemployed or unemployable. The working poor try to scrape by on the minimum wage or on more than one low-paying job, and are sometimes better off if they go on social assistance. Rather than raising the minimum wage, however, some provincial governments actually reduced welfare benefits in the last half of the 1990s, and only Quebec provides an adequate daycare program. By the turn of the new century, most governments were giving priority to tax cuts, even at the expense of social programs. On this point, the Centre for Social Justice asserts:

> *For the poorest 10 percent of families raising children, tax cuts completely miss the point: they have no taxable income. For the next 10 percent, they have negligible taxes on minimal incomes. How ironic that those families who most heavily paid the price of the war on the deficit now don't get a cut of the peace dividend.*[15]

One of the great weaknesses of the poor in the political system is that they are generally unorganized and collectively inarticulate. They lack the skills to organize effectively as pressure groups, primarily because they are without the education, money, and time to develop such skills. Because of their low voter turnout rate, they tend to be ignored by both federal and provincial governments. Three main pressure groups exist to speak for the poor in the cacophony of the political process: the Canadian Council on Social Development, the National Council of

Welfare, and the National Anti-Poverty Organization. Nevertheless, no one should expect any degree of equality in the struggle among interest groups representing different classes.

DISCUSSION QUESTIONS

1. What should be the role of the federal government in overcoming Canada's great distances and divisions?
2. To what extent are regional and provincial complaints about federal policies justified?
3. What can be done to lessen the problem of regional economic disparities?
4. Do the economic elite owe their wealth and power to their own efforts or to exploitative forms of profitmaking and manipulation of the political system?
5. Why is union membership among the working class not higher? Why is class consciousness in Canada relatively low?

FURTHER READING

Abella, Irving, ed. *On Strike*. Toronto: James Lewis & Samuel, 1974.

Braid, Don, and Sydney Sharpe. *Breakup: Why the West Feels Left out of Canada*. Toronto: Key Porter Books, 1990.

Clement, Wallace, ed. *Understanding Canada: Building on the New Canadian Political Economy*. Montreal: McGill–Queen's University Press, 1996.

Kilgour, David. *Inside Outer Canada*. Edmonton: Lone Pine Publishers, 1990.

McQuaig, Linda. *Behind Closed Doors*. Toronto: Penguin, 1987.

Palmer, Bryan. *Working-Class Experience: The Rise and Reconstitution of Canadian Labour, 1800–1980*. Toronto: Butterworths, 1983.

Ross, David P., Katherine J. Scott, and Peter J. Smith. *The Canadian Fact Book on Poverty—2000*. Ottawa: Canadian Council on Social Development, 2000.

Notes

1. For example, Pierre Berton, *The National Dream* and *The Last Spike* (Toronto: McClelland and Stewart, 1970 and 1971, respectively); Robert Chodos, *The CPR: A Century of Corporate Welfare* (Toronto: Lorimer, 1973).
2. Task Force on Canadian Unity, *A Future Together* (Ottawa: Supply and Services, 1979), 26–27.

3. Wallace Clement and Daniel Drache, *A Practical Guide to Canadian Political Economy* (Toronto: Lorimer, 1978), 9–14.

4. David Kilgour, *Uneasy Patriots: Western Canadians in Confederation* (Edmonton: Lone Pine Publishers, 1988) and *Inside Outer Canada* (Lone Pine, 1990); Don Braid and Sydney Sharpe, *Breakup: Why the West Feels Left out of Canada* (Toronto: Key Porter Books, 1990).

5. Donald Smiley, *The Federal Condition in Canada* (Toronto: McGraw-Hill Ryerson, 1987), 159.

6. Roger Gibbins, *Prairie Politics and Society* (Toronto: Butterworths, 1980), 191.

7. "The Wealth Report." National Post Online, May 2001 http://www.nationalpost.com/features/wealth/top_10.html (Retrieved on 15 Sept. 2001).

8. *The Globe and Mail Report on Business*, July 2001, lists 50 CEOs who received over $6.5 million! In the same year that Nortel Networks laid off thousands of workers and lost most of the value of its shares, President John A. Roth collected direct compensation of over $70 million.

9. Linda McQuaig, *Behind Closed Doors* (Toronto: Penguin, 1987).

10. *Exposing the Facts of Corporate Rule: A Handbook on How to Challenge the Big Business Agenda* (Centre for Social Justice: Toronto, 1998).

11. Irving Abella, *On Strike* (Toronto: James Lewis & Samuel, 1974); Walter Stewart, *Strike!* (Toronto: McClelland and Stewart, 1977), chap. 4.

12. Human Resources Development, *Directory of Labour Organizations in Canada* (Ottawa: Minister of Public Works and Government Services Canada, 1998), 15.

13. Gad Horowitz, *Canadian Labour in Politics* (Toronto: University of Toronto Press, 1968).

14. *The Canadian Fact Book on Poverty—2000.* (Canadian Council on Social Development: Ottawa, 2000), 2.

15. Armine Yalnizyan, *Canada's Great Divide: The Politics of the Growing Gap between Rich and Poor in the 1990s* (Toronto: Centre for Social Justice, 2000).

Chapter 3

French Canada and the Quebec Question

Among all the ethnic/cultural/linguistic issues in Canadian politics, it is the English–French cleavage that has always been of greatest significance. The prominence given to concerns of French Canadians primarily reflects the large number of people involved, their historical rights, and the territorial base of Canada's francophones in Quebec. The French–English cleavage is at least as problematic as the regional economic cleavage in Canadian politics, and both reinforce each other in the question of Quebec's place in Confederation.

Chapter Objectives

After you have completed this chapter, you should be able to:

Outline the historical evolution of French–English interaction in Canada

Enumerate the French–English crisis points in our history

Explain and appreciate the concept of Quebec nationalism

Contrast the values, attitudes, and demands of the Québécois before and after the Quiet Revolution

Distinguish between contrasting approaches to protect and promote the French language and culture in Canada

Comment on the responses of federal, Quebec, and other provincial governments to francophone demands

Outline the main provisions in the Meech Lake and Charlottetown Accords

Discuss the prospects of Quebec remaining part of Canada in the 21st century

....

Historical Overview of French–English Relations
Pre-Confederation Developments

Almost every Canadian political decision for over 200 years has reflected the French–English division to some extent, and the tensions that currently threaten the continued existence of the country are best understood in historical context. The French first colonized what is now the province of Quebec, and populated it with farmers, clergy, and seigneurs. But when the British defeated the French on the Plains of Abraham in 1759, the conquerors took control of the non-agricultural economy and the government.

Time Line

Constitutional Developments 1759–1867

1759   British conquest of Quebec
1774   Quebec Act
1791   Constitutional Act
1840   Act of Union
1867   British North America Act (Constitution Act, 1867)

The people, however, continued to speak French and attend the Roman Catholic Church, which became a highly influential and autonomous organization. It would probably have been impossible to make Quebec into an Anglo-Protestant colony; in any case, the British, after a brief attempt at assimilation, exhibited a policy of tolerance and accommodation, and in the 1774 **Quebec Act,** they guaranteed the French their religious rights and their own system of civil law.

A large component of "English" immigrants—especially the United Empire Loyalists from the new United States—moved into what is now Ontario in the 1780s. The colony was thus divided into two by the **Constitutional Act** of 1791: Lower Canada (Quebec) would be essentially French-Catholic, and Upper Canada (Ontario) would be Anglo-Protestant. In the 1830s, conflict erupted in both colonies between the assembly and the executive, which in the case of Lower Canada translated into discord between French (assembly) and English (executive). The colonies were reunited by the 1840 **Act of Union** on the recommendation of Lord Durham who believed that the ethnic problem in Canada could be solved only by another attempt to assimilate the French. This objective was quickly abandoned, and the French language came to be used alongside

English in the government of the pre-Confederation period. Cabinets were usually alliances between English and French leaders, and the legislature operated on the informal principle of the double majority—legislation had to have the approval of a majority of members from both sections of the colony.

Given this historical evolution, the federal union incorporated in the British North America Act (BNA Act), now called the **Constitution Act, 1867,** is perfectly understandable. As a separate province, Quebec would have considerable autonomy, although not all Quebec participants were satisfied that the autonomy provided by the division of powers between the federal and provincial governments was sufficient. Most adhered to the "compact theory of Confederation," according to which Confederation was a compact between two equal founding nations, and any change in the Constitution would require unanimous provincial consent, or at least that of Quebec.

As for cultural guarantees, both French and English were given official status in all operations of the federal Parliament, and laws were to be passed in both languages. Both languages could also be used in whatever federal courts were later established, as well as in the legislature and courts of Quebec.

Post-Confederation Conflicts

Although the two language groups have been regularly accommodated in government circles since 1867, a number of serious linguistic/ethnic conflicts erupted from the time of Confederation to the Second World War. The first of two Riel Rebellions, led by French-Catholic Métis Louis Riel, precipitated the creation of the province of Manitoba in 1870. In 1884–85, he re-emerged in what is now Saskatchewan to lead the second Riel Rebellion on behalf of western Natives and Métis who had been treated shamefully by the government. After quelling the rebellion, the federal government charged Riel with treason. This raised ethnic and religious tensions across the country to a fever pitch, for while Anglo-Protestants regarded Riel as a murderer, traitor, and madman, French-Catholics believed he was a patriot and a saint. Riel's hanging heightened the level of French-Catholic outrage across the country, especially in Quebec, and permanently damaged the close attachment of the people of that province to the Conservative Party.

The second linguistic conflict occurred in Manitoba. The small settlement was about equally divided between French and English, and at Riel's insistence, the 1870 Manitoba Act followed the Quebec precedent of giving the two languages official status in the new province's legislature and courts. After its

Time Line

Post-Confederation French–English Conflicts to 1945

1870   First Riel Rebellion
1885   Second Riel Rebellion
1890   Manitoba's Official Language Act
1913   Ontario's Regulation 17
1917   First Conscription Crisis
1944   Second Conscription Crisis

creation, however, Manitoba attracted thousands of English-speaking immigrants and others who chose to identify with the anglophone community. Hence, in 1890, the anglophone majority passed the Official Language Act, removing the official status of French.

The third linguistic conflict concerned minority French-language education rights in Ontario. In 1913 the Whitney government's Regulation 17 virtually abolished the use of French in the Ontario school system; English was to become the sole language of instruction after the third year, and the study of French as a subject was limited to one hour a day.

The **conscription crisis** of the First World War was the fourth major French–English confrontation. Having little in the way of standing armed forces, the Canadian military effort rested on appeals for volunteers. These appeals initially had promising results, but as reinforcements were needed later in the war, few recruits came forward. The government therefore decided to resort to conscription—compulsory military service—in 1917. Isolated from Europe, even France, for centuries, French Canadians felt that the war was not of any concern to them and certainly did not justify the risk of their lives. Prime Minister Robert Borden knew that French Canada generally felt indifferent to the conflict and that conscription would divide the country along ethnic lines. He therefore appealed to Liberal leader Wilfrid Laurier to join him in a coalition government. Laurier refused the offer, although most English-speaking Liberal MPs did join in a Union Government. The subsequent enforcement of conscription entailed considerable violence, including a riot in Quebec City in the spring of 1918 that left four people dead and many others injured. This confrontation destroyed what little French-Canadian support for the Conservative Party was left after the execution of Louis Riel.

Ontario repealed Regulation 17 in 1927, and French–English tensions returned to their normal, controllable level until they were inflamed by the fifth ethnic conflict, another conscription crisis during the Second World War. But in 1939 Canada was led by Liberal Prime Minister Mackenzie King, with a strong contingent of ministers and MPs from Quebec. King knew that French Canada would resist conscription, so on the basis of the slogan "conscription if necessary, but not necessarily conscription," he held a national referendum in 1942 to release his government from an earlier pledge not to conscript. Happily, King then managed to postpone the adoption of compulsory military service until almost the end of the war.

....

Quebec Nationalism

Central to the question of French–English relations and the position of Quebec in Canada is the phenomenon of Quebec nationalism. This feeling of primary loyalty to the French-Canadian nation of Quebec emanates from the widely held notion that Quebec is a distinctive French-Canadian nation, centred on language, ethnicity, culture, and territory, and—prior to 1960—religion. Over the centuries, Quebec nationalism has taken many twists and turns, but it remains a driving force in both provincial and federal politics, where it always stood for a substantial degree of political autonomy or self-determination. Quebeckers valued autonomy because Quebec was different and because they felt such autonomy had been guaranteed in 1867. Quebec sometimes also considered itself to be morally superior to the rest of the country, and often believed that it was fighting for its life. Before 1960, Quebec nationalism was largely inward-looking and defensive, primarily concerned with ensuring that the federal government kept out of that province's affairs. After 1960, it was activist and self-confident, as the province wanted to take over many federal responsibilities. Quebec nationalism also sought to address the dominance of Anglo and external economic power in the province. Moderate nationalists now advocate the protection and promotion of the French language and culture, increased powers for the province, and more French-Canadian control of the economy. More extreme nationalists fight for provincial sovereignty with a loose connection to Canada or outright separation. Somewhat complicating the picture, however, is the declining French-Canadian birthrate in Quebec and the presence in the province of about one million residents (including Aboriginal peoples, anglophones, and those of other origins) who do not embrace the same ethnic-linguistic-cultural objectives. As noted in Chapter 2,

Quebec has recently fallen below a symbolic 25 percent of the total Canadian population.

....

The French–English Cleavage, 1960–82
The Quiet Revolution: Quebec in the 1960s

Until 1960, Quebec was a traditional, conservative, rural, poorly educated, patronage-oriented society, heavily influenced by the Roman Catholic Church. Dominated by the authoritarian Premier Maurice Duplessis from 1935 onward, the inward-looking population was taught that only he could protect them from evil external influences, such as Ottawa. The Quebec of the past 40 years, however, is a different province and society. Since 1960, Quebec francophones have experienced a **Quiet Revolution,** consisting of a dramatic change of values and attitudes—especially toward the state—a new collective self-confidence, and a new brand of nationalism. These features of the new Quebec had many implications for French–English relations in both the Quebec and Canadian political systems.

QUEBEC'S CHANGES AND DEMANDS

The government of Jean Lesage (1960–66) took over many functions previously administered by the Church.[1] The most important of these, education, was radically modernized, and health and welfare programs were also made public rather than charitable responsibilities. With the nationalization of private power companies, Hydro-Québec became a huge Crown corporation supplying all the electricity in the province and serving as an engine of economic development. Lesage also reformed almost every piece of legislation on the books, especially labour and electoral laws, added reams of new ones, and created many government agencies. All these new and expanded public responsibilities required substantial additional revenues, and Lesage put immense pressure on Ottawa to increase federal–provincial grants, to allow Quebec to opt out of the conditions attached to them, and to give the province a greater share of joint taxation. In areas of provincial jurisdiction, Quebec began to move toward distinctive programs, designing its own pension plan, which was then used as a model for the Canada Pension Plan. As time went on, the province began to demand ever larger jurisdiction, leading to perpetual federal–provincial discord.

Time Line

French–English Relations, 1945–70

1945–59	Opposition to Maurice Duplessis grows
1960–66	Quiet Revolution
1963–68	B & B Commission
1968	Pierre Trudeau becomes PM
1968–69	Official Languages Act
1970	FLQ crisis

Federally oriented Quebec francophones such as future prime minister Pierre Trudeau began to demand that French be used as a language equal to English in the corridors of power in Ottawa. This group of Québécois was also concerned about the fate of francophone minorities in the other provinces. The new self-confidence of the Québécois inspired these dwindling minorities to greater self-assertiveness.

FEDERAL RESPONSES

During the 1960s, the federal government grappled somewhat haphazardly with these demands. The Diefenbaker government (1957–63) introduced simultaneous interpretation into Parliament, began printing federal government cheques in a bilingual format, and appointed a French-Canadian governor general. Immediately upon taking office, the Pearson government (1963–68) established the Royal Commission on Bilingualism and Biculturalism (the B and B Commission). Pearson also gave Quebec and the other provinces more federal funds and taxation powers, removed conditions from many shared-cost programs, and permitted Quebec to make international arrangements with France and other francophone countries. Since the federal Parliament and courts were already theoretically bilingual, the main gap in official bilingualism at the national level was in the executive branch, where English was essentially the working language of the public service, at least at policymaking levels. Pearson therefore introduced the **Official Languages Act** to make the Canadian public service bilingual, and since its passage under Trudeau in 1969 Canada has become officially and effectively bilingual in its federal institutions. Ottawa also began to assist francophone minorities in other provinces in order to try to stem their increasing assimilation into the anglophone majorities as well as to support French immersion educational programs.

The question of French–English relations, or "national unity," was the principal political issue throughout the Trudeau era (1968–79, 1980–84). At that point, it became clear that two basic models existed to deal with the problem. The first was to recognize Quebec as the homeland of French Canada and to give that province powers and resources to protect and promote its linguistic and cultural distinctiveness. Quebec would be essentially "French" and the rest of Canada primarily "English." The second option was to treat Quebec as "une province comme les autres" and to promote bilingualism at the federal level and in the other provinces so that any Canadian could use either language anywhere in the country. English Canadians had difficulty accepting these demands, which seemed excessive and contradictory: making Quebec more French and more autonomous at the same time as promoting French in Ottawa and the other provinces. Most English Canadians did not understand that the two demands came largely from two different groups of francophones, the vast majority concentrating on Quebec and a minority that wanted to expand French Canada beyond that province. Trudeau was not representative of mainstream thought in Quebec in his fighting against the recognition of Quebec as the homeland of French Canada and in his opposition to giving that province any special status or power on the grounds that this would be the first step toward separation. Part of Trudeau's popularity in English Canada stemmed from the perception that he was "anti-Quebec," but he was passionately "pro-French" in promoting French power and bilingualism in Ottawa and across the country.[2]

THE SEPARATIST OPTION

During the 1960s, advocates of a third option—Quebec separatism—began to emerge, most committed to democratic processes. One wing of the separatist movement, however, the **Front de Libération du Québec (FLQ),** believed that the normal political process was not responding quickly enough to the demands of the Quiet Revolution, and resorted to violence. Its periodic bombings killed two people and injured many others. In October 1970, two small cells of the FLQ kidnapped a British diplomat, James Cross, and abducted and murdered Quebec Cabinet Minister Pierre Laporte. Trudeau invoked the **War Measures Act,** giving the police and armed forces special powers to quell the violence—arresting over 400 innocent, peaceful separatist supporters in the process. By crushing the FLQ, by giving French Canadians more clout in Ottawa, and by guaranteeing pan-Canadian bilingualism in the Constitution in 1982, Trudeau hoped to undercut any Quebec demand for special status or separatism in the defence of French Canada.

Quebec–Canada Relations, 1970–82

The first Robert Bourassa government in Quebec (1970–76) passed Bill 22 to give primacy to the French language in many spheres in the province, such as in the operations and documents of public authorities. As far as education was concerned, immigrant children were generally forced to attend French-language schools. This was an attempt to have such children join the majority French linguistic group in the province rather than become "English," as so many previous immigrants had done. In fact, relying on immigration to bolster the francophone segment of the population became a vital point after the French-Canadian birthrate plummeted in the 1960s. Bill 22 also aimed at the francization of the private sector by pressuring companies to use French as the language of internal corporate operations. The more that Quebec moved in the direction of French unilingualism, of course, the greater English Canada's resistance to Trudeau's policy of national bilingualism, and the greater the number of anglophones who left Quebec.

Time Line

Quebec–Canada Relations, 1970–82

1976	Election of Parti Québécois
1977	Quebec Bill 101
1980	First Quebec Referendum
1982	Constitution Act, 1982

The Parti Québécois was elected to office in 1976 under René Lévesque with an even more nationalistic program.[3] Faced with a hostile Trudeau government in Ottawa, the PQ made few gains in provincial autonomy. But in 1977 it passed **Bill 101,** the Charter of the French Language, which considerably extended Bill 22 in making French the predominant language in the province. The Bill generally turned the persuasive and optional aspects of Bill 22 into coercive and mandatory ones. It made French the only official language of the legislature (although laws continued to be translated unofficially into English); only individuals (not corporations) could use English in Quebec courts; essentially the only children who could go to English schools in the province were those who had at least one parent who had done so; and all commercial signs had to be in French only. All four of these clauses were subsequently ruled unconstitutional by the courts, but they were modified to comply with the court decisions, and in other ways Bill 101 still stands, so that French continues to be the official language of the province.

In 1980, the PQ government held a **referendum** on the question of pursuing a more independent relationship with Canada called **sovereignty-association.** Many prominent politicians, including Trudeau, Justice Minister Jean Chrétien, and several provincial premiers, encouraged Quebeckers to defeat the PQ proposal, promising them "constitutional renewal" if they did so. When sovereignty-association was turned down by a vote of 60 percent to 40 percent, new federal–provincial constitutional negotiations began, culminating in the **Constitution Act, 1982.**[4] Ironically, even though the whole effort was supposed to appeal to the residents of Quebec, that province alone objected to the act as reflecting the Trudeau vision of a bilingual Canada rather than recognizing the distinctive francophone character of Quebec. Nevertheless, it became law in all parts of the country. As far as language was concerned, the act reinforced official bilingualism at the federal level and in New Brunswick, and guaranteed **minority language education rights** in all provinces wherever numbers warranted. Many Quebeckers never forgave Trudeau and Chrétien for adopting such a significant constitutional document without Quebec's consent.

....

French–English Relations in the Other Provinces

The distribution of French and English communities in the various provinces is shown in Table 3.1. Defined by mother tongue, francophone minorities are located primarily in Ontario (500 000) and New Brunswick (242 400); as percentages they are largest in New Brunswick (33.2 percent), Ontario (4.7 percent), and Manitoba (4.5 percent).

The Quebec government and most Quebeckers have been more concerned about internal linguistic matters than about what happened to French minorities in other provinces. Nevertheless, the Quiet Revolution led francophones outside Quebec to make a last-ditch attempt to preserve their language and culture. Often under pressure from Prime Minister Trudeau, some provincial premiers hoped that by extending rights or services to their francophone minority, they would help to forestall separatism in Quebec. Thus, many provinces have made considerable improvement in minority francophone rights since 1965. As mentioned, all were bound by the Constitution Act, 1982 to provide education in the minority official language where numbers warrant. All provinces were also committed to provide for criminal trials in French if demanded by the accused.

New Brunswick went farthest with its own Official Languages Act of 1969, which was constitutionalized at provincial request in 1982. New Brunswick also

TABLE 3.1 MOTHER TONGUE AND HOME LANGUAGE BY PROVINCE, 1996 (PERCENTAGES)

	Mother Tongue		Home Language	
	English	French	English	French
Newfoundland	98.5	0.5	99.2	0.2
Prince Edward Island	94.1	4.3	97.2	2.3
Nova Scotia	93.2	4.0	96.3	30.5
New Brunswick	65.3	33.2	68.9	82.8
Quebec	8.8	81.5	10.8	2.9
Ontario	73.1	4.7	83.6	2.1
Manitoba	74.7	4.5	88.3	0.6
Saskatchewan	84.4	2.0	94.6	0.7
Alberta	81.5	2.1	91.1	0.5
British Columbia	76.1	1.5	86.5	1.8
Yukon	86.8	3.8	95.4	1.0
Northwest Territories	56.7	2.2	68.8	22.6
Total	59.8	23.5	67.6	

Source: "Mother Tongue and Home Language by Province, 1996 (Percentages)," adapted from the Statistics Canada Web site www.statcan.ca/Daily/English/971202/d971202.htm (Retrieved 15 Sept. 2001).

improved the Acadian educational system at all levels and provided provincial government services in both languages.

Even before Trudeau, Ontario began to provide for French-language secondary schools, and later established the right of every Franco-Ontarian to go to a French-language school. Ontario then guaranteed French trials in the provincial courts and gradually extended French-language provincial services. Bill 8, becoming effective in 1989, provided for provincial government services in French in designated regions of the province as well as for the translation of laws. Meanwhile, simultaneous interpretation in the legislature began in 1987, and Franco-Ontarians were granted the right to have their French-language schools run by trustees elected by the francophone population.

Manitoba moved very slowly in this direction on its own, but was pushed by a series of Supreme Court of Canada decisions beginning in 1979. The result was that the 1890 Official Language Act was declared unconstitutional, all laws had to be passed in both languages, trials had to be available in French, and most government documents had to be bilingual.

Quebec–Canada Relations since 1982

Three years after the controversial adoption of the Constitution Act, 1982, Quebeckers defeated the Parti Québécois and put Robert Bourassa's Liberals back in power. The second Bourassa government was first able to persuade the more receptive Mulroney government to allow Quebec to play a fuller part in the international French-speaking community, the Francophonie. Then, in 1988, the Supreme Court of Canada declared the sign provision of Bill 101 to be unconstitutional as a violation of freedom of expression, even "commercial expression." Bourassa responded by using the "notwithstanding clause" in the federal and Quebec charters of rights to pass Bill 178, providing for French-only outdoor signs but allowing some bilingual signs indoors. Violating a constitutional right of anglophones in this way produced a vehement reaction among Anglo-Quebeckers and an anti-Quebec and anti-French response in the rest of the country. On the other hand, some aspects of Bill 101 were voluntarily relaxed in 1983, and in 1986 Quebec ensured the provision of social and health services in English to its anglophone minority. Moreover, when the five-year limit on Bill 178 ran out in 1993, Bourassa replaced it with Bill 86, which allowed bilingual signs outside as well as inside stores.

Time Line

Quebec–Canada Relations Since 1982

1987–90	Meech Lake Accord
1992	Charlottetown Accord and national referendum
1995	Second Quebec referendum
1996	Calgary Declaration
1998	Supreme Court decision on Quebec independence
2000	Clarity Act

The Meech Lake Accord

The Constitution Act, 1982, including the Charter of Rights and Freedoms, was operative in Quebec even though the government of that province refused to endorse it. When he became prime minister, however, Brian Mulroney was determined that Quebec should symbolically rejoin the Canadian constitutional family "with honour and enthusiasm." He included several Quebec nationalists in his cabinet, and in 1985, asked Bourassa to outline his conditions for such a reunion.

The Quebec government proceeded to make five demands:

1. constitutional recognition of Quebec as a "distinct society" within Canada
2. increased jurisdiction over immigration
3. participation in Supreme Court appointments
4. power to veto constitutional amendments
5. right to opt out, with compensation, of national programs within provincial jurisdiction

Mulroney called the premiers together at Meech Lake in April 1987, where they unexpectedly agreed to a document that addressed Quebec's demands and became known as the **Meech Lake Accord.**[5] The prime minister secured unanimous provincial consent by extending to the other provinces the same rights as were demanded by Quebec, except for the distinct society clause. The document would also have constitutionalized the Supreme Court of Canada, guaranteed annual first ministers' conferences on the Constitution and the economy, and at the behest of the Alberta delegation, provided for provincial participation in Senate appointments.

CRITICISM OF MEECH LAKE

Despite the relative ease with which it was drafted, the Meech Lake Accord generated much controversy. Led by ex-prime minister Trudeau, its critics did not approve of Quebec's designation as a distinct society within Canada, and especially objected to the phrase that it was the role of the government and legislature of Quebec to "preserve and promote" that distinctiveness. No one was sure what implications the **distinct society clause** would have for the federal–provincial division of powers, leaving it for judicial clarification on an issue-by-issue basis. Some felt that in a federation all provinces had to have exactly equal status, and many argued that, armed with the distinct society clause, Quebec would immediately begin to challenge federal powers in a variety of fields. Others worried about the status of the English and Aboriginal minorities within Quebec, as well as of the francophone minorities in other provinces, and many women outside Quebec feared that the distinct society clause might endanger gender equality in Quebec, a fear not shared by women within that province.

A second objection to the Accord was that it enlarged the list of subjects that required unanimous provincial consent in the constitutional amending formula. Many critics felt that Senate reform and the transformation of the northern territories into provinces would be virtually impossible if such changes required agreement of all 10 provinces instead of only 7.

Much concern was expressed about the provision allowing provinces to opt out of national programs within provincial jurisdiction and be compensated by Ottawa. Fears were expressed that satisfactory new national social programs (such as daycare) would never materialize because provinces would be compensated for programs that merely met national objectives, not national standards.

Apart from criticizing what was in the Accord, many opponents faulted it for what was left out. The North was not allowed to nominate senators or Supreme Court judges; Aboriginal rights were not strengthened; and multiculturalism was ignored.

Others condemned the process through which the Accord had emerged—a behind-the-scenes gathering of (male) first ministers. In the post-Charter era, individual Canadians in all parts of the country insisted on being part of the constitutional amendment process; moreover, the primacy of Quebec's concerns was rejected by those given constitutional standing by the Charter—women, Aboriginal peoples, and multicultural and other minorities.[6] The public now demanded more meaningful participation in the process of constitutional change.

In Defence of Meech Lake

Those who defended Meech Lake argued that it would symbolically bring Quebec back into the constitutional fold and overcome the isolation and betrayal that many residents of that province felt after 1982. Indeed, it was the most modest list of demands ever to come out of Quebec. Defenders called this the "Quebec round," and argued that Aboriginal, Northern, Western, and other concerns would be the next items on the constitutional agenda. Rather than promote incremental separatism, they felt that the Accord would give Quebec the flexibility to remain satisfied within Confederation. Supporters contended that in demographic, linguistic, and cultural terms, the distinctiveness of the Quebec society could not be denied. Those who felt that Trudeau's concept of official bilingualism was unrealistic for certain parts of the country thought that the Accord, in noting that French-speaking Canadians are centred in Quebec, might lessen linguistic tensions and the pressure for bilingualism in inappropriate places.

Many political scientists and others had long argued that the provinces should have a say in the appointment of senators and Supreme Court judges. In the former case, this was because the Senate was intended to represent the provinces within Ottawa's decisionmaking structure; in the latter, because the Supreme Court rules on federal–provincial disputes and its judges should not be unilaterally appointed by one side. Many true federalists also contended that Ottawa should not be able to invade provincial jurisdiction with its spending power and set up national programs without provincial consent, as had often happened in the past.

According to the constitutional amending formula adopted in 1982, the Accord then had to be approved by the federal and all provincial legislatures within three years, that is, before June 1990. In most cases such legislative approval came rather easily, but new governments in Newfoundland, New Brunswick, and Manitoba had reservations about the Accord. In the end, Clyde Wells did not allow it to come to a vote in the Newfoundland legislature, while in Manitoba, Aboriginal MLA Elijah Harper delayed passage beyond the deadline because of the absence of any advance for Native peoples.

The Charlottetown Accord

With the death of the Meech Lake Accord, many Quebeckers felt betrayed again, and nationalist and separatist sentiment in Quebec mushroomed. Both the Quebec Liberals and Parti Québécois issued more nationalistic constitutional positions, and demands arose for a referendum on sovereignty to be held in 1992. Meanwhile, several Quebec members of Parliament quit the Conservative and Liberal parties to sit as Quebec indépendantistes in the Bloc Québécois led by Lucien Bouchard, a former minister in the Mulroney cabinet.

Prime Minister Mulroney appointed Joe Clark as the minister responsible for Constitutional Affairs, and Clark tried to develop a collective federal–provincial–

André-Philippe Côté (*Le Soleil*). Reproduced with permission.

territorial–Aboriginal response to offer to Quebec before its constitutional refer-endum. After several rounds of negotiations, Clark, the nine premiers, and terri-torial and Aboriginal leaders all agreed on a comprehensive constitutional proposal in July 1992. Overcoming its previous refusal to participate, Quebec then joined a full-fledged constitutional conference in Ottawa in August. After nearly a week of hard bargaining, the leaders unanimously signed a new constitutional accord upon which they put the final touches in Charlottetown a week later.[7] The **Charlottetown Accord** had four main parts, two of primary concern to Quebec: the **Canada clause** and changes to the division of powers.

The Canada clause that began the Accord would recognize Quebec as a dis-tinct society within Canada as well as enumerate the other fundamental values and characteristics of the country. These included democracy, the rule of law, par-liamentary and federal systems, the Aboriginal peoples of Canada and their enhanced rights, official language minorities, cultural and racial diversity, indi-vidual and collective rights, gender equality, and the equality and diversity of the provinces.

The second main issue of interest to Quebec was the federal–provincial divi-sion of powers. As in the Meech Lake Accord, provinces could opt out of new national shared-cost programs set up within provincial jurisdiction and receive federal financial compensation if the programs met national objectives. In addi-tion, Ottawa offered to withdraw from six fields at provincial request—forestry, mining, tourism, recreation, housing, and municipal and urban affairs—again with financial compensation. Culture and labour-market training would essen-tially become provincial powers, and the two levels would share jurisdiction in immigration, telecommunications, and regional development. Thus, beyond the immigration power in Meech Lake, provinces would now have full or partial power over 10 additional fields of public policy. In return for this increased decen-tralization of powers, Ottawa hoped to strengthen the economic union by elimi-nating interprovincial trade barriers, but had to settle for agreement in principle, with the issue to be negotiated later.

The other two major components of the Charlottetown Accord, Aboriginal self-government and the Triple-E Senate (equal provincial representation, elected, and effective), are dealt with elsewhere in this book, but it is appropriate to men-tion here some of the other ingredients in the Accord. Provisions of Meech Lake with respect to the Supreme Court of Canada were included, along with those con-cerning an annual meeting of first ministers, and changes in the constitutional amending formula, except that the creation of new provinces would no longer require unanimous consent. Ontario premier Bob Rae was successful in having a social charter added to the Constitution to guarantee rights to health care, social services, and education, along with workers' rights and protection for the environment. The guarantee of equalization payments was strengthened, and the federal reservation, disallowance, and declaratory powers were essentially removed.

THE 1992 NATIONAL REFERENDUM

The Accord would be of no effect until ratified by Parliament and the 10 provincial legislatures. Before ratification, however, the federal government announced that a national referendum would be held on the new constitutional deal on October 26, 1992. The decision to hold such a nationwide referendum was based on several considerations. First, Quebec was already committed to a referendum on constitutional change on that date, while Alberta and B.C. laws required a referendum on constitutional amendments. If these three provinces would be voting on the Accord in any case, the opportunity had to be extended to the others. Second, a referendum would avoid the criticism that Meech Lake had lacked public input, and public approval would lend legitimacy to the agreement and spur the 11 legislatures into speedy affirmative action.

On a national basis, the referendum result was 55 percent no and 45 percent yes. Majorities voted no in Quebec, Nova Scotia, the four western provinces, and the Yukon. Even though the referendum was not legally binding, there was no point in bringing the constitutional package before legislatures for ratification: the Charlottetown Accord was dead.

Public opinion polls showed that rather than basing their decision on the contents of the Accord as such, many of the people who voted "no" did so to vent their anger and frustration against Prime Minister Mulroney, the premiers, and politicians and governments in general. Voters were not in a generous frame of mind, and rather than seeing it as a multi-sided compromise, they generally felt that the Accord gave too much to others and not enough to themselves. Thus, the negative vote in Quebec was largely based on the view that the Accord did not give Quebec sufficient new powers, but many outside Quebec argued that that province got too much. Many Westerners did not see the proposed reforms to the Senate as sufficient protection of their interests in Ottawa, and many Aboriginal Canadians were dissatisfied with the provisions on Aboriginal self-government. Indeed, while the Accord was primarily designed to address the constitutional insecurity of Quebec, Aboriginal Canadians, and western and smaller provinces, a majority in all three groups believed that their elites had not bargained hard enough on their behalf.[8]

The Chrétien Government Record and the 1995 Referendum

After this disheartening if not traumatic experience, leaving the constitutional issue alone was determined to be a wise choice by all federal parties, especially the Chrétien Liberals elected a year later on the promise that they would concentrate on improving the economy. In 1994, however, the Parti Québécois was returned to power in Quebec. With Ottawa largely ignoring the issue, the new Quebec premier, Jacques Parizeau, wanted a quick vote on a clear-cut separatist position. Others, however, including Bloc Québécois leader Lucien Bouchard, preferred a scheme that retained significant ties to Canada. When the polls showed that Parizeau could not achieve the support of a majority of Quebec voters on the question of his choice, he succumbed to the pressure of public opinion (and of Bouchard), and promised an extensive list of continuing links to Canada.

Parizeau's referendum was held in October 1995. The proposal involved a convoluted and unclear question incorporating a kind of sovereignty that retained significant ties to the rest of Canada. In the final week of the campaign, Prime Minister Chrétien finally woke up to the possibility of a PQ victory, and made a vague promise of reform if the "no" vote prevailed. The result of the referendum could not have been closer: 50.6 percent voted "no," while 49.4 percent voted "yes." Even this narrow defeat precipitated premier Parizeau's abrupt resignation, and Lucien Bouchard moved from leading the BQ in Ottawa to the PQ in Quebec. Parizeau's departure was hastened by negative reaction to his televised remarks on referendum night to the effect that the defeat could be blamed on "money and the ethnic vote."

Fulfilling his last-minute promises, but not being able to persuade all provinces to make an actual amendment to the Constitution, Chrétien had Parliament pass a resolution recognizing Quebec as a distinct society within Canada. He also promised that regardless of the official constitutional amending formula, no constitutional amendments would be passed without the approval of each region of the country (including Quebec). Labour-market training was then transferred from federal to provincial jurisdiction. After the 1997 election campaign that saw the Chrétien government returned to power, the prime minister referred a hypothetical question to the Supreme Court of Canada, asking it to rule on the legality of a unilateral declaration of independence by Quebec.

Nine provincial premiers (excluding Lucien Bouchard) gathered in Calgary in September 1997 and produced the **Calgary Declaration.** It tried to reconcile the "unique character of Quebec society" with the equality of all the provinces. While substituting "unique" for "distinct" and emphasizing provincial equality might attract some support in English Canada as a recipe for constitutional reform, however, it was less certain that it would appeal to most Quebeckers.

In August 1998, the Supreme Court answered the question previously submitted by Chrétien: "secession of a province 'under the Constitution' could not be achieved unilaterally." Quebec would have to use the constitutional amending formula and seek the approval of the other participants in Confederation to its exit. Neither did Quebec gain such a right under international law because its residents did not constitute an oppressed people. On the other hand, if Quebec obtained a clear majority vote in a provincial referendum on a clear question in favour of secession, it would be hard for the rest of the country to ignore.[9]

In the Words of the Court

"Quebec does not meet the threshold of a colonial people or an oppressed people, nor can it be suggested that Quebeckers have been denied meaningful access to government to pursue their political, economic, cultural and social development ... [But] a clear majority vote in Quebec on a clear question in favour of secession would confer democratic legitimacy on the secession initiative which all of the other participants in Confederation would have to recognize."

Source: Reference re Secession of Quebec, [1998] 2 S.C.R. 222.

Bouchard was re-elected three months later, and threatened another referendum as soon as "winning conditions" prevailed. This led Chrétien to introduce a controversial **Clarity Act,** which essentially translated the Supreme Court decision into legislation. Although it stopped short of articulating what a "clear majority" would be in numerical terms, the Act did specify that the federal government would not recognize a Quebec referendum result that did not involve a clear expression of the will of the population that the province should cease to be part of Canada. The federal government would not tolerate a question that involved continuing economic or political arrangements with Canada nor support a constitutional amendment that did not address the division of assets and liabilities; border changes; the rights, interests, and territorial claims of Aboriginal peoples; and the protection of minority rights. Chrétien believed such legislation was required because the questions asked in the Quebec referendums of 1960 and 1995 were deliberately vague. In fact, the new Act did not incite the inflammatory backlash in that province that some opponents had expected.

The year 2000 ended well for those committed to national unity when the Liberals out-polled the Bloc Québécois in the November federal election. The next year started with Lucien Bouchard's resignation from public life, having failed to persuade Quebeckers of the wisdom of sovereignty. His successor, Bernard Landry, began his premiership on a more aggressive separatist note, but soon realized that most Quebec residents were not interested.

··

The Future of French–English Relations

Given that francophones constitute nearly 25 percent of the Canadian electorate, and given their historic constitutional rights, their geographic concentration in Quebec, and majority control of such a large province, and their modern-day self-consciousness and self-confidence, the French in Canada cannot be ignored. If English Canada wants Quebec to remain part of the country, it cannot go back to the easy days of pre-1960 unilingualism and federal government domination.

Despite much confusion on the question, five alternatives can be identified:

- complete independence of Quebec (Parizeau)
- sovereignty of Quebec with links to Canada (Bouchard)
- Quebec as a distinct society within Canada (Bourassa, Mulroney)
- all provinces equal; strong central government; national bilingualism (Trudeau)
- all provinces equal; strong provinces; no bilingualism outside Quebec (Preston Manning)

It appears to this writer and many others that the only way to accommodate the French presence within Canada is the "middle way."[10] Given that 85 percent of French Canadians are located in Quebec and that 82 percent of Quebeckers are French-speaking, it is logical to recognize that Quebec is the heartland of French Canada. In the words of Brian Mulroney and Robert Bourassa, Quebec constitutes a "distinct society within Canada." This approach would give that province special recognition and responsibility to protect itself in the North American English linguistic environment. Justified or not, Quebec has something of a "siege mentality" with respect to its language and culture, and language has replaced the Church as the focus of the French identity. The Quebec corporate elite is now a francophone group, and they, along with the new middle class in the Quebec public sector, see themselves benefiting from increased provincial autonomy.[11] Due to the oratory of Pierre Trudeau and Preston Manning, however, English-Canadian opinion has probably hardened toward the idea of recognizing Quebec as a distinct society despite the passage of the parliamentary resolution to this effect.

DISCUSSION QUESTIONS

1. Which of the options listed above is closest to your vision of Canada?
2. How far would you be willing to go in recognizing Quebec's distinctiveness in the Constitution? Is such a designation unfair in any way to other provinces?
3. To what extent should individual provinces operate on a bilingual basis?
4. If a future referendum were won by the separatists, what sort of scenario do you see unfolding?

FURTHER READING

Cairns, Alan C. *Disruptions: Constitutional Struggles, from the Charter to Meech Lake*. Toronto: McClelland and Stewart, 1991.

Clarke, Harold D., Allan Kornberg, and Peter Wearing. *A Polity on the Edge: Canada and the Politics of Fragmentation*. Peterborough: Broadview Press, 2000.

Fraser, Graham. *René Lévesque and the Parti Québécois in Power*. Toronto: Macmillan, 1984.

Johnston, Richard, et al. *The Challenge of Direct Democracy: The 1992 Canadian Referendum*. Kingston: McGill–Queen's University Press, 1996.

McRoberts, Kenneth. *Misconceiving Canada: The Struggle for National Unity*. Toronto: Oxford University Press, 1997.

McRoberts, Kenneth. *Quebec: Social Change and Political Crisis*. 3rd ed. Toronto: McClelland and Stewart, 1993.

McRoberts, Kenneth, and Patrick Monahan, eds. *The Charlottetown Accord, the Referendum and the Future of Canada*. Toronto: University of Toronto Press, 1993.

McWhinney, Edward. *Canada and the Constitution 1979–82: Patriation and the Charter of Rights*. Toronto: University of Toronto Press, 1982.

Romanow, Roy, J. Whyte, and H. Leeson. *Canada … Notwithstanding: The Making of the Constitution 1976–1982*. Toronto: Methuen, 1984.

Russell, Peter. *Constitutional Odyssey: Can Canadians Become a Sovereign People?* 2nd ed. Toronto: University of Toronto Press, 1993.

Notes

1. Dale Thomson, *Jean Lesage and the Quiet Revolution* (Toronto: Macmillan, 1984).
2. Kenneth McRoberts, *Misconceiving Canada: The Struggle for National Unity* (Toronto: Oxford University Press, 1997).
3. Graham Fraser, *René Lévesque and the Parti Québécois in Power* (Toronto: Macmillan, 1984).
4. Roy Romanow, J. Whyte, and H. Leeson, *Canada … Notwithstanding: The Making of the Constitution 1976–1982* (Toronto: Methuen, 1984); Edward McWhinney, *Canada and the Constitution 1979–82: Patriation and the Charter of Rights* (Toronto: University of Toronto Press, 1982).

5. Patrick J. Monahan, *Meech Lake: The Inside Story* (Toronto: University of Toronto Press, 1991).

6. Alan C. Cairns, *Constitution, Government, and Society in Canada* (Toronto: McClelland and Stewart, 1988); *Disruptions: Constitutional Struggles, from the Charter to Meech Lake* (Toronto: McClelland and Stewart, 1991).

7. Kenneth McRoberts and Patrick Monahan, eds., *The Charlottetown Accord, the Referendum and the Future of Canada* (Toronto: University of Toronto Press, 1993); Peter Russell, *Constitutional Odyssey: Can Canadians Become a Sovereign People?* 2nd ed. (Toronto: University of Toronto Press, 1993).

8. Richard Johnston, *The Challenge of Direct Democracy: The 1992 Canadian Referendum* (Kingston: McGill–Queen's University Press, 1996).

9. *Reference re Secession of Quebec*, [1998] 2 S.C.R. 217.

10. McRoberts, *Misconceiving Canada: The Struggle for National Unity*.

11. Thomas Courchene, "Market Nationalism," *Policy Options* (October 1968).

Chapter 4

Aboriginal Peoples, Other Ethnic Groups, and Gender Issues

The French–English question has been a constant of Canadian politics since before Confederation, but until recently Aboriginal and other ethnic issues were largely ignored. Similarly, once women achieved the vote around 1920, the system paid little attention to them. About 1970, however, Aboriginal, other ethnic, and gender issues suddenly became prominent items on the political agenda. This chapter explores these three new concerns: the first part examines Canada's Aboriginal peoples; the second discusses other ethnic groups; and the last section deals with the women's movement and other gender issues.

Chapter Objectives

After you have completed this chapter, you should be able to:

Discuss the historical evolution of Aboriginal–European interaction and the factors that have contributed to the deplorable state of life of many Aboriginals in Canada

Understand different kinds of Aboriginal land claims and the concept of Aboriginal self-government

Distinguish between pre-1970 and post-1970 Canadian immigration patterns

Trace the evolution of multiculturalism policy

Enumerate the milestones of women's political participation in Canada, as well as the factors that have inhibited such participation

Discuss the issues that have concerned the women's movement since 1970

Understand the public policy concerns of the gay and lesbian communities

....

Canada's Aboriginal Peoples
History and Numbers

The Native or Aboriginal peoples who have inhabited Canada for as long as 40 000 years are an extremely varied group. They are officially categorized as North American Indians, Inuit, and Métis, but none of these groups is homogenous. Because the early explorers mistakenly thought they were in India and named the local inhabitants accordingly, most of the native people now prefer to be known by the term "Aboriginal" or "First Nations." Before Europeans came to the continent, the Natives were self-sufficient and self-governing. They made decisions on the basis of consensus rather than by voting, and in many cases women (sometimes called clan mothers) played a significant role. In their close attachment to the land, they did not think in terms of private ownership; instead, they believed in the shared use of land and saw themselves as trustees of it for future generations. The fur trade, which led to the invasion by Europeans, was devastating for the Aboriginal peoples, totally disrupting their way of life and introducing new diseases that severely reduced their population.

In the **Royal Proclamation of 1763,** which divided up the territory acquired by Britain, an attempt was made to define Indian lands. In a large area called Indian Territory, the purchase or settlement of land was forbidden without Crown approval, that is, without a treaty between the Crown and the Aboriginal peoples concerned. As we know, this policy was not always followed, and Europeans often occupied Indian land without a treaty. Even when treaties were signed, there was much question about the fairness of the negotiations. Later on, the Crown set aside reserves in exchange for the cession of Indian land, in addition to providing benefits such as the right to hunt and fish on unoccupied Crown land.

The 1867 Constitution Act gave jurisdiction over Indians and lands reserved for the Indians to the federal government. In 1876, Parliament passed the **Indian Act,** providing for federal government control of almost every aspect of Aboriginal life. The Indian Act aimed to assimilate Aboriginals into the new white majority and represented a colonialist mentality—the exploitation, domination, and subjugation of a people by an imperial power. One of its provisions allowed for "enfranchisement," which encouraged Indians to give up their Indian status. Thus began the distinction between "status Indians," those registered with the federal government according to the terms of the Indian Act, and "non-status Indians," those not so registered.

Meanwhile, the treaty-making process continued apace, covering most of northern Ontario and the Prairie provinces. These treaties were designed primarily to clear Aboriginal title so that the transcontinental railway could be built and western immigrant settlement could begin. In return for surrendering title to the lands involved, Indians received tracts of land for reserves as well as other benefits such as small annuities, gratuities, schools, hunting and fishing rights, agricultural implements, cattle, and ammunition. In retrospect, almost everyone agrees that the Aboriginal peoples were taken advantage of in these negotiations; the land given them for reserves was usually small, remote, and lacking in resources.[1] Even worse off, however, were those Indians in much of British Columbia and the Arctic with whom no treaties were signed at all.

The Métis were the descendants of European fur traders and Indian women. Found largely on the Prairies, Métis combined nomadic hunting with farming. Not covered by the Indian Act or by treaties, they were left to the mercy of new white settlers and provincial and territorial governments. It is not surprising that Louis Riel, leader of the rebellion that led to the creation of Manitoba in 1870, took up their cause in 1884–85 in the second Riel Rebellion in Saskatchewan. After having been crushed, they remained in an even weaker position.

In the 1996 census, some 1.1 million people, or 3.7 percent of the total Canadian population, reported Aboriginal origins, but only 800 000 (2.8 percent of the total population) identified with an Aboriginal group. Canada's Aboriginal population breaks down as follows: about 75 percent North American Indian, about 20 percent Métis, and about 5 percent Inuit. The Department of Indian and Northern Affairs reported a slightly higher number of Aboriginal peoples in 1998: approximately 1.6 million, or 4.5 percent of the population. These numbers were distributed as follows: status Indians on reserve, 400 000; status Indians off-reserve, 260 000; non-status Indians, 425 000; Métis, 212 100; and Inuit, 60 000.[2] There are over 2500 reserves in Canada, with an average size of about 1150 hectares. They are divided among some 610 bands, with an average band population of about 600 persons.

The Condition of Aboriginal Peoples

The above statistics present only part of the picture. Of equal significance are the distressing statistics on Aboriginal poverty. Many reserve families have incomes far below the poverty line, and apart from a few urban professionals, the same is true for most of those who live off-reserve. Related to this level of poverty are alarming rates of Aboriginal alcoholism, low educational attainment, and unemployment. The overall life expectancy of Aboriginal Canadians is seven years shorter than of non-Aboriginals, largely a result of poor health services and housing on reserves that is overcrowded and lacking in running water, indoor toilets, and central heating. The infant mortality rate among registered Indians is almost twice that of the Canadian population as a whole, and Aboriginal peoples suffer far more than non-Aboriginals from tuberculosis and many other diseases. The suicide rate among Aboriginal youth is at least five times the national average, and Aboriginal peoples are much more likely to be murdered or die from accidents, poisoning, or violence.

Much of the condition of Aboriginal peoples in Canada can be traced to the Indian Act. Having lost their land, original livelihood, and culture, and being placed on unproductive reserves, many Aboriginals find themselves with little to do. The resulting unemployment, idleness, and reliance on welfare often lead them to seek solace in substance abuse. In this intoxicated state, many resort to family and other violence, which in turn brings them into trouble with the law. Not being able to pay their fines, and subject to discrimination at the hands of the police, the courts, and other aspects of the justice system, they then go to jail where they become even more alienated, depressed, and abused. Aboriginal peoples have suffered from untold discrimination and indignity at every turn, and the Indian Act requires non-Aboriginal bureaucratic approval for almost any band decision. In the past, Aboriginal babies were frequently removed from the reserves to be adopted by non-Aboriginal parents, and Aboriginal children were forced to go to residential schools where they were punished, sometimes to the point of assault, for speaking their Aboriginal language or engaging in Aboriginal customs. Aboriginal languages and cultures have been systematically discouraged, and traditional forms of government and medicine have been outlawed. Indians living on reserves did not even have the right to vote in federal elections until 1960, and between 1927 and 1951, the Indian Act made it an offence for them to hire a lawyer to bring a claim against Canada without government consent. Another factor contributing to the disruption of Aboriginal peoples' lives is the exploitation of Indian lands by mining, petroleum, and lumber companies.

Aboriginal Political Issues since 1970

Although they struggled against public policies from the time of the Riel rebellions, it was not until 1970 or so that governments in Canada began to pay much attention to Aboriginal peoples and their problems. Aboriginal peoples registered unprecedented offense at the Trudeau–Chrétien **White Paper on Indians** of 1969 that called for their complete integration into the wider Canadian society. With the proposed repeal of the Indian Act and treaties, they would become equal, ordinary Canadian citizens. On the other hand, Aboriginal peoples were encouraged by the sympathetic Berger Inquiry into the proposed Mackenzie Valley gas pipeline in 1977. By this time, their problems had become so serious that they simply could no longer be ignored, and the incidence of sit-ins, roadblocks, rallies, court cases, hunger strikes, and international protests increased. Thus, several Aboriginal organizations came into existence, especially the **Assembly of First Nations,** to spearhead the demand for change. Such post-1970 Aboriginal issues are primarily related to land and to governance.

LAND ISSUES

In most of the country, as noted earlier, North American Indians signed treaties with the Crown under which they ceded the land to the government in return for protected reserves. But, especially in British Columbia and the North, few such treaties were signed, leaving Indians and Inuit in these regions without a land base, similar to the Métis who have never legally possessed any land. This gives rise to the issue of **Aboriginal title,** that is, a claim to land on the basis of traditional occupancy and use rather than treaty. The existence of such Aboriginal title was first recognized in the *Calder* case in 1973 in connection with the Nisga'a band in British Columbia. In response, the government of Canada announced its intention to negotiate Aboriginal title. A great many Aboriginal land claims have therefore been launched in the past 30 years. They fall into two categories: comprehensive claims based on Aboriginal title (that is, traditional use and occupancy of land) that have not been dealt with by treaty or other legal means; and specific claims arising from misinterpretation or nonfulfillment of the terms of Indian treaties and other lawful obligations.

Such claims have moved relatively faster in the North than in the south, since north of the 60th parallel the federal government has jurisdiction over the land as well over the Aboriginal peoples. In fact, agreement in principle has been achieved in several comprehensive land claims in the North. Besides providing land and money, such comprehensive claims clarify Aboriginal hunting, fishing, and trapping rights, and clear obstacles to future economic development.

In the south, where Ottawa has responsibility for Aboriginal peoples and lands reserved for the Indians but where the provinces have jurisdiction over public lands, such claims have moved more slowly. Aboriginal peoples have generally found provincial governments even less sympathetic to their issues than Ottawa, and conflict has often developed between Indian bands and large natural resource companies as well as other non-Aboriginals who now live on the land in question. Ottawa insists that the provinces be party to such settlements and contribute to their costs. Thus far, relatively few comprehensive land claim successes can be reported below the 60th parallel.

The first main provincial comprehensive land claim settlement was the 1975 **James Bay Agreement** between the Cree and Inuit and the government of Quebec. The James Bay Agreement gave the Aboriginal peoples exclusive use of 13 700 km^2 of land and an additional 450 000 km^2 of exclusive hunting, fishing, and trapping rights, along with $225 million in cash in return for allowing Quebec to construct a giant hydro development project in the area. One terrible side effect of the development was the mercury poisoning of the fish, due to an unanticipated chemical reaction between water and rock in the flooded land, and of the Aboriginal peoples who ate them. This problem and the growing perception that the deal may otherwise have been less generous to the Aboriginal community than originally thought led the Cree of Quebec to reject the second, "Great Whale" phase of the James Bay project in the 1990s.

Since the province of British Columbia contains a large proportion of North American Aboriginal peoples who have not signed treaties, the comprehensive land claims issue has been particularly significant there. Progress was slow until the *Delgamuukw* case established a definition of Aboriginal title and approved the admissibility of oral history evidence in making such a claim. The Nisga'a tribe in northwest B.C., which had been seeking recognition of their Aboriginal title for over 100 years, finally arrived at an agreement in principle in 1996. The treaty ratified by the federal and provincial governments in 2000 provided the Nisga'a with 1930 km^2 of land and $190 million in cash, along with self-governing powers outlined below.

Figure 4.1 is a map of Indian Treaties, but perhaps it is most significant in revealing which parts of the country are without them. Specific land claims are those resulting from dissatisfaction with treaties—especially when bands did not receive the full amount of land that the treaties promised. Between 1973 and 1998, Canada settled over 200 specific land entitlement claims amounting to $900 million, leaving several hundred others under negotiation or assessment.

Another dimension of land issues concerns what treaties allow Aboriginals to do on public or Crown lands. Aboriginal **treaty rights,** especially hunting and fishing rights, frequently conflict with provincial law. After many court cases, some progress has been made on this front, including the issue of logging trees, although the issue of Aboriginal peoples' fishing out of season has repeatedly erupted in Burnt Church, New Brunswick, in recent years. In the *Marshall* cases,

●●●

Figure 4.1   Map of Historic Indian Treaties

Historic Indian Treaties

Treaty 11
1921

Murray Treaty
1760

Treaty 8
1899

Treaty 10
1906

1908
Treaty 5
1875

Treaty 6
1876   1889

1929–1930
Treaty 9
1905

Robinson-Huron
Treaty – 1850

Treaty 7
1877

Pre-Confederation
Vancouver Island Treaties
14 Treaties – 1850-1854

Treaty 4 –1874
Treaty 2 –1871

Treaty 1
1871

Treaty 3
1873

Robinson-Superior
Treaty – 1850   Manitoulin
Island Treaty
1862

Upper Canada
Treaties

Williams
Treaties
1923

Pre-Confederation
Maritime Peace and
Friendship Treaties

Treaty of
Swegatchy
1760

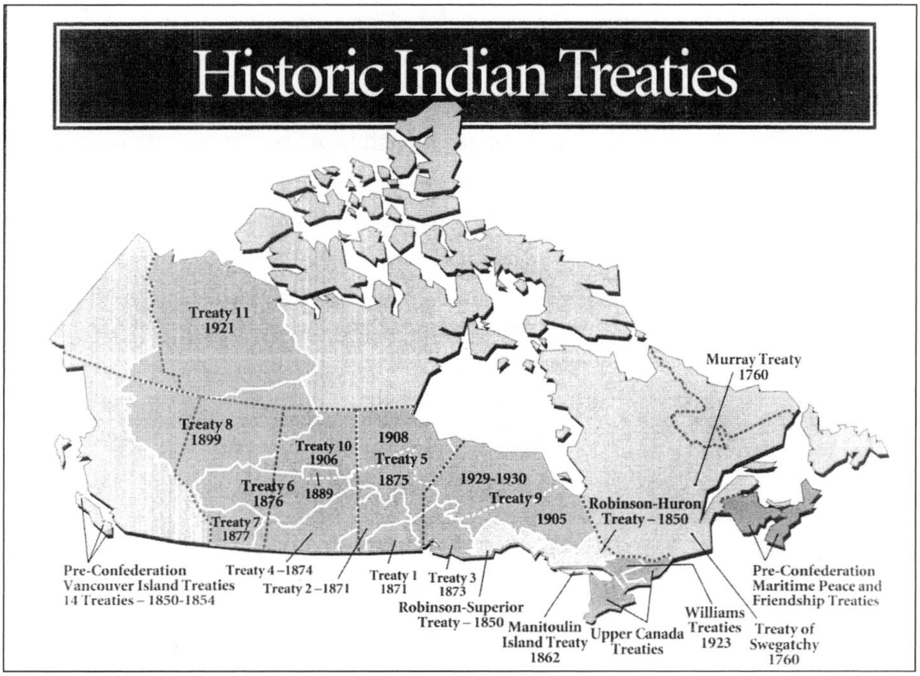

Source: Indian and Northern Affairs Canada, 2001. Reproduced with the permission of the Minister of Public Works and Government Services Canada, 2001.

the Supreme Court of Canada recognized a treaty right for local Aboriginals to make a moderate livelihood from the sea, but it also acknowledged that the Department of Fisheries and Oceans could regulate the fishery in the interests of conservation.

Yet another aspect of the land question arose in the conflict at Oka, Quebec, in the summer of 1990, the most serious Aboriginal–government conflict of modern times.[3] The municipal council's decision to expand a golf course on land claimed by resident Mohawks as sacred ground led to an armed standoff between Mohawk warriors and the Quebec Provincial Police, during which one police officer was killed, presumably by the fire of a fellow officer. The Canadian Armed Forces were later brought in, and Aboriginal demonstrations took place across the country. Five years later, an unarmed Aboriginal, Dudley George, was killed by a police officer in a peaceful land claims demonstration at Ipperwash, Ontario. The controversy over the involvement of the Harris government in this affair continues.

GOVERNANCE ISSUES

Aboriginal Canadians have long demanded improvements in government health, social, and educational services, and some minor improvements have been made over the years. Aboriginal peoples began to feel, however, that they were too constrained by the Indian Act and that their problems required Aboriginal solutions. They were tired of living at the mercy of politicians and bureaucrats. Yet most Aboriginals did not want to gut the Indian Act and existing government programs until they had something better to put in their place.

Shortly after their rejection of the 1969 White Paper, Aboriginal peoples began to argue that they should be able to choose their own decisionmaking processes, for they could hardly be expected to support the apparatus that created their current problems. Before the passage of the Indian Act, they had sophisticated and distinctive forms of government; many wanted to return to such traditional ways, feeling that the system of elected band councils was an alien imposition. But going well beyond such decisionmaking machinery, they also wanted **Aboriginal self-government.** Although most Aboriginal peoples demand more control over their own affairs, the specific structures of such proposed self-government are not clear-cut. Some advocates would accept a kind of super-municipality, but others have more ambitious plans that would be harder to fit into the Canadian constitutional framework. For the moment, the demand is for a "two-track" approach: constitutional recognition of the inherent right of Aboriginal self-government stemming from their unique history as Canada's original inhabitants, plus concurrent progress toward greater community-based control at the local level. In this way, an array of self-government arrangements and institutional models can be developed within the existing constitutional setup. Self-government would also help Aboriginal peoples take action to preserve Aboriginal languages that are in danger of becoming extinct.

The first improvement in the constitutional recognition of Aboriginal rights occurred in the Constitution Act, 1982. Section 25 guaranteed that Charter rights would not be construed so as to abrogate or derogate from any Aboriginal, treaty, or other rights or freedoms that pertained to the Aboriginal peoples of Canada, including any rights recognized by the Royal Proclamation of 1763, and any rights or freedoms "that now exist by way of land claims agreements or may be so acquired." Section 35 recognized and affirmed the existing Aboriginal and treaty rights of the Aboriginal peoples of Canada, including the Indian, Inuit, and

Adrian Raeside (*Victoria Times-Colonist*). Used with permission.

Métis peoples. Inspired by the equality rights clause in the Charter, the Indian Act was amended to rescind the clause that had previously removed Indian status from Aboriginal women who married white men but granted such status to white women who married Indian men. Bill C-31 led to the reinstatement of nearly 100 000 Aboriginal women and their children, but since bands were allowed to control who could actually live on the reserve, many of those reinstated in status had difficulty in returning to the reserve. Otherwise, the Charter of Rights and its interpretation by the courts has been of limited help to Aboriginal peoples, despite their inclination to take their claims to court when dealing with uncooperative politicians and bureaucrats.[4]

Although mid-1980s constitutional talks on Aboriginal self-government broke down, two pieces of legislation were passed to provide for self-government in specific localities. The 1984 Cree-Naskapi (of Quebec) Act set in place self-government arrangements for the Aboriginal peoples of Quebec who were parties to the James Bay land claim agreement, and the 1986 Sechelt Indian Band Self-Government Act allowed the Sechelt band in British Columbia to assume control over their lands, resources, health and social services, education, and local taxation in what is usually called the "municipal model."

THE MEECH LAKE AND CHARLOTTETOWN ACCORDS AND BEYOND

Canadian Aboriginal peoples were understandably opposed to the 1987 Meech Lake Accord, which addressed Quebec's constitutional demands but completely overlooked their own. Even supporters of the Accord found it hard to blame Elijah Harper for withholding unanimous consent to extend the usual sitting time when it came before the Manitoba legislature for approval in 1990. This action, together with the Oka affair, precipitated a dramatic breakthrough in constitutional concern with Aboriginal issues and in the participation of Aboriginal leaders in constitutional negotiations. Aboriginal leaders were given the same status as premiers in the talks leading up to the 1992 Charlottetown Accord, and that document addressed Aboriginal concerns in a more extensive and satisfactory way than it did the demands of Quebec.

The ill-fated 1992 Charlottetown Accord would have recognized the inherent right of Aboriginal peoples to self-government within Canada and that such Aboriginal governments constituted a third order of government in Canada, analogous to provinces. The document provided for self-government agreements to be negotiated among the three levels of government. Federal and provincial laws would remain in place until superseded by Aboriginal laws, but the latter would have to be consistent with the preservation of peace, order, and good government in Canada.

Since the rejection of the Charlottetown Accord, activity in the area of Aboriginal governance has been limited to legislative and administrative changes, such as experiments in delegating federal or provincial government powers to Aboriginal bands. For example, a framework agreement was signed in 1994 by the Minister of Indian Affairs and the Grand Chief of the Assembly of Manitoba Chiefs to dismantle the Department of Indian Affairs as it affected Aboriginal peoples in that province. The Department is essentially withdrawing from the exercise of its functions at the request of local Aboriginal governments. A year later, the Chrétien government formally launched a negotiating process to implement the inherent right of self-government, with arrangements varying from one group to another. Some 80 Aboriginal groups are involved in these negotiations, such that Aboriginal peoples have increased their control over how federal funding is spent and have assumed responsibility for delivering many of their own educational, social, and health care services.

Much hope for the solution of Aboriginal problems was placed in the Royal Commission on Aboriginal Peoples, appointed in 1991 and reporting in 1996. It endorsed Aboriginal self-government in its widest sense and the basic separation of Aboriginal and non-Aboriginal societies. Among other things, it proposed an Aboriginal Parliament, dual Canadian–Aboriginal citizenship, an independent lands and treaties tribunal, an Aboriginal development bank, an action plan on health and social conditions, and an Aboriginal-controlled education system.

Matthew Coon Come, Grand Chief of the Assembly of First Nations (Andrew Vaughan/CP Picture Archive)

Whether because of the magnitude or the direction of the recommendations, the Chrétien government seemed reluctant to rush into their implementation. It did, however, issue a Statement of Reconciliation, apologizing for past wrongs, especially the horrors of the residential school system.

Comprehensive land claims and self-government agreements are now often negotiated simultaneously, and two prominent examples should be mentioned. In **Nunavut** in the eastern Arctic, the land claim was finalized in 1993; meanwhile, a plebiscite in 1992 had ratified the division of the Northwest Territories. In 1999 the territory of Nunavut was separated from the NWT. It has all the governmental institutions associated with a province or territory, but represents a kind of Aboriginal self-government in the sense that the population is almost completely composed of Inuit. The 2000 Nisga'a Treaty incorporated self-government powers at least analogous to municipal governments, but secured by federal-provincial-Aboriginal agreement. It also contained sections on forestry, mining, wildlife and the environment, the administration of justice, finance, and taxation (including Aboriginals' surrendering their tax-exempt status).

ABORIGINAL JUSTICE

Aboriginal peoples comprise between 15 and 20 percent of the inmates of Canadian correctional institutions, compared to about 4 percent of the population. Thus, one aspect of self-government raised is the concept of a parallel Aboriginal justice system. Aboriginal cases would be diverted from the regular judicial process to allow convictions and sentences based on Aboriginal values and community traditions. Support for this concept has come from many provincial inquiries into the treatment of Aboriginal peoples in the regular judicial system—especially the Donald Marshall Inquiry in Nova Scotia and the Aboriginal Justice Inquiry in Manitoba in 1991. Marshall was a Micmac imprisoned for over 10 years for a crime he did not commit. The Manitoba inquiry centred on the rape and murder of Helen Betty Osborne, an Aboriginal girl in The Pas, by four white men who were protected from prosecution, and on the shooting of an Aboriginal leader by a Winnipeg police officer. More recent cases in Saskatoon and Toronto involving police mistreatment of Aboriginal peoples have even attracted the ire of Amnesty International. These inquiries and cases, and others, documented incidents of misunderstanding, prejudice, harassment, abuse, and brutality by police, courts, and jails. A precedent for the coexistence of two legal systems could perhaps be found in the distinctive civil law system in Quebec.

While governments have generally ruled out a wholesale parallel Aboriginal justice system, several provinces have allowed experimental judicial processes involving Aboriginal input. More Aboriginal peoples have been hired as police officers; some reserves have their own Aboriginal police force; and a few even maintain their own correctional facilities. Increasingly, judges dealing with Aboriginal defendants are following Aboriginal traditions such as sentencing circles or consulting with elders in imposing sentences, including restitution or banishment. Perhaps with the high rate of Aboriginal incarceration in mind, Parliament amended the Criminal Code in 1995 to read: "All available sanctions other than imprisonment … should be considered for all offenders, with particular attention to the circumstances of Aboriginal offenders."

Other Ethnic Groups and Multiculturalism

A third aspect of ethnic cleavage, involving other ethnic groups and multiculturalism, increasingly vies with the French–English and Aboriginal questions on the political agenda. The three principal issues in this area are immigration policy, preserving and promoting the identity of ethnic groups (or multiculturalism), and ensuring that individuals belonging to such groups are treated equitably in law and society.

Canadian Immigration Patterns

The first dramatic surge of immigrants, besides the French and the British, arrived during the 1880s, including Danes, Dutch, Icelanders, Poles, Ukrainians, Finns,

Norwegians, and Swedes. In British Columbia, Asians were a leading group: between 1881 and 1884 nearly 16 000 Chinese were brought in as contract labourers to work on the CPR. Nova Scotia and Ontario also became home to a substantial number of Blacks escaping from slavery in the United States.

An even larger number and variety of immigrants arrived between 1903 and 1914, and the prosperous 1920s were another active decade on the immigration front. Table 4.1 shows immigration arrivals by decade. After the Second World War was over, another huge wave of immigrants came to Canada, largely from southern Europe. They were supplemented by postwar refugees from around the world. Table 4.2 indicates the changing nature of immigration to Canada by decade (see page 76).

TABLE 4.1 IMMIGRANT ARRIVALS IN CANADA BY DECADE

1860–69	156 384
1870–79	328 876
1880–89	846 615
1890–99	372 474
1900–09	1 398 989
1910–19	1 857 269
1920–29	1 264 220
1930–39	252 044
1940–49	428 733
1950–59	1 544 642
1960–69	1 369 304
1970–79	1 444 914
1980–89	1 259 054
1990–99	2 203 949

Source: Citizenship and Immigration, *"Facts and Figures 2000: Immigration Overview,"* http://www.cic.gc.ca/english/pdffiles/pub/facts2000.pdf (Retrieved Sept. 15, 2001). Reproduced with the permission of the Minister of Public Works and Government Services Canada, 2001.

Overall, Britain was the leading source of immigrants between 1900 and 1965. Until 1967, immigration policy favoured British, American, and European newcomers, since they were considered well educated and skilled, and, being predominantly Caucasian, better able to assimilate. After the Immigration Act was significantly amended in 1967, Canadian immigration patterns changed radically, as Table 4.2 shows. In 1957, over 90 percent of immigrants were from Britain or continental Europe, a figure that fell to 72 percent in 1967, 35 percent in 1977,

TABLE 4.2 COMPARISON OF BRITISH, EUROPEAN, AND ASIAN IMMIGRANTS TO CANADA IN SELECTED YEARS (PERCENTAGE)

	Britain	Continental Europe	Asia
1957	38.6	52.6	1.3
1967	28.0	43.8	9.3
1977	15.7	19.8	21.0
1987	5.6	19.1	44.3
1997	2.1	15.8	54.3

Source: Citizenship and Immigration Canada, *Immigration Statistics 1992*, and "Facts and Figures 1999: Immigration Overview," http://www.cic.gc.ca/english/pub/facts99/index.html (Retrieved 15 Sept. 2001).

25 percent in 1987, and 17.9 percent in 1997. In contrast, Asian immigrants were less than 2 percent of the total in 1957, increasing to 9 percent in 1967, 21 percent in 1977, 44 percent in 1987, and 54 percent in 1997. The top 10 source countries over the 1998–2000 period can be seen in Table 4.3. This result was the term **"visible minorities,"** defined as "persons, other than Aboriginal peoples, who are non-Caucasian in race or non-white in colour."

Nearly three-quarters of the visible minorities in Canada reside in the three largest cities, Toronto, Vancouver, and Montreal. Indeed, over 30 percent of the population of Toronto and Vancouver now comprises visible minorities. Immigrant groups can be subdivided between the more recent visible minorities,

TABLE 4.3 TOP TEN SOURCE COUNTRIES, 1998–2000

Country	Number
China	85 607
India	58 859
Pakistan	31 559
Philippines	27 431
Korea	19 761
Iran	18 288
Taiwan	16 166
U.S.A	16 110
Hong Kong	14 607
Sri Lanka	13 882

Source: Citizenship and Immigration Canada, "Facts and Figures 2000: Immigration Overview," (calculations by author) http://www.cic.gc.ca/english/pub/english/pdffiles/pub/facts2000.pdf (Retrieved 15 Sept. 2001).

essentially those from Asia, Africa, the Caribbean, South America, and the Middle East, and those that came earlier from Britain and continental Europe. Some public policies, such as multiculturalism, apply to both groups, while others, such as employment equity, apply only to visible minorities.

Multiculturalism and Related Policies

With the revision of the Immigration Act in 1967, the composition of the Canadian population changed significantly. Such an increase in the numbers of people of "other" ethnic origin naturally gave them more leverage to push for changes in areas where they encountered indifference or discrimination.

Due largely to pressure from Ukrainian Canadians, the 1963 Royal Commission on Bilingualism and Biculturalism was ultimately asked to examine the contribution made by other ethnic groups to the cultural enrichment of Canada and the measures that should be taken to safeguard that contribution. While focusing primarily on English and French, the Commission recommended that increased government attention be given to other ethnic groups, including public funding in certain areas. With this encouragement, such groups began to demand public financial assistance in addition to verbal or moral support, and the term "multiculturalism" came into use.

In 1971, the Trudeau government announced a new policy of multiculturalism within a bilingual framework. Multiculturalism is the official recognition of the diverse cultures in a plural society; it involves encouraging immigrants to retain and foster their linguistic heritages and ethnic cultures instead of abandoning them. The government argued that the Canadian identity would not be undermined by multiculturalism; on the contrary, cultural pluralism was the very essence of the Canadian identity. Multiculturalism is based on the virtues of having a population of diverse origins who make Canada a more interesting place to live. By providing links to virtually every other country in the world, such a population also enhances Canada's international image and influence.

The policy of multiculturalism legitimized demands for many other changes both in terms of promoting ethnic identities and removing barriers to equity. Next was the creation of the Canadian Human Rights Commission in 1978 to complement equivalent bodies at the provincial level. Another advance for multiculturalism was the Charter of Rights and Freedoms in 1982, which provided constitutional protection against discrimination by federal and provincial governments in the **equality rights** clause, section 15. Moreover, the Charter endorsed affirmative action programs in order to overcome past discrimination.

New Canadians take the oath of citizenship (Aaron Harris/CP Picture Archive)

After intense pressure from various ethnic groups, another section was added to the Charter to the effect that it would be interpreted "in a manner consistent with the preservation and enhancement of the multicultural heritage of Canadians" (section 27). The Multiculturalism ministry that began to take form in the 1970s gradually increased in status, and 1988 saw the passage of a new Canadian Multiculturalism Act.

On a different front, the 1986 federal **Employment Equity** Act designated visible minorities along with women, people with disabilities, and Aboriginal peoples as groups that could benefit from affirmative action programs with respect to hiring in the public service. While some ethnic leaders criticized the lack of specific goals and timetables in the legislation, those not included complained about reverse discrimination. Removing legal barriers to equity and/or giving visible minorities an occasional boost, however, does not ensure that they will not encounter discrimination in the daily interactions of life. Besides instances of personal abuse, they still encounter situations where their skills are underutilized and not fairly remunerated.

In 1988, the Mulroney government took action to compensate Japanese Canadians for their mistreatment during the Second World War. Unjustly suspected of being loyal to Japan, Canadian citizens of Japanese background were uprooted from the West Coast, interned in "relocation centres," and had their property confiscated. The 1988 Japanese Redress Agreement provided $21 000 for each of the surviving internees. This led to demands from other ethnic groups that they be similarly compensated for wartime discrimination in Canada.

Reaction against Multiculturalism and Immigration

If the responses to demands from the multicultural community were largely positive in the 1970s and 1980s, such was not the case in the 1990s. Opposition surfaced toward immigration in general and visible minority immigration in particular, including multiculturalism, employment equity, and other policies and practices.[5]

This opposition was partly in response to the recession of the early 1990s and the continuing high unemployment rate afterward. Whatever the real merits of immigration in economic terms, ordinary voters saw recent immigrants in jobs that they felt would otherwise have gone to Canadian residents of longer duration. As for the source of immigrants, while the level of Canadian acceptance and tolerance of nontraditional immigrants is high, it is not unlimited. The Reform Party (now the Canadian Alliance) was the first to break ranks with an all-party consensus on this issue and called for a sizable cut in annual immigration levels, with a greater emphasis on skills. The Chrétien government reduced the immigration level from about 250 000 to about 200 000 in 1994. It also announced that it would place greater emphasis on attracting those with the capacity to settle quickly and contribute to Canada's economy. By the turn of the century, however, over 225 000 immigrants were arriving annually.

The policy of official multiculturalism has been criticized, especially in an era of government fiscal restraint. Even some members of the multicultural community have spoken out against the policy, especially writer Neil Bissoondath. He maintains that official multiculturalism is divisive, ghettoizes visible minorities, fosters racial animosity, and detracts from national unity.[6] Critics argue that it is not appropriate for the government to be fostering the maintenance of foreign traditions while starving national cultural institutions; the money might be better spent teaching immigrants about basic Canadian values. Less opposition to visible minorities was evident at the turn of the new century, even as the number of visible minorities increased. This could have been the result of a more prosperous economy and/or the growing recognition that immigration was essential to economic growth.

The Women's Movement and Other Gender Issues
Evolution of Women's Rights to 1970

Men and male-oriented issues virtually monopolized Canadian politics before 1900. In those early years, when all women were expected to marry and then become chattels of their husbands, they first had to fight for educational and occupational rights, such as admission to universities and to the medical and legal professions. Women demanded the right to make contracts and to own property, and increasingly began to work in factories and offices and to become teachers and nurses; others continued to make major contributions on the farm. About 1900, farm women in particular became active in reform organizations of many kinds, including those that pressed for the prohibition of alcohol and the establishment of new public health facilities, better housing, and improved working conditions for women and children.

As influential as women were in promoting these causes, many began to feel that their impact would always be limited until they could vote. Thus, in what is sometimes called the "first wave" of the women's movement, women demanded the franchise. After the outbreak of the First World War, proponents of female suffrage had an additional argument: women should be rewarded for their contribution to the war effort. Thus, Manitoba, Alberta, and Saskatchewan, the three prairie provinces, containing some of the most articulate women of the day, pioneered the female franchise in 1916; Ontario and British Columbia joined them in 1917; and all the other provinces except Quebec followed shortly afterward.

At the federal level, the Borden government deliberately manipulated the franchise for the 1917 election, in part by giving the vote to women in the armed services (mostly nurses) and by allowing soldiers fighting abroad to appoint their nearest female relative at home—women who would likely support the war effort—to cast their vote by proxy. A year later the vote was extended to all women (except those excluded for ethnic reasons, such as Aboriginal peoples and Asians), and they had their first chance to exercise this new right in the 1921 election.

Two women were elected to the Alberta legislature in 1917, but they were exceptional. Agnes Macphail became the first woman elected to the House of Commons in 1921, but she served alone until 1935, when a second woman was elected. Macphail stayed on until 1940 and then became the first woman elected to the Ontario legislature in 1943. Vigorous and articulate, Macphail promoted

Time Line

Milestones in Women's Rights

1916	Women obtain vote in three provinces
1917/18	Women obtain vote in federal elections
1921	First woman MP
1929	*Persons* case
1940	Women obtain vote in Quebec
1957	First woman federal Cabinet minister
1967/70	Royal Commission on Status of Women
1982	First woman on Supreme Court
1989	First woman federal party leader
1993	First woman prime minister

radical and progressive causes of many kinds, but she could do only so much by herself to advance women's issues in such an entrenched male bastion.

It was not until 1940 that Quebec women were enfranchised in provincial elections. Moreover, the legal status of a married woman under the Quebec Civil Code was such that until 1955 she could not seek a separation on grounds of adultery by her husband, and until 1964 she had no right to carry on a trade without her husband's consent.

The number of women who won seats in the House of Commons was minuscule right up to 1970, and many of those elected were the widows or daughters of male members of Parliament. Female political participation was inhibited by many factors. First, both sexes were traditionally socialized into the view that politics was a masculine pursuit and that women should remain in the home. Second, most women were constrained by the responsibilities of homemaking and childrearing. Such roles had little prestige and prevented women from accumulating the money, contacts, and experience that political careers usually require. The long hours and unpredictable schedules of politicians conflicted with most women's family commitments, which prevented them from being away from home for any length of time. Third, political parties discouraged female candidacies, and when consciousness of the lack of female candidates increased, parties frequently nominated them as sacrificial lambs against a strong male incumbent.

Until the late 1920s, no women had been appointed to the other house of Parliament, the Senate. When an enterprising group of Western women took this issue to court, the Supreme Court of Canada ruled that women were not "qualified persons" within the meaning of s. 24 of the 1867 Constitution Act and were therefore ineligible to sit in the Senate. This decision was appealed to the Judicial Committee of the Privy Council, which in the 1929 *Persons* Case overruled the Supreme Court. The women's movement continues to celebrate this decision to this day in the form of the "Person's Day Breakfast." Prime Minister Mackenzie King immediately appointed Cairine Wilson to the Senate, but the second woman was not appointed until 1935, and 18 years would pass before three more received the call.

In the Words of the Court (the Judicial Committee of the Privy Council)

"The exclusion of women from all public offices is a relic of days more barbarous than ours ... [T]heir Lordships have come to the conclusion that the word "persons" in s. 24 includes members both of the male and female sex ..." (*Henrietta Muir Edwards v. Attorney-General for Canada*, better known as the "*Persons* case").

It was not until 1957 that the first woman, Ellen Fairclough, was appointed to the federal cabinet; she was followed by Judy LaMarsh in 1963. The advance of women to the cabinet at the provincial level was generally even slower. Nevertheless, gradual improvements continued to be made in federal and provincial legislation and programs of benefit to women. The federal Family Allowances Act of 1944, for example, provided a small monthly payment to each Canadian mother to help care for her children, and often represented the only independent income the woman possessed. In 1952, Ontario passed the first equal pay legislation, to be followed by federal legislation two years later. Amendments to the Criminal Code in 1969 made it legal to advertise birth control devices in Canada, and a new Divorce Act made it easier to get out of an unfulfilling marriage.

The Women's Movement since 1970

By 1970 attitudes had changed sufficiently that it was possible to speak of a **women's movement,** and the word "feminist" became common. In their most general sense, such terms are used to apply to those who seek to establish complete gender equality, to free men and women from restrictive gender roles, and to end any semblance of the subordination of women.

This "second wave" of the women's movement coincided with the Royal Commission on the Status of Women, appointed in 1967 and reporting in 1970. That report "provided a solid statistical base and a framework for most of the feminist action that followed during the 1970s"[7] and made 167 recommendations. Since that time, gender issues have become an important, daily factor in Canadian politics, and most governments now designate a minister responsible for women's issues. Ottawa issued a Federal Plan for Gender Equality in 1995.

The number of women's groups has increased remarkably in recent years, the foremost pressure group being the **National Action Committee on the Status of Women (NAC).** NAC was established in 1972, largely because of government inaction on the Status of Women report, and functions as an umbrella lobbying group for over 650 local and national member groups representing over three million women. Although large in membership, its chronic shortage of funds has hampered its effectiveness, a problem exacerbated by the withdrawal of much federal government funding in recent years.

POLITICAL REPRESENTATION

In the post–1970 era, women's participation in politics and government increased substantially and, for the first time, regularly. Table 4.4 charts this progress (see page 84). Many of the factors mentioned above that inhibited women from becoming politicians before 1970 are still present, although in recent years most parties have created special funds to support female candidates.

At the cabinet level, a few more women were appointed during the 1970s, but by the 1980s, the one or two token female ministers were clearly considered to be insufficient. Brian Mulroney appointed six women to his 1984 cabinet, for example, while in the provinces the number of women ministers gradually increased too. Bob Rae came close to gender equality in his Ontario NDP cabinet in 1990.

It was also in the post–1970 period that Canada finally saw women elected as political party leaders. Alexa McDonough (NDP, Nova Scotia) led the way in 1980, to be followed by Sharon Carstairs, Elizabeth Weir, Barbara Baird-Filliter, Lynda Haverstock, Lyn McLeod, Rita Johnston, Catherine Callbeck, Pam Barrett, and Nancy MacBeth. After Rosemary Brown made a serious stab at the NDP national leadership in 1975 and Flora Macdonald sought the PC's in 1976, it remained for Audrey McLaughlin to make history when she was elected leader of the federal New Democratic Party in 1989, the first woman to lead a major national party. Alexa McDonough moved from Nova Scotia to succeed her in 1995.

TABLE 4.4 REPRESENTATION OF WOMEN IN THE HOUSE OF COMMONS, 1921–2000

Election	Number Elected	Election	Number Elected	Election	Number Elected
1921	1	1953	4	1974	9
1925	1	1957	2	1979	11
1926	1	1958	2	1980	14
1930	1	1962	4	1984	27
1935	2	1963	4	1988	39
1940	1	1965	3	1993	53
1945	1	1968	1	1997	62
1949	0	1972	4	2000	62

Source: Status of Women Canada, *A Canadian Chronology*, 1994, supplemented by 1997 and 2000 election results. Reproduced with the permission of the Minister of Public Works and Government Services Canada, 2001.

Three women have become first ministers: Rita Johnson (B.C.), Catherine Callbeck (P.E.I.), and Prime Minister Kim Campbell. Jeanne Sauvé was the first woman Speaker of the House of Commons and first woman governor general; Bertha Wilson became the first woman to sit on the Supreme Court of Canada (1982). Women judges have been appointed at an ever-increasing rate in other courts, and in 1999, about 20 percent of federally appointed judges were women. In 2000, Beverley McLachlin became the first female Chief Justice.

Within the federal bureaucracy, the first women joined the RCMP in 1974, and the first woman deputy minister was appointed in 1975; women gradually became eligible for full combat roles in the armed forces, and the first woman general was named in 1988. In 1993, Jocelyne Bourgon became the first woman to hold the top public service position in Ottawa, Clerk of the Privy Council and Secretary to the Cabinet.

EMPLOYMENT ISSUES

Since about 70 percent of women of working age are now in the labour force, and because women constitute about 46 percent of the labour force, one major feminist concern is employment. Women have traditionally been discriminated against in pay, underrepresented in managerial positions, and discouraged from undertaking nontraditional occupations. In 1985, full-time female workers earned on average 65.5 percent of what men earned, leading women to demand "equal pay for work of equal value" or **pay equity.** Most Canadian governments now have pay equity legislation, and by 1998, women's full-time earnings had risen to an average of 72.2 percent of men's.[8]

Beyond pay equity is the broader subject of **employment equity,** that is, the elimination of discrimination in hiring and promoting women. Employment equity is sometimes combined with affirmative action programs to give women preference in order to make up for past inequities. In 1983, affirmative action with respect to the hiring of women was made mandatory in all federal government departments, and the 1984 Royal Commission Report, *Equality in Employment*, became the foundation of the 1986 Employment Equity Act. It extended employment equity requirements to all Crown corporations, all federally regulated companies with over 100 employees, and other large companies in receipt of major government contracts. Nevertheless, while women now constitute about 50 percent of the federal government workforce, they occupy only 25 percent of executive-level jobs. Ontario passed an even more extensive Employment Equity Act in 1993, but it was quickly repealed by the new Conservative government of Mike Harris.

The area in which women are most severely underrepresented is at the top of private corporations. A 1999 survey of the top 500 industrial companies in Canada found only 13 women who held the position of chief executive officer. Notable examples were Maureen Kempston Darkes at General Motors and Heather Reisman at Indigo Books and Chapters.

LEGAL, REPRODUCTIVE, SEXUAL, AND VIOLENCE ISSUES

As the 1982 Charter of Rights and Freedoms emerged from federal–provincial negotiation, gender equality was to be lumped into section 15's equality rights with such other factors as race, religion, and age, which governments would be allowed to override with the notwithstanding clause. Such treatment at the hands of 11 male first ministers galvanized the women's movement as never before; as a result of its tremendous pressure, section 28 was added to the final document to give gender equality a place of its own, protected from the notwithstanding clause.[9]

There followed a series of feminist challenges to laws that women believed discriminated against them. The government itself encouraged such legal activity with the Court Challenges Program, under which it subsidized the Legal Education and Action Fund (LEAF) in making such challenges. Women have not won every such case, but among their victories was the right to maternity leave under the Unemployment Insurance Act.

One of the main feminist rallying cries of the post–1970 period is that women must be able to control what happens to their own bodies. Many women's organizations supported Dr. Henry Morgentaler in his long fight to reform the Criminal Code's provisions on abortion.[10] Although amendments were made in 1968, feminists did not regard these as sufficient, and the Supreme Court of Canada threw out the abortion law in the famous 1988 *Morgentaler* case. In 1990, the Mulroney government introduced a compromise abortion law, but it was defeated in the Senate, leaving Canada with no federal law restricting abortion. Even so, access to abortion varies widely across the country. The Mulroney government also appointed a Royal Commission on New Reproductive Technologies, whose 1993 report generally endorsed a cautious approach to this controversial subject. Prostitution and pornography have also been subject to judicial decision, while sexual stereotyping, sexual harassment, and physical and sexual assault are other major issues of concern to women. They gained a partial victory in "rape-shield" sexual assault cases, when questions to defendants about past sexual history were somewhat restricted.

THE FEMINIZATION OF POVERTY AND DAYCARE

Chapter 2 revealed the large extent to which Canada has experienced the "feminization of poverty." As pointed out there, about 56 percent of sole-support mothers raise their children below the poverty line. With or without a male partner, large numbers of women with pre-school children find it necessary to work outside the home to support themselves and their families.[11] This continued even after the National Child Tax Benefit was added to the income tax system to replace the Family Allowance for lower-income families. To decrease the incidence of women living in poverty, measures such as pay equity, employment equity, higher minimum wages, increased unionization, and improved job training and literacy programs will be required.

One of the major unresolved women's issues today is that of daycare for children of parents working outside the home, especially children of single mothers. Of course, some single mothers or two-parent families are happy to rely on relatives, friends, or other unlicensed facilities, but it is clear that a serious shortage of childcare spaces exists. Both PC and Liberal governments have reneged on promises of a national daycare program.

Gay and Lesbian Issues

A variety of issues related to homosexuality have arisen in recent years, and these also figure prominently on today's political agenda. In most cases, politicians are reluctant to deal with demands coming from the gay, lesbian, and bisexual communities, leaving such groups to take their concerns directly to the courts.

One of the group's first demands was for protection in human rights codes from individual discrimination, and somewhat surprisingly, the breakthrough came in Quebec. When the Charter of Rights and Freedoms was adopted in 1982, section 15 prohibited discrimination by government or in law on the basis of sex, but sexual orientation was not explicitly included. In the 1995 *Egan* case, however, the Supreme Court of Canada ruled unanimously that the clause did indeed include sexual orientation, although it was subject to reasonable limits. By the late 1990s, whether by legislation or court action (as in the *Vriend* case in Alberta), sexual orientation had been added to all the human rights codes in Canada. Such federal and provincial legislation protects homosexuals from discrimination in the private sector.

The next phase of the battle for equality in this area centred on gay and lesbian couples. In two cases from Ontario, the *Rosenberg* case and M. *v. H.*, the courts recognized same-sex equality rights in pension benefits after death and in financial support after separation. In the latter case, the Supreme Court advised Ontario to amend other laws that continued to treat same-sex couples differently from others. Thus, in 1999 and 2000, Quebec, Ontario, and the federal government all passed omnibus legislation to make such amendments across the board. In some cases, however, they continued to define "marriage" as a union between a man and a woman, and made a distinction between a "same-sex partner" and a "spouse." A number of homosexual couples challenged such distinctions, as well as restrictions on adoption, issues that remain unresolved.

In the meantime, the 2001 census included a question on same-sex partners for the first time. Regardless of the Constitution and the law, many employers in both the public and private sectors have extended employee benefits (health, dental, and retirement plans) to same-sex couples. No government has yet made this practice mandatory by law, and an attempt to do so was defeated in the Ontario legislature in 1994.

DISCUSSION QUESTIONS

1. To what extent should Aboriginal peoples in Canada be self-governing?
2. To what extent should Canada pursue the policy of multiculturalism?
3. To what extent do we need employment equity laws in support of women, Aboriginal peoples, visible minorities, and people with disabilities?

4. What are the most significant current public policy issues of interest to women?
5. How far should we go in public or private policies recognizing same-sex relationships?

FURTHER READING

Aboriginal Peoples

Alfred, Taiaiake. *Peace, Power, Righteousness: An Indigenous Manifesto*. Toronto: Oxford University Press, 1999.

Berger, Thomas. *A Long and Terrible Shadow: White Values, Native Rights in the Americas*. Vancouver: Douglas and McIntyre, 1991.

Boldt, Menno. *Surviving as Indians: The Challenge of Self-Government*. Toronto: University of Toronto Press, 1993.

Frideres, James S. *Aboriginal Peoples in Canada: Contemporary Conflicts*. 5th ed., Scarborough: Prentice-Hall Canada, 1998.

Long, David, and Olive Dickason. *Visions of the Heart: Canadian Aboriginal Issues*. Toronto: Harcourt Brace, 1996.

Mercredi, Ovid. *In the Rapids: Navigating the Future of First Nations*. Toronto: Viking, 1993.

Morrison, Andrea. *Justice for Natives: Searching for Common Ground*. Montreal: McGill-Queen's University Press, 1997.

Other Ethnic Groups

Bissoondath, Neil. *Selling Illusions: The Cult of Multiculturalism in Canada*. Toronto: Penguin, 1994.

Driedger, Leo. *Multi-Ethnic Canada: Identities and Inequalities*. Toronto: Oxford University Press, 1996.

Elliott, Jean Leonard, and Augie Fleras. *Multiculturalism in Canada: The Challenge of Diversity*. Scarborough: Nelson Canada, 1991.

Troper, Harold, and Morton Weinfeld. *Ethnicity, Politics and Public Policy*. Toronto: University of Toronto Press, 1999.

Gender

Andrew, Caroline, and Sanda Rodgers, eds. *Women and the Canadian State*. Montreal: McGill-Queen's University Press, 1997.

Bashevkin, Sylvia. *Women on the Defensive*. Toronto: University of Toronto Press, 1998.

Dobrowolsky, Alexandra. *The Politics of Pragmatism: Women, Representation, and Constitutionalism in Canada*. Toronto: Oxford University Press, 1999.

Herman, Didi. *Rights of Passage: Struggles for Lesbian and Gay Legal Equality*. Toronto: University of Toronto Press, 1994.

Johnson, Holly. *Dangerous Domains: Violence against Women in Canada*. Scarborough: Nelson Canada, 1996.

MacIvor, H. *Women and Politics in Canada*. Peterborough, Ont.: Broadview, 1996.

Sharpe, Sydney. *The Gilded Ghetto: Women and Political Power in Canada*. Toronto: HarperCollins, 1994.

Smith, Miriam. *Lesbian and Gay Rights in Canada: Social Movements and Equality-Seeking, 1971–1995*. Toronto: University of Toronto Press, 1999.

Notes

1. Thomas R. Berger, *A Long and Terrible Shadow: White Values, Native Rights in the Americas* (Vancouver: Douglas and McIntyre, 1991).
2. "Basic Departmental Data, 1999," Department of Indian Affairs and Northern Development Web site http://www.ainc-inac.gc.ca/pr/sts/bdd99//index_e.htm (Retrieved 15 Sept. 2001).
3. Geoffrey York and Loreen Pindera, *People of the Pines: The Warriors and the Legacy of Oka* (Toronto: Little Brown, 1991); Craig MacLaine and Michael Baxendale, *This Land Is Our Land* (Toronto: Optimum, 1990).
4. For example, the two Marshall decisions: R. v. Marshall, [1999] 3 S.C.R., 456 and R. v. Marshall, [1999] 3 S.C.R., 533, and a 2001 Supreme Court decision that rebuffed the Akwesasne Mohawks' claim of an Aboriginal right to import goods from the United States without paying duties.
5. Jean Leonard Elliott and Augie Fleras, *Multiculturalism in Canada: The Challenge of Diversity* (Scarborough: Nelson Canada, 1991).
6. Neil Bissoondath, *Selling Illusions: The Cult of Multiculturalism in Canada* (Toronto: Penguin, 1994).
7. Penney Kome, *Women of Influence* (Toronto: University of Toronto Press, 1985), 86.
8. "Average Earnings by Sex and Work Pattern," Statistics Canada Web site www.statcan.ca:80/english/Pgdb/People/Labour/labor01b.htm (Retrieved 15 Sept. 2001). Two other useful Statistics Canada sources are *Women in Canada 2000* (cat. No. 89-503-XPE) and *The Persistent Gap: New Evidence on the Canadian Gender Wage Gap* (cat. no. 11F0019MPE, no. 157).
9. Penney Kome, *The Taking of Twenty-Eight* (Toronto: Women's Educational Press, 1983); Women of Influence, ch. 10.
10. Janine Brodie et al., *The Politics of Abortion* (Toronto: Oxford University Press, 1992).
11. David P. Ross, Katherine J. Scott, and Peter J. Smith, *The Canadian Fact Book on Poverty—2000* (Ottawa: Canadian Council on Social Development, 1990).

Chapter 5

The Global Context of Canadian Politics

Canada does not exist in a vacuum; instead, it is linked to the rest of the world by all sorts of political, economic, defensive, cultural, demographic, individual, and technological ties. In colonial times, all basic governmental decisions for the country were made in Britain. As Canada emerged into a sovereign state, however, the world was becoming increasingly interdependent, so that even though it gained the legal powers to make decisions for itself, Canada became particularly susceptible to influence from the United States. Nowadays, the external constraints are much more numerous, and could be said to constitute the "global" environment of the Canadian political system. A multitude of states, international organizations, international agreements, and transnational corporations have an ever-increasing impact upon it, complicating the efforts of governments to pursue their own policy preferences. This was evident even before Canada joined the "war against terrorism" after September 11, 2001.

Chapter Objectives

After you have finished this chapter, you should be able to:

Trace the evolution of Canadian autonomy from Britain

Discuss the American influences on Canadian defence and foreign policies

Contrast the arguments in favour of and opposed to foreign investment in Canada

Comment on American influences on other aspects of Canadian economic policies

Identify policies adopted to promote and protect Canadian culture

Discuss the concept of globalization and its effects on Canadian policy-making

··

The Road to Canadian Sovereignty from Britain

The British North American colonies were largely self-governing in internal affairs even before 1867. Contrary to popular belief, the British North America Act of 1867 (that is, the **Constitution Act, 1867**) did not directly advance the cause of Canadian independence. Although the act of confederation made Canada a more respectable and viable entity and ultimately strengthened its case for greater autonomy, it did not alter the British–Canadian relationship. In theory, the British government could still overturn any statute passed by the Canadian Parliament, although in practice, it rarely did so.

In external relations, Canada had succeeded in claiming the right to control its own tariffs even before Confederation, and between 1867 and 1914 it became increasingly autonomous in making treaties with other countries. By the turn of the century, Canada sent an official contingent to the South African (Boer) War more in response to Canadian public opinion than to British pressure. In the Alaska Boundary dispute of 1903, however, the British representative on the Anglo-Canadian half of the judicial tribunal voted with the three American representatives to award the United States a long strip of the northern British Columbia coastline.

The ultimate independence of Canada and several other British colonies is usually attributed to developments connected to the First World War. Although Canada was automatically at war in 1914 as a result of British action, a series of conferences of Dominion prime ministers began in 1917 as Canada and the other Dominions demanded a say in return for their wartime contributions. Prime Minister Robert Borden and his counterparts participated in the Paris Peace Conference and signed the peace treaties, and the Dominions became individual members of the League of Nations. Thus, by 1919, Canada had gained new international status as a result of accomplishments on the battlefield and subsequent demands for recognition at the conference table.

The Imperial Conference of 1926 ended with a proclamation of the complete equality of the United Kingdom and the Dominions in internal, international, and imperial affairs. They were proclaimed

> *autonomous Communities within the British Empire, equal in status, in no way subordinate one to another in any aspect of their domestic or external affairs, though united by a common allegiance to the Crown, and freely associated as members of the British Commonwealth of Nations.*[1]

Besides giving Canada complete autonomy in all policy fields, the developments of 1926 had implications for the position of governor general. This official would no longer be an agent of the British government, but rather only a representative of the Crown. These arrangements were refined at another conference in 1930 and then constitutionalized in the **Statute of Westminster** of 1931.

After 1931, therefore, Canada was completely independent of Britain, but a number of anomalies helped to disguise this fact. First, Canada continued to share a head of state with Britain, although from the Canadian perspective, that person was King or Queen of Canada. Of more importance, since Canada had not been able to decide how to amend the B.N.A. Act within Canada, such amendments still had to be passed by the British Parliament, albeit only at Canadian request. Also of great significance, but due to Canadian inaction, the Judicial Committee of the Privy Council remained Canada's final court of appeal until 1949.

Canada made an autonomous decision to take part in the Second World War, after which British–Canadian ties declined. Later, Canada's population became more diversified in its ethnic origins, Britain occupied a diminished role in world affairs, and Canada drew closer to the United States.[2] The 1982 Constitution Act removed the Constitution from any kind of British custody, with a new formula for amending it in Canada. After that, Canada shared only the Queen with Britain (and several other states), but in her capacity as the Canadian head of state, she provides no official link between the two countries.

Time Line on Canadian Independence

1919	Member of the League of Nations
1926	Imperial Conference confers autonomy on Dominions
1931	Statute of Westminster
1949	Supreme Court of Canada becomes final court of appeal
1982	Made-in-Canada constitutional amending formula

The American Sphere of Influence

Even before becoming fully autonomous from Britain, Canada began its slow but steady absorption into the U.S. sphere of influence. The United States not only pressures Canada on a daily basis but also serves as a model for many Canadians.

Its influence can thus be seen in such areas as defence and foreign policy, economic policy, and culture.

Defence and Foreign Policy

After the Second World War, the United States became increasingly obsessed with containing Soviet communism, and in 1949 persuaded Canada and most western European countries to form a new military alliance, the North Atlantic Treaty Organization (NATO). Commitments to NATO required a great increase in the size of the Canadian armed forces. U.S. attention was then drawn to the confrontation between North and South Korea, and the United Nations military intervention in the Korean War was effectively a U.S. effort to which Canada made a significant military contribution, losing 1550 lives.

The next phase of the North Americanization of Canadian defence was a series of radar screens built across the United States and Canada during the 1950s to intercept anticipated Soviet bombers. These arrangements logically led to what is now called the North American Aerospace Defence Command (NORAD) of 1958. The agreement provided for a joint Canada–U.S. air defence system with headquarters in Colorado. A Defence Production Sharing Program was added to these collaborative schemes in 1959.

Prime Minister John Diefenbaker encountered two serious missile crises with the United States in the 1957–63 period. When U.S. President John F. Kennedy used the establishment of Soviet missile bases in Cuba as an excuse to announce a naval blockade of that country, the Canadian cabinet waited three days before putting its armed forces in a state of highest alert. Kennedy's anger at this delay was compounded by American annoyance at Canada's stand with respect to BOMARC missiles. These had been established by the United States at two bases in Canada as part of the NORAD Agreement and were intended to be armed with nuclear warheads. Some cabinet ministers argued that to place the warheads on Canadian soil would appear to proliferate the nuclear arms race, and the Canadian–American defence relationship thus became a prominent issue in the 1962 and 1963 election campaigns. The Diefenbaker government fell apart over the issue in 1963 and was defeated on a nonconfidence motion. The Liberals won the resulting election under Lester Pearson, and the new prime minister had the warheads installed as part of Canada's international commitments.

Pearson's successor, Pierre Trudeau, removed the warheads, cut military spending, and, in a new emphasis on protecting domestic sovereignty, halved Canada's NATO contingent. Nevertheless, the NORAD Agreement was repeatedly renewed. Trudeau then allowed the United States to test yet another new weapon, the Cruise missile, over Canadian territory because of the resemblance of its terrain to that of the Soviet Union.

The Mulroney government promised to make defence a much higher priority and published a hawkish White Paper on the subject in 1987. Public opposition and budgetary considerations prevented the paper's implementation, however, a decision that appeared to have been farsighted when the Cold War effectively ended a year or so later. Canada participated in the U.S.–led Gulf War coalition, and then in the various phases of the Balkan war. Even in the new century, Canada is under pressure to agree to a new U.S. missile defence system (NMD— National Missile Defence), and responded quickly to the call to join the American-led "war on terrorism."

Thus it is clear that for at least 50 years the United States exerted significant pressure on Canadian defence policy. Even though Canada did not always respond as energetically as the United States wished, such external demands influenced Canadian political outcomes. Some Canadians were satisfied with the arrangement because the country was essentially protected by the U.S. military arsenal and had to pay relatively little for its own defence. Others did not like the U.S. pressure and the loss of control of a vital aspect of public policy.

To the extent that foreign policy can be distinguished from defence policy, the degree of U.S. influence in this field has also been a controversial question. Canada sees itself as a "middle power" that has staked out an independent position on recognizing and/or trading with countries such as China, Cuba, and the Soviet Union. On the other hand, the United States tends to view Canadian support of its initiatives as automatic. The Canadian government was quick to respond to U.S. demands to contribute to its military efforts in Kuwait and its peacekeeping mission in Somalia, both ostensibly in the name of the United Nations. Moreover, the United States continued to retaliate against Canadian companies that did business in Cuba.

More independently, Canada responded to international pressure and made a major humanitarian contribution in the Bosnian civil war, as well as in Rwanda. Canada was also a leader in the campaign to ban anti-personnel landmines and to establish an International Criminal Court.

Economic Policy

The economic influence of the United States on Canada is even more pervasive than its impact on defence and foreign policy. This influence is felt in almost every aspect of Canadian life, including investment, trade, environment, and energy. In many ways, Canada constitutes a zone within the American economy rather than a distinctive national economy.

FOREIGN INVESTMENT

A new country is not likely to produce enough domestic capital to finance all the development projects desired. Therefore, in the early years, a great deal of investment in Canada came from Britain. Some of this foreign capital consisted of British companies operating in Canada, such as the Hudson's Bay Company, but to a large extent it took the form of Canadian borrowing in the London bond market. Interest had to be paid on such loans, but ownership remained largely in Canadian hands.

   Later, the main source of foreign investment shifted from Britain to the United States. Moreover, the form of investment switched from loans to "direct" or "equity" investment, that is, control through the ownership of shares. Table 5.1 indicates the shift from British to U.S. investment in Canada between 1900 and 1999. To a large extent, the Canadian economy has come to consist of branch plants of U.S. parent corporations; since these companies typically operate in many other countries, they therefore gain the label of "multinational" or "transnational" corporations.

TABLE 5.1 PERCENTAGE OF BRITISH, U.S., AND OTHER FOREIGN INVESTMENT IN
            CANADA, 1900–1999

	1900	1914	1930	1939	1946	1950	1960	1967	1985	1999
U.S.	13.6	23.0	61.2	60.0	71.8	75.5	75.2	80.7	75.6	72.2
U.K.	85.2	72.4	36.3	35.8	23.2	20.1	15.1	10.3	9.5	5.9
Other	1.1	4.6	2.4	4.1	4.9	4.2	9.6	8.9	14.9	21.8

Source: Privy Council Office, Foreign Direct Investment in Canada, 1972, p. 15 and Statistics Canada, Canada's International Investment Position, cat. no. 67-202, March 2000, p. 40. Reproduced with permission of the Minister of Public Works and Government Services, 2001.

   This pattern of economic development was fostered in the first instance by the **National Policy** of 1879, which put a tariff on imported manufactured goods. Rather than export to Canada from the United States and pay the tariff, U.S. companies set up branch plants within Canada behind the tariff wall. This was advantageous for the creation of employment in Canada and contributed to the general prosperity of the country, especially Ontario. As time went on, however, considerable capital was generated within Canada, but the degree of foreign ownership continued to increase.

It was not only U.S. manufacturers that moved into Canada but also foreign companies that sought to exploit Canadian natural resources. "A large proportion of the investment in resource exploitation reflected the needs of the United States investors for raw materials for their processing and manufacturing plants in the United States." This integration often had the practical impact "of reducing the likelihood of further processing activity of Canadian natural resources in Canada."[3] Thus, along with many aspects of manufacturing, the mining, forestry, and petroleum industries came to be characterized by a high degree of foreign, mostly American, ownership. In fact, Canada has more foreign ownership than any other advanced industrial country, although, as the table shows, the sources of recent international investment in Canada are more diversified than in the past.

The 10 largest multinationals operating in Canada in 2000 are identified in Table 5.2. Other familiar foreign-owned corporate names include Wal-Mart, Mitsui, Cargill, Mobil Oil, Costco, DuPont, Fletcher Challenge, General Electric, McDonald's, Toyota, Kraft, Hewlett-Packard, and Pratt & Whitney. In total, 27 of the top 100 companies in Canada in terms of 1999 sales were foreign owned.

TABLE 5.2 TEN LARGEST MULTINATIONAL COMPANIES IN CANADA, 2000

General Motors of Canada Ltd. (U.S.)	Sears Canada Inc. (U.S.)
Ford Motor Co. of Canada Ltd. (U.S.)	Honda Canada Inc. (Japan)
DaimlerChrysler Canada Inc. (U.S.)	Shell Canada Ltd. (Netherlands)
Imperial Oil Ltd. (U.S.)	Canada Safeway Ltd. (U.S.)
Imperial Tobacco Canada Ltd. (U.K.)	Canadian Ultramar Co. (U.S.)

Source: The *National Post*, *The Business 500*, Summer 2000. Reproduced with the permission of the *National Post*.

Most advocates of the capitalist system are enthusiastic boosters of unlimited foreign investment. They claim that maximum efficiency results from capital being able to flow to wherever it will yield the greatest returns. In this case, defenders of foreign investment argue that Canada still needs foreign capital and that such investment creates jobs, which in turn raise the Canadian standard of living. They also claim that efficiency is enhanced when multinationals transfer "state-of-the-art" technology as well as well-trained managers and management techniques to their branch plants.

Others take the view that these advantages are short-term or short-sighted.[4] First, multinationals are likely to purchase supplies and component parts from the parent company or parent country, rather than buying them and creating employment in Canada. Second, their plants usually remain small and inefficient because they are designed to serve only the Canadian market rather than being encouraged to compete in export markets with the parent plant or with branches set up in other countries. Critics also claim that a branch-plant economy suffers because most of its research and development (R & D) is done in the parent plant in the parent country. This limits the number of interesting and challenging jobs in science, engineering, and technology located in Canada. As convenient as it is to import such technology, this process hinders Canadian innovative efforts to develop distinctive export products, for most studies indicate that R & D is the secret of future economic success. Critics of the situation also worry that if layoffs or shutdowns are necessary, these are usually slated for branch plants first.

The ultimate symbolic disadvantage of foreign-owned companies is that they may occasionally choose or be required to conform to the laws of the country in which their parent is located rather than those of Canada. The extension of U.S. laws to branch plants located in Canada is called extraterritoriality, and has regularly occurred, especially in the case of the *Trading with the Enemy Act* and the *Helms-Burton Act*. When branch plants in Canada have tried to do business with countries on the U.S. "enemy list" (Cuba, in terms of Helms-Burton), they have been told that they must follow U.S. law, thus reducing production and job opportunities in Canada.

The policies that Canadian governments have adopted to counter this threat of U.S. or other foreign ownership of the Canadian economy can be divided into four main categories. First, Crown corporations—government-owned enterprises—have been established to ensure that the company involved remains in Canadian hands. Atomic Energy of Canada Ltd. and Petro-Canada were created by the federal government in response to demands that a Canadian presence in strategic industries be retained.

Second, while leaving other corporations to function privately, the federal government often created regulatory agencies. The main such agency was the Foreign Investment Review Agency (FIRA), established in the early 1970s. FIRA screened foreign takeovers of larger Canadian companies and new ventures by foreign firms in Canada, approving the deal if it involved "significant benefit to Canada." In fact, FIRA rarely disallowed any such initiatives and imposed minimal conditions, but even so it became a major irritant to the United States, and the Mulroney government replaced it with Investment Canada. However, in its new form, the agency's goal was to attract increased foreign investment to Canada. Other regulatory agencies include the National Energy Board and the Canadian Nuclear Safety Commission (formerly the Atomic Energy Control Board), which were designed to protect the Canadian national interest in certain important respects.

Third, ownership restrictions and tax incentives have been introduced. Maximum foreign-ownership limits exist in fields such as broadcasting, financial institutions, newspapers and publishing, and (before the Free Trade Agreement) banking. Incentives to Canadian ownership were exemplified by the **National Energy Program (NEP)** of 1980, under which, largely via tax write-offs, the Reichmann brothers bought Gulf Canada from its American owners. Finally, the government has established funding agencies such as the Business Development Bank of Canada, whose mandate is to encourage Canadian entrepreneurship when the commercial banks are not interested.

Many of these policies were half-hearted and others were later diluted under U.S. pressure. Many were weakened or withdrawn by the Mulroney government, both to increase foreign investment and to remove irritants in the Canada–U.S. relationship. The proportion of foreign control has increased since 1984, and the low value of the Canadian dollar has made Canadian firms ripe for sale to foreigners. Thus, economic nationalists regard the situation as more critical than ever, while others remain indifferent or take the opposite side of this issue, seeing foreign investment as the source of badly needed jobs and a natural aspect of globalization.

TRADE

Because of geographic proximity, it is only logical that Canada and the United States are closely linked by trade. It is even more likely because of their complementary resources and industries—the abundance of primary resources in Canada and the extent of manufacturing in the United States. Thus, Canadian dependence on the United States as a market for its exports and as a source of its imports has gradually increased over time. Indeed, most provinces now trade more with neighbouring states than with each other, although much of this trade is of an intrafirm character rather than truly international.

Canadian exports to the United States exceeded those to the United Kingdom after 1921 and edged up to over 82 percent of all exports by 1994. Imports from the United States constituted nearly 50 percent of the Canadian total from the start and rose to 75 percent in 1994 and since. The 2000 proportions can be seen in Figure 5.1.

. . . .

Figure 5.1   Canada's Imports and Exports, 2000

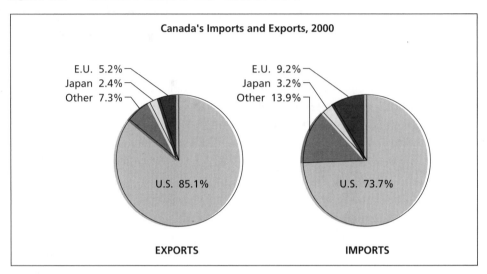

Source: "Imports and Exports of Goods on a Balance-of-Payments Basis," Statistics Canada Web site www.statcan.ca/english/Pgd/Economy/Internation/glec02a.htm (Retrieved 15 Sept. 2001).

Given the degree to which Canadian prosperity depends on export trade, it is advantageous to have ready access to the U.S. market; it is also convenient to have such a close supply of goods that are not produced in Canada. On the other hand, to have so many eggs in one basket means that in times of U.S. recession, demand for Canadian goods falls off and the Canadian economy declines, whereas in prosperous periods, U.S. inflation also tends to increase prices in Canada. Furthermore, protectionist pressure in the United States for new or increased tariffs or quotas against Canadian exports can have a devastating effect on certain industries, such as softwood lumber.

THE ENVIRONMENT

Canadians have seriously damaged their own environment over the years, but the situation has been aggravated by proximity to the United States and by some of its even less restrictive anti-pollution laws. The largest transboundary environmental issue is that of acid rain. Canadian research generally shows that about 50 percent of the acid rain falling north of the border is caused by U.S. sources, primarily coal-fired power plants in the Midwest. These emissions fall into Canadian lakes and rivers, killing plant and animal life and damaging trees, cars, and buildings. Thus, after pressing the issue for many years, Canada welcomed the U.S.

Clean Air Act of 1990 as a step forward in controlling North American air pollution; however, it was not a complete solution.

The pollution of the Great Lakes is the other serious bilateral environmental problem. Here again, each side is to blame, but most of the chemicals are discharged from the larger number of factories and waste dumps situated on the U.S. shores of the lakes. Phosphorous levels were reduced in the 1970s, but the Great Lakes are still in a critical state because of toxic pollution. Indeed, recent government cutbacks in environmental protection on both sides of the border have made the problem worse.

Canada has been involved in many offshore fishing disputes, especially on the Atlantic coast, and often not involving Americans. But in the late 1990s, the major confrontation in this field was the "salmon war" with the United States on the Pacific coast.

ENERGY

In the energy sector, the voracious U.S. industrial complex usually wants to import Canadian electric power, oil, and natural gas. Governments in Quebec, New Brunswick, Manitoba, and B.C. have been eager to export electricity, and those of Alberta, Saskatchewan, B.C., Nova Scotia, and Newfoundland want to supply oil and natural gas. The federal government has normally approved these sales with little hesitation, although the National Energy Board is charged to ensure that long-term Canadian needs will not be compromised in the process. Native and environmental groups in some provinces have not been so favourably disposed toward the hydro or nuclear plants necessary to produce the electricity, however, and Canadian nationalists worry about the future supply of petroleum for domestic purposes as well as rising prices because of such exports. George W. Bush's obsession with energy has pleased Alberta petroleum exporters and put pipelines to transport northern petroleum to the United States back on the political agenda.

The degree of U.S. ownership of the Canadian petroleum industry has also caused considerable conflict between the two countries. The National Energy Program of 1980 set a target of 50 percent Canadian ownership of the oil and gas industry by 1990 and gave certain preferences to Petro-Canada and private Canadian firms. U.S. petroleum companies in Canada protested, and their government pressured Canada to remove these incentives to Canadianization. The Mulroney cabinet dismantled the NEP completely and began the privatization of Petro-Canada; more recently, there have been many American takeovers of Canadian oil companies.

TRADE UNIONS

Historically, Canadian trade unions have been just as closely allied with those in the United States as the corporations for which their members worked. Many unions in Canada, such as the United Steelworkers and the United Food and Commercial Workers, are part of "international unions" with their headquarters in the United States. The Canadian union movement justified the relationship by arguing that as long as it had to bargain with multinational corporations, it needed the support of international unions, especially their larger strike funds. Membership in international unions peaked in 1965 at 67 percent of all union members in Canada. Since then, however, a nationalist trend has been apparent in the Canadian labour movement, and several unions have cut their ties with the international headquarters. Bob White's creation of an autonomous Canadian Auto Workers union is the most striking example. Thus, by 1998, only 1 177 000 or 30 percent of Canadian union members belonged to international unions,[5] and the current president of the United Steelworkers of America is a Canadian.

American Influence on Canadian Culture

People around the world enjoy U.S. popular culture. Canadians are a particularly captive market, given their geographical proximity, their linguistic similarity, their small domestic market, their chronic feeling of dependence and inferiority, and the degree of economic integration between the two countries. The general public has little consciousness of the origin of most pop culture fare, and even less concern that so much of it comes from the United States. But many nationalists among the intellectual elite are disturbed by the high proportion of television, magazines, movies, books, and music in Canada that emanates from the United States, as seen in Figure 5.2. They claim that this cultural invasion stifles the development of a distinctive Canadian national identity, worry about its influence on Canadian attitudes and values, and wonder how long a separate political system can be maintained in these circumstances.

Television was the most significant cultural institution of the second half of the 20th century. Today, the average Canadian watches about 22.8 hours of television per week, and 60 percent of that is foreign (mostly American) programming.[6] Broken down by language group, anglophones watch 70 percent foreign programs, and francophones watch only 33.5 percent. Some Canadians live close enough to the U.S. border to receive U.S. channels directly; failing that, most Canadian stations broadcast a large proportion of U.S. programming. As well, about 75 percent of Canadian households have purchased cable television that

• •

Figure 5.2   Market Share of Content by Origin in the Cultural Industries of Canada

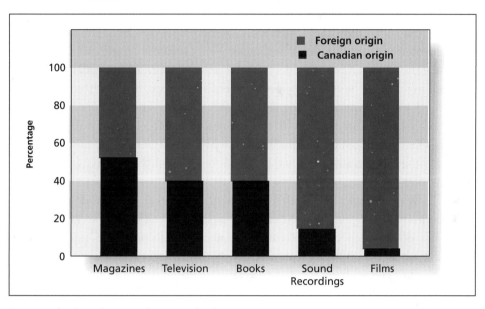

Source: Based on figures from assorted sources cited in the text.

normally offers them all the U.S. networks as well as additional Canadian channels. Beyond cable, many Canadians have pay television, which extends the U.S. content. Finally, satellite dishes can deliver even more U.S. channels through direct-to-home satellite transmission.

Canadian television networks broadcast so much U.S. programming for two reasons. First, it is much cheaper to buy a U.S. show or series than to produce a Canadian one—about one-tenth the cost. Second, while Canadians watch their own news, public affairs, and sports programs quite conscientiously, U.S. programs shown in Canada attract a larger audience. They therefore command higher advertising rates than the Canadian programs. In fact, Canadian television has a higher reputation abroad than it does at home, and those few Canadian series that are produced are readily sold to foreign networks.

Magazines are perhaps the second most important vehicle of popular culture, and this Canadian industry is also permeated by U.S. content. While Canadian magazines lead foreign magazines in subscriptions in Canada, foreign magazines account for the bulk of English-language newsstand sales. Overall, Canadian magazines constitute about 50 percent of the total circulation, but as with television, the picture is much more positive in French-speaking Canada than in English-speaking areas.

The Canadian motion picture industry is even weaker than television or magazines, and the average Canadian moviegoer has rarely, if ever, seen a Canadian feature film. Less than 5 percent of screen time in Canadian movie theatres is devoted to Canadian films, and most of that is in the large Toronto and Montreal markets. U.S. movie producers make many feature films in Canada every year, taking advantage of its low prices, scenic locations, and technical expertise, but these are almost always disguised as U.S. movies. The problem has many causes, including the fact that the film distribution system is U.S.–controlled, the undeniable Canadian fascination with Hollywood, the small Canadian market, and a shortage of funds. Canadian productions do slightly better in the home video market.

When it comes to books, the Canadian market is again dominated by U.S. content. It is estimated that 60 to 70 percent of the Canadian book market consists of imported books.[7] Both Canadian-owned companies and foreign-owned publishers operating in Canada sell foreign as well as Canadian titles, for books are like television shows: they are cheaper to import than to make domestically. Most Canadian bookstores make little effort to sell Canadian books, and paperback books at newspaper stands, drug and cigar stores, and supermarkets come almost entirely from the United States because the publisher-distributors who control the supply are U.S.–owned companies.

As for sound recording, about 15 foreign-controlled companies have over 80 percent of sales in Canada, even though 170 Canadian-controlled companies are also in business. More significantly, sales with Canadian content or by Canadian artists constituted only about 14.5 percent of total sales in 1995–96, and among new releases, 828 contained Canadian content compared to 5827 that did not.[8]

In short, in the five cultural industries of television, magazines, movies, books, and sound recordings, Canadian-owned companies produce virtually all of the Canadian output. But these companies are marginal players in a market dominated by subsidiaries of large, mainly U.S., multinationals. That there is a Canadian presence at all in such industries is primarily the result of demands made by the nationalist minority for protection from U.S. domination and for promotion of Canadian content.

COUNTERING THE U.S. INFLUENCE

The Crown corporation is a nationalistic instrument in the cultural field, as it is in economic matters. The **Canadian Broadcasting Corporation (CBC),** in its radio and television networks, and Radio-Canada, its French-language equivalent, is perhaps the most crucial agent of Canadian cultural expression. Today, CBC radio has virtually 100 percent Canadian content, and can be heard in almost every part of the country. Its programs are widely regarded as crucial links in keeping the country together. CBC television is less successful, mainly because the television medium is so expensive. The Mulroney government slashed millions of dollars from the CBC budget after 1984, making the corporation's task even harder. Every study of the problem has said that the CBC should receive stable, multi-year public funding to enable it to fulfill its mandate, but the Chrétien government cut its budget even further.

Another Crown corporation, the National Film Board, has also had an illustrious existence, making impressive Canadian films and winning many international awards. It has two serious disadvantages, however: insufficient funding to make feature films, so that it has specialized instead in documentaries and shorts; and no effective mechanism for giving the general public access to its films.

A second policy instrument to protect and promote Canadian culture is a regulatory agency, the **Canadian Radio-television and Telecommunications Commission (CRTC).** This agency issues broadcasting licences and Canadian-content regulations, the latter being more stringent for the CBC than for private stations and networks. CBC television has recently aired all-Canadian programs in prime time, whereas news, public affairs, and sports take up most of the required

By Adrian Raeside (*Victoria Times-Colonist*). Used with permission.

Canadian time on the private television networks, which produce very little Canadian drama. The CRTC also requires that radio stations play 35 percent Canadian music, a regulation that is generally seen as the catalyst for the explosion of the Canadian musical industry over the past 35 years.

Because the CRTC has been under strong industry and popular pressure to allow more U.S. outlets in Canada, it permitted cable and pay television that diluted the audiences of Canadian channels. In 1995, the CRTC also authorized direct-to-home (DTH) satellite services. Many nationalists fear for the fate of Canadian content in the not-too-distant future when the largely American 500-channel universe is beamed directly into Canadian homes.

A third policy instrument consists of Canadian ownership restrictions and financial incentives. Ownership restrictions in the cultural field apply to radio, television, and newspaper companies in Canada. In addition, Canadian magazine policy from 1965 allowed firms to deduct magazine advertising expenses from their income tax only if those advertisements are placed in Canadian magazines. The same policy also prohibited the entry into Canada of split-run editions of foreign magazines containing advertisements directed at Canadians. In the 1990s, however, *Sports Illustrated* started to produce a Canadian split-run edition that challenged the law because such editions could now be physically printed in Canada via satellite. Capitulating to U.S. pressure and a WTO ruling, the Chrétien government allowed foreign magazines sold in Canada to carry up to 18 percent of Canadian ads without any Canadian editorial content and raised the limit on foreign ownership of a Canadian magazine from 25 to 49 percent.

A fourth device to promote Canadian culture is the funding agency. The Canada Council for the Arts, set up in 1957, gives life-saving grants to hundreds of individual writers, artists, musicians, and playwrights, as well as to almost every orchestra, theatre centre, art gallery, ballet and opera company in the country, while Telefilm Canada subsidizes the production of feature films.

Globalization

In the new millennium, Canada has to contend with many external influences beyond those of the United States. These can be lumped together under the label of **globalization.** Globalization is usually understood to be based on the following new developments:

- Comprehensive free trade agreements, involving removal of state controls on corporate behaviour

- Massive diffusion of computerization and other technological change
- Mega-mergers of large transnational corporations, cross-border capital and investment flows, and world-wide corporate competition

Such globalization can be discussed under four headings: foreign governments, international organizations, international agreements, and transnational corporations.

Foreign Governments

Foreign governments make decisions every day, in both foreign and domestic policy, that can have some effect on Canada. Sometimes this impact is deliberate, but often it is unintentional. It is the responsibility of our foreign affairs department to put pressure on such governments so that their decisions are not harmful to Canada. The case of the United States has already been discussed, but such influences now come from all directions. For example, the European Union, Canada's second largest trading partner, has raised objections of many kinds. These include banning the import of furs from animals caught using leg-hold traps, rejection of our lumber exports because of concern about Canadian forestry practices, and the labelling of champagne. The pressure that the United States, the European Union, and many other foreign governments apply to Canada to change its policies are often made on behalf of their own multinational corporations. On the other hand, Canada has complaints of its own, especially the over-fishing by a number of European countries in Canadian territorial waters, and the unmatchable subsidies that European and American governments pay their wheat farmers.

International Organizations

Canada has joined a multitude of international organizations with the aim of taking advantage of opportunities to influence other countries' policies, to expand our external trade, and to promote joint objectives with other states. Nevertheless, such membership often entails obligations and responsibilities that influence Canadian domestic or foreign policies. The United Nations is probably the most important of such organizations. It gives a middle-ranking country such as Canada a platform to promote its altruistic as well as its self-interested objectives. But the UN also makes claims on Canada, such as to answer the call whenever it decides to set up a peacekeeping force in trouble spots around the world. Moreover, the UN has criticized several domestic Canadian policies, including

Students confront riot police at the Summit of the Americas, Quebec City, 2001 (Kevin Frayer/CP Picture Archive)

Quebec language legislation, and federal and provincial laws on labour, Aboriginal people, and women, as well as the deterioration of social programs. Of course, many Canadians welcomed these criticisms in an effort to change such laws.

In 1947, Canada was among the signatories of the General Agreement on Tariffs and Trade (GATT) under which countries pledged to remove trade restrictions on a multinational basis. The successor to GATT, the **World Trade Organization (WTO),** can actually order its members to change their trading practices. The WTO has disallowed a large number of Canadian laws and policies in recent years in connection with agricultural marketing boards, magazines, dairy products, drug patents, aircraft company subsidies, and even the Canada–U.S. Auto Pact. The WTO has thus become a huge impediment to the pursuit of Canadian government policies, that is, to Canadian **sovereignty,** in a wide range of sensitive fields. The WTO has attracted opposition around the world from those who feel that its decisions prevent countries from making reasonable policies in their own national public interest and that, instead, it acts in the interests of transnational corporations.

Other international organizations also have an effect on Canadian policy: the International Monetary Fund, the Asia-Pacific Economic Cooperation Council (APEC), the Summit of the Americas, and even those to which Canada does not belong, such as the Organization of Petroleum Exporting Countries (OPEC). The leaders of the G7 (the Group of Seven leading Western industrialized countries) and the Summit of Eight (the G7 plus Russia) meet annually to try to come to a consensus on economic and other matters. Especially after September 2001, global terrorist organizations have forced Canada and other states to change many of their policies and practices.

International Agreements

Canadian policymakers had been concerned for some time that the country was being left out of the regional trading blocks being formed, especially the European Union. Then, in the early 1980s, a protectionist mood descended upon the U.S. Congress, and new barriers to many Canadian exports were imposed: on shakes and shingles, softwood lumber, potash, potatoes, fish, and specialty steel. Such protectionist measures were among the factors that converted Brian Mulroney to the concept of free trade. Mulroney found another advocate of free trade in the White House, so he and Ronald Reagan set the negotiations in motion. The **Canada–U.S. Free Trade Agreement (FTA)** was finalized in October 1987 and took effect on January 1, 1989. It was a wide-ranging pact covering almost every aspect of the relationship between the two countries—far more than "trade."[9] It was clearly designed to enshrine neoconservative values, give corporations more leeway from government regulation, and prevent the recurrence of such national-istic measures as FIRA and NEP.[10]

The agreement removed almost all barriers to the flow of goods and services between the two countries over a 10-year period. Firms in each country could henceforth send their products to the other without tariffs, quotas, or other impediments. Each country had to treat the other's firms the same as its own (the "national treatment" principle), but each continued to apply its own tariffs to imports from other states.

In the area of financial services, a significant change was the elimination for U.S. investors of the 25 percent ceiling on foreign ownership of Canadian banks. As for other investment, U.S. businesses would now be able to start new opera-tions in Canada without restriction (and vice versa); Investment Canada could only screen acquisitions of firms with a value over $150 million and could not impose any performance requirements.

Energy, agriculture, the Auto Pact, and cultural industries were four of the other most controversial sections of the agreement. A North American energy pool was created in which Canada had to sell oil, gas, or electricity to the United States at the Canadian domestic price, and if cutbacks were ever necessary, domestic sales had to be reduced by the same proportion as exports. In agriculture,

Canada had to remove import restrictions on chickens, turkeys, and eggs, as well as tariffs on processed food, and the agreement enunciated the goal of ultimately eliminating all subsidies that distort agricultural trade. The Auto Pact was also changed to some extent in order to incorporate U.S. concerns. In theory, the agreement did not affect existing cultural programs; however, any new support of cultural industries could be met by retaliation of equivalent value by the other country.

For any future conflicts in trade between the two countries, a complex dispute-settlement mechanism was set up that involved binational panels and binding arbitration. If either country refused to abide by the final decision of the arbitrators, however, the other could retaliate ("countervail"), as before.

The "free trade debate" was heated for many years, with proponents regarding the agreement as the salvation of all Canadian economic problems and the source of perpetual prosperity, while opponents saw it as leading to the complete integration of Canada and the United States.[11] Over 10 years later, the results seem to be mixed. Ontario did lose some 200 000 manufacturing jobs in the early 1990s, but how much of this was due to the free trade agreement, as such, and how much to the recession and other globalizing factors is hard to determine.[12] More significantly, the number of conflicts under the agreement has been large. Some of the same issues that precipitated the Free Trade Agreement have continued to be problems, especially Canadian exports of softwood lumber, on which the United States placed a 19.3 percent import duty in 2001. Other areas of dispute include uranium, beer, government procurement, magnesium, steel, swine, wheat, sugar, peanut butter, tobacco, milk, meat, paper, salmon and herring, poultry products, magazine publishing, and country-music television. On the other hand, trade between the two countries has expanded enormously in both directions, and few of the most dire predictions have come to pass.

The ink was hardly dry on the Canada–U.S. Free Trade Agreement when the Mulroney government entered talks with the United States and Mexico that produced the **North American Free Trade Agreement (NAFTA).** It essentially extended FTA to Mexico; most provisions in the two agreements were identical. This initiative was not so much Canada's choice; Canada entered it mainly to preclude the other partners from endangering its position, although some corporations saw it as a means of enhancing the efficiency of their operations. Opponents feared that companies would move from Canada to Mexico because of the low wages and environmental standards in that country, and they complained that Mexico was able to negotiate a stronger energy clause with the United States than Canada had under the FTA. Despite pre-election fanfare, the new Chrétien government was content with minor changes in the pact once in office.[13]

Under Chapter 11 of NAFTA, a foreign company can sue a country on the grounds that a government policy reduced its profits. Canada has lost at least two multimillion dollar lawsuits in this connection, the most infamous involving the gasoline additive MMT. Ethyl Corporation of Virginia used such NAFTA rules to force Canada to roll back its ban on this ingredient, which is widely regarded as a hazard to health.

In the wake of these agreements, Canada signed the "Open Skies" agreement with the United States in 1995, which deregulated the cross-border airline industry, giving U.S. and Canadian companies equal access to routes between the two countries. The Chrétien government also signed a separate free trade deal with Chile, and participated in talks aimed at establishing a Free Trade Area of the Americas, encompassing the 34 countries of the whole hemisphere. To this end, the Summit of the Americas was held in Quebec City in April 2001, and amid considerable anti-globalization violence in the streets, the assembled governments set a target date of 2005 to have the treaty completed.

Transnational Corporations

As noted, the pressures exerted by a foreign government are often made on behalf of corporations with head offices in that country, and international agreements are often about removing government controls on corporate behaviour. Indeed, the essence of globalization is the changed role of **transnational corporations.** More and more companies are outgrowing their domestic state; they are introducing new forms of technology at an incredible rate; they are merging and taking each other over; and they are opening or closing operations strictly on the basis of economic efficiency and without regard to traditional location. Most importantly, they are persuading governments to develop comprehensive free trade agreements that remove state controls on corporate activity. The world is increasingly becoming one integrated global economic unit in which national boundaries are much less significant than in the past. Corporate money, banking, finance, and investment flow between countries almost at will. In these circumstances, it is becoming more difficult for national or provincial governments to maintain distinctive labour, tax, or environmental laws because such companies (and their senior employees) regularly threaten to move to other jurisdictions that they find more congenial.[14] Opposition to further globalization, whether under the auspices of the WTO or the Summit of the Americas, has led to many demonstrations, the most violent being in Seattle during the WTO summit in late 1999.

On the other hand, many observers feel that governments do not have to cave in completely to such corporate blackmail.[15] The forces of globalization suffered at least a temporary setback in 1998 with the abandonment of the Multilateral Agreement on Investment (MAI). To its supporters, the MAI was merely an international investment agreement that would set rules for the operation of the global economy. But its critics argued that governments would be hobbled in their objectives of taxing, regulation and setting standards, and that Canada would no longer be able to give preference to its own people via tax breaks, subsidies, grants, or other support to promote employment, research and development, or Canadian content. These critics around the world engaged in a remarkable effort of multinational grassroots organization largely via the Internet (perhaps an example of the more positive side of globalization), such that the sponsors of MAI abandoned the project, although it may resurface again in another form.[16]

Other Canadians who accept the inevitability of globalization have suggested refinements: the process of globalization should be more open or transparent than it has been to date, involve a commitment to democracy and human rights, and ensure a fairer distribution of the increased wealth that globalization generates.

DISCUSSION QUESTIONS

1. On balance, have the free trade agreements been good or bad for Canada?
2. How much scope does globalization leave to nation-states to make distinctive domestic policies?
3. What are the advantages and disadvantages of the close cultural relationship between Canada and the United States?

FURTHER READING

Barlow, Maude, and Tony Clarke. *Global Showdown: How the New Activists are Fighting Global Corporate Rule*. Toronto: Stoddart Publishing, 2000.

Cameron, Duncan, and Mel Watkins, eds. *Canada under Free Trade*. Toronto: Lorimer, 1993.

Canada among Nations. Toronto: Lorimer until 1998, and then Oxford University Press, annual.

Chodos, Robert, et al. *Canada and the Global Economy*. Halifax: Lorimer, 1995.

Doern, G. Bruce et al., eds. *Border Crossings: The Internationalization of Canadian Public Policy*. Toronto: Oxford University Press, 1996.

Doern, G. Bruce, and Brian Tomlin. *Faith and Fear: The Free Trade Story*. Toronto: Stoddart, 1991.

Dorland, Michael, ed. *The Cultural Industries in Canada: Problems, Policies and Prospects*. Halifax: Lorimer, 1996.

McQuaig, Linda. *The Cult of Impotence: Selling the Myth of Powerlessness in the Global Economy*. Toronto: Viking, 1998.

Watson, William. *Globalization and the Meaning of Canadian Life*. Toronto: University of Toronto Press, 1998.

Notes

1. R. McGregor Dawson, *The Government of Canada*, 5th ed., rev. Norman Ward (Toronto: University of Toronto Press, 1970), 54.

2. Donald Creighton, *Canada's First Century* (Toronto: Macmillan, 1970); George Grant, *Lament for a Nation: The Defeat of Canadian Nationalism* (Toronto: McClelland and Stewart, 1965); J.L. Granatstein, *How Britain's Weakness Forced Canada into the Arms of the United States* (Toronto: University of Toronto Press, 1989).

3. Canada, *Foreign Direct Investment in Canada* (Ottawa: Supply and Services, 1972), 14.

4. The pioneer of this theme was Kari Levitt, *Silent Surrender: The Multinational Corporation in Canada* (Toronto: Macmillan, 1970).

5. Human Resources Development Canada, *Directory of Labour Organizations in Canada 1998*, cat. no. L2-2/1998.

6. Statistics Canada, *Canada's Culture, Heritage and Identity: A Statistical Perspective*, cat. no. 87-211-XPB, 1997.

7. Victor Rabinovitch, "The Social and Economic Rationales for Canada's Domestic Cultural Policies," in Dennis Browne, ed., *The Culture/Trade Quandary: Canada's Policy Options* (Ottawa: Centre for Trade Policy and Law, 1998), 30.

8. *Canada's Culture, Heritage and Identity: A Statistical Perspective*.

9. G. Bruce Doern and Brian Tomlin, *Faith and Fear: The Free Trade Story* (Toronto: Stoddart, 1991).

10. Glen Williams, "Regions within Region: Continentalism Ascendant," in Whittington and Williams, eds., *Canadian Politics in the 1990s*, 4th ed. (Scarborough: Nelson Canada, 1995).

11. Duncan Cameron and Mel Watkins, *Canada under Free Trade* (Toronto: Lorimer, 1993); John Warnock, *Free Trade and the New Right Agenda* (Vancouver: New Star Books, 1988).

12. An April 2001 report by the Economic Policy Institute in Washington, D.C. found that by the end of the 1990s, manufacturing employment in Canada was still below the 1989 level, and that new jobs were largely part-time and in the low-paying service sector

13. Government of Canada, *The North American Free Trade Agreement at a Glance*, cat. no. E75-56/1-1993E; Jeffrey M. Ayres, *Defying Conventional Wisdom: Political*

Movements and Popular Contention against North American Free Trade (Toronto: University of Toronto Press, 1998).

14. G. Bruce Doern et al., eds., *Border Crossings: The Internationalization of Canadian Public Policy* (Toronto: Oxford University Press, 1996).

15. Stephen McBride and John Shields, *Dismantling a Nation: Canada and the New World Order* (Halifax: Fernwood Publishing, 1993); William Watson, *Globalization and the Meaning of Canadian Life* (Toronto: University of Toronto Press, 1998); Linda McQuaig, *The Cult of Impotence: Selling the Myth of Powerlessness in the Global Economy* (Toronto: Viking, 1998); Maude Barlow and Tony Clarke, *Global Showdown: How the New Activists are Fighting Global Corporate Rule* (Toronto: Stoddart Publishing, 2000).

16. Andrew Jackson and Matthew Sanger, eds., *Dismantling Democracy: The Multilateral Agreement on Investment and Its Impact* (Toronto: Lorimer, 1998).

PART 2

Linking People to Government

Having outlined the societal context in which Canadian politics operate, we are now ready to examine how people are linked to the government—the study of Canadian politics. The three traditional elements of Canadian politics are the electoral system, political parties, and pressure groups. At a minimum, each citizen can have a modest impact on the government by voting in an election. If people wish to have more influence on government policy, they can join or support the political party that is closest to their way of thinking or choose the vehicle of social movements and pressure groups. Each of these three links between people and government is discussed in its own chapter in the following section.

But the context of values, attitudes, opinions (and how they are acquired), and patterns of political participation must also be examined. Moreover, no one can deny the importance of the mass media and public opinion polls in linking people to government. Thus we begin with chapters on the Canadian political culture, socialization and participation, and the media and public opinion polls.

Chapter 6

Political Culture, Socialization, and Participation

Understanding how Canadians feel about politics and government, how they develop such feelings, and how they participate politically provides a useful context in which to study elections, political parties, and pressure groups. This chapter therefore examines Canadian political values and attitudes—the Canadian political culture; how these values and attitudes are acquired—political socialization; and the related subject of patterns of Canadian political participation.

Chapter Objectives

After you have completed this chapter, you should be able to:

Define democracy and discuss the extent to which Candians are committed to it

Enumerate the principal differences that have been identified between basic Canadian and American political values

Evaluate the extent to which the traditional political culture remains intact, and comment on the forces that threaten it

Identify the main agents of political socialization

Comment on variations in the vote turnout rate and reasons for voting or not voting

Enumerate forms of nonelectoral participation

....

Political Culture

Political culture can be defined as the sum total of the political values, beliefs, attitudes, and orientations in a society. Vague and elusive as these values and attitudes may be, most political scientists think they are worthy of analysis because they influence what is done within a political system.

Political culture includes feelings people have toward the overall political community of Canada, such as their reaction to national symbols—flag, anthem, Constitution—and feelings of patriotism, nationalism, and pride. It also includes how people feel toward their province as opposed to the whole country. A second aspect of political culture involves beliefs regarding the role of the state—how large a part Canadians want it to play in their lives. Another variable consists of orientations to the decision-making apparatus. Are people aware of it, and to what extent do they want to control it? How do Canadians feel, in general, about the police, the bureaucracy, the courts, and the politicians? Do citizens trust them? Do people feel that their participation in the political system can make any difference? When such values and attitudes are widely shared, they can be said to constitute the collective political culture. While political culture is usually considered to be fairly stable, it will also be necessary in the Canadian case to sketch how it seems to be changing.

Democracy

The first conclusion that emerges from a quest for Canadian political values is that almost all Canadians believe in **democracy.** The preamble to the Charter of Rights and Freedoms acknowledges democracy to be a foremost value in the country when it speaks of Canada as a "free and democratic society," but the Charter is not very specific about what this means. "Democracy is derived from the Greek words "demos" (people) and "kratia" (power), and in the modern Western world usually includes the following elements:[1]

- popular sovereignty
- political equality
- political freedom
- majority rule

POPULAR SOVEREIGNTY

Popular sovereignty means that the people have the final say, which in large, modern political systems usually takes the form of elections at specified intervals.

For most Canadians, this is a sufficient opportunity for the exercise of popular sovereignty, although few would be content with anything less. Some states use plebiscites or referenda on a regular basis, but these devices have largely been foreign to the Canadian mentality. Only three national **referenda** have occurred since 1867 (prohibition in 1898, conscription in 1942, and the Charlottetown Accord in 1992), although the incidence is slightly higher at the provincial and municipal levels. Popular sovereignty is thus normally exercised in periodic elections that are essentially opportunities to select those who will make the big political decisions over the next four years or so, although any effective democracy also involves popular participation between elections. At least in the past, Canadians cherished **representative democracy** in which such elected and appointed authorities made decisions on their behalf.

POLITICAL EQUALITY

Given the significance of elections as the means of implementing the principle of popular sovereignty, a second aspect of Canadian democracy is **political equality**—that is, everyone is equal on election day. In essence, this means that each person has one vote. It is only in relatively recent times, however, that Canada has met this ideal, and at one time or another in the past several groups were excluded.

POLITICAL FREEDOM

The 1982 Charter of Rights and Freedoms provided an explicit constitutional statement of **political freedom** in Canada. It says: "Everyone has the following fundamental freedoms: freedom of conscience and religion; freedom of thought, belief, opinion and expression, including freedom of the press and other media of communication; freedom of peaceful assembly; and freedom of association." The Charter did not create these political freedoms, however; it put into writing the freedoms that Canadians had always enjoyed, and it provided a new means of protecting them—using the courts to invalidate legislation that infringed them rather than having to persuade politicians to do so.

MAJORITY RULE

Canadian democracy also incorporates the notion of **majority rule**—that is, in case of dispute, the larger number takes precedence over the smaller number. This principle is generally accepted in elections and in the legislatures that result from elections. Of course, if the number of options is greater than two, as in the case of Canadian elections, the winning candidate or party may not actually have a majority (over 50 percent), but just a plurality.

On the other hand, it is sometimes felt necessary to protect minorities from the actions of the majority, so that specific minority rights are given constitutional protection. The Constitution Act, 1867, recognized certain religious and linguistic minority rights, while the Charter of Rights and Freedoms extended constitutional minority rights to a considerable degree.

Distinguishing between Canadian and American Values

Once we get beyond the consensus on democracy, it is difficult to find widespread agreement on other Canadian political values. One approach that bears promise, however, is to contrast widely held Canadian values with those of the United States. Canadian and American values are, of course, very much alike. But some analysts have found at least subtle differences that have their foundation in the revolutionary origins of the United States and in the Canadian reaction against that revolution.

Many have made the point that the American Declaration of Independence lists the objectives of "life, liberty and the pursuit of happiness," while Canada's Constitution Act, 1867 talks about "peace, order and good government." Seymour Martin Lipset goes on to outline a basic distinction: "Canada has been and is a more class-aware, elitist, law-abiding, statist, collectivity-oriented, and particularistic [group-oriented] society than the United States."[2] Pierre Berton has similarly noted that Canadians are law-abiding, peaceful, orderly, deferential toward authority, cautious, elitist, moralistic, tolerant, diffident, and unemotional.[3] The results of a 1995 Allan Gregg survey of what ordinary Canadians thought was distinctive about Canada included nonviolence, tolerance of minorities, humane treatment of the poor and disadvantaged, official bilingualism, and reluctance to boast.[4] This approach leads us to identify five basic Canadian values that can be distinguished from those in the United States:

- Canadians prefer a closer balance between individualism and collectivism.
- Canadians are more tolerant of minorities and value variety more than homogeneity.
- Canadians are more deferential toward authority.
- Canadians have a stronger belief in egalitarianism.
- Canadians are more cautious, less confident, and less violent.

Balance between Individualism and Collectivism

If there is one value other than democracy to which most Canadians adhere, it is probably that of **individualism,** liberalism, or capitalism, often expressed as the sanctity of private enterprise or individual economic freedom. Canadians generally believe that those with the greatest talent or those who work hardest should reap the benefits of their abilities and/or labour. The extent of such commitment can be best gauged, however, in comparison to the United States.

While both countries have "mixed economies" today—that is, a combination of private enterprise and government involvement—the United States remains the world's last stronghold of individualism, with a relatively smaller public sector than other modern states. Canada, on the other hand, has been less hostile toward public intervention and more inclined to rely on government. This is partly because of the distinctive geographic environment of the Canadian political system and the desire to protect Canada from various U.S. influences. But it also stems from the basic Canadian value of **collectivism,** or community, derived in the first instance from the United Empire Loyalists who opposed the American Revolution. They saw society not as a mass of grasping, ambitious, "free" individuals, but as an organic community in which all people had their place and did their respective part to contribute to the welfare of the whole. It is not part of the Canadian psyche to be instinctively suspicious of the state; indeed, Canadians have not seen the government in terms of an alien imposition but as the authorized agent to respond to their individual and collective demands.

Canada is generally less collectivist than Western Europe, and the difference between the two North American countries should not be overstated, but much concrete evidence of a significant variation exists. The Canadian public health insurance system stands out in great contrast to that of the United States; the Canadian social security system is considered more adequate; and the extent of federal and provincial Crown corporations is unheard of south of the border. Taxes in Canada are generally higher in order to finance such collective activity. In just about every policy field, in fact, the extent of government intervention is greater in Canada than in the United States.

Tolerance of Minorities and Appreciation of Diversity

A second difference between the basic values of the two countries is commonly expressed in terms of the melting pot and the mosaic: immigrants to the United States are urged to become "unhyphenated" Americans, whereas Canada encourages the retention of cultural diversities. Canada celebrates heterogeneity in society and tolerance of minorities, and expects its public institutions to accommodate immigrants' practices and beliefs. The distinctiveness of the French-Canadian Roman Catholic community based in Quebec was the original basis of this value, but it has now spread to policies of multiculturalism and recognition of other group rights, including Aboriginal rights. Multiculturalism is seen as a means of enriching and enlivening the country, encouraging new Canadians to feel at home, promoting tolerance and minimizing discrimination, and perhaps enhancing Canada's contribution to world harmony.

Diversity also has a territorial dimension—the fact that Canadian provinces are much stronger than the American states relative to the central government. Decentralization in Canada is accompanied by stronger regional or provincial loyalties and identities, due again to the example set by Quebec. Most studies have indicated that Ontarians are more oriented to Canada than to their province, while the residents of Quebec, Newfoundland, and Alberta identify most with their province. Even so, the provincial orientations of Albertans or Quebeckers should not be overstated. In a recent survey, 67 percent of Albertans disagreed with the suggestion that the province should replace national programs with its own, and 87 percent of Albertans had a strong sense of belonging to Canada.[5] Table 6.1 reveals how francophone Quebeckers balanced loyalties to Quebec and Canada in a February 2001 survey.

TABLE 6.1 FRANCOPHONE QUEBECKERS ATTITUDES TO QUEBEC AND CANADA, 2001

Question: Which of the following do you consider yourself?	
Solely a Quebecker	29%
A Quebecker first, then a Canadian	29%
Equally a Quebecker and a Canadian	24%
A Canadian first, then a Quebecker	12%
Solely a Canadian	5%

Source: Leger marketing poll, *The Globe and Mail*, February 9, 2001, p. 4. Used with permission.

DEFERENCE TO AUTHORITY

Another fundamental difference between Canadian and American values is the greater **deference to authority** in Canadian society. Canadians demonstrate more respect toward the law, judges, police, religious leaders, and many others with "legitimate power." Peace, order, and good government rather than individual liberty is the Canadian ideal, and many observers have noted that Canada is probably the only country where a police officer is a national symbol. Less obsessed with material success than Americans, Canadians are more likely to obey a law even if they do not like it. Crime rates are considerably lower in Canada (the homicide rate typically being one-quarter that of the United States on a per capita basis), gun control laws are stronger, and the drug problem is less severe.

EGALITARIANISM

Canada values **egalitarianism** more than the United States. That is, Canada is more concerned with removing barriers that prevent individuals or groups from achieving their full potential. One striking example is in the constitutional equality of women. Canada adopted a strong guarantee of gender equality (including affirmative action) in the 1982 Canadian Charter of Rights and Freedoms at the very time that a similar proposal failed in the United States. The health and welfare programs that flow from Canadian collectivism similarly ensure a greater degree of socioeconomic equality for the poor and working classes. Studies of income distribution in the two countries consistently reveal smaller disparities between rich and poor in Canada. For example, in the late 1990s, the wealthiest 10 percent of family units held 53 percent of all personal wealth in Canada, whereas this highest group in the United States had two-thirds of the total net worth. Even in the realm of higher education, Canada now appears to be more egalitarian than the United States: in contrast to earlier times, a larger proportion of young adults in Canada have access to higher education.[6] Canada also extends this redistributive egalitarianism to have-not provinces through equalization payments.

CAUTION, DIFFIDENCE, AND NONVIOLENCE

A final value difference to emerge from this analysis relates to Canadian caution and diffidence, sometimes called a national inferiority complex. It includes a historical dependence on other countries and the absence of a spirit of innovation and risk-taking. Canadians delight in the security of savings and understatement. Of course, there have been many Canadian "winners" in all walks of life, in whose accomplishments Canadians vicariously share: Margaret Atwood, Céline Dion, Glenn Gould, Anne Murray, Wayne Gretzky, Karen Kain, Bryan Adams, Frederick Banting, Lester Pearson, John Polanyi, and others. But Canadians are obsessed with "survival" rather than success; they are especially good at deprecating themselves, and almost always think things American are superior.

Brian Gable (*The Globe and Mail*).
Reprinted with permission from *The Globe and Mail*.

Canadians are prudent and cautious, sober and solemn, introverted, uncertain, and always questioning themselves. Most Canadians take quiet satisfaction in their achievements—the 1995 survey showed that 89 percent of Canadians felt proud when they saw the Canadian flag or heard the national anthem—but they rarely proclaim it aloud.

Along similar lines, although Canada made major contributions to two world wars, Canadians are not a warlike people and abhor violence at home and abroad. We have tried to be peacemakers and peacekeepers in international relations, putting special emphasis on the United Nations, trying to reduce the militancy of the foreign policy of the United States in quiet, backroom diplomacy (though perhaps not as hard as we should have), and helping to remove the causes of war through assistance to developing countries.

The Changing Canadian Political Culture

As Canada approached the 21st century, many aspects of this traditional value structure seemed to be changing. Different concepts of democracy emerged, and the distinction between Canadian and American values appeared to be in decline. Much of this transformation can be attributed to the presence of the United States, directly or indirectly, although some of it is part of a worldwide change in political values.

As far as democracy is concerned, the 1990s saw an upsurge in interest in the means of more direct popular participation. The most common prescription in this regard is the referendum, in which legislators would be guided or bound by the frequent referral of policy questions to the electorate as a whole. Quebec has used this device repeatedly on the question of sovereignty; certain other provinces now require it for approval of constitutional amendments, and some have prescribed its use for other issues such as significant tax increases. Somewhat similarly, British Columbia has established a mechanism for the "recall" of MLAs between provincial elections.

As for the distinctions between Canadian and American values, these are threatened in at least three ways. First, given the extent of U.S. control over Canada and Canadian exposure to the United States, values implicit in that country's popular culture, as transmitted by television, movies, books, magazines, and music, are likely to have considerable impact on those north of the border. It is debatable whether distinctive Canadian values can withstand the homogenizing force of modern technology, especially that emanating from the south. Second, Canadian nationalists see all these influences increasing under free trade agreements with the United States, which restrict government intervention. Third, some observers feel that the adoption of a U.S.–style Charter of Rights and Freedoms will further diminish distinctive Canadian values by challenging rather than deferring to government authority.

In a country that articulates its basic values so diffidently to start with, these powerful threats are not to be taken lightly. There are several recent indications that support for collectivism and feelings of deference in Canada are already on the decline.[7] Although it cannot be blamed entirely on Americans (for the Business Council on National Issues and others have also been involved), the obsession with government debts and deficits at both federal and provincial levels has seriously eroded social programs, and shifted the basis of pensions and child benefits from universality to selectivity. Privatization of Crown corporations and deregulation have also become rampant. Moreover, Canadians seem increasingly concerned with the legal equality of all citizens, rather than with their socioeconomic equality or well-being.

Political Socialization

Political socialization is the process through which individuals acquire their political values, attitudes, information, and opinions. The process consists in part of direct, individual exposure to political phenomena, but is mostly performed by intermediaries or agents of socialization. It is relatively easy to identify the main agents of political socialization in Canada, but much more difficult to evaluate their relative impact. We begin with the four traditional agents—family, school, peers, and the media—and then examine other such influences.

Agents of Socialization

THE FAMILY

Despite many modern pressures that have transformed the role of the family, including the increasing incidence of mothers working outside the home and the high divorce rate, it remains the basic cell of Canadian society. Parents, stepparents, or sometimes grandparents are the first major influence on a child's attitudes and values. Most children absorb attitudes and values, some of which are of political significance, in a kind of osmosis from their family's talk and behaviour. Parents' casual comments about politics, politicians, parties, and police are good examples. Some parents also deliberately try to indoctrinate their children with certain political values or to support a particular political party. It seems, however, that what children pick up unconsciously and unintentionally is just as significant as what parents try to teach. For example, if parents talk about politics in the home, with or without attempting to guide their children's orientations, their children will usually become more politically interested later in life. Nevertheless, the political impact of the family should not be overemphasized, for political socialization is a process that continues throughout one's life.

THE SCHOOL

The school is the second main agent of political socialization. All school systems in Canada and elsewhere deliberately attempt to inculcate certain basic values and attitudes, including some of a political nature, such as a feeling of affection or support for the country, the governmental apparatus, the head of state, the police, the flag, and the national anthem. Like the family, the school is an early enough influence that it may shape basic lifelong values.

The fact that students are now entering some form of institutionalized educational setting earlier than in previous generations has probably increased the school's importance relative to the family, a phenomenon that may be of particular importance in immigrant households.

Given the diversity of Canadian society, many questions arise about the role of the school in the political socialization process. Since the provinces have jurisdiction over education, for example, do they deliberately contribute to the development of distinctive provincial political cultures at the expense of the overall country? The radically different accounts of certain historical events found in French and English textbooks are often cited as an example of the biased role of formal education in this process.[8] One point is clear: the forces of dualism, regionalism, and continentalism in Canadian society make it difficult for the school system to develop any pan-Canadian sense of national identity.[9]

Just as happens in the family setting, the school also contributes to the development of attitudes and values informally and unintentionally. Such unconscious transmissions occur in teachers' remarks beyond the formal curriculum, in class discussions and excursions, and in extracurricular activities. Moreover, different attitudes toward participation and dissent would likely result from exposure to an authoritarian teacher or principal than in a more democratic setting. Corporations are also becoming increasingly involved in the educational system, promoting their own goods, services, and values.

Students are not only starting school at a younger age but also staying in school longer. The 1996 census showed that only 35 percent of the population had not completed high school, down from 48 percent in 1981. University graduates represented 16 percent of the population, while 24 percent were graduates of postsecondary colleges and trade schools.

Political socialization in the classroom setting

PEERS

Peers are the third main agent of political socialization. Peers are simply friends, acquaintances, and associates. The concept of "peer pressure" is probably most familiar at the adolescent level, and is not usually concerned with political values, attitudes, and opinions. But we are all susceptible to peer influence at any stage of our lives. In any group setting, including peer-group discussions that turn to politics, one person often becomes dominant, whether because of knowledge, position, or strength of character. At this stage, given the likelihood that basic values have already been established, attitudes and opinions are most open to persuasion.

THE MASS MEDIA

The **mass media** are the fourth main agent of socialization. They are more often instruments of entertainment than enlightenment, however, and personal interaction with family members, teachers, or peers normally carries greater impact than passive, impersonal exposure to the media. When it comes to politics, the media primarily transmit opinions on topical issues and personalities, and are less likely to influence lifelong values and attitudes. Nevertheless, there is evidence that Canadians do learn from this coverage,[10] and such short-term stimuli are becoming more important in determining how people vote.

Once again, media influence can be divided between the unconscious and the deliberate. In their editorials, newspapers explicitly attempt to influence opinions, while on the other pages of the paper, Canadians generally expect news coverage to be as unbiased and factual as possible. Whether newspapers can keep such a fine line between subjective editorials and objective reporting is an interesting question, and some observers have detected bias in the headlines, positioning, pictures, and selection of items to be included or excluded. Even though television does not usually have editorials as such, it has much greater scope for presenting biased news coverage than do newspapers, as noted in the fuller account of the mass media in Chapter 7. Moreover, some observers argue that the images portrayed on television, even in its provision of entertainment, convey powerful messages with political implications.

OTHER AGENTS OF POLITICAL SOCIALIZATION

The family, school, peers, and media are probably the main agents of political socialization in Canada, but certainly not the only ones. Political parties, churches, groups of various kinds, corporations, and the government itself are secondary influences on political attitudes, values, information, and opinions.

Political parties practise the art of persuasion and seek to influence opinions and party preferences on a daily basis. Those people who already identify with a particular party find that the simplest means of forming an opinion on any issue is by taking their cue from the party leader.

The Roman Catholic Church strongly influenced political values, attitudes, and opinions in Quebec prior to 1960. It had a close relationship with political authorities and did not hesitate to tell its members how to behave politically. The influence of religion in Canadian society may be on the decline, but its political role remains significant. For example, witness the interest in the religious convictions of Canadian Alliance leader Stockwell Day.

Over half the population belongs to an organized group of some kind, and although the orientation of such groups is primarily nonpolitical, all have the potential to influence their members' political views. Some, such as the Catholic Women's League, the Canadian Medical Association, and the Canadian Labour Congress, are quite determined to do so. As with parties and churches, taking one's opinions from the urging of a group leader obviates the need to make further individual effort to understand the issue. Other groups such as the Boy Scouts or Girl Guides try to instill in children an informed affection for the country.

Like political parties, individual corporations are in the business of persuasion, trying to sell their own goods and services. Sometimes, however, companies also try to influence political attitudes and opinions, an effort that is called **advocacy advertising.** Many corporations were involved in the free trade debate, especially during the 1988 election campaign, expressing their support through "speeches, debates, letters, advertisements, information sessions with employees, and inserts in newspapers."[11] Employers sometimes try to influence the voting preferences of their own employees with internal memos about how different parties or policies would affect the firm.

Finally, the government itself is often engaged in efforts to influence public views and behaviour. Sometimes this is widely recognized as legitimate, such as encouraging physical fitness, and discouraging smoking, impaired driving, racial discrimination, domestic violence, and the use of drugs. Sometimes it is done for broadly acceptable political purposes, such as promoting vacations in Canada, the purchase of Canadian-made goods, or national unity. Governments are also expected to inform the public about new laws, regulations, and programs, but it is a fine line between providing simple information and extolling the virtues of such initiatives for partisan purposes. The Mulroney government, for example, spent large sums of public funds promoting the merits of the Free Trade Agreement and the Goods and Services Tax in advertising campaigns that most observers felt were excessive and self-serving. In the latter case, the Speaker declared such advertising to be an affront to the House of Commons, as it took place even before debate there had concluded.

How Canadians individually and collectively acquire their political values, attitudes, and opinions is a complicated question. Because the process is so haphazard and complex and the stimuli in each person's own environment so diverse, no deliberate effort is guaranteed to be successful. Instead, Canadians acquire many of their political values, attitudes, and opinions in a completely unconscious way. Moreover, many Canadians are only semi-socialized: they simply do not have many political values, attitudes, and opinions or much political information. The general level of political awareness is not high, which in turn is reflected in patterns of political participation.

··

Political Participation

Political participation consists "of those voluntary activities by citizens that are intended to influence the selection of government leaders or the decisions they make."[12] Numerous avenues of political participation exist, but actual participation takes initiative and effort, which many people are too lazy to exert. Participation is also related to the possession of **political efficacy**—a sense of political competence and a feeling that one can have some impact on the system. In a recent survey, for example, two-thirds of respondents complained that politics was too complicated for them to understand, that people like themselves had no say about what government did, and that government did not care about their opinions.[13] Participation also depends on the possession of such resources as time, money, and information, although perhaps not as much as many people think. Regrettably, the opportunities for participation in Canada far exceed actual levels of involvement.

Electoral Participation

Voting on election day is a crucial aspect of democracy and is the most common form of political participation in Canada. The voter turnout rate is also one of the few forms of participation that can be regularly and reliably measured. The overall average national turnout rate between 1900 and 1988 was about 73 percent, or nearly three-quarters of those eligible to vote. These figures disguise the fact that the turnout rate varied considerably from one province to another. Prince Edward Island stands out with the highest average turnout, while the rate in Alberta, the

North, and Newfoundland was much lower. The rate for each federal election between 1974 and 2000 is provided in Table 6.2.[14]

TABLE 6.2 PERCENTAGE VOTER TURNOUT IN FEDERAL ELECTIONS, 1974–2000

Year	Turnout	Year	Turnout
1974	71	1988	75
1979	76	1993	70
1980	69	1997	67
1984	75	2000	61

Source: Data compiled from Chief Electoral Officer of Canada, Reports of the Chief Electoral Officer. Material reproduced with permission of the Chief Electoral Officer of Canada, 2001.

Those who do not vote have consistently been shown to be alienated from or uninformed about the political system, and primarily include the young, the poor, and the working classes. Other traditional reasons for not voting include lack of interest, unappealing alternatives, weak party identification, passivity engendered by watching television, feelings that government is irrelevant to one's life or is not listening, or thinking the result is a foregone conclusion. The voter turnout rate dramatically decreased over the 1990s to an all-time low of 61 percent in 2000. Perhaps the alternatives have become even less attractive, or maybe this decline is due to the feeling that it is not worth the trouble to vote. Due to the "dismantling of the state," including globalization, government performs fewer functions than it used to, leaving people with less confidence in it and fewer expectations. Canada's turnout figure falls between the extremes of other countries, as revealed in Table 6.3 (on page 132). Canada is well above the United States in voter turnout, but behind most comparable states including Britain.

Within the group who do vote, we can distinguish other degrees of electoral involvement. For one thing, the level of information of the typical voter should not be overestimated. Even if around 80 percent claim to have exposed themselves to television or newspaper coverage of the election campaign, only about 20 percent follow politics closely on a daily basis between elections.[15]

A study of the 1984 election found that, as a national average, voters could name 3.3 provincial premiers, and 36 percent could define the concepts of "left" and "right" and place the NDP as the furthest left of the three main parties. The level of factual and conceptual knowledge increased with level of education and reading about politics in newspapers and magazines, but viewing political programs on television was of negligible impact.[16] Beyond those who cast an

TABLE 6.3 PERCENTAGE VOTER TURNOUT RATES IN EIGHTEEN COUNTRIES, 1990s

Italy	90.2	Netherlands	75.2
Belgium	84.1	Germany	72.7
Australia	82.7	United Kingdom	72.4
Sweden	82.6	Ireland	70.2
Denmark	81.7	France	60.6
New Zealand	80.4	**Canada**	**60.1***
Austria	79.6	Japan	57.0
Spain	79.0	United States	44.9
Norway	75.7	Switzerland	37.7

*This Canadian figure is lower than the official figures given in Table 6.2 because IDEA uses a different methodology, comparing turnout to the census population eligible to vote rather than to the names on the voters' list. By this measure, the turnout rate in the 2000 election would have been about 50 percent!

Source: International Institute for Democracy and Electoral Assistance (IDEA) Web site, Voter Turnout: A Global Survey, http://www.idea.int/ (Retrieved 15 Sept. 2001). Used with permission.

"informed vote," a smaller proportion of the electorate actually becomes actively involved in the election campaign: attending an all-candidates meeting; joining a political party; voting at the party's local nomination meeting; contributing money to a political party; or helping a local candidate to do mailing, telephoning, door-to-door canvassing, and election-day work. A small number in each constituency become totally preoccupied with the local campaign; these people, including candidates themselves, are sometimes called "gladiators" as distinct from the great bulk of the population who are primarily "spectators."

Table 6.4 indicates the number of individuals who contributed money to national parties and local candidates in 1997. Since some made contributions to both parties and candidates, the total of those who made financial contributions is probably no more than 250 000 out of an electorate of 19 million, or slightly more than 1 percent.

Nonelectoral Participation

The political participation of most Canadians peaks at election time, but many avenues are open between elections in which to make demands or otherwise become involved in the political process. One option would be to join a political party. Most Canadian political parties do not maintain reliable lists of their mem-

TABLE **6.4** NUMBERS OF INDIVIDUALS MAKING FINANCIAL CONTRIBUTIONS TO PARTIES AND CANDIDATES, 1997

	To National Parties	To Local Candidates
PC	25 352	20 353
Liberal	34 429	21 906
NDP	50 434	15 119
Reform	75 587	20 624
BQ	18 885	13 215
Total	202 687	91 217

Sources: Elections Canada, *Registered Political Parties' Fiscal Returns for 1997.* Extrapolation and analysis rests with the author. Reproduced with permission of the Chief Electoral Officer of Canada, 2001.

bers, but Ken Carty estimates that about 2.7 percent of the population belong to a party.[17] It is known, however, that many people sign up before or during the campaign, often to participate in the nomination of candidates, and then let their membership lapse.

Another means of political participation is to join an organized interest group, an action that some 60 percent of Canadians claim to do. As seen in Chapter 10, any group, whatever its primary orientation, can become a pressure group, so that membership in any group is potentially political. Even if the group itself takes a political turn, however, passive members rarely do more than send the occasional preprinted postcard to their MP or the prime minister.

On the other hand, the purpose of some groups is primarily political, and political activists increasingly prefer social movement and interest group to party involvement. Active executive and staff members of such groups may become highly involved in political campaigns and the pressure-group politics that goes on in Canada every day. Even more initiative is required to form such a group, usually to protest against some political decision or lack of action at the municipal, provincial, federal, or even global level.

Such group participation usually involves communicating with the authorities in routine ways, but occasionally it takes the form of peaceful demonstrations (locally or on Parliament Hill), sit-ins and other types of civil disobedience, and the rare case of violent protest. As noted above, Canadians are generally a peaceful lot, and political violence is uncommon. The main historical incidents of such violence in Canada were the Riel Rebellions of 1870 and 1885, the conscription riots in Quebec City in 1918, the Winnipeg General Strike of 1919, the

Regina Riot of 1935, the various FLQ incidents of the 1960s culminating in the
FLQ crisis of 1970, and the Mohawks' armed standoff at Oka in 1990.[18]

Canadians can also participate politically between elections as individuals—
writing, faxing, or e-mailing letters to MPs or the prime minister, writing letters
to the editors of newspapers, calling radio or television phone-in shows, signing
petitions, or telephoning or meeting an MP. As with so many other aspects of
political participation, however, it is difficult to obtain solid data on the degree of
individual involvement in these activities. In general, few people take the initiative to do any of these things, one survey reporting about 20 percent.[19]

The relationship between degree of participation and social status is notable.
Table 6.5 indicates five forms of participation broken down by level of income,
education, and occupational status. In almost any measure of participation,
whether discussing politics, working for a party, signing a petition, or engaging in
marches, rallies, or sit-ins, the degree of involvement increases with level of
income and education and from blue-collar to white-collar to professional and
managerial occupations. Possession of money often provides such resources as
leisure time, political information, and contacts that facilitate such high levels of
participation. Such a pattern exists even for political protests.

TABLE 6.5 PERCENTAGE LEVEL OF PARTICIPATION IN SELECTED POLITICAL ACTIVITIES,
1993, BY OCCUPATION, INCOME, AND EDUCATION

	Discuss Politics	Party Work	Sign Petition	March/ Rally	Sit-In
Occupation					
Blue Collar	75	4	71	26	9
White Collar	89	6	76	26	7
Professional/Managerial	86	9	78	37	10
Income					
Under $20 000	70	5	54	21	7
$70 000 & over	87	12	79	30	7
Education					
Elementary or less	68	9	34	14	5
Complete secondary	82	8	69	19	6
University degree	86	7	86	45	13

Source: Mishler and Clarke, "Political Participation in Canada," 137. Used with permission.

DISCUSSION QUESTIONS

1. Are periodic elections a sufficient means of exercising the principle of popular sovereignty? In what situations are referenda appropriate?
2. To what extent are basic Canadian political values still distinct from those in the United States?
3. Thinking about the relative importance of the agents of political socialization in your own life, can you decipher your own socialization process?
4. How high a level of political information and political participation does a democracy require?

FURTHER READING

Bell, David. *The Roots of Disunity: A Look at Canadian Political Culture*. Rev. ed. Oxford University Press, 1992.

Berton, Pierre. *Why We Act Like Canadians*. Toronto: McClelland and Stewart, 1982.

Friedenberg, Edgar J. *Deference to Authority*. White Plains, N.Y.: M.E. Sharpe, 1980.

Lipset, Seymour Martin. *Continental Divide*. New York: Routledge, 1990.

Nevitte, Neil. *The Decline of Deference*. Peterborough: Broadview Press, 1996.

Ostry, Sylvia. "Government Intervention: Canada and the United States Compared." *Policy Options* (March 1980): 26–31.

Thomas, David, ed. *Canada and the United States: Differences That Count*. Peterborough: Broadview Press, 2nd ed., 2000.

Notes

1. Henry B. Mayo, *An Introduction to Democratic Theory* (New York: Oxford University Press, 1960), ch. 4.
2. Seymour Martin Lipset, *Continental Divide* (New York: Routledge, 1990), 8.
3. Pierre Berton, *Why We Act Like Canadians* (Toronto: McClelland and Stewart, 1982).
4. *Maclean's* (1 July 1995): 15.
5. Canadian Information Office, Government Communications Survey-Wave IV: Final Survey Findings, Fall 1999 (CIO Web site) www.infocan.gc.ca/survey/pubop_e.html (Retrieved 15 Sept. 2001); Shawn McCarthy, "Albertans embrace federation," (*The Globe and Mail*, 14 February 2001).
6. Statistics Canada. *Canadian Social Trends*, cat. No. 11-008 (Autumn 1993); Statistics Canada, *The Survey of Financial Security*, cat. No. 13-595 (March 2001), p. 9.
7. Neil Nevitte, *The Decline of Deference* (Peterborough, Ont.: Broadview Press, 1996).

8. Marcel Trudel and Genevieve Jain, *Canadian History Textbooks: A Comparative Study* (Ottawa: Royal Commission on Bilingualism and Biculturalism, 1970).

9. Ronald Landes, "Political Education and Political Socialization," in Jon Pammett and Jean-Luc Pépin, eds., *Political Education in Canada* (Halifax: Institute for Research on Public Policy, 1988), 17.

10. Frederick Fletcher, "The Mass Media and Political Education," in Pammett and Pépin, 92.

11. Alan Frizzell et al., *The Canadian General Election of 1988* (Ottawa: Carleton University Press), 69.

12. William Mishler and Harold D. Clarke, "Political Participation in Canada," in Michael Whittington and Glen Williams, eds., *Canadian Politics in the 1990s*, 4th ed. (Scarborough: Nelson Canada, 1995), 130.

13. Ibid., 134.

14. The 1993 rate may not be entirely accurate, because a year-old voters' list from the 1992 referendum was used.

15. Mishler and Clarke, "Political Participation," 134, 143.

16. Ronald D. Lambert et al., "The Social Sources of Political Knowledge," *Canadian Journal of Political Science* (June 1988): 359–74.

17. R. Kenneth Carty, *Canadian Political Parties in the Constituencies*. Royal Commission on Electoral Reform and Party Financing Research Studies, Vol. 23, cat. no. 21-1989/2-41-23E.

18. Judy Torrance, *Public Violence in Canada* (Montreal: McGill–Queen's University Press, 1986).

19. Mishler and Clarke, "Political Participation," 134.

Chapter 7

The Mass Media and Public Opinion Polls

The **mass media,** principally television, newspapers, and radio, are the primary source of most Canadians' knowledge and opinions about topical political issues and current political personalities. Public policymakers in turn depend on the media for information, as well as for transmitting the messages that they want the public to hear. The media thus provide an important two-way communications link between the governors and the governed. A second crucial link is the public opinion poll. Although political parties rely heavily on polls to guide their actions immediately before and during election campaigns, governments and the media also seek to discover Canadians' opinions on a daily basis. This chapter examines both of these important features of the political system, which are frequently interconnected.

Chapter Objectives

After you have completed this chapter, you should be able to:

Discuss the agenda-setting function of the media

Outline the ownership of different media and evaluate the significance of public, private, and concentrated ownership

Distinguish between the virtues of newspapers and television in the eyes of both the general public and media analysts

Understand the mutually dependent relationship between politicians and the media

Appreciate the extent to which public opinion is not well informed

Enumerate the practitioners and discuss the techniques of public opinion polling

Evaluate the extent to which public opinion polls influence voting behaviour and the policies adopted by governments

The Mass Media
The State of the Media

In surveying the newspaper, radio, and television industries today, it should first be noted that the privately owned media exist primarily to make a profit, and that whatever political functions they serve are incidental to that purpose. In addition, since the media—even television—usually rely on words and language, and since a majority of Canadians are unilingual, the country is characterized by a "media apartheid," in which English and French are virtually two solitudes.

NEWSPAPERS

The Canadian daily newspaper industry has been characterized by chain owner-ship for several decades, but the owners have frequently exchanged papers in recent years. An earlier era was dominated by the Ken Thomson and Southam newspaper chains. The pride of the Thomson chain was *The Globe and Mail*, which calls itself "Canada's National Newspaper" and publishes a national edition transmitted by satellite to several printing locations so that it is available every morning in all major centres across the country. But in 1996 Thomson sold most of his newspapers (except the *Globe*) to Conrad Black, who operated the Hollinger chain, had previously purchased the Southam chain, and proceeded to establish a national competitor to *The Globe and Mail* called the *National Post*.

Then, in 2000, Izzy Asper, proprietor of CanWest Global Television, bought about half of Black's Canadian dailies, and in 2001 Black sold 16 others to Michael Sifton. In the same year, Thomson sold *The Globe and Mail* to BCE (Bell Canada Enterprises), which had previously taken possession of the CTV televi-sion network. At of the time of writing, therefore, the CanWest Global chain encompassed about 27 daily newspapers, and Sifton's Osprey Group, 16.

The third-largest chain, with 15 dailies, is Quebecor, owned by the Péladeau family of Quebec and centred on the English-language *Sun* chain. Conrad Black still has 12, after which come the Desmarais chain with seven Quebec papers, led by *La Presse* of Montreal; TorStar, with five in Ontario; and the four-paper Irving chain in New Brunswick. In addition, there are approximately 15 independents or members of smaller chains.

Thus, some of the wealthiest families in Canada—Asper, Black, Irving, Desmarais, and Péladeau—control most of the country's newspaper industry. Moreover, one chain or another often has an overwhelming dominance in a single province, such as Irving in New Brunswick and Asper in Saskatchewan,

Newfoundland, and Prince Edward Island. Such concentrated ownership of Canadian newspapers has always caused considerable concern. Many fear that the owner of several papers will gain an unhealthy degree of influence over public opinion by establishing a common point of view for all papers in the chain. The Trudeau government appointed the Kent Royal Commission on Newspapers to investigate this question, but responding to strong pressure from the industry, that government abandoned a bill aimed to restrict concentrated media ownership. Some observers welcomed the Asper purchase of Black properties because they expected the new owner to be less inclined to provide such right-wing ideological editorial direction, but all conglomerate-owned newspapers are likely to betray a pro-business bias.[1]

Most of these newspaper-owning families have substantial holdings beyond newspapers. This leads to the question of whether such newspapers provide fair coverage of the firms' other operations. Especially in the small confines of New Brunswick, for example, it has been charged that Irving newspapers refrain from critical comment on all the family's other holdings. Moreover, many media analysts find the new trend toward companies owning both television networks and daily newspapers to be somewhat troubling.

RADIO AND TELEVISION

The radio and television industries are distinct from newspapers in two respects: the degree of public ownership and the government regulation involved.[2] As for public ownership, the **Canadian Broadcasting Corporation** operates 49 radio stations in English and 24 in French, and through transmitter stations, its coverage is almost nationwide. CBC radio has a relatively large and sophisticated audience, and plays a major role in transmitting information and opinion among its listeners. The CBC/Radio-Canada television network has 24 stations across the country, with English production centred in Toronto and French production in Montreal. These are supplemented by agreements with 24 other privately owned affiliated stations, which agree to telecast a certain amount of CBC programming.

Apart from CBC/Radio-Canada, the Canadian radio industry consists of nearly 500 local AM and FM stations. These stations used to be independently owned, but are increasingly characterized by chain ownership, just as in the newspaper industry. Ownership changes quite frequently, but by 1990, fully half of the radio market in Canada was controlled by the 10 leading firms. Like newspapers, radio stations must be Canadian-owned, but the limited Canadian content on private radio stations became a problem, with the result that the CRTC issued Canadian content rules, as noted in Chapter 5.

The privately owned CTV network, centred on CFTO in Toronto, consists of 28 television stations. Once the property of the Eaton family, the network is now owned by BCE and run by Ivan Fecan. The Toronto-based CanWest Global system is owned by Izzy Asper of Winnipeg, who succeeded in cobbling together a third national English-language network of 11 television stations in eight provinces. Several major cities also have an unaffiliated, independent private English station. On the French side, the equivalent of CTV is nine-station TVA network, now owned by Péladeau, and whose focal point is Télé-Métropole in Montreal; a second private French network is Quatre Saisons.

The **Canadian Radio-television and Telecommunications Commission (CRTC)** is the federal regulatory agency in this field. The commission requires Canadian television stations to be domestically owned and to telecast 50 percent or more Canadian content. But such regulations are virtually meaningless when almost all residents are within reach, either directly or via cable, of a large assortment of U.S. television channels. On this point, Fred Fletcher talks of "American images crowding out Canadian ones,"[3] and Ed Black writes of the problem of trying to serve a small population in two language groups "who live in tempting, embarrassing, and almost smothering proximity to [10 times as many] Americans who speak the language of Canada's majority ... They also have the world's most penetrating and effective system for transmitting ideas en masse."[4] Peter Trueman adds, "Think of the overwhelming preponderance of American programming, which in an unobtrusive way pumps us full of American values, American hopes, American history, even American patterns of speech."[5]

CBC television has a strong commitment to Canadian programming, but suffers from a chronic shortage of funds. After severe bloodletting under the Mulroney government, the CBC hoped for better treatment under the Chrétien regime. Instead, that government slashed the CBC budget even further, precipitating the resignation of the Corporation's president.

Private stations and networks realize that profits can be maximized by telecasting as much U.S. programming as the CRTC will allow. Nevertheless, the importance and popularity of CBC, CTV, and Global national newscasts, *The Morning News*, *The Fifth Estate*, *Marketplace*, *Royal Canadian Air Farce*, *This Hour Has 22 Minutes*, *Téléjournal*, *Le Point*, *Canada AM*, and *W5* should not be underestimated. Figure 7.1 illustrates the percentage of time spent watching Canadian-content programs in 1997. The overall percentage is 40 percent, but this varies from 66.5 percent among francophones to 30 percent for anglophones. In every category, francophones watch more Canadian content than anglophones, although the latter do watch more Canadian than foreign coverage in two main

Figure 7.1   Percentage of Time Spent Watching Canadian-Content Programs, Anglophones and Francophones, 1997

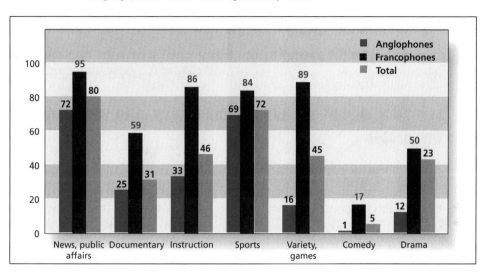

Source: "Percentage of Time Spent Watching Canadian-Content Programs, Anglophones and Francophones, 1997," adapted from the Statistics Canada Web site http://www.statcan.ca/english/IPS/Data/87F0006KPB.htm

categories: news and public affairs and sports. What is probably most troubling is the low proportion of Canadian viewing in the drama category, especially by anglophones.

The establishment of CBC Newsworld in 1989 (and a French equivalent in 1995) was another effort to strengthen Canadian television content. These all-news channels cover many political events live and more extensively than regular CBC, with which they work closely, and provide much regional coverage, documentaries, and in-depth interview programming. While their audience is small, most members of the political elite tune in regularly. The national parliamentary channel on cable is now called CPAC; in some provinces another channel carries provincial legislative proceedings, and several provinces have an educational television channel.

About 75 percent of Canadian homes are hooked up to (and hooked on) cable television, more than in any other country. The CRTC regulates which channels cable systems carry, but cable television brings the major U.S. networks into most Canadian homes and permits subscribers to watch U.S. news, public affairs, and sports programs. The Canadian cable industry is essentially dominated by three regional giants: Rogers Communications, Shaw Cablesystems, and Vidéotron. The variety of other channels on cable television is constantly increasing, and some of them are of Canadian origin, as CBC, CTV, Global, and others have established their own specialty channels. CRTC approval of new specialty channels, including "pay-per-view," and direct-to-home (DTH) satellite services, has further served to dilute the audience of the conventional Canadian television stations.

The Changing Media World: Convergence in Canadian Media Ownership

Probably few aspects of the political system are in such a state of rapid change as the mass media. The first change is the convergence of technologies and corporations, as television, telephone, satellite, cable, computer, and Internet companies merge.[6] Spectacular mega-media conglomerations have taken place in the United States in recent years (which in themselves have a considerable impact on Canada), but in this respect Canada is not far behind. The merging of BCE with CTV, Sympatico, and *The Globe and Mail*, and the purchase of half the Black newspapers by CanWest Global Television represent similar cross-media conglomerates, as seen in Table 7.1. The increased concentration of ownership of such sources of public information is not a healthy development in any democ-

TABLE 7.1 FOUR LARGEST MEDIA CONGLOMERATES IN CANADA

CanWest Global	Bell Globemedia	Quebecor	Rogers Communications
11 conventional TV stations	CTV television network	15 daily newspapers	Cable television
Specialty channels	Specialty channels	TVA television network	Specialty channels
27 daily newspapers	*The Globe and Mail*	Internet Services	Internet service
Southam magazines	Teleglobe TV satellite	Publishing houses	Magazines
Internet services	Bell ExpressVu satellite service	Cable television	Radio stations
	Internet services	Magazines	
	Quatre Seasons television network	Video rentals	

racy that values the maximum diversity of opinions. Moreover, it tends to reduce the resources devoted to news and investigative reporting at the expense of profit-oriented entertainment.

On the other hand, the opposite trend toward a fragmentation of audiences allows individuals to ignore broader public questions as they expose themselves to media coverage of only a few personal interests through specialized television channels. The same criticism also applies to the Internet, whose political impact is not yet entirely clear. While it is a liberating force that permits people to gain information from around the world, connect with others having similar concerns, and provide direct feedback to government, it can also be used for antisocial purposes.

The Media and the Public

The influence of the mass media on the political system is profound and appears to be constantly increasing.[7] Most of the information Canadians receive about the political process comes from television, newspapers, or radio, and perhaps *Maclean's*, rather than from direct observation or other sources such as books or magazines. Some recipients may be able to separate this information from whatever commentary or biases accompany it, but many are swayed by the particular perspective that the media give to the data they present.

The current consensus on the role of the media is that they set the political agenda for the country.[8] In other words, the media tell people what to think about, what the important issues are, and which political personalities are significant. They help to define what is political.[9] This is a function that the media share with political parties, and while parties may be more important as initiators of issues, these will not likely remain on the agenda without media attention. The **Parliamentary press gallery** seems to have a "herd instinct" or to engage in "pack journalism" in developing a consensus about what these significant issues are.[10] In part, this reflects the influence of the daily oral Question Period in the House of Commons, which provides them with short, superficial, and controversial issues that are well suited to television coverage.

When asked to choose among the various media, a majority of people say they prefer to get their political information from television rather than newspapers. Those who prefer television feel it is most fair and believable for all kinds of information, and most complete, except perhaps for business and economic news.[11] These results are somewhat distressing to those who know the real advantages and disadvantages of the three media in question. Because of cost and time

Peter Mansbridge—most Canadians get their political information from television (Frank Gunn/CP Picture Archive)

constraints, television must present a shorter and more superficial account of political events than either radio or newspapers. Coverage of any item rarely exceeds a 60- to 90-second "news clip" with a 10-second "sound bite" of the voice of political leaders, in which *how* something is said is usually more important than *what* is said. The transcript of a 30-minute newscast would make up about one-third of a single newspaper page.[12] Moreover, because it is a visual medium, television must seek out colourful, dramatic, emotional, conflictual, or entertaining pictures. Riots, demonstrations, and political conventions usually make good television, but the daily routine of politics does not lend itself so well to compelling visual coverage. Witness the efforts taken by politicians, protesters, and the media to find contrived and engaging settings in which to stage political happenings, make announcements, or tape interviews.

Television portrays images and impressions, and is therefore much better at dealing with political leaders and personalities than with issues. When Liberal leader John Turner issued a 40-point policy manifesto just before the 1988 election, for example, "the electronic media, which have trouble transmitting more than a single idea in a 30-second clip, could not cope with such a cornucopia of ideas that had not been pre-digested into a simple theme wrapped around a few easily grasped issues."[13] These characteristics make television the most open of the three media to distortion and exploitation, so that it is actually the *least* believable and—however unintentionally—the *most* biased.[14] Television meets the needs of the average citizen with a short attention span who is looking for visual stimulation and does not wish to invest much effort in understanding the political system.

This situation is exacerbated by the increasing tendency of political parties and politicians to gear their activities to the demands of television rather than the other media or the public. Press conferences are now dominated by television lights and cameras; leaders' tours during election campaigns are "photo opportunities" designed to generate a sound bite on the evening news; and party conventions and leaders' debates are scheduled at the television networks' convenience. In preparing for elections, parties put greater effort into designing television commercials and trying them out before focus groups than in devising solutions to the country's problems. The leaders' debate has become the single most important event in an election campaign because elections usually turn more on leader images than issues, policies, local candidates, or other leading figures in the party. The appearance, style, and general image of the party leader, including the ability to perform on television, has become of crucial importance. This emphasis on appearance is often said to trivialize politics.

It would be too soon, however, to write off the political importance of newspapers. Daily newspapers generally offer more comprehensive coverage of political events, and they excel at covering issues, which they can do at length, in depth, and in detail, presenting both greater factual information and a wider range of interpretation. While the "average" Canadian relies on television for political information, those with political influence, whether in government, parties, pressure groups, or peer-group situations, depend on newspapers. Those who prefer newspapers over television have higher educations, higher incomes, and are better informed. Furthermore, even though print journalists must often defer to the paraphernalia of their television colleagues, the broadcast media and opposition parties tend to take their cues from newspapers.

It should be added that the degree of political participation increases sharply with a person's level of newspaper consumption. In other words, those who make the effort to increase their political information by reading a newspaper (as opposed to sitting passively in front of a TV set) are not only better informed but also most likely to go on to engage in some form of political participation.[15]

The Globe and Mail is read by most of the top-level decisionmakers and media executives across the country; it thus tends to set the agenda for other news organizations. Over the past few years, however, it has had competition from the *National Post*. The independent but financially troubled *Le Devoir* occupies a similarly influential position in French Canada, and it has always been an advocate of Quebec nationalism. In fact, all French-language media in Quebec have played a part in communicating a sense of the French-Canadian nation, from the famous Plouffe family television series in the 1960s to the federally owned Radio-Canada.

The Media and the Politicians

Politicians and their bureaucratic advisers need publicity and therefore have a great interest in how the media cover their behaviour. Even though they have their own direct sources, they also depend on the media to provide information they need about what is happening at home and abroad. The media in turn often rely on government sources for most of their information, and much media reporting of politics is of the "government handout" variety, which raises concern.

OWNERS, EDITORS, AND JOURNALISTS

The Canadian daily newspapers are expected to present news coverage in an objective manner, and reserve the opinions of the owner or editor for the editorial page. Even so, one can often detect slight biases in the tone or selection of news items, such as a rightward slant in *The Globe and Mail* and a left, Liberal inclination in the *Toronto Star*. Conrad Black made such biases more overt when he assumed ownership of the Southam chain, especially in his creation of the *National Post*: a clear-cut preference for the Reform/Alliance party and its right-wing policies pervaded the whole paper.

In principle, reporters should remain distant from politicians to cover them objectively; on the other hand, it is often necessary to cultivate close relations in order to get the kind of information the media seek. Allan Fotheringham writes that "the narrowest line in journalism is the line between exploiting your sources (without ever destroying them) and being captured by them."[16] Furthermore, since politicians often confidentially seek out the opinions of working reporters, the latter sometimes have to agonize over whether to reveal information that was given to them "off the record," that is, in the expectation that it would not be used.

The media also have to confront the issue of politicians' privacy. When do excessive drinking, sexual infidelity, or family and financial problems begin to interfere with a politician's public functions, and when should they be revealed? Beyond personal privacy is the question of whether the media should transmit information they are not supposed to have, such as when Global Television came into advance possession of a summary of the 1988 budget.

THE GOVERNMENT SIDE: NEWS MANAGEMENT

The increasingly common problem of **news management** and manipulation relates especially to the deliberate timing and selective distribution of government information. It includes exaggerating the positive while keeping secret or delaying release of that which is negative, giving preference to friendly reporters over others, making prime ministerial requests for network television time for less than important announcements, or outright lying. News management also involves putting the best face on a deficient government action or politician's performance by having a partisan official tell the media how successful it actually was, in the hope that the media will transmit this evaluation to their audience.

Those involved in such efforts are often called media handlers or **spin doctors,** because they try to put the best face, or "spin," on any event.

News leaks are another issue in news management. When governments do not know what course to follow, they sometimes leak a proposal to the media as a "trial balloon," hoping for guidance from the public reaction received. Ed Black points out that this practice is helpful in these days when politicians usually have little time to respond to problems or give them comprehensive consideration.[17]

The ultimate problem in media–government relations is political interference with the "freedom of the press," one of the sacred principles of democracy, as discussed in Chapter 6. The most blatant examples of such political interference have occurred at the provincial level. In Quebec, Premier Maurice Duplessis kept the press under control by awarding advertising and printing contracts to newspaper owners and financial gifts to members of the press gallery. In Alberta, the Social Credit party in the 1930s tried to force newspapers to retract any criticisms of the government. Occasional attempts have apparently been made by the Prime Minister's Office over the years to have the CBC take a certain perspective on a vital national issue. The most celebrated case in English Canada was the cancellation in 1966 of the highly popular but critical CBC public affairs program *This Hour Has Seven Days*.[18] The Trudeau government accused the Radio-Canada network of being riddled with separatists who gave a biased interpretation of federal–provincial relations. Although there was probably some truth to the charge, it smacked of political interference. Short of actual political interference or government censorship is the highly secretive tradition of Canadian governments. In 1982, the Access to Information Act made it somewhat easier for the media as well as other interested parties to obtain access to government information, but the secrecy habit is difficult for politicians and bureaucrats to overcome.

Public Opinion Polls

The phrase **public opinion** sometimes implies that a unanimous, informed view on a particular issue is held by all members of the public. In actuality, many opinions are held on any issue, and each issue interests only a certain segment of the population. Furthermore, most political opinions are not well informed. They are based on little information, they are simplifications of complex issues, and they are often internally contradictory. Indeed, people often form their opinions first and then look for information to confirm them; at the very least, they "seek out information that conforms to their predispositions ... and avoid or reinterpret any contrary and non-supportive messages."[19] Nevertheless, public opinions about topical issues frequently influence the actions of government.

Measuring Public Opinion

Given this great conglomeration of viewpoints, public opinion is very difficult to gauge. Haphazard methods such as reading editorials or letters to the editor or listening to open-line programs are obviously unreliable, but so are many amateur public opinion surveys. On the other hand, professional polling agencies claim to be able to select a small representative sample of people, ask carefully worded questions, and report with a high degree of accuracy the opinions of the whole population. Such polls have assumed an immense importance in contemporary Canadian politics: "no political party plans campaign strategy without them, no government is prepared to risk major policy initiatives without gauging public opinion, and for major news organizations they are an indispensable reporting tool, both between and during elections."[20]

Beyond the now common procedure for conducting a **public opinion poll,** two special techniques deserve mention. The first is "tracking," which entails telephoning samples of 100 to 500 people nightly during an election campaign in order to see how day-to-day developments are affecting them. The second is the "focus group," in which a small number of people are gathered together behind a one-way mirror with a group leader who encourages them to voice their "gut" reaction to various leaders, issues, and slogans. Their responses are recorded and then analyzed. The importance of polls and focus groups to construct a party's campaign message and even the language to be used to convey that message can hardly be overemphasized.

Who are these professional pollsters? The leading pollsters all do much nonpolitical polling as well, and a number of lobbying firms also do polling as part of their comprehensive consulting work. Professional pollsters include

- Environics Research Group (Michael Adams and Donna Dasko)
- POLLARA (Michael Marzolini, the official Liberal Party pollster)
- Ekos Research Associates Inc.
- Ipsos-Reid (formerly Angus Reid)
- Léger Marketing (formerly Léger and Léger Group, leading Quebec pollsters)
- ComQUEST Research
- Goldfarb Consultants (Martin Goldfarb, the original Liberal pollster)
- Compas Inc.

How accurate are the polls? The only way a survey's accuracy can really be tested is through a comparison of its results immediately prior to an election with the electoral outcome itself. The immediate pre-election findings of most professional agencies have usually been within the range of accuracy claimed—typically plus or minus 4 percent 19 times out of 20. The way a question is worded, the optional responses available, the sequence of the questions, the degree to which respondents are telling the truth, and many other variables can influence the results.

Such discrepancies in results give rise to a concern that those with ulterior motives can deliberately manipulate polling results by tailoring the sample or the wording of the questions. Moreover, those with significant financial resources can resort to advocacy advertising and then continue polling until the correct "public opinion" is forthcoming.

Impact of Polls on the Public

Perhaps the main issue that arises in the discussion of polls and pollsters is whether their pre-election predictions influence the election results. This question cannot be answered categorically, but it is unlikely that their direct effect is that great. First, most voters do not pay much attention to poll results; second, not everyone believes them; and third, it is not important to everyone to vote for the winning side even if this is clear in advance. While some voters may want to jump on the victorious bandwagon—the **bandwagon effect**—at least a few are likely to switch to the predicted loser—the "underdog effect"—either out of sympathy or to try to prevent an overwhelming victory for the prospective winner.[21]

On the other hand, the polls probably have a significant indirect effect on the election results. The media are just as obsessed with the polls as the politicians are, and survey results may well entice the media to concentrate on those parties and politicians who are in the lead and to ignore those who are trailing. Furthermore, polls have a considerable impact on party morale. A positive poll usually generates greater enthusiasm and effort, better candidates, and larger financial contributions, while a negative poll saps the spirit of leaders, candidates, and foot soldiers alike. Such results affect the subtle "momentum" of the campaign.

Another issue can be addressed more categorically: polls definitely detract from the discussion of real issues in the election campaign.[22] The media are fascinated by polls primarily because they are good for business, and given the media's ability to influence the political agenda even during election campaigns, they

....

Figure 7.2   Final Federal Voting Preference, 2000 Election

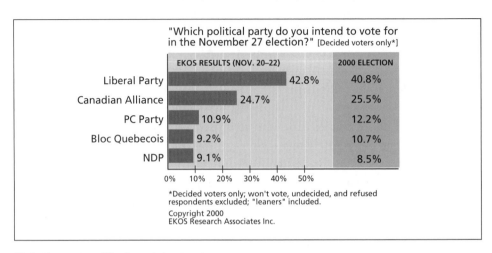

Used with permission of Ekos Research Associates Inc.

emphasize the **horse-race effect** of the contest. Media tend to spend more time on who is ahead than on comparative analysis of party platforms, asking leaders to comment on the latest poll results, for example, rather than how the party would deal with a particular public problem. Now that the media actually hire or own polling firms, survey results are becoming major news items in themselves.

Many political losers have blamed their fate on negative public opinion polls, and some have called for the prohibition of polls during part or all of the campaign. Such bans do exist in many countries. Whatever their faults, however, polls enliven the campaign and increase the information available, and to prohibit their publication in the media would not prevent parties, candidates, and others from conducting their own surveys. The main effect of a publication ban would be to give certain crucial information to those who could afford a survey and to deny it to the general public, a rather undemocratic suggestion.

One of the amendments to the Canada Elections Act made in the wake of the Royal Commission on Electoral Reform was to prohibit, in the final three days of the campaign, the broadcast, publication, or dissemination of public opinion poll results. This restriction was soon challenged by the Thomson and Southam newspaper chains as a violation of freedom of the press, and their objection was upheld by the Supreme Court of Canada. The revised Canada Elections Act of 2000 prohibits the publication of polling results only on election day itself.

Impact of Polls on the Authorities

The other main question in the study of public opinion is the relationship between it and the response of the authorities. For nearly 100 years after Confederation, governments had to act in the absence of a reliable survey, but it now sometimes seems that they are reluctant to make any decision until it can be based on a poll. Even with such polling results, however, opinion is likely to be considerably divided, so that clear-cut guidance cannot always be found.

Sometimes, even when public opinion is clearly in favour of a certain course of government action, the authorities will decide to do otherwise. This may be the consequence of the politicians' own convictions, the recommendations of the public service, the pressure of lobbyists and interest groups, or the rigidity of party discipline. Indeed, some hold the view that even in a democracy, politicians are not obliged to follow public opinion; they may also lead it. This is especially true now that we realize how uninformed, superficial, and changeable most public opinions really are. While politicians and bureaucrats may be accused of acting in their own self-interest if they do not follow a clear preference among the public, they may actually be relying on a deeper understanding of the issue, the greater information at their disposal, a more sophisticated analysis of its implications, or a concern for minority rights. For example, capital punishment has been an issue on which public opinion clearly supported one side but on which the authorities repeatedly went their own way. Should Parliament reinstate capital punishment in response to popular opinion based on a mistaken impression about rising crime rates, a desire for retribution, and a questionable assumption of deterrence? Most political issues are even more complicated than capital punishment, and on most, public opinion is much more divided; thus the correlation between public opinion and public policy is not as strong as might be expected.

In his book *Margin of Error,* Claire Hoy reveals just how many public policies were adopted over the years and how many election dates were set on the basis of public opinion polls. He also shows how important polls were in the 1988 election campaign. First, the governing Conservatives used many publicly funded polls to determine their election platform. Second, the Liberals surveyed public opinion in Quebec to see if a Senate veto of the Free Trade Agreement would detract from their support in that province. Third, the NDP avoided the Free Trade issue (and left the Liberals to capitalize on it) because party polling indicated that the NDP lacked public credibility on economic issues.[23] Indeed, the NDP used focus groups as early as 1984 to find that the phrase "ordinary Canadians" was preferable to "working Canadians" to use as its slogan.[24] When even the NDP starts to base its slogans and strategies on focus groups and public opinion polls, it is hard to overstate their significance.

Indeed, the incidence of and government reliance on public opinion polls severely undercuts the argument in favour of referenda. Public opinion polls already provide a quick, cheap, frequent, and accurate picture of the public's views.

DISCUSSION QUESTIONS

1. Is there something distinctive about media companies that suggests concentrated ownership should be more restricted than in other industries?
2. What are the advantages and disadvantages of obtaining political information from television and newspapers?
3. Should public opinion polls be prohibited at some stage of an election campaign? Should the authorities always do what public opinion polls show a majority wants?

FURTHER READING

Fotheringham, Allan. *Birds of a Feather: The Press and the Politicians*. Toronto: Key Porter Books, 1990.

Frizzell, Alan, et al. *The Canadian General Election of 1997*. Toronto: Dundurn Press, 1997.

Levine, Allan. *Scrum Wars: The Prime Ministers and the Media*. Toronto: Dundurn Press, 1993.

Lorimer, Rowland, and Mike Gasher. *Mass Communications in Canada*, 4th ed. Don Mills: Oxford University Press, 2001.

Miller, John. *Yesterday's News: How Canada's Daily Newspapers Are Failing Us*. Halifax: Fernwood Publishing, 1998.

Nash, Knowlton. *Trivia Pursuit: How Showbiz Values Are Corrupting the News*. Toronto: McClelland and Stewart, 1998.

Nevitt, Neil, et al. *Unsteady State: The 1997 Canadian Federal Election*. Toronto: Oxford University Press, 2000.

Taras, David. *The Newsmakers*. Scarborough: Nelson Canada, 1990.

Taras, David. *Power and Betrayal in the Canadian Media*. Peterborough: Broadview Press, 1999.

Winter, James. *Democracy's Oxygen: How Corporations Control the News*. Montreal: Black Rose, 1997.

Notes

1. David Taras, *Power and Betrayal in the Canadian Media* (Peterborough: Broadview Press, 1999); James Winter, *Democracy's Oxygen: How Corporations Control the News in Canada* (Toronto: McClelland and Stewart, 1980); John Miller, *Yesterday's News: How Canada's Daily Newspapers Are Failing Us* (Halifax: Fernwood Publishing, 1998).
2. Rowland Lorimer and Mike Gasher, *Mass Communications in Canada*, 4th ed. (Don Mills: Oxford University Press, 2001).
3. Frederick J. Fletcher and Daphne Gottlieb Taras, "Images and Issues: The Mass Media and Politics in Canada," in Michael Whittington and Glen Williams, eds., *Canadian Politics in the 1990s*, 3rd ed. (Scarborough: Nelson Canada, 1990), 229.
4. Edwin R. Black, *Politics and the News: The Political Functions of the Mass Media* (Toronto: Butterworths, 1982), 80.
5. Peter Trueman, *Smoke and Mirrors: The Inside Story of Television News in Canada* (Toronto: McClelland and Stewart, 1980), 161.
6. Taras, *Power and Betrayal*, ch. 3.
7. The general thrust of David Taras in *The Newsmakers* (Scarborough: Nelson Canada, 1990).
8. Ibid., 30–31.
9. Fletcher, *The Newspaper and Public Affairs*, 16; Fletcher and Taras, "Images and Issues," 222; Black, *Politics and the News*, 183; Peter Desbarats, *Guide to Canadian News Media*, 2nd ed. (Toronto: Harcourt Brace Jovanovich, 1990), 149; Arthur Siegel, *Politics and the Media in Canada* (Toronto: McGraw-Hill Ryerson, 1983), 14.
10. Taras, *The Newsmakers*, ch. 3; Allan Levine, *Scrum Wars: The Prime Ministers and the Media* (Toronto: Dundurn Press, 1993).
11. Environics Media Study (Environics Research Group, December 1986), cited by Desbarats, *Guide to Canadian News Media*, 28; and its *1991 Media Study*.
12. Taras, *The Newsmakers*, 102.
13. Alan Frizzell et al., *The Canadian General Election of 1988* (Ottawa: Carleton University Press, 1989), 33.
14. Taras, *The Newsmakers*, ch. 4; Knowlton Nash, *Trivia Pursuit: How Showbiz Values Are Corrupting the News* (Toronto: McClelland and Stewart, 1998).
15. Henry Milner, "Civic Literacy in Comparative Context," *Policy Matters*, Vol. 2, no. 2, (Montreal: Institute for Research on Public Policy, 2001).
16. Allan Fotheringham, *Birds of a Feather: The Press and the Politicians* (Toronto: Key Porter Books, 1989), 139.
17. Black, *Politics and the News*, 12; Taras, *The Newsmakers*, 234.
18. Desbarats, *Guide to Canadian News Media*, 41.
19. Black, *Politics and the News*, 168.
20. Frizzell, *1988*, 91.

21. John Turner's success in Vancouver Quadra in the 1984 election is often cited as an example of the underdog effect, given that all polls in the constituency indicated that he would lose. Joe Clark's personal victory in 2000 might be another such example.
22. Taras, *The Newsmakers*, 187, 192–94; Desbarats, *Guide*, 138.
23. Claire Hoy, *Margin of Error* (Toronto: Key Porter Books, 1989), 1–5.
24. Howard R. Penniman, ed., *Canada at the Polls, 1984* (Durham, N.C.: Duke University Press, 1988), 131.

Chapter 8

Elections and the Electoral System

Elections are one of the most important features of a democratic political system, and usually one of the most exciting. This chapter examines the formal, legal aspects of the electoral system, as well as the party campaign organization at both the national and local levels. It also contains an evaluation of the electoral system and suggestions for reform; a discussion of party and election finance; and an assessment of electoral behaviour and party support.

Chapter Objectives

After you have completed this chapter, you should be able to:

Outline the redistribution process

Understand how the formal election machinery is organized at both national and local levels

Comment on how parties organize their election campaigns at both national and local levels

Understand the concern of political scientists about the relationship between a party's popular vote and the percentage of seats it wins

Enumerate and evaluate the main provisions of the law on party and election finance, including the problem of "third-party" advertising

Assess Canadian voting behaviour

Discuss any enduring relationships between socioeconomic variables and party support in Canada

....

The Election Organization
Drawing the Electoral Map

Canadian elections are based on single-member electoral districts. Hence, before Canadians go to vote, an electoral map must be established to divide the country into electoral districts or **constituencies.** The term **redistribution** is used to describe this process. It involves two stages: first, deciding how many seats in the House of Commons to allot to each province and territory, and second, drawing constituency boundaries within them.

The Constitution Act, 1867 requires that the readjustment process be repeated after each decennial census, such as after 2001 and 2011. Given the federal character of Canada with its strong provincial loyalties, the search for a reasonably fair means of distributing seats in the House of Commons among the provinces has been a long and unsatisfactory one. The formula used following the 1991 census and the one that resulted in the current 301 seats in the House of Commons for the 2000 election involved the four following steps:

1. Starting with 282 seats, 1 seat is allocated to each of the Northwest Territories, Nunavut, and the Yukon, leaving 279 seats.
2. The total population of the 10 provinces is divided by 279 to obtain the electoral quota or quotient.
3. This electoral quota is divided into the population of each province to obtain the number of seats each is entitled to.
4. Additional seats are then awarded so that each province has as many House of Commons seats as it has senators, and as many seats as it had in 1985.

Thus, for the 2000 election, the House of Commons seats were distributed as follows: Ontario, 103; Quebec, 75; British Columbia, 34; Alberta, 26; Manitoba and Saskatchewan, 14 each; Nova Scotia, 11; New Brunswick, 10; Newfoundland, 7; Prince Edward Island, 4; Northwest Territories, 1; Nunavut, 1; and Yukon, 1. Because the territories and smaller provinces are overrepresented as a result of points 1 and 4, the four largest provinces actually deserve more seats than they have been given.[1]

The second phase of the redistribution process, drawing constituency boundaries within each province, was historically the prerogative of the politicians. They regularly engaged in the process of "gerrymandering," that is, manipulating constituency boundaries so as to ensure as far as possible the re-election of the members of the government party. A new system was adopted in the Electoral

Boundaries Readjustment Act of 1964, however, so that this task is now performed by non-partisan commissions. An electoral boundaries commission is appointed for each province, chaired by a judge, with the other two members of each commission appointed by the Speaker of the House of Commons. All commissions draw extensively on the support staff of Elections Canada.

The commissions swing into action as soon as the provincial population figures are available from the census. Theirs is a very delicate task of trying to arrive at a design that will provide constituencies of approximately equal population size throughout the province at the same time as accounting for geographic characteristics, or identity and historical patterns; for example, not dividing a town into two separate electoral districts. The most difficult problem is in dealing with sparsely populated rural or northern regions at the same time as concentrated urban centres. In recognition of this problem, the commissions are allowed to deviate from the average population figure in any province to a maximum tolerance of plus or minus 25 percent, and even to exceed this limit in extraordinary circumstances. Thus, rural and northern constituencies tend to be below the provincial quotient and southern, urban ones somewhat above it. In Ontario in 2000, for example, the number of people on constituency voters lists varied from 50 242 to 99 682. In general, since it takes fewer votes in smaller provinces and in rural parts of all provinces to elect a member of Parliament, such votes are worth more than those in large provinces or in urban areas. Whether out of charity, ignorance, or recognition of the fact that the population is peculiarly distributed, Canadians seem generally unconcerned about this deviation from the principle of representation by population or political equality.

The Official Election Organization

SETTING THE DATE

The prime minister normally has the prerogative to call the election within five years of the previous one. Largely based on the government party's standings in the public opinion polls, the election is typically called about four years after the previous campaign. Going into the fifth year, especially to the five-year limit, is usually a sign that the government expects to be defeated. Public opinion polls can be wrong, of course, or public opinion can change between the calling of the election and the actual voting day, since Canadian party preferences are highly volatile. The apparent advantage for the party in power in choosing the date is

Paul Lachine. Reproduced with permission.

therefore not absolute, as several prime ministers and premiers have discovered to their chagrin. Nevertheless, allowing the governing party the discretion to choose the election date gives it an advantage in terms of readiness, the ability to "bribe" the electorate at the last minute with new spending and other initiatives, and the opportunity to use government money for advertising.

The governor general must approve the prime minister's request to **dissolve Parliament** in order to call an election, but this is normally automatic. Only once in Canadian history (1926), in rather peculiar circumstances, did a governor general refuse such a request. The defeat of a government in a nonconfidence vote in the House of Commons is the alternative method of precipitating an election, in which case the prime minister's leeway is limited to choosing the exact date.

ELECTION OFFICIALS

The **Chief Electoral Officer** is responsible for the overall administration of the election and must act with absolute impartiality. On the other hand, the **returning officers,** who organize the election in each of the 301 electoral districts (also called constituencies or ridings), are chosen by the cabinet on a partisan basis. Once appointed, however, they are expected to function in a nonpartisan fashion. The 2000 U.S. presidential election, whose results remain questionable to this day, reinforced the wisdom of having Canadian federal elections run on a uniform basis by Elections Canada.

THE VOTERS LIST

In Canadian federal elections, the voters list used to be compiled from scratch by means of a door-to-door enumeration after the election writ was issued. Reforms introduced in 1996 provided for a permanent National Register of Electors, the base of which was compiled in one last door-to-door enumeration in April 1997. Ever since, it has been automatically updated from such sources as income tax returns, citizenship and immigration files, and driver's licence and vital statistics files. Although such a permanent voters list is considered less reliable than a door-to-door enumeration, it made it possible to reduce the length of the election period to 36 days. Homeless people were allowed to vote in federal elections for the first time in 2000.

NOMINATION

Most candidates are nominated by a political party, but they must submit formal **nomination** papers endorsed by 100 people on the local voters list accompanied by a $1000 deposit. Candidates are now reimbursed for the full $1000 upon filing their financial statement after the campaign. Official candidates of registered parties must obtain the party leader's endorsement in order to use the party name on the ballot. This requirement was adopted mainly to make it easier for voters to identify candidates with their party, but it effectively gives the leader a veto over nominations.

ELECTION DAY

After nomination day, the returning officer arranges for the ballots to be printed and allows people to vote in advance polls or by special ballot. Recent reforms have made voting much more convenient for those not expecting to be at home on election day, including those living or travelling outside the country. The returning officer also hires and trains deputy returning officers and poll clerks to look after each polling station on election day and finds appropriate polling station locations.

Canadian federal elections are held on Mondays, and the polls used to be open from 9 a.m. to 8 p.m. local time. Because voters in the Western part of the country complained that the winner was often decided even before their votes had been counted, a system of staggered hours for different time zones was introduced in 1997. This means that the polls close at approximately the same time all across the country, and ballots can be counted and the results announced more or less simultaneously. As before, however, broadcasters are not allowed to report results from other regions until the polls close in their own time zone. Voters are entitled to three consecutive hours off work in which to cast their ballot, and the sale of liquor is no longer prohibited during polling hours.

Voters mark their X in private with a pencil on the ballots provided, and when the polls close, the deputy returning officer and poll clerk count them by hand, usually in the company of scrutineers from the various candidates who are allowed to challenge unorthodox markings on ballots and generally keep the whole process honest. Results are announced an hour or two after the polls close, and the candidate with the most votes, the first past the post, is declared elected. The winner usually does not actually have a majority of the votes cast, only a plurality. If the difference between the first and second candidate in any electoral district is less than 1/1000 of all votes cast, an automatic recount is held.

THE BALLOT

The secret ballot was introduced in federal elections in 1874. The candidates are listed in alphabetical order, and since 1970 the ballot has contained their party affiliation, if any. The chief electoral officer keeps a registry of political parties; only parties that run at least 12 candidates are allowed to use the party label on the ballot. Such parties must also register their national and constituency official agents and auditors for the purposes of keeping track of the party's and candidates' finances. Twelve parties were registered for the 1988 election, 14 for 1993, 10 for 1997, and 11 for 2000.

Figure 8.1   **A Sample Ballot**

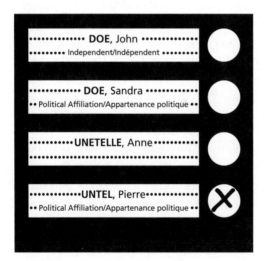

Source: Elections Canada. Used with permission.

THE FRANCHISE

The extension of the franchise, the right to vote, beyond males with substantial property was mentioned in earlier chapters. This process was complicated by the use of different provincial franchises in federal elections between 1867 and 1917.

Moreover, the franchise was manipulated in 1917 so as to maximize support for the incumbent government; the vote was extended to women serving in the war as well as to female relatives of men overseas, but denied to Canadian citizens who had come from "enemy alien" countries. In 1918, all women were granted the federal vote, and since 1920 a uniform federal franchise has existed. Even so, until all such restrictions were removed by 1948, most Canadians of Asian ancestry (especially those from Japan, China, and India) were denied the right to vote in federal elections because the federal law disqualified anyone who for reasons of race was denied the vote under provincial electoral statutes. The vote was extended to Inuit people in 1953 and to Indians living on reserves in 1960. The voting age was reduced from 21 to 18 in 1970, and British subjects who were not Canadian citizens lost their vote in 1975.

By that time, the Canada Elections Act mainly disqualified returning officers (except in the case of a tie), federally appointed judges, prison inmates, those deprived of their liberty by reason of mental disease, and those convicted of corrupt or illegal electoral practices. In the course of the 1988 campaign, however, three of these disqualifications were challenged in the courts in terms of the Canadian Charter of Rights and Freedoms, which guarantees the vote to every Canadian citizen. In the case of judges and those in mental institutions, the provisions of the act were declared unconstitutional and the disqualifications were removed. The courts made a number of contradictory decisions on whether prison inmates should be able to vote, and the 1993 amendments gave the vote (in federal elections, at least) to inmates serving sentences of less than two years. The new Canada Elections Act of 2000 gave returning officers a vote, and in case of a tie, a **by-election** would be held in the constituency. By-elections are otherwise precipitated by the resignation or death of an MP between elections.

The National Party Campaign

At the national level, political parties usually set up a campaign committee about two years before they expect the election to be called. They start to think about strategy, policy, image, and budget, as party headquarters conduct public opinion polls to see how the voters perceive the various leaders, parties, and issues.[2] For the party in power, such polls are central to deciding when to call the election in the first place, and for all major parties, polls serve to guide general strategy, media advertising, and the selection of priority ridings once the campaign begins.

Another national activity that begins before the calling of the election is the search for good candidates. While party headquarters rarely impose a candidate on an unwilling constituency association, they may try to guide the local decision or even parachute a few "star" candidates into safe seats. Parties usually run a full slate of candidates, so where local organizations are weak, the national level of the party sometimes has to take the initiative to find a candidate for them. In order to ensure a minimum number of candidates of cabinet calibre, especially women, and to avoid nominations falling into the wrong hands, Jean Chrétien had the party give him the power to appoint candidates in certain cases.

The NDP once hoped to achieve gender parity in its candidates, but was later content with nearly 50 percent being either women or visible minorities. Meanwhile, because of the Reform Party's tendency to attract a certain number of extremists, that party made prospective candidates complete a form detailing their background, a practice continued by the successor Canadian Alliance. If an "undesirable" person still manages to get nominated, the party leadership may have to expel a candidate, as it did in one case of an alleged racist in 1993.

Party headquarters organize training sessions for campaign managers and candidates (right down to personal deportment), and produce mounds of election material for local candidates. One of the Liberals' great assets in the 1993 campaign was their election platform, commonly called the "Red Book." It provided a tremendous prop for a leader who was otherwise not overly policy oriented in his public appearances.[3] "Red Book II," used in 1997, was less effective, and "Red Book III," in 2000, even less so.

THE LEADER'S TOUR AND ITS MEDIA COVERAGE

Once the campaign begins, party headquarters organize each leader's tour and the party's national media campaign, and gear up for the televised leaders' debate. Each party leader crisscrosses the country over the campaign period in an effort both to give a boost to promising local candidates and to generate daily stories for the national media. Such "free" coverage is eagerly sought, and parties spare no trouble or expense to obtain it.

The leader is accompanied by a horde of strategists and support staff, as well as by reporters who pay to travel aboard the party-chartered plane or bus. In general, national television newscasts contain one item per leader per day, and have usually provided almost equal time to the main parties.

NATIONAL MEDIA ADVERTISING

Each party also buys media advertising during (and sometimes immediately before) the campaign, and most parties spend huge amounts of money on the production of television commercials alone. The purchase of broadcast time is regulated by the Elections Act, requiring each broadcaster to make available, for purchase by registered political parties, six and one-half hours of prime time during the campaign. The broadcasting arbitrator allocates time among the parties based primarily on the number of seats held in the House of Commons and on the popular vote received in the previous election, but no party can receive more than one-half of the total time. As a result of a Reform Party court challenge, parties can now purchase more than these allotments, subject to their overall expense ceiling, so that the significance of the allocation of time has diminished. In addition to purchasable time, parties are awarded free radio and television time in the same proportions.

THE LEADERS' DEBATE

The other main aspect of the national campaign is the televised leaders' debate. The debates have become crucial aspects of the campaign because of the combined importance of leaders and television. Separate debates are held in English and French, putting a premium on a party leader's bilingual capacity.

The debates are not mentioned in the law, so the consortium of television stations that carry them essentially sets the rules. The debates have to fit into the television networks' schedule and are held when least advertising revenue would be lost. In 1993, with a large number of parties in the race, the consortium agreed that only five parties would take part—that is, those represented in Parliament and having had a consistent impact in public debates and public opinion. Mel Hurtig, leader of the new National Party of Canada, went to court to try to force his way into the debate, but did not succeed. The leaders of the same five parties participated in 1997 and 2000.

The frontrunner in the campaign basically tries to avoid a knockout punch, while the other party leaders attempt to score one. After the debate, each party sends forth its **spin doctors** to persuade reporters that its leader won, but whether the public makes up its own mind on the winner or awaits the verdict of media commentators is not certain. About two-thirds of the electorate watched at least one debate in both 1984 and 1988, and nearly 60 percent in 1993.[4] Although 45 percent of respondents told a *Maclean's* poll that the 1988 debate had helped them decide how to vote,[5] mostly to the advantage of the Liberals, much of this advantage had worn off by election day. The Conservatives had strategically insisted on having the debate early in the campaign in case they needed time to recover from just such an inferior performance. The 1997 and 2000 debates were of little significance in the overall result.

The Local Candidate Campaign

NOMINATION

At the local level, each party's first priority is to nominate its candidate. Holding the nomination meeting even before the election is called allows many preparations to be made ahead of time, so the campaign can get off to a strong and early start.

THE LOCAL CAMPAIGN

Once the nomination has taken place, each party sets up a campaign committee under a campaign manager (see Figure 8.2). The official agent is responsible for ensuring that the candidate complies with the Canada Elections Act. In most campaigns the other key official is the canvass organizer, who organizes the door-to-door "foot canvass" to distribute literature and/or a telephone canvass. Whether canvassers contact voters on the doorstep or on the phone, the object is both to spread the party's message and to seek out its own supporters. Armed with a voters list, canvassers put a positive, negative, or "undecided" mark beside the name of all voters contacted. To cover an entire constituency in this fashion requires a veritable army of volunteers and an elaborate organization. If money is more plentiful than volunteers, the local campaign may rely instead on media advertising. In recent elections, some parties in targeted constituencies engaged in local polling and computer-assisted mail and telephone campaigning directed

Figure 8.2   Structure of a Typical Local Campaign Committee

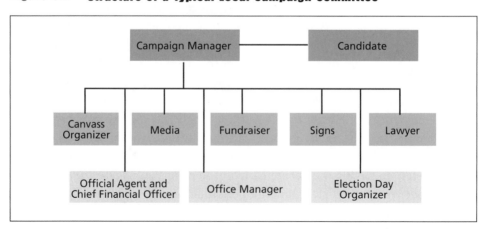

to members of key groups. In the past, much of this work was voluntary, but parties increasingly engage paid staff, sometimes consisting of "volunteers" paid by a business or union. The local campaign is a complex operation requiring ever more sophistication, staffing, and funding.

All this activity culminates on election day, when the organization tries to have a party scrutineer placed in each of the polls. Ideally, an inside scrutineer keeps track of which people on the list have cast their ballot, while an outside scrutineer periodically collects this information and heads out to round up all those previously identified as party supporters.

Evaluating the Electoral System

In each constituency, the candidate with the most votes wins—the **first past the post,** even if this is less than 50 percent. Among the advantages of this electoral system are its simplicity, its quick calculation of results, and its provision for each constituency of a clear-cut representative. When all the local results are cumulated nationally, however, the proportion of seats a party wins does not necessarily bear much relationship to its overall share of the total **popular vote.** Take as an extreme, hypothetical example a two-person race in each constituency in which the Liberal candidate beat the Conservative candidate by one vote in every case: the Liberal Party would then win 100 percent of the seats from just over 50 percent of the vote, and the Conservative Party would have 0 percent of the seats from just under 50 percent of the vote. In fact, this example is not so hypothetical: in the New Brunswick election of 1987, the Liberals won 100 percent of the seats with about 60 percent of the popular vote. Many political scientists and other observers are therefore concerned that such overall disparities can occur between percentage of seats won and percentage of popular vote.

Alan Cairns analyzed the disparities for both the national and provincial levels.[6] Overall, in 24 elections starting in 1921, the party with the largest popular vote won more seats than it deserved on 23 occasions. The system also typically favoured third parties with concentrated regional support (Social Credit, Reform/Alliance, and the BQ), but those with broad national support usually lost out, and the CCF/NDP, for example, regularly received only about half as many seats as its popular vote merited.

Some observers tolerate these disparities because this first-past-the-post electoral system usually produces a **majority government**—the leading party obtaining more than 50 percent of the seats—even though a party rarely wins over 50 percent of the popular vote. Table 8.1 indicates that on 3 occasions (1940,

TABLE 8.1 COMPARISON OF PERCENTAGE OF POPULAR VOTE AND PERCENTAGE OF SEATS BY PARTY FOR FEDERAL ELECTIONS 1921–2000

	Liberals		Conservatives		CCF/NDP	
	% Vote	% Seats	% Vote	% Seats	% Vote	% Seats
1921	41	49	30	21	—	—
1925	40	40	46	47	—	—
1926	46	52	45	37	—	—
1930	45	37	49	56	—	—
1935	45	71	30	16	9	3
1940	52	74	31	16	9	3
1945	41	51	27	27	16	11
1949	49	74	30	16	13	5
1953	49	64	31	19	11	9
1957	41	40	39	42	11	9
1958	34	18	54	79	10	3
1962	37	38	37	44	14	7
1963	42	49	33	36	13	6
1965	40	49	33	36	18	8
1968	45	58	31	27	17	8
1972	38	41	35	40	18	12
1974	43	53	36	36	16	6
1979	40	40	36	48	18	9
1980	44	52	33	37	20	11
1984	28	14	50	75	19	11
1988	32	28	43	57	20	15
		Liberal	PC	NDP	Ref/All	BQ
1993	% Vote	41.3	16.0	6.9	18.7	13.5
	% Seats	60.0	0.7	3.1	17.6	18.3
1997	% Vote	38.4	18.9	11.1	19.4	10.7
	% Seats	51.4	6.6	7.0	19.9	14.6
2000	% Vote	40.8	12.2	8.5	25.5	10.7
	% Seats	57.1	4.0	4.3	21.9	12.6

Source: Data compiled from Chief Electoral Officer of Canada, Reports of the Chief Electoral Officer. Material reproduced with permission of the Chief Electoral Officer of Canada, 2001. Extrapolation and analysis rests with the author.

1958, and 1984) the winning party obtained at least 50 percent of the vote, and this automatically produced a majority government. On 13 other occasions out of 24, this electoral system manufactured a majority government in terms of seats, even though the leading party did not win a majority of the vote. This left only 8 occasions when a **minority government** resulted. While applauding the system for its tendency to produce majority governments, however, we should note that it weakens the opposition. Moreover, on three occasions (1957, 1962, and 1979) the party with the second-largest popular vote ended up with more seats than the party that came first, and therefore went on to form the government.

It is worth noting that if parties had received as many seats as their popular vote justified in 1993, the PCs and NDP would have been recognized as official parties in the House of Commons, and the Reform Party, instead of the Bloc Québécois, would have been the Official Opposition. The 1997 and 2000 elections rectified these points, but continued to underrepresent the PCs and NDP. In 1997, for example, the PCs and Reform were virtually tied in votes, but they were awarded 20 and 60 seats respectively. In 2000, if seats were awarded in proportion to votes, the Liberals would have won about 50 fewer seats, the Bloc, about 5 less; the Alliance, at least 10 more; the NDP, twice as many; and the PCs, three times as many.

Another set of disparities between popular vote and seat figures exists on a province-by-province basis. Alan Cairns was particularly struck by the disparity between the Conservative vote and seats in Quebec (1896–1984) and the disparity between the Liberal vote and seats in Western Canada (since 1957). Table 8.2 provides the figures for the 2000 election, and Figure 8.3 shows the 2000 election results in graphic form.

Cairns observed that such disparities affect parties in three principal ways: image, strategy, and policy. When the Conservatives had virtually no members from Quebec prior to 1984, they gained an anti-French image, even though they usually obtained at least 13 percent of the popular vote in that province. Similarly, after 1957, the Liberals acquired the image of an anti-Western party because they rarely elected members west of Ontario, even though they normally received over 20 percent of the Western vote.

As far as strategy is concerned, when Conservatives despaired of electing members from Quebec and felt they could form a government without much representation from that province, they ignored it. The Liberals have often similarly felt that campaigning in the West was a waste of time and money, and concentrated their effort elsewhere. Jean Chrétien did not bother to make a single

TABLE 8.2 COMPARISON OF PERCENTAGE OF SEATS WON AND VOTES IN 2000 ELECTION BY PROVINCE

	Liberals			Alliance			PC			NDP			BQ		
	Seats	%S	%V	Seats	%S	%V	Seats	%S	%V	Seats	%S	%V	Seats	%S	%V
Nfld	5.0	71.0	44.9	–	–	3.9	2.0	29.0	34.5	–	–	13.1	–	–	–
P.E.I.	4.0	100.0	47.0	–	–	5.0	–	–	38.4	–	–	9.0	–	–	–
N.S.	4.0	36.0	36.5	–	–	9.6	4.0	36	29.1	3.0	27.0	24.0	–	–	–
N.B.	6.0	60.0	41.7	–	–	15.7	3.0	30.0	30.5	1.0	10.0	11.7	–	–	–
Quebec	36.0	48.0	44.2	–	–	6.2	1.0	1.0	5.6	–	–	1.8	38	51	39.9
Ontario	100.0	97.0	51.5	2.0	2.0	23.6	–	–	14.4	1.0	1.0	8.3	–	–	–
Man.	5.0	36.0	32.5	4.0	29.0	30.4	1.0	7.0	14.5	4.0	29.0	20.9	–	–	–
Sask.	2.0	14.0	20.7	10.0	71.0	47.7	–	–	4.8	2.0	14.0	26.2	–	–	–
Alta.	2.0	8.0	20.9	23.0	88.0	58.9	1.0	4.0	13.5	–	–	5.4	–	–	–
B.C.	5.0	15.0	27.7	27.0	79.0	49.4	–	–	7.3	2.0	6.0	11.3	–	–	–
NWT	1.0	100.0	45.6	–	–	17.7	–	–	10.0	–	–	26.7	–	–	–
Nunavut	1.0	100.0	69.0	–	–	–	–	–	8.2	–	–	18.3	–	–	–
Yukon	1.0	100.0	32.5	–	–	27.7	–	–	7.5	–	–	31.9	–	–	–
Total	172.0	57.1	40.8	66.0	21.9	25.5	12.0	4.0	12.2	13.0	4.3	8.5	38.0	12.6	10.7

Source: Data compiled from Report of the Chief Electoral Officer of Canada, 2000. Material reproduced with permission of the Chief Electoral Officer of Canada, 2001. Extrapolation and analysis rests with author.

campaign stop in Calgary, for example, in the 2000 election campaign. These strategies are not good for keeping the country together, one of the functions that political parties and elections are supposed to perform.

Finally, since the elected members of the party have a major role to play in the development of party policy, Conservative policy did not reflect the concerns of French Canada when the party lacked francophone and Quebec MPs, just as Liberal policy tended to ignore Western concerns. This is especially serious for the party that forms the government, for it has few or no MPs from a province or region to put into the cabinet. Because of such regionalized party standings between 1962 and 1984, either Quebec or the West was effectively left out of national decisionmaking at the cabinet level. Residents of those neglected regions understandably felt that national policy did not reflect their interests and turned to provincial governments to defend these interests or started to think in separatist terms.

In 2000, the Liberals succeeded in electing at least two MPs from each province—enough to ensure minimal cabinet representation. Even so, they

Figure 8.3   Seats Won by Party by Province, 2000

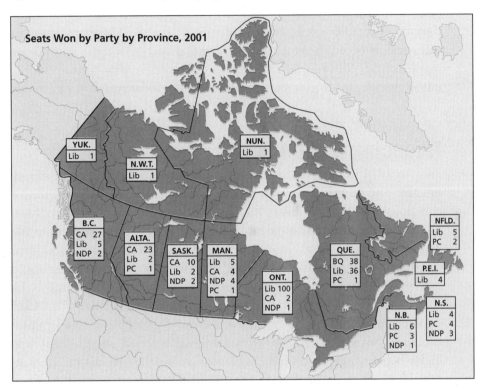

Seats Won by Party by Province, 2001

YUK.	
Lib	1

NUN.	
Lib	1

N.W.T.	
Lib	1

B.C.	
CA	27
Lib	5
NDP	2

ALTA.	
CA	23
Lib	2
PC	1

SASK.	
CA	10
Lib	2
NDP	2

MAN.	
Lib	5
CA	4
NDP	4
PC	1

ONT.	
Lib	100
CA	2
NDP	1

QUE.	
BQ	38
Lib	36
PC	1

N.B.	
Lib	6
PC	3
NDP	1

NFLD.	
Lib	5
PC	2

P.E.I.	
Lib	4

N.S.	
Lib	4
PC	4
NDP	3

received more votes but fewer seats than the Bloc in Quebec; the Alliance had only two seats to show for its 24 percent of the vote in Ontario; and the Liberals gained 25 percent of the vote in the West, but were rewarded with only 14 of 88 seats.

Since Cairns first brought these problems to scholarly attention, reform of the electoral system has been frequently discussed. Many observers would like to overcome the lack of representation of important segments of opinion in party caucuses and the cabinet, as well as to avoid the sense of regional–ethnic alienation that stems from this situation. A full-scale system of proportional representation is probably too extreme a reform in the circumstances, but a hybrid scheme combining constituency MPs with "supplementary MPs" based on popular vote has much merit.

Several authorities have suggested the addition of 50 or 60 supplementary MPs, who would overcome the worst problems of the existing system but still make majority government possible. This system would start with the regularly elected constituency MPs who are necessary to ensure the representation of all parts of Canada. But the supplementary MPs would be added, to be distributed on the basis of popular vote by party by province. They would correct the greatest discrepancies between the proportion of seats and votes. For the party in power, such supplementary MPs could provide provincial representation in the cabinet.[7] They might also be used to correct gender or minority imbalances.

....

Financing Elections

Prior to 1974 Canada had virtually no laws with respect to party and election finance. The Liberal and Conservative parties relied almost completely on contributions from big business at the national level, which usually produced a surplus to be distributed to candidates' campaigns as well. Candidates were otherwise dependent on donations from local small firms. Both parties had fundraisers or "bagmen"—often senators who could exploit their corporate connections and make use of their abundant spare time—assisted by corporate volunteers. Business also made contributions in kind, such as skilled personnel. The CCF/NDP depended primarily on individual membership fees supplemented by union contributions, but in this case the flow of funds was reversed, and the local candidates had to help finance the central campaign. Overall, the Liberals and Conservatives raised and spent far more than the CCF/NDP, both at the national and local levels.

The secrecy surrounding party and election finance before 1974 makes it difficult to know exactly how many irregularities and scandals actually took place, but they were probably numerous. Small-scale scandals in the 1960s, together with increasing public expectations of political morality, caused the Pearson government to appoint a commission on the subject of party and election finance in 1964. Opposition pressure in the minority government period of 1972–74 finally forced the reforms that commission recommended. Amendments to the Canada Elections Act were passed in 1974 but did not take effect until the election of 1979. The legislation has six basic provisions, some of which have been adjusted since:

- ceiling on candidate spending
- ceiling on party spending
- disclosure of the identity of those contributing over $200
- tax credit for contributions

- public subsidy for candidates winning at least 15 percent of vote
- public subsidy for major parties

While no limit is placed on the size of contributions, a ceiling is imposed on how much a national party can spend; a ceiling is also placed on each candidate's expenditures. A disclosure provision requires that the names of those contributing over $200 be filed with the chief electoral officer and that such records be open to public inspection. A tax credit provision gives contributors a 75 percent income tax credit for contributions up to $200, a 50 percent tax credit for contributions between $200 and $550, and a 33 percent credit for contributions over $550 to a maximum tax credit of $500. Candidates who receive at least 15 percent of the vote have roughly 50 percent of their expenses subsidized by the public purse. Finally, parties that win at least 2 percent of the popular vote are subsidized for 22.5 percent of their total national expenditures.

The objectives of the legislation are thus to increase the fairness, openness, and participatory nature of the electoral system. Fairness is enhanced in limiting national party and candidate spending, as well as by the public subsidy provision; the disclosure clause makes it difficult for large secret contributions to be made in return for some favourable government decision, policy, or grant; and the tax credit encourages individual contributions, reducing Liberal and Conservative dependence on corporations. For all the difficulties and loopholes remaining in the act, it has produced a more honest, equitable, and participatory system of election finance. Table 8.3 shows the total amount spent by the local and national campaigns of each of the main parties in 2000, but it should be remembered that the BQ ran candidates only in Quebec.

The results are fairer than they would be in the absence of such legislation, but the disparities are of continuing concern to many observers. Preliminary data

TABLE 8.3 TOTAL ELECTION EXPENSES OF FIVE MAIN PARTIES, 2000 ELECTION (DOLLARS)

	Candidates	National	Total
Liberal	14 348 433	12 525 174	26 873 607
Alliance	9 395 054	9 669 648	19 064 702
PC	4 404 500	3 983 301	8 387 801
NDP	3 905 361	6 334 585	10 269 946
Bloc	4 188 211	1 968 692	6 156 903

Source: Chief Electoral Officer, Contributions and Expenses of Registered Political Parties and Candidates, 2000, http://www.elections.ca (Retrieved on 15 Sept. 2001). Extrapolation and analysis rests with the author.

from the 2000 election show that the Liberals received $12 million from corporations of their total intake of $20 million, and the Canadian Alliance had $7 million from corporations of a $19 million total. Those two parties vastly outspent the others, and this heavy reliance on the corporate sector gives rise to many suspicions about what those corporations expect from government in return. Meanwhile, new parties find it particularly difficult to compete with the five main established ones in the raising of funds. Since taxpayers ultimately pay for much of these party expenditures via tax credits and tax rebates, an argument can be made that government financing of the whole campaign would not cost the public purse much more than it does already and would eliminate the suspicions of sleaze. Alternatively, contributions could be limited to individuals, as is the case in provincial elections in Quebec and Manitoba.

Third-Party Advertising

Another major problem in the realm of election finance is **third-party advertising.** Legislation in 1993 prohibited all advocacy-group spending during an election campaign that was not channelled through a party or candidate campaign. It was argued by sponsors of the legislation that the only way party and candidate spending ceilings could be effective was if any spending on their behalf was included in the parties' budgets. But in the 1980s more and more groups began to advertise on their own, for or against various parties or candidates. While such advertising was clearly a violation of the spirit of the law as well as its specific terms, the National Citizens' Coalition (NCC) challenged these sections of the legislation in an Alberta court. The court ruled the clauses unconstitutional as a violation of the freedom of expression provisions of the Charter of Rights and Freedoms.

Third-party advertising increased enormously in the 1988 election campaign, especially in the case of the pro–free trade group, the Canadian Alliance for Trade and Job Opportunities. With only the Conservative Party in favour of free trade, any advertising that promoted the Free Trade Agreement also promoted the Conservative Party. Thus the Conservatives benefited from some $5 million in advertising by advocacy groups on top of its own national budget of nearly $8 million. Such third-party advertising made a mockery of party spending ceilings and is widely thought to have helped the Conservatives achieve re-election by turning the momentum of the campaign back in their favour.

In response to widespread public criticism of this problem and to address other electoral issues, the Mulroney government appointed a Royal Commission on

Electoral Reform and Party Financing shortly after the 1988 election. On this issue, the Royal Commission recommended that spending by individuals or organizations other than candidates and political parties be restricted to $1000 during the election period. The commission argued that given the significance of the issue, to limit paid advertising of such advocacy groups during 36 days every four years was a "reasonable limit" on freedom of expression and would stand up to judicial scrutiny. The law was so amended just prior to the 1993 election, but successfully challenged by the NCC again. The amendments of 2000, however, allowed third parties to spend up to $150 000, of which no more than $3000 could be spent in each electoral district on advertising for or against candidates. The Supreme Court of Canada upheld this new law in the middle of the 2000 campaign, although an Alberta court challenged it afterward.[8]

....

Electoral Behaviour and Party Support
Electoral Behaviour

Given the fact that the Liberals were so regularly victorious in Canadian federal elections between 1935 and 1984 and again since 1993, it is tempting to believe that a large proportion of voters have a strong identification with that party and that any result other than a Liberal triumph is unlikely. Research in psephology— the study of voting behaviour—shows, however, that more and more voters—at least 50 percent—have no enduring **party identification.** A majority of voters constitute a large pool ready to be moved by the particular issues, candidates, and leaders in the campaign.[9] The overall aggregate stability, therefore, masked "the potential for significant variation in electoral outcomes,"[10] as became evident in the 1984 Conservative landslide. Other factors that add flexibility to the system are the group that votes in one election but not the next, as well as the newly eligible voters in each election. Table 8.4 summarizes the lack of durability among the electorate between the 1993 and 1997 elections. Only 42 percent of 1997 voters supported the same party as in 1993.

In most other Western democracies the degree of voter identification with a specific party is much higher, and the flexibility of the Canadian electorate demands explanation. Jon Pammett accounts for this phenomenon as follows:

> *The most basic [factor] is that Canadian political culture is relatively apolitical. While Canadians are moderately interested in politics, this interest does not translate for most into substantial political involvement.*

TABLE 8.4 1997 Voter Preference Compared with 1993 (Percentage)

Voted same party	42
Switched parties	18
Previous voters not voting	7
Previous non-voters voting	14
Not voting either time	9
Newly eligible voters	10

Source: Jon H. Pammett, "The Voters Decide," in Alan Frizzell and Jon H. Pammett, *The Canadian General Election of 1997* (Toronto: Dundurn Press, 1997). Used with permission.

> *The amount of detailed political information possessed by the average Canadian is low. Studies of children's political learning, or socialization, show a relatively weak transference of preference for a political party from parent to child ... because these feelings may not be strongly or persistently held in the adult "socializer."*[11]

The voting decision is an extremely complex and subtle one that is not easily explained. Nevertheless, voters are often asked which factor was most influential in helping them make up their mind—party, leader, issues, or local candidate. For all but those with the strongest party identification, it is usually the leader or issues that are most important. The local candidate is not normally a crucial factor. Voters will often say that they were moved by the issues, but many have trouble identifying the issues that supposedly influenced them. The relative importance of issues and leaders also varies from one election to another. In short, as Lawrence LeDuc writes, "the Canadian electorate continues to be one with relatively weak long-term attachments to political parties, low ideological commitment, and high responsiveness to short-term forces such as leaders, issues, or political events."[12] Such flexibility means that over half of the electorate makes up its mind during the course of the campaign, and that elections remain highly unpredictable.

These revelations also cast doubt on the question of whether elections provide a policy **mandate** for the successful party. First, Canadian parties rarely present a comprehensive election platform in the campaign. Next, victorious parties do not seem to feel bound by the specific policies that they proposed. In the third place, the limited extent to which issues play a part in the campaign seriously detracts from the claim of any government that it has a mandate to pursue a particular policy. Finally, even on the rare occasion that a single issue figures prominently, the winning party almost never obtains a majority of the total votes cast, and certainly not a majority in all regions of the country. The free trade issue in 1988 provided the closest thing to a policy mandate for any Canadian government in recent times, yet the Conservatives received only 43 percent of the overall popular vote and less than 40 percent in six provinces and territories. The Liberals made much of their Red Book during the 1993 campaign, but even though a large part of it was unfulfilled, the electorate returned them to office in 1997.

Party Support

The other aspect of electoral behaviour that has attracted much attention from political scientists is the relationship between voters' regional, cultural, and socioeconomic background and their party preference. This relates to the cleavages encountered in earlier chapters. At least until the 1984 federal election, certain fairly clear-cut patterns of socioeconomic support for the three main parties could be identified.

First, there were wide variations in regional support. The Liberals dominated Quebec and the Conservatives excelled in the West, especially Alberta. While these respective patterns were not quite as dramatic in terms of popular vote as in the proportion of seats won, they were still significant. Liberal support in Quebec had been virtually unchanged since 1900, but the Conservative popularity in the West was primarily a legacy of the leadership of John Diefenbaker in the 1950s and 1960s. Such party strongholds resulted in the situation that election campaigns were most heatedly contested in Ontario, which could swing either way.

A second marked pattern in Canadian voting behaviour was religion. Roman Catholics have been strongly inclined to vote Liberal, whether they were French, English, or of other ethnic background, and regardless of where they lived in the country. This situation is especially striking when one considers that no serious religious issues divided the parties in Canadian federal politics for generations.

Ethnicity was another significant factor in Canadian electoral behaviour. The French-Canadian preference for the Liberal Party is well known and exists outside as well as within Quebec. Among those of non-British and non-French origins, the Liberals also did best, especially among post–Second World War immigrants (largely of Mediterranean and Indian subcontinental origins), who apparently reacted with gratitude to the fact that the Liberal Party was in office when they arrived.

A final demographic factor is social class, the expectation being that upper-class citizens would vote Conservative (or Alliance), the middle class would support the Liberals, and the working and poorer classes would vote NDP. In most Western democracies such a pattern is quite significant, but it is not borne out well in Canada.[13] The Liberal Party has usually attracted nearly the same degree of support from all classes except farmers. Only a small proportion of the working class actually votes for working-class parties. The NDP, for example, normally gets relatively more support from skilled and unskilled labour than from other groups, but not as much as does each of the other parties. The low level of **class consciousness** and class-based voting in Canada is quite striking, and many explanations have been offered.[14]

The 1984 and 1988 elections ran counter to generations of traditional voting patterns, especially with Quebec French-Canadian Roman Catholics preferring the Conservatives over the Liberals. The 1993 election then saw the West abandon the Conservatives for Reform, and Quebec switch to the Bloc Québécois. Thus, such regional and socioeconomic patterns of party support as were once evident seem to have vanished. But this new pattern of regional party support was reinforced in 1997, especially in terms of elected MPs, with Reform dominating the West, the Liberals overwhelming Ontario, the Bloc doing well in Quebec, and the NDP and PCs reviving in Atlantic Canada. The 2000 results were not substantially different, although the Liberals won more votes than the Bloc in Quebec, and the Canadian Alliance won two seats in Ontario.

DISCUSSION QUESTIONS

1. Is the current Canadian "first-past-the-post" electoral system fair to parties and conducive to national unity? If not, what changes could be made to improve it?
2. What changes should be made to the law governing party and election finance?
3. What could be done to give more emphasis to the substance of each party's campaign (i.e., its platform) and less to its presentation (personality, image, and advertising)?

FURTHER READING

Cairns, Alan C. "The Electoral System and the Party System in Canada." *Canadian Journal of Political Science* (March 1968): 55–80.

Clarke, Harold D., et al. *Absent Mandate: Canadian Electoral Politics in an Era of Restructuring*, 3rd ed. Toronto: Gage, 1996.

Courtney, John C., et al., eds. *Drawing Boundaries: Legislatures, Courts, and Electoral Values*. Saskatoon: Fifth House Publishers, 1992.

Elections Canada. Assorted publications.

Frizzell, Alan, and Jon H. Pammett, eds. *The Canadian General Election of 1997*. Toronto: Dundurn Press, 1997.

Frizzell, Alan, and Anthony Westell, eds. *The Canadian General Election of 1984*. Ottawa: Carleton University Press, 1985.

Frizzell, Alan, Jon H. Pammett, and Anthony Westell, eds. *The Canadian General Election of 1988*. Ottawa: Carleton University Press, 1989.

———. *The Canadian General Election of 1993*. Ottawa: Carleton University Press, 1994.

Milner, Henry, ed. *Making Every Vote Count: Reassessing Canada's Electoral System*. Peterborough: Broadview Press, 1999.

Nevitte, Neil, et al. *Unsteady State: The 1997 Canadian Federal Election*. Toronto: Oxford University Press, 2000.

Pammett, Jon. "Class Voting and Class Consciousness in Canada." *Canadian Review of Sociology and Anthropology* 24, no. 2 (1987): 269–90.

Notes

1. Three hundred and one constituencies distributed purely on the basis of population would have resulted in the following representation based on the 1991 population: Ontario 111; Quebec 76; B.C. 36; Alberta 28; Manitoba 12; Saskatchewan 11; Nova Scotia 10; New Brunswick 8; Newfoundland 6; P.E.I. 2; and the North 1.

2. Alan Frizzell and Jon Pammett, eds., *The Canadian General Election of 1997* (Toronto: Dundurn Press, 1997).

3. Stephen Clarkson, "Yesterday's Man and His Blue Grits: Backward into the Future," in Alan Frizzell, *The Canadian General Election of 1993* (Ottawa: Carleton University Press, 1994), 33.

4. Lawrence LeDuc and Richard Price, "Great Debates: The Televised Leadership Debates of 1979," *Canadian Journal of Political Science* (March 1985).

5. Ibid.; Frederick Fletcher, "The Media and the 1984 Landslide," in Howard Penniman, ed., *Canada at the Polls, 1984* (Durham, N.C.: Duke University Press, 1988), 181; *Maclean's* (5 December 1988).

6. Alan C. Cairns, "The Electoral System and the Party System in Canada," *Canadian Journal of Political Science* (March 1968): 55–80.

7. William Irvine, *Does Canada Need a New Electoral System?* (Kingston: Institute of Intergovernmental Relations, Queen's University, 1979) proposes a more extreme reform. See also Henry Milner, ed., *Making Every Vote Count: Reassessing Canada's Electoral System* (Peterborough: Broadview Press, 1999).

8. On this issue, and well as for figures on election finance in general, see the Web site of Elections Canada: http://www.elections.ca.

9. Lawrence LeDuc, "The Flexible Canadian Electorate," in Penniman, *Canada at the Polls, 1984,* 40.

10. Frizzell, *The Canadian General Election of 1988,* 109.

11. Jon H. Pammett, "Elections," in M. Whittington and G. Williams, eds., *Canadian Politics in the 1990s,* 4th ed. (Scarborough: Nelson Canada, 1995), 242.

12. LeDuc, "The Flexible Canadian Electorate," 51.

13. Jon Pammett, "Class Voting and Class Consciousness in Canada," *Canadian Review of Sociology and Anthropology* 24, no. 2 (1987): 269–90; Keith Archer, "The Failure of the New Democratic Party: Unions, Unionists, and Politics in Canada," *Canadian Journal of Political Science* (June 1985): 353–66.

14. See the section on class-based parties in Chapter 9 of this book; Janine Brodie and Jane Jenson, *Crisis, Challenge and Change: Party and Class in Canada Revisited* (Ottawa: Carleton University Press, 1988); Pammett, "Class Voting;" and Archer, "The Failure."

Political Parties

Political parties are integral to the operation of almost every aspect of a modern political system, and are mentioned in almost every chapter of this book. This chapter discusses them in five main sections: the functions of political parties, the historical evolution of Canadian political parties; the number and kinds of parties in Canada; party organization; and party ideology. Party and electoral finance and the role of parties in the electoral campaign, including electoral behaviour and party support, were discussed in Chapter 8.

Chapter Objectives

After you have completed this chapter, you should be able to:

Understand the functions and roles of political parties

Trace the evolution of the Canadian party system

Differentiate between one-party dominant, two-party, two-plus, and multiparty eras

Discuss the pros and cons of broker and class-based parties

Discuss the various theories accounting for the numerous minor parties in Canada

Enumerate the factors that are contributing to the decline in the importance of parties

Contrast parties in terms of membership, leadership selection and review, policymaking, and general structures and operations

Define the concepts of left, right, liberalism, conservatism, democratic socialism, collectivism, individualism, equality, and inequality, and apply them to Canadian parties

....

The Functions of Political Parties

A **political party** can be defined as an organized group that nominates candidates and contests elections in order to influence the policy and personnel of government. Its truly distinctive feature is that it runs candidates in an election campaign. When one sees political parties at their worst, for example, in the televised daily Question Period in the House of Commons, it is sometimes tempting to ask why we have them at all, or to ask why we cannot make up a government consisting of the best people from each party. Why do we have political parties, and what do they do?

First, parties recruit and train politicians. While many ambitious or public-spirited persons would likely seek public office without them, parties ensure that we have candidates for federal (and provincial) elections. In the best-case scenario, parties provide qualified, representative candidates, nominating the best person they can find, and, time permitting, educating that candidate in the issues of the day. In so doing, parties avoid some of the problems of municipal elections: they eliminate acclamations, filter out kooky candidates, and give voters a notion about what the candidate stands for.

Second, political parties provide experienced political leadership. The most able and successful MPs eventually become potential party leaders. Again, in an ideal case, those who seek the leadership of the party and the country will have served in the House of Commons for an extended period of time, so that they are experienced in the operation of the complex government machine. Parties usually serve to preclude the situation where a person will become prime minister out of the blue.

The third function of political parties flows from the earlier points and from the definition above: each provides a united team of people attached to a coherent policy platform. Parties simplify the electoral process as each one aggregates a number of interests together in its platform, thus providing a limited number of alternative packages from which voters can choose. In the process of combining, consolidating, or appealing to many different interests, parties also help to integrate the country, and reduce the number of demands to a manageable quantity sometimes called "issues." In the exchange of election rhetoric, as well as in the partisan crossfire in Parliament, parties educate the public about the issues and help to ensure that the electorate is exposed to a variety of viewpoints.

Besides these electoral functions of parties, they are crucial to the operation of government once the election is over. It is hard to imagine that a cabinet could make efficient, coherent decisions without the shared bond of party loyalty, or that the House of Commons could organize its business without a strong element of party discipline. A Parliament of 301 Independents would be a recipe for chaos, and although coalition governments work well in some countries, a cabinet made up of the best MPs from each party is likely to be unstable.

Finally, political parties keep government accountable. One or more opposition parties in Parliament criticize government decisions on a daily basis, providing fodder for media coverage so that the public can remain well informed. Such opposition parties ultimately provide an organized alternative for the voters to support in the next election if they are dissatisfied with the incumbent government's performance.

Of course, political parties rarely live up to the theoretical ideals listed above. But given the fact that they are engaged in a serious struggle for power, some inadequacies or excesses are to be expected. That political parties develop in virtually all national political systems in the world, even where not provided for in the Constitution or the law, surely attests to the utility or necessity of such organizations.

··

Historical Evolution of Canadian Political Parties

A brief outline of the historical evolution of Canadian political parties would probably be useful here. This evolution can be divided into three periods.

1867–1921

The first 30 years of Confederation were dominated by Sir John A. Macdonald's Conservative party. Hence, the period from 1867 to 1896 is often labeled as a **one-party dominant** system. After Macdonald was disgraced in the Pacific scandal over fundraising practices, the Liberals took office between 1873 and 1878 under Alexander Mackenzie, but his government reflected a lack of party cohesion. Although Macdonald returned to power in 1878, his decision to execute Louis Riel caused French-Canadian support to fall away from the Conservative Party, helped by the fact that an appealing French Canadian, Wilfrid Laurier, became leader of the Liberal Party shortly afterward. Macdonald died in 1891, and his party experienced a period of great instability in the subsequent five years. Thus, with the Liberals finally showing the marks of a well-organized national party, it is not surprising that Laurier won the watershed election of 1896. At that time Canada moved to a classic **two-party system** in which Liberals and Conservatives competed on equal terms.

Time Line

Prime Ministers, 1867–1921

John A. Macdonald	Conservative	1867–73
Alexander Mackenzie	Liberal	1873–78
John A. Macdonald	Conservative	1878–91
John Abbott	Conservative	1891–92
John Thompson	Conservative	1892–94
Mackenzie Bowell	Conservative	1894–96
Charles Tupper	Conservative	1896
Wilfrid Laurier	Liberal	1896–1911
Robert Borden	Conservative	1911–20
Arthur Meighen	Conservative	1920–21

Laurier governed quite successfully until he was beaten in 1911 by Robert Borden's Conservatives. The new government was soon confronted with the monumental task of managing Canada's war effort. After three years of war, Borden concluded that conscription would have to be adopted. Most English-speaking Liberal MPs agreed to join the Conservatives in a Union Government in 1917, but Laurier and the French-Canadian Liberals remained aloof. With conscription, the Conservative party almost totally alienated French Canada, at the same time as the policies of both parties upset the farming community in English Canada, notably the West. On the other hand, when Mackenzie King succeeded Laurier as Liberal leader, he skillfully pursued party reconciliation.

1921–93

Mackenzie King led the Liberals back to victory in 1921. That election marked the end of the two-party system in Canada, however, as farmers entered the contest with their own Progressive Party candidates. Because various minor parties made their presence felt but did not seriously challenge the dominance of the Liberals and Conservatives between 1921 and 1993, the Canadian party system during that period can be called a **two-plus** or **two-and-one-half party system.**

By the late 1920s, most of the Progressive MPs had either become Liberals or been defeated. The Liberals themselves were defeated in 1930, primarily because of the onset of the Depression. The unlucky victors, the Conservatives led by R.B. Bennett, could not cope with the unemployment, poverty, and general devastation wrought by the Depression. Along with almost every other government in office during this period, they were defeated in the next election.

The Depression was also the catalyst for the creation of a number of new political parties. The Co-operative Commonwealth Federation (CCF) was formed in 1932, an amalgam of farmer and Labour MPs, Eastern intellectuals, and various farmer, labour, and socialist groups and parties, primarily from the West. The party elected several MPs in 1935 and took office in Saskatchewan in 1944 under T.C. Douglas.

The Social Credit Party was born in Alberta in 1935 around charismatic evangelist William Aberhart. The party was originally concerned with the reform of the banking system as a means of dealing with the Depression, but all attempts to do so were disallowed by the courts or the federal government. Alberta soon became prosperous with the discovery of oil, and Social Credit transformed itself into an orthodox conservative party under E.C. Manning. The party remained in power in Alberta for 36 years, came to power in British Columbia in 1952, and repeatedly elected several Western MPs.

None of these developments impeded the Liberal Party at the federal level, as Mackenzie King led his party back to power in 1935. King's conciliatory skills were severely tested during the Second World War (1939–45), but his government avoided a serious second conscription crisis. After also presiding over the initiation of the Canadian welfare state, he retired in favour of Louis St. Laurent in 1948.

The Conservative Party floundered for 20 years after 1935, having previously alienated French Canada, and having been blamed, however unfairly, for the Depression. It changed leaders repeatedly, changed party policy to some extent, and changed the party name to Progressive Conservative in 1942, all to no avail. The political climate was suddenly transformed in 1956, however, with the choice of John Diefenbaker as party leader. Benefiting from the public's increasing resentment of Liberal arrogance and complacency, especially over the "Pipeline scandal," Diefenbaker led the Conservatives to victory in 1957. But his government fell apart over defence policy in the early 1960s and was defeated in 1963.

Meanwhile, the CCF had seen its fortunes decline throughout the 1950s and decided to combine its efforts with those of the new Canadian Labour Congress. The result was the creation of the New Democratic Party (NDP) in 1961. T.C. Douglas was persuaded to leave the premiership of Saskatchewan to become the first national NDP leader.

Lester Pearson's Liberals were elected in 1963 and re-elected in 1965, but always denied a majority of seats. Nonetheless, Pearson tackled many controver-

Time Line

Prime Ministers 1921–93

Mackenzie King	Liberal	1921–26
Arthur Meighen	Conservative	1926
Mackenzie King	Liberal	1926–30
R.B. Bennett	Conservative	1930–35
Mackenzie King	Liberal	1935–48
Louis St. Laurent	Liberal	1948–57
John Diefenbaker	Progressive Conservative	1957–63
Lester Pearson	Liberal	1963–68
Pierre Elliott Trudeau	Liberal	1968–79
Joe Clark	Progressive Conservative	1979–80
Pierre Elliott Trudeau	Liberal	1980–84
John Turner	Liberal	1984
Brian Mulroney	Progressive Conservative	1984–93
Kim Campbell	Progressive Conservative	1993

sial issues, particularly the new nationalism in Quebec, the Canada Pension Plan, medicare, and a new Canadian flag. One opposition party or another supported each of Pearson's measures, so that he was able to continue in office until he retired in 1968.

The Liberals then gained a majority government under their new leader Pierre Elliott Trudeau. After 11 years in office, however, the Liberals were defeated in 1979 by the Conservatives, now led by Joe Clark. Nine months later, the Clark government fell with parliamentary rejection of its Budget, and Trudeau led his party back to power in early 1980.

After helping to defeat the 1980 referendum proposal of the Parti Québécois, Trudeau patriated the Constitution, together with a Charter of Rights and Freedoms, but without the consent of the Quebec government. He also alienated the West with his controversial National Energy Program. Upon his retirement in 1984, the Conservatives won a landslide victory under their new leader, Brian Mulroney, which included a startling majority of the seats in Quebec. After the negotiation of the Canada–U.S. Free Trade Agreement and the Meech Lake Accord, Mulroney led his party to a second successive majority in 1988, in which the free trade issue played a pivotal role. But by 1990, Meech Lake failed to acquire the unanimous approval of new provincial governments, and in 1992 the successor Charlottetown Accord failed to gain the support of a majority of Canadians.

1993–Present

The Liberal Party's obsession with Quebec was the main reason that the West preferred the Conservatives after 1957. But when the Mulroney Conservatives proved to be primarily concerned with holding on to their unprecedented Quebec support after 1984, many Westerners turned to the new Reform Party, headed by Preston Manning, son of the former Social Credit premier of Alberta. Besides being an expression of Western alienation, Reform was a manifestation of right-wing populism in its opposition to big government, its desire for lower taxes, and its concern with law and order.

Profile of a New Party

A group of Western Canadians, upset with various decisions of both Liberal and PC parties, met in Vancouver and Winnipeg in 1987, and founded the Reform Party of Canada with Preston Manning as its leader. After disappointing results east of Manitoba in the 1993 and 1997 elections, Manning unveiled a plan to broaden the party, especially seeking to attract the support of Conservative party sympathizers in a "United Alternative." This idea was supported by a majority of delegates at a convention in February 1999 and in a subsequent referendum in May. In January 2000, another convention chose the name "Canadian Reform Conservative Alliance," which was supported in another referendum of Reform Party members. In a two-stage leadership vote among party members in mid-2000, Stockwell Day defeated Manning for the leadership of the new party, since referred to as the "Canadian Alliance."

With the collapse of the Meech Lake Accord in 1990, sovereignist sentiment increased in Quebec, giving rise to a second new federal party, the separatist Bloc Québécois. Thus, five parties of considerable strength contested the 1993, 1997 and 2000 federal elections, and produced unusual results: the Liberals did especially well in Ontario; the Bloc Québécois displaced the Conservatives in Quebec; and the Reform Party/Canadian Alliance usurped the Conservatives in the West. It seemed that a new highly regionalized Canadian-style **multiparty**

system had developed.[1] In the 2000 election, the Liberals won seats in every province and territory, but lacked depth west of Ontario; the Bloc weakened its grip on Quebec; and the Alliance made modest gains east of Manitoba, winning two seats and 24 percent of the vote in Ontario. The post-2000 election period was characterized by four weak opposition parties—the NDP on the left, the BQ in Quebec, and the competition between the PCs and Alliance on the right. Moreover, the Alliance lost much of its popular support because of decreasing confidence in its leader, Stockwell Day.

··

The Number and Kinds of Parties

Political scientists have proposed several perspectives on the number and kinds of political parties in Canada. They have also theorized about the future of such parties.

Broker Parties

One kind of political party that has been identified is the **broker party.**[2] Those who advocate such a type of party start with the multiple cleavages in Canadian society and the function of parties to aggregate interests. These advocates argue that political parties in Canada should be conciliators, mediators, or brokers among such cleavages as regions, ethnic and linguistic groups, classes, and genders. They suggest that maximizing their appeal to all such groups is not only the best way for parties to gain power but also necessary in order to keep the country together. Thus, in their search for power, parties should act as agents of national integration and attempt to reconcile as many divergent interests as possible.

Throughout most of Canadian history, the two overriding cleavages that have concerned people as well as parties have been region and culture. Thus, broker parties make appeals to the different regions and try to bridge the English–French divide in their election platforms, government policies, and party leadership. Now that other interests have also claimed a place on the political agenda—Aboriginal people, other ethnic groups, and women, for example—they must also be accommodated. The one cleavage that tends to get overlooked by broker parties is that of class, but defenders of the broker system argue that parties should not foment artificial class conflicts and ideological differences in a country that is already seriously divided; they should bring people together rather than drive them apart.

However appealing the broker system may seem, its implications should not be overlooked. By concentrating on regional and ethnic cleavages, parties minimize the role of ideology in Canadian politics. Such parties are opportunistic and prag-matic rather than offering the electorate a choice of principles and genuinely dis-tinctive programs. They do not generate innovative policy approaches, but are content instead to respond to public opinion polls and interest group demands. What parties offer to the electorate in the place of alternative solutions to national problems are alternative leaders and slogans. Especially in a television age, leader images, unfortunately, have often become the focus of election campaigns.

Class-Based and Ideological Parties

A second kind of political party is one that is based on a set of principles (an ide-ology) or that seeks the support of a particular socioeconomic class. There is usu-ally a direct or indirect connection between class and ideology, such that these can be called **class-based parties**.[3] Class analysts expect that in the pre-democ-ratic period of any country all parties will defend the capitalist system, but when the vote is extended to the working class, a new working-class party will emerge. It will generally force politics to take on an ideological and class-based character, an evolution that clearly occurred in Britain.

Malcolm Mayes. *artizans.com*

When the vote was extended to the working class at the turn of the century in Canada, some isolated labour, socialist, and communist political activity occurred, and by 1920 new class-based farmer and labour parties existed. But the newly enfranchised working class did not manage to create a successful class-based party because the Liberals and Conservatives did everything in their power to discourage such a development, using both seductive and coercive techniques. Eventually, the farmers' interest in politics declined, and the working class mostly supported the two old-line parties on ethnic/religious and regional grounds, rendered content by the occasional piece of social legislation.

The Depression represented the collapse of the capitalist system, and the CCF emerged to become the most sustained working-class, left-wing party to that point in time. As unionization expanded significantly in the 1940s, the CCF achieved its highest popular standing. After this point, however, Liberal welfare initiatives helped to draw off working-class support. This decline led to the creation of the NDP in 1961, but even with the NDP's organic link to the labour movement, most working-class Canadians continued to vote Liberal or PC (or, later, for other parties).

Analysts have proposed many reasons for the lack of class-consciousness among the Canadian working class.[4] Those who defend the lack of such consciousness argue that other divisions legitimately take precedence in Canada, that the system permits social mobility, that most people feel themselves to be middle class, that material benefits are widely shared, and that the Liberal and Conservative parties have accommodated working-class interests along with ethnic, religious, and regional interests in the broker system. Those who decry the lack of working-class consciousness contend that the Liberals and Conservatives were firmly entrenched when the franchise was extended to the working class and had already defined politics around social differences other than class. These two parties diverted attention from class-based issues either by appealing to one or more ethnic/religious and regional groups or by developing pan-Canadian appeals, such as the argument that national unity was the primary issue. These parties have been accused of deluding voters into the belief that they belonged to the middle class and of giving them the false impression of inclusion and social mobility.

Advocates of a class-based party system thus point out that the existing system is partially class-based—the upper and upper middle classes are conscious of their class position and vote accordingly; it is just that the working class does not vote appropriately. These advocates claim that a class-based system would provide ideological alternatives in elections, making them more meaningful. Moreover, when the Liberals and Conservatives are unsuccessful as brokers, the separation of one or more ethnic-regional units is possible. In such circumstances, class and ideology could be the integrating ingredients, uniting the people of various regions and ethnic groups around nationwide poles of left and right.[5]

Class-based parties are one kind of ideological party, but it is possible for a party to be based on a set of principles of some other kind, such as nationalism (e.g., the PQ and BQ) or populism (part of the Reform/Alliance focus). It is also quite likely in real life that some—perhaps most—parties will combine elements of both the broker and class-based or ideological models.

One-Party Dominance

Until 1993, Canada basically possessed a two-party system, or two-plus, as mentioned above. H.G. Thorburn maintains, however, that the Canadian party system has really been dominated not by two major parties but by one—the Liberals—since about 1900.[6] The Liberals are the government party, power oriented rather than issue oriented, attracting "winners" and "successes" as supporters and candidates, and maintaining themselves in office with the help of public service expertise, public opinion polls, and the chance to choose election day. Writing before 1993, Thorburn saw the Conservatives as the opposition party, ordinarily having to settle for the role of critic and being elected to office only on those rare occasions when the people get thoroughly fed up with the Liberals. However, with their divisiveness, "opposition mentality," and lack of preparedness to govern, the Conservatives never remain in power very long. Finally, he termed the NDP the innovative party, not really having a chance to govern nationally, but being responsible for introducing new left-wing ideas from beyond the range of current ideological conformity, often at the provincial level. In the light of the 1993, 1997, and 2000 elections, the Liberals were more dominant than ever, but the PCs and NDP have been eclipsed to a large extent by the Reform/Alliance with its innovations from the right.

Minor Parties

Because Canada has had more minor parties than other similar political systems, political scientists have developed several theories to account for them. Essentially, these parties can all be explained by the fact that at one time or another, ethnic, regional, or class grievances have gone unsatisfied by the broker parties. Moreover, new minor parties are to be expected when party identification is weak, and in the context of the ideological stagnation and opportunism of the broker system. In particular, if the working class never managed to establish a major party in Canada, it is not surprising that minor working-class parties would be created. The principal factors responsible for the rise of the various minor parties in Canada involve regional or ethnic alienation, class or ideology, a poor economy, and charismatic leadership. As seen in Table 9.1, more than one of these factors is often involved.

TABLE 9.1 FACTORS INVOLVED IN THE RISE OF MINOR PARTIES

	Region	Ethnicity	Class/Ideology	Economy	Leader
Progressives	*		*	*	
CCF			*	*	
Social Credit	*		*	*	*
Reconstruction			*	*	
Bloc Populaire	*	*			
NDP			*		
Créditistes	*	*	*	*	*
Libertarian			*		
Christian Heritage			*		
Green			*		
Confederation of Regions	*	*			
Reform/Alliance	*	*	*		*
Bloc Québécois	*	*			*

The Decline of Parties?

Some political scientists, including John Meisel, regretfully detect a decline of political parties.[7] He suggests a number of reasons why this is the case and why traditional party functions have been taken over by other institutions. Perhaps because voters perceive that parties no longer serve their interests, people seem to prefer to participate directly in specialized voluntary associations. The result is that interest groups have greatly increased in number and strength. The quantity and complexity of information with which governments must deal have come to mean that generalist politicians can no longer cope with it, leaving them increasingly dependent upon the bureaucracy. This culminates in a situation in which interest groups confer with bureaucrats to work out policies that the politicians can neither understand nor alter, further reducing the role of political parties in the policymaking process. Federal–provincial conferences and committees have become the forum in which many public policies are ironed out, and once certain political and bureaucratic compromises have been made, there is little that other politicians or parties can do about them.

Meisel also notes that parties now gear most of their activity to the demands of the media, and to the extent that elections are dominated by leader images and leader debates, the need for traditional party organizations diminishes. Similarly, public opinion polls provide better feedback to politicians than their traditional discussions with party activists. Investigative journalism has reduced the role of the opposition in Parliament, direct-mail appeals have replaced traditional forms of party fundraising, and modern transnational corporations are beyond the control of any party or government. Other recent developments that have contributed to the decline of parties are the increasing power of the prime minister, the influence of election strategists and other specialist advisers, and the new role of the courts and the Charter of Rights and Freedoms.

Party Organization

A political party has been defined as an organized group, but the structure of such a group requires clarification. Two main components of each party can be identified: the parliamentary party or **party caucus,** that is, the party's elected representatives in Parliament, and the **extra-parliamentary party** organization made up of party activists, the party staff, and ordinary party members. These extra-parliamentary organizations of the various parties can be distinguished in a variety of ways.

Party Membership

All parties strive to sign up members, but most fall far short of their expectations. No more than 3 percent of Canadians actually carry a party membership card, and only a few will make a small contribution of time or money at election time.

The NDP takes the concept of party membership more seriously than the other parties, often putting considerable effort into an annual membership drive. New members must take an oath that they support the party's principles, and strict rules apply with respect to the right to vote at nomination meetings. Constituency association representation at party conventions is based on the size of the local membership, and the party is unique in also having affiliated members, that is, members of trade unions that have voted to affiliate with the party.

Like the NDP, the Canadian Alliance has a 30-day membership qualification period for voting at nomination meetings, and its convention representation is also based on the number of local members.

The Liberals and Conservatives are normally more casual about the annual renewal of party memberships. For the most part, their members sign up in connection with a meeting to nominate a candidate for the next election or to choose delegates to a national convention. Although the Liberals are usually more restrictive in their rules than the Conservatives, it is typical for aspiring Liberal candidates or delegates to recruit large numbers of new members (often from ethnic groups in large urban centres) just prior to the deadline.

Party Leadership

In the new millennium, there are essentially two methods of choosing party leaders in Canada. The traditional way is at a national convention, to which constituency associations elect delegates.[8] Amid a great abundance of speeches, socializing, and twisting of arms, delegates engage in several rounds of voting until one candidate has at least 50 percent of the votes. There is much to be said for a traditional leadership convention, such that it attracts free media attention, usually raises the morale of party members, and can have a unifying effect on the party as the delegates gradually come together around the successful candidate.

The more recent procedure for choosing party leaders has been to allow every card-carrying member of the party to cast a vote. This avoids much of the cost of

Stockwell Day, the beleaguered leader of the Canadian Alliance
(Fred Chartrand/CP Picture Archive)

holding a national convention; eliminates the unholy fight among various candidates for delegates at the constituency level; and ensures that the decision is not left to the more affluent members of the party who can afford the travel costs. The Parti Québécois was the first party to move to a "one member–one vote" leadership selection process, and many provincial party leaders have now been elected on this basis. At the national level, the PC party and the Canadian Alliance have both used this system, in which it is common to issue party members a personal identification number (PIN) and have them telephone in their choice. Such procedures have potential problems of their own, however, including technological breakdowns, an unrepresentative electorate, and the involvement of voters who have no knowledge of the candidates or who actually support other parties. Many partisans also feel that the loss of the publicity value of a nationally televised convention is too high a cost, and suggest that by imposing spending limits on candidates and subsidizing delegates' expenses, some of the worst features of conventions can be avoided. Some parties try to combine the best of both worlds: giving every member a vote, but also having a leadership convention. Both the Liberals and NDP adopted such hybrid procedures in the 1990s.

Most parties also have **leadership review** mechanisms in their constitutions, although these vary in detail. The NDP opens nominations for the position of leader at their national convention every two years, so that an unsatisfactory leader can be immediately replaced. However, in the absence of a concrete challenger, no vote is needed. The Conservatives put the question "Are you in favour of having a leadership convention?" at the first convention following an election that the party loses. The Liberals ask the same question at the first national party convention after each election, win or lose, while the Reform/Alliance asks the question at every biennial national assembly. Many members of the Canadian Alliance wanted to get rid of Stockwell Day even before the scheduled vote.

Party Policymaking

All political parties have difficulty designing their policymaking process. On the one hand, they want to give ordinary party members an opportunity to contribute to party policy. But on the other, each party worries that the issues are too complex to be guided exclusively by ordinary members' views, and no party wants to be saddled with unrealistic policy commitments. Thus, they all struggle to combine grassroots input with the influence of the party elite.

Liberal and Conservative national conventions or general meetings usually include a policy session and sometimes focus primarily on policy. But even if specific resolutions are debated and passed, party leaders or cabinets retain the right to determine official party policy. The Liberals' Red Book, used as the party platform in the 1993 election, drew substantially from party policy meetings over the previous two years but was not bound by them. As part of its rebuilding process after 1993, the PC Party designed a new policymaking process combining greater membership input with expert advice. A certain tension exists in the

Reform/Alliance between its populist intentions and the dominance of its leader and elite. The party has an elaborate policymaking process in which resolutions can originate at the constituency level, from caucus, from party task forces, and from the executive council. Discussion of party policy takes up a considerable portion of the agenda at its national assemblies, but discrepancies have been found between official party policy and the election platform.

The NDP always claimed to be particularly distinctive in the realm of party policymaking. It has regular policy sessions every two years, which are the predominant item on the convention agenda. Constituency associations are invited to submit resolutions in advance, and resolutions passed by the convention are considered to be official and binding on the leader and the parliamentary party. Even in the NDP, however, constituency resolutions are now vetted by the party's policy committee with its considerable resources before being transmitted to the council and convention.

Party Conventions

All parties have constitutions that outline their objectives, structures, and procedures. In theory, at least, the ultimate power in each party is held by the convention that all parties try to hold at regular two-year intervals. The convention agenda normally includes the election of the party executive, constitutional amendments, and policy discussions, but such conventions also serve important social and morale-building purposes. In the Liberal and Conservative parties, each constituency association is entitled to an equal number of delegates, while in the NDP and the Canadian Alliance, representation is based on the size of the local membership. All parties include certain ex-officio delegates such as MPs, while in the NDP, affiliated labour unions also send delegates. Women's, youth, campus, Aboriginal peoples', and ethnic groups may also send delegates to certain party conventions.

Federal–Provincial Party Links

The federal nature of Canada and the existence of two levels of government at which political parties seek to influence policy and personnel raises the question of the relationship between national and provincial party organizations. To oversimplify the situation somewhat, the federal and provincial PC parties are essentially independent. There is virtually no formal organizational or financial link between the two wings of the party, and there is no provincial Conservative Party at all in Quebec. Thus, federal and provincial party memberships are usually separate, and a complete set of federal riding associations and executives coexists with provincial party organizations at the grassroots level.

By contrast, the NDP could be called an "integrated" party because, with the exception of Quebec, one joins the NDP at the provincial level and automatically becomes a member of the national party. Provincial offices of the party serve the needs of both federal and provincial parties, and the two levels of the party are integrated financially. In Quebec, however, federal and provincial wings of the party are quite separate.

The Liberal Party is characterized by two different federal–provincial relationships. In Quebec, Ontario, Alberta, and British Columbia, the party is split into federal and provincial wings, each with separate finances, memberships, constituency associations, executives, conventions, and offices. In the other provinces and territories, the party is more "unitary." Where the federal and provincial wings of the Liberal party are organizationally separate, as in the PCs, there is less inclination to be ideologically compatible or to be helpful to each other in their respective election campaigns.

Preston Manning wanted to concentrate all of Reform's attention at the national level, and persuaded his members to back his objection to provincial party branches. Nevertheless, a provincial party in British Columbia had previously adopted the "Reform Party" label and continued to operate with a similar platform, but without organic links to the federal party. When Reform transformed itself into the Canadian Alliance, it retained the same policy with respect to provincial branches of the party, hoping to curry close relations with provincial Conservative organizations, especially in Alberta and Ontario.

Party Ideology

For the purposes of this discussion, ideology can be defined as a coherent set of ideas or principles about how a society ought to function, with particular reference to the role of the state. If Canadian politics has been dominated by broker parties, one would not expect the role of ideology to be of fundamental importance. Nevertheless, it can be argued that genuine ideological differences do exist in Canada, and that such ideologies as liberalism, conservatism, and democratic socialism can be found to differentiate the three traditional parties, as well as the Reform/Alliance.[9] The ideological continuum can be sketched in diagrammatic form as in Figure 9.1, based on the contending principles of collectivism and individualism on the one hand, and egalitarianism and inequality on the other.

···

Figure 9.1   The Ideological Continuum in Canada

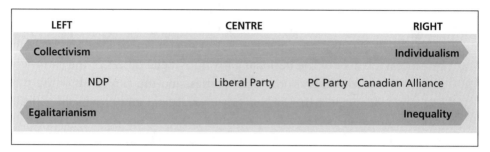

LEFT	CENTRE	RIGHT
Collectivism		Individualism
NDP	Liberal Party	PC Party Canadian Alliance
Egalitarianism		Inequality

This perspective suggests that the overwhelming ideology in Canada is **liberalism,** but that traces of **democratic socialism** and **conservatism** also exist and that each of the ideologies is represented by a corresponding party. Liberalism seeks to liberate the individual and maximize each individual's freedom and potential, something that almost all Canadians would support. The differences that emerge essentially centre on the role of the state.

Democratic socialism seeks to liberate the individual from the inequalities and exploitation of the capitalist system; it believes in equality of condition, not merely equality of opportunity; and it prescribes a large element of state action or **collectivism** in order to achieve such liberation and equality.

In discussions of political ideology, these views are generally referred to as being on the left. In particular, democratic socialism emphasizes government planning, regulation, ownership of some of the major industries of the country, progressive taxation, and redistribution of income via social programs. Democratic socialists are sometimes subdivided between "socialists" and "social democrats," depending on the extent to which they wish the state to intervene and the extent of equality they wish to effect. The CCF/NDP take credit for introducing public hospital and medical insurance when they formed the government of Saskatchewan, pressing for other social programs, advocating a more progressive taxation system, creating a variety of Crown corporations in the provinces where they held power, and supporting the establishment of new government bodies in Ottawa.

Liberalism, too, has a dual personality and can be subdivided into "welfare" and "business" variants. Business liberals believe that the state inhibits individual self-fulfillment and that its role should therefore be minimized so that individualism can prevail. Welfare liberals, on the other hand, take the view that the state can be a positive agent in liberating individuals from the constraints of other forces including the private-enterprise economy. Welfare liberals therefore stand for a combination of individualism and collectivism and a combination of equality and inequality that they usually label "equality of opportunity." The Liberal Party is thus composed of business and welfare liberals, leaving it in the centre of the Canadian ideological continuum. While Liberals obviously hold the private enterprise system in greater esteem than does the NDP, Liberal governments introduced old age pensions, family allowances, and many other social welfare programs over the years, although many observers saw a rightward shift after 1993.

Conservatism also has two variants. On the one hand, conservatives seek to liberate the individual from the restrictions of the state. Reducing the role of the state to a minimum and allowing capitalistic market forces to determine the distribution of power and wealth is often labelled **individualism.**

If this results in inequalities, conservatives are generally unconcerned; inequalities are both natural and deserved—some people are more talented and work harder than others. These attitudes are labelled as being on the **right,** and these conservatives can be called "business liberals." The second wing of the Canadian Progressive Conservative Party is the "progressive" element, people who are sometimes called **red tories.** These Conservatives combine beliefs in privilege and collectivism, seeing society as an organic whole, emphasizing community values as well as individualism, and standing for order, tradition, and stability. They believe in hierarchy—that everyone should occupy his or her place—but they also have a paternalistic concern for the condition of all the people. This aspect of conservatism is not unique to Canada, being found quite commonly in Britain and the rest of Europe; it stands out only in contrast to a lack of such sentiment within American conservatism.

Thus, the ideology of the Canadian Conservative party is not as clear-cut as the diagram indicates and is divided as much as the other two parties. Furthermore, the red tory element overlaps to some extent with welfare liberalism and even social democracy. While the Mulroney government pursued a fairly consistent business-liberal agenda—privatization, deregulation, deficit reduction, and cutting of social programs—its Conservative predecessors sometimes exhibited a red tory touch, such as in the creation of the RCMP, CBC, CNR, the National Energy Board, the Bennett New Deal, and the Stanfield proposal for government controls on wages and prices.

If liberalism in the United States lacks the collectivist touch, how does one explain its presence in all three of the traditional Canadian party ideologies? One explanation focuses on the United Empire Loyalists, who removed most of the collectivist tendencies from the U.S. political culture when they migrated to

Canada, and left behind undiluted business liberalism in that country. The United Empire Loyalists rendered ideological diversity legitimate in Canada and, because of their early predominance, made collectivism a respectable and important element in the Canadian political culture. In fact, they added to the collectivist approach already found in the feudal background of French Canada, that is, the ideas of hierarchy, order, stability, and community. Collectivism was reinforced by subsequent waves of British immigration whose intellectual baggage included both red tory and socialist views, along with the influence of the Social Gospel movement. Such collectivist tendencies were discussed in Chapter 6.

Over the past decade, the whole ideological spectrum has shifted to the right. In Canada, this began with the Mulroney government, which pursued a business-liberal or **neoconservative** agenda in which renewed reliance was placed on market forces and the extent of government intervention was reduced. For the first time in Canadian history, social programs were cut back rather than expanded; Crown corporations were privatized rather than created; regulations were repealed rather than promulgated; public debts and deficits were reduced rather than increased; and public servants were fired rather than being hired. The whole phenomenon could be called the "dismantling of the state." The new ideology went beyond one or two parties; it affected governing parties of all ideological persuasions: PCs, Liberals, the Parti Québécois, and even the NDP in Saskatchewan.

The Reform Party was very much part of this shift to the right, and exerted great influence at both federal and provincial levels even though it did not form the government. The other leaders of this right-wing crusade, Conservatives Ralph Klein in Alberta and Mike Harris in Ontario, also followed the Reform lead. In 2000, Reform transformed itself into the Canadian Alliance, but without any significant change in policy. It believed in reducing the role of government, reducing taxes, reducing regulation, privatizing Crown corporations, laying off public servants, reducing the debt and the deficit, and cutting back on social programs. This is all consistent with a belief in individualism, which is unconcerned about whether it leads to socioeconomic inequalities. (Ironically, the Reform/Alliance is a strong believer in treating everyone, including provinces, equally *in law*.) What distinguishes the Reform/Alliance from other Canadian parties is therefore an almost complete absence of the collectivist value. In this respect, it is a clone of the U.S. Republican Party, with which it maintains contact.

A second strand of Reform/Alliance ideology is social conservatism, such as in its opposition to abortion and gay rights and its promotion of "family values" and censorship. This bundle of issues led to internal divisions within the party in the 2000 leadership race and election because to some extent this position contradicts the neoconservative one. Social conservatism advocates a strong role for the state in moral regulation by maintaining law and order and upholding conventional values. New-right governments in Canada, like that of Harris and Klein, have strengthened the state by centralizing power in the hands of the cabinet. Witness the changes to education in Ontario that have disempowered school boards and teachers and given the provincial cabinet the power to infuse the educational curriculum with corporate values and to impose strict codes of student comportment.

A third aspect of Reform/Alliance ideology is its populist streak. It is against political elitism and professes to value the wisdom of ordinary people, giving them direct participation in decisionmaking via referenda, for example. This, too, is an Americanism, as opposed to the traditional Canadian belief in **representative democracy.** The final main concern of the Reform/Alliance Party is a territorial rather than ideological issue—that the West was getting shortchanged within Confederation.

The other new party, the Bloc Québécois, has one main objective: Quebec sovereignty. The question of nationalism generally overwhelms the left–right ideological approach in Quebec, but the BQ and PQ have usually been placed on the left side of the continuum, somewhere between the Liberals and the NDP.

As a result of the shift to the right, the NDP now occupies the previous position of the Liberal Party. The Chrétien government pursued the same kind of leaner government that it previously condemned under Mulroney, and Finance Minister Paul Martin dismembered many of the social programs that were largely the creation of his father, a long-time "welfare" Liberal cabinet minister. A crush occurred on the right-wing side of the spectrum, and the Conservative Party found it difficult to identify its own ideological space between the Chrétien Liberals and Manning's Reform Party or Stockwell Day's Canadian Alliance. Despite this movement, however, no single party emerged to embrace the predominant right-wing ideology.

DISCUSSION QUESTIONS

1. What sort of future do you see for the political left in Canada? Should the right unite?
2. Canadian political parties appear to be increasingly regionalized. If this is not a good thing, what can be done about it?

3. Is it possible in this complex, information-driven age for ordinary party members to make useful policy suggestions within the political parties to which they belong?

FURTHER READING

Brodie, Janine, and Jane Jenson. *Crisis, Challenge and Change: Party and Class in Canada Revisited*. Ottawa: Carleton University Press, 1988.

Campbell, Colin, and William Christian. *Parties, Leaders, and Ideologies in Canada.* Toronto: McGraw-Hill Ryerson, 1996.

Flanagan, Tom. *Waiting for the Wave: The Reform Party and Preston Manning*. Toronto: Stoddart, 1995.

Thorburn, H. G. and Alan Whitehorn, eds. *Party Politics in Canada*, 8th ed. Scarborough: Prentice-Hall Canada, 2000.

Whitehorn, Alan. *Canadian Socialism: Essays on the CCF and the NDP*. Toronto: Oxford University Press, 1992.

Notes

1. In traditional European terms, a multiparty system implies that no party has a majority, leading to coalition governments. That is clearly not the case in Canada.

2. H. G. Thorburn, "Interpretations of the Canadian Party System," in H. G. Thorburn, ed., *Party Politics in Canada*, 6th ed. (Scarborough: Prentice-Hall Canada, 1991).

3. Janine Brodie and Jane Jenson, *Crisis, Challenge and Change: Party and Class in Canada Revisited* (Ottawa: Carleton University Press, 1988); Charles Taylor, *The Pattern of Politics* (Toronto: McClelland and Stewart, 1970); Gad Horowitz, "Toward the Democratic Class Struggle," in Trevor Lloyd and Jack McLeod, eds., *Agenda 1970* (Toronto: University of Toronto Press, 1968).

4. Jon Pammett, "Class Voting and Class Consciousness in Canada," *Canadian Review of Sociology and Anthropology* 24, no. 2 (1987): 269–90; Keith Archer, "The Failure of the New Democratic Party: Unions, Unionists, and Politics in Canada," *Canadian Journal of Political Science* (June 1985): 353–66.

5. Horowitz, "Toward the Democratic Class Struggle," 254.

6. Thorburn, "Interpretations of the Canadian Party System"; Reginald Whitaker, *The Government Party: Organizing and Financing the Liberal Party of Canada 1930–58* (Toronto: University of Toronto Press, 1977); George Perlin, *The Tory Syndrome: Leadership Politics in the Progressive Conservative Party* (Montreal: McGill–Queen's University Press, 1980). The decline of the Tories in 1992–93 had additional causes.

7. John Meisel, "Decline of Party in Canada," in H. G. Thorburn, ed., *Party Politics in Canada*, 5th ed.; John Meisel, "The Dysfunctions of Canadian Parties: An Exploratory Mapping," in Thorburn, 6th ed.; John Meisel and Matthew Mendelsohn, "Meteor? Phoenix? Chameleon? The Decline and Transformation of Party in Canada," in H. G. Thorburn and Alan Whitehorn, eds. *Party Politics in Canada*, 8th ed. (Toronto: Prentice-Hall, 2001).

8. John C. Courtney, *Do Conventions Matter? Choosing National Party Leaders in Canada* (Montreal: McGill–Queen's University Press, 1995); Maureen Mancuso et al., eds., *Leaders and Leadership in Canada* (Toronto: Oxford University Press, 1994).

9. Louis Hartz, *The Founding of New Societies* (New York: Harcourt, Brace and World, 1964); Gad Horowitz, "Conservatism, Liberalism and Socialism in Canada: An Interpretation," *Canadian Journal of Economics and Political Science* (May 1966): 143–71; Colin Campbell and William Christian, *Parties, Leaders, and Ideologies in Canada* (Toronto: McGraw-Hill Ryerson, 1996).

Chapter 10

Pressure Groups and Lobbying

Pressure groups or interest groups develop in almost every political system when individuals with common concerns band together in order to strengthen their cause. This chapter will identify some of the leading Canadian pressure groups and social movements, outline their targets and methods, assess their resources, and then give an account of the activity of new lobbying firms.

Chapter Objectives

After you have completed this chapter, you should be able to:

Understand the prominence of pressure groups in the political system

Provide examples of leading pressure groups in a variety of fields

Distinguish between institutionalized and issue-oriented groups, public interest and self-interested groups, and social movements

Discuss how the structure of government affects the way pressure groups are organized

Enumerate the targets of pressure group activity and the methods used to reach them

Discuss the importance of different group resources

Distinguish between old and new forms of lobbying and enumerate the provisions of the Lobbyists Registration Act

Comment on unsavoury aspects of the professional lobbying scene

···

The Functions of Pressure Groups and Lobbying

A **pressure group** or **interest group** (terms used interchangeably here) can be defined as any group that seeks to influence government policy without contesting elections, that is, without putting forward its own candidates. Alternatively, pressure groups have been defined by Paul Pross as "organizations whose members act together to influence public policy in order to promote their common interest."[1] The term **lobbying** is generally used to refer to any organized attempt to influence the decisionmakers, an activity that is most commonly undertaken by pressure groups but could also be done by individuals, companies, or other political actors. Increasingly, however, pressure groups have been joined by professional lobbying firms in this activity.

Pressure groups are primarily involved in the function of "interest articulation"; they normally have a narrow focus and are organized around a single interest that they try to impress upon those in authority. As society becomes more complex, Canadians increasingly demonstrate a preference to form or join such specialized, functional groups in order to transmit their demands to government, rather than rely on the broader and largely territorial representation of parties and elections. Thus, in the promotion of interests, pressure groups provide a supplementary kind of "functional" representation, especially between elections.[2]

···

The Array of Canadian Pressure Groups

The number of interest groups operating in Canada is in the thousands. Only some of the largest and most influential are listed in Table 10.1.

Business Groups[3]

In the case of business, nothing prevents individual companies from lobbying on their own behalf for grants, subsidies, tariff protection or free trade agreements, loan guarantees, tax write-offs, government contracts, or policy changes, and many firms do so on a regular basis. In addition, the firms within almost every industry have organized a common pressure group to promote the interests of the industry as a whole. It is estimated that more than 600 business groups are active in Canadian politics.[4] Superimposed upon these industrial groupings are such "peak" organizations as the **Business Council on National Issues,** the Canadian Alliance of Manufacturers and Exporters, the Canadian Chamber of Commerce, and the Canadian Federation of Independent Business. They each represent a

TABLE 10.1 LEADING NATIONAL CANADIAN PRESSURE GROUPS

Business	Business Council on National Issues
	Canadian Alliance of Manufacturers and Exporters
	Canadian Chamber of Commerce
	Canadian Federation of Independent Business
	Canadian Bankers' Association
	Canadian Association of Broadcasters
	Canada's Research-Based Pharmaceutical Companies
Agriculture	Canadian Federation of Agriculture
Labour	Canadian Labour Congress
Professions	Canadian Bar Association
	Canadian Medical Association
	Canadian Federation of Students
Ethnic	Assembly of First Nations
	Canadian Ethnocultural Council
	National Congress of Italian Canadians
Religious	Canadian Council of Churches
	Canadian Conference of Catholic Bishops
	Canadian Jewish Congress
Causes	John Howard Society
	Canadian Civil Liberties Association
	National Action Committee on the Status of Women
	Pollution Probe
	Mothers against Drunk Driving
	Non-Smokers' Rights Association
	Council of Canadians

wide range of business interests. In agriculture, nearly 100 active organizations vie for influence, the leading group being the Canadian Federation of Agriculture.

Nonbusiness Groups

The **Canadian Labour Congress** functions as a common voice for organized labour, but only about 59 percent of union members in Canada belong to unions

Profile of a Business Pressure Group: The Business Council on National Issues

The Business Council on National Issues (BCNI) was formed in 1976, and its membership comprises the chief executive officers of the 150 leading Canadian corporations. With about 1.3 million employees and over $2 trillion in assets, it bills itself as "the senior voice of Canadian business on national and global issues." The president and chief executive is Tom d'Aquino, who is the Council's chief of policy and strategy and manages its day-to-day affairs. Both the Council and observers of the Council give it credit for setting the agenda for all recent Canadian governments. First, it promoted the idea of free trade between Canada and the United States, then pressured the government to balance the budget, and then advocated tax cuts. Each of these high-pressured campaigns resulted in a reduction in the size and role of the state.

For more information on the council go to: http://www.bcni.com

affiliated with the CLC. Another 6 percent belong to the Quebec-based Conseil des syndicats nationaux, while most of the rest have not joined any central labour organization. The CLC maintains a link to the New Democratic Party, as do many of its individual unions, a unique relationship among Canadian pressure groups.

Many of the ethnic groups in Canada have their own organized associations, such as the National Congress of Italian Canadians. Most of these have been brought together, with government support, in the umbrella organization, the Canadian Ethnocultural Council. The largest of several Aboriginal groups is the **Assembly of First Nations.** The English and French are organized only where they are minorities—the anglophone Alliance-Quebec and the Fédération des communautés francophones et acadienne du Canada, incorporating provincial units such as the Association canadienne-française de l'Ontario (ACFO). Religious denominations in Canada also function as pressure groups from time to time, with the Canadian Conference of Catholic Bishops, the United Church of Canada, the Canadian Council of Churches, and the Canadian Jewish Congress probably being most influential. Most professions have organizations that speak for their members on relevant issues, the Canadian Medical Association and Canadian Bar Association being two of the oldest and most important. A large proportion of postsecondary students belong to the Canadian Federation of Students.

Other Categorizations of Pressure Groups

However much any of the above-mentioned groups claim to be pursuing the public interest, they can be generally categorized as "self-interested" groups because in most cases their principal concern is to improve their own, usually economic, position. The true "public-interest" group exists to promote causes that it sees as beneficial to society as a whole and that do not directly benefit its own members, such as the John Howard Society (improving prison conditions and the lot of ex-inmates), the Canadian Council on Social Development (promoting better social policy), the Canadian Civil Liberties Association (protecting civil liberties from government infringement), and a variety of environmental groups.

With some exceptions, those named above and many others are called **institutionalized groups** because they are permanent, well-established, formal organizations. Almost all maintain a head office in Ottawa with a full-time staff, a sizable budget, and a reasonably stable membership. Most have developed continuous links with the authorities, and represent their members' interests on a daily basis, year after year.

In contrast, some groups spring up spontaneously around a specific issue, and once the issue is resolved, they fade away. Such **issue-oriented groups** lack the institutionalized groups' permanence, office, staff, budget, membership, and access to the authorities. Instead, they more likely resort to attracting public attention to their cause through media coverage of such actions as demonstrations. Examples of issue-oriented groups include the Stop Spadina group that opposed extension of the Spadina Expressway in Toronto in the early 1970s and "Bread Not Circuses," which objected to Toronto's bid to host the 1996 (and 2008) Olympic Games. In the 1980s, when Finance Minister Michael Wilson attempted to de-index the old age pension, an ad hoc group of seniors organized across the country and forced him to back down. If their issue is not resolved, or if they anticipate further challenges, such groups may become a more permanent fixture.[5]

Political scientists often find it useful to distinguish between pressure groups and social movements. Many of the issue-oriented groups referred to are, in fact, part of larger unstructured social movements, of which the environmental, women's, and peace movements have been most prominent. Other examples include the Aboriginal, gay, and animal rights movements. A **social movement** has been defined as an informal network of organizations and individuals who on the basis of a collective identity and shared values engage in political and/or cultural struggle and undertake collective action designed to affect both state and society.[6] Social movements begin at the margins of the political system, possess an alternative vision of "the good life," and usually consist of coalitions of small local groups that have not yet hardened into a cohesive national group.

The National Action Committee on the Status of Women is a somewhat institutionalized coalition of some 650 member groups, while the Canadian Environmental Network contains over 2000 groups. Such movements run into much bureaucratic and political party resistance because of a reluctance to consider radical new ideas, and often do not achieve immediate success. In the long run, however, they widen the scope of public discourse, and parties and other mainstream political institutions eventually respond. Take recent improvements in legislation with respect to women and the environment, for example, and changes in public attitudes toward war, Aboriginal peoples, gays and lesbians, and the treatment of animals.

Other categorizations are also sometimes useful in discussing pressure groups. Most groups are "autonomous" in the sense that they develop without government initiative, although they may later seek government financial support. But politicians or bureaucrats are sometimes involved in the creation of interest groups, whether for personal gain or in the hope of promoting a certain public policy objective. In the late 1960s, for example, the federal government began to fund antipoverty, women's, minority official language, Aboriginal, and other ethnic groups to ensure that these interests would be involved in the political marketplace.[7] The Trudeau and Mulroney governments cut back on grants to Aboriginal, women's, and poor and disabled people's groups both for fiscal and ideological reasons or when a particular group became too critical of the hand that fed it. Canada has been something of a world leader in government support of critical interest groups, but such grant reductions reveal the dangers that arise if a group becomes too critical and too dependent.

Pressure Group Structures

As far as the structure of pressure groups is concerned, issue-oriented groups can burst forth anywhere an issue arises—at the international, federal, provincial, or municipal level. Institutionalized groups, on the other hand, tend to be organized wherever government decisions regularly affect them. The federal nature of the country means that authoritative decisions are made at two or more levels of government, and most institutionalized groups parallel the federal structure of government. They find it advantageous to be organized at both levels because the division of powers between the federal and provincial governments is so blurred. The Canadian Medical Association is composed of 10 autonomous provincial

Profile of a Social Movement: The Council of Canadians

The Council of Canadians is a citizens' movement that provides a critical voice on key national issues such as safeguarding social programs, promoting economic justice, renewing democracy, asserting Canadian sovereignty, preserving the environment, and promoting alternatives to corporate-style free trade. It has been active on such issues as free trade, public pensions, bank mergers, concentrated media ownership, the use of growth hormones in cattle, and other aspects of genetically modified food. One of the Council's priorities is to persuade federal and provincial governments to prohibit the bulk export of Canadian water.

The Council is part of the Action Canada Network and the Alternative Federal Budget movement, along with the CLC, CFS, NAC, NAPO, unions and environmental groups. The AFB hammers out a detailed and sophisticated alternative federal budget each year, which is published by the Canadian Centre for Policy Alternatives, one of the few think tanks on the left.

The Council and its allies also put much effort into stopping the Multilateral Agreement on Investment (MAI), working successfully with similar grassroots groups around the world. The Internet facilitates both national and international grassroots political campaigns, and such social movements and networks are often seen as one of the few counterweights to corporate globalization in the modern world.[8] In fact, opposition to globalization via new free trade agreements that primarily benefit transnational corporations is the very issue that increasingly inspires social movements.

For more information on the Council, go to http://www.canadians.org/

divisions (such as the Ontario Medical Association); the Canadian Chamber of Commerce has strong provincial branches (such as the Alberta Chamber of Commerce), as does the Canadian Labour Congress (the Nova Scotia Federation of Labour). These latter two groups in particular also maintain municipal organizations—local chambers of commerce or boards of trade in every sizable community, and over 100 local labour councils across the country.

Many pressure groups, including teachers, nurses, and students, are actually more strongly organized at the provincial level than in Ottawa. This is because they are more affected by decisions of provincial governments than by federal ones. Some, such as the medical and legal professions, are even delegated powers by provincial governments to regulate themselves.

The Canadian Federation of Students demonstrates against rising tuition fees (Steve Russell/CP Picture Archive)

Students may even organize protests at the campus level to try to change university or college decisions. In recent years, such protests have often focused on increases in tuition fees or exclusive rights contracts granted to individual corporations (like Coke or Pepsi) to advertise or provide a service on campus.

Targets and Methods of Pressure Group Activity

Besides being affected by federalism, Canadian interest groups are very much influenced in their operations by the fact that they exist in a parliamentary system. This system, despite its name, places most of the decisionmaking power in the hands of the bureaucracy and the cabinet. Pressure groups that understand this basic truth direct most of their attention to these two branches of government.

In this connection, Paul Pross's conception of **policy communities** should be mentioned.[9] This concept is based on the premise that each field of public policy is discrete and specialized, with its own constellation of participants. Each policy community consists of a grouping of government agencies, pressure groups, corporations, institutions, media people, and individuals who have an interest in that particular policy field and attempt to influence it. These actors initially attempt to establish their legitimacy with the lead government agency, and if they achieve such recognition and status, they may be made part of the agency's information flow. Once such groups are given the privilege of consultation and access to strategic information, they normally behave quite cooperatively, and the whole policy community becomes cohesive and mutually supportive. All the actors involved, including the lead agency, prefer to keep the issues that concern them within the "community" and have a strong incentive to resolve any problems there rather than open the issues up to cabinet discussion or, even worse, public debate and confrontation.

The Bureaucracy

As discussed in Chapter 14, the bureaucracy advises the cabinet on almost all of its decisions. It drafts legislation and regulations according to the cabinet's general instructions; it proposes budgets and spends government money; and it implements policies and programs once they have been given cabinet and/or legislative approval. All of these areas hold considerable scope for bureaucratic discretion. It is for this reason that institutionalized groups in particular direct the bulk of their messages at the bureaucratic target. Many pressure group demands involve technical matters that only the bureaucracy understands and that it may be able to satisfy without reference to the politicians.

Such groups try to cultivate close relationships with senior public servants, hoping to be able to contact these officials on an informal, direct, day-to-day basis via telephone calls, faxes, meetings, letters, and business lunches. Although bureaucrats may be suspicious of their motives, the relationship between a pressure group and its most relevant government department may ultimately become a reciprocal one, as desirable for the public service as it is for the group.

Thus, what is called a **clientele relationship** often develops between such groups as the Canadian Federation of Agriculture and the Department of Agriculture, the Canadian Medical Association and the Department of Health, the petroleum and mining associations and the Department of Natural Resources, and big business organizations and the Department of Finance. The relations between such a department or agency and its allied pressure groups may even become so close that it is difficult to tell them apart. The department or agency almost becomes an extension of the pressure group, making policy in the interest of the group and promoting the interest they both represent within the higher councils of government. The minister, deputy minister, and Department of Finance speak for the business community, while the minister, deputy minister, and Department of Agriculture speak for the farming community, and so on.

In return for the various ways in which the bureaucracy responds to group demands, the group may pass on information that the department needs or desires in order to do its work. Many issues become too complex for politicians—ministers or MPs—to understand, especially as larger numbers of issues, constituents, and obligations eat up their time. As a consequence, legislation is increasingly drafted in skeletal form with the specifics delegated to the bureaucracy to be added later in the form of **regulations** or "delegated legislation." Bureaucrats regularly consult institutionalized pressure groups as they draft legislation, design programs, and draw up regulations. The group may also be a valuable ally in persuading other bureaucratic agencies or ministers to do what the department wants.

Although pressure groups are usually seen in terms of their "input" function of making demands, they also perform various "output" functions. A group may be better equipped to inform its specialized membership about new laws, regulations, or programs than a department that is restricted to the media or other regular channels of communication. In addition, the cooperation of the group might be indispensable to the successful execution of a program. In some cases, as noted, certain groups are even delegated powers of self-regulation.

When public servants themselves are members of interest groups, it naturally assists the group in maximizing its influence. For example, medical bureaucrats often belong to the Canadian Medical Association and legal bureaucrats to the Canadian Bar Association. In fact, considerable movement of personnel takes place between interest groups and the higher levels of the public service: officials often move from pressure group jobs to the bureaucracy or vice versa.

The Cabinet

The cabinet is the second-most frequently targeted branch of government because it makes the major governmental decisions in a parliamentary system. Since it is now virtually impossible to meet the prime minister and cabinet as a whole, groups often find it productive to submit single-issue representations to individual ministers, who spend much of their time in meetings with such groups. If a minister stays in one position long enough, a pressure group may be able to construct a more personal, informal relationship, as the Canadian Federation of Agriculture did with Jimmy Gardiner, who served as minister of Agriculture from 1935 to 1957. The social scene in Ottawa should also be mentioned, for parties and receptions provide excellent opportunities for cabinet ministers, deputy ministers, and established pressure group representatives (especially corporate ones) to meet and mingle.

The Trudeau government established the precedent of encouraging various groups to meet with the minister of finance prior to the preparation of the annual Budget, a practice that was even more widespread under Mulroney's first finance minister, Michael Wilson. As noted below, pressure groups are now encouraged to appear before the House of Commons Standing Committee on Finance, but that does not preclude a private meeting with the minister of finance.

It is sometimes claimed that most public decisions in Canada emerge from the interaction of three agents: the cabinet, the senior public service, and pressure groups, especially in the business field.[10] The individuals who occupy the top positions in these sectors are elites both in the sense of being small numbers of people with disproportionate amounts of power (compared to ordinary citizens) and in the sense of their exclusive socioeconomic backgrounds, coming from families of higher social class, higher incomes, and higher educations. Robert Presthus thus postulates that the common backgrounds and values of political, bureaucratic, and corporate leaders help to facilitate agreement among them. Commanding the heights of these sectors of society, they easily accommodate each other in the working out of public policies. Lobbyists from professional lobbying firms also fit perfectly into this arrangement.

Parliament

The third main branch of the government is the legislature or Parliament, but as discussed in Chapter 15, it largely legitimizes decisions previously taken by the executive. That being the case, the House of Commons is not as often the target of interest group activity, but it does remain the object of considerable attention, especially for groups lacking access to the executive branch. One of the main reasons that a bill is usually sent to a legislative committee during its passage is to allow interest groups to make representations on it. The Standing Committee on Finance, with its pre-budget hearings, is now integrated into the expenditure management system, and provides an excellent opportunity for pressure groups to make their case.

Especially in a majority government situation, however, ministers have traditionally been reluctant to accept amendments proposed at the legislative stage, so that groups are better advised to make their case at the executive level before the bill is made public. It has even been said that the sight of a pressure group at the legislative level in Canada is a sign that the group already failed at the level of the bureaucracy and the cabinet. Nevertheless, groups converge on MPs in their offices or inundate them with letters, telegrams, or postcards. For example, although not ignoring the cabinet and bureaucracy, the Canadian Chamber of Commerce is particularly adept at applying pressure on MPs through its base in almost every constituency across the country. Pressure groups also meet with individual party caucuses, and certain MPs may already belong to a group, in which case they can be expected to speak on its behalf.

The upper chamber of Parliament, the Senate, is also involved in the lobbying process. Because many senators have close corporate connections and function regularly as lobbyists for big business, the Senate has been called "a lobby from within."[11] During passage in that chamber, much legislation is considered by the Senate Committee on Banking, Trade and Commerce, many of whose members hold directorships in Canadian banks and other large corporations. Such holdings have not deterred Committee members from active consideration of questions relating to financial institutions in what many observers see as a classic case of conflict of interest.

Other Targets

Interest groups have many targets beyond these three main branches of government. If they can find a legal or constitutional angle to their demand, for example, such groups may take cases to the courts. Corporations have sometimes challenged federal or provincial legislation in the courts as a violation of the division of powers; francophone groups have used the courts to uphold constitutionally guaranteed minority language rights; and Aboriginal groups are increasingly using the courts to uphold or broaden the meaning of treaty and other Aboriginal rights. The Charter of Rights and Freedoms provides added potential for targeting the courts by actually inviting individuals and groups to challenge federal or provincial legislation that they consider to be discriminatory. The tobacco industry, for example, was somewhat successful in arguing that the law banning tobacco advertising violated the companies' freedom of expression.

Denny Pritchard. Reproduced with permission.

As mentioned, only the Canadian Labour Congress has seen fit to attach itself formally to a political party. But this strategy may have reduced the group's impact on Liberal and Conservative governments as it awaited an NDP victory. Other groups remain scrupulously nonpartisan so that they can exert equal influence on whatever party is in power, which is not to say that business groups in particular have any difficulty in gaining access to any party. Another target of pressure group activity is the **royal commission.** These elaborate investigations of public problems normally invite pressure groups and experts to submit briefs in public hearings, supplementing whatever original research the commission itself undertakes.

Besides their direct representations to government, pressure groups and corporations increasingly try to influence public opinion in what is called **advocacy advertising** in the hope that the authorities will respond to a clear message from the public. In 1991, for example, both the Pharmaceutical Manufacturers Association and the rival Canadian Drug Manufacturers' Association took out media advertisements to make their case on the question of patent protection for new drugs, and since then, other groups have used this device regularly.

Many pressure groups increase their public profile once an election has been called. This phenomenon, discussed in Chapter 8, is usually called **third-party advertising.** Pressure groups often seek the response of parties and candidates to questions of concern to the group and then indicate their support or opposition in media advertising. The National Citizens' Coalition regularly does so, contrary to the spirit of expenditure ceilings in the Canada Elections Act, while the Canadian Alliance for Jobs and Trade Prospects and its anti–free trade counterpart, the Pro-Canada Network, were particularly visible in 1988. National or local pressure groups sometimes target particular politicians, especially ministers, for defeat.

If all else fails, a group may resort to demonstrations, protest marches, tractor parades, sit-ins, and road and bridge blockades. Some of these are peaceful and legal, such as the orderly demonstrations that are an almost daily occurrence on Parliament Hill and frequently greet prime ministers on their travels. But the frustration of Aboriginal, environmentalist, and radical or issue-oriented groups increasingly takes the form of civil disobedience. The 1990 armed standoff at Oka, Quebec, was one of the rare occasions in which a group resorted to violence, but only after governments failed to respond to the Mohawks' verbal protests.

In recent years, globalization and free trade agreements that are claimed to benefit only transnational corporations have attracted much violent protest. At the World Trade Organization (WTO) Summit in Seattle in late 1999, at the Summit of the Americas in Quebec City in April 2001, and at the G7/G8 summit in Genoa three months later, hundreds of protestors took to the streets. While most acted in a nonviolent fashion, some were intent on shutting the meetings down. Such demonstrations attract much media and public attention and may be the only way to make a point about certain issues, but are not the most common form of pressure group activity.

....

Group Resources and Determinants of Success

It is hard to determine why some groups are successful and others are not; however, factors accounting for success and failure include the following:

- members
- cohesion
- money
- information
- sympathy of the government and popularity of the cause
- financial position of government
- absence of opposition

The size of the group is usually important, considering that numbers represent votes. The authorities feel comfortable ignoring very small groups, for example, because the electoral consequences would be minimal. In this respect, the Canadian Labour Congress and the National Action Committee on the Status of Women should be regularly successful in having the authorities respond to their demands because, with about 2.5 and 3 million members respectively, they are the largest pressure groups in Canada.

The fact that the CLC is not usually very influential points to the equal importance of the cohesiveness of the organization. First, as previously mentioned, the labour movement as a whole is not very cohesive, and even among those who are members of the CLC, unity, commitment, and militancy are notoriously lacking. Moreover, on those occasions when the CLC "declared war" on the government, the bulk of its members continued to vote for parties other than the NDP. Liberal and Conservative governments apparently feel that the CLC is so incapable of mobilizing its members behind the demands issued by its leadership that it can often be ignored. In contrast, the Royal Canadian Legion and the Canadian Chamber of Commerce are able to mobilize their members to inundate the authorities with demands for concerted action.

As in other aspects of politics, money is an important resource. In the case of pressure groups, money can buy staff, offices, organization, expertise, publicity, and other useful weapons with which to get the group's message across. The

Business Council on National Issues, the Canadian Alliance of Manufacturers and Exporters, and the Canadian Chamber of Commerce are all financially strong, giving them the capacity to both generate information to strengthen their case and transmit it to relevant targets. Except for those representing big business or highly paid professions, most groups have financial problems.

Information is a fourth crucial resource in pressure group politics. Especially at the bureaucratic level, where much of this politics takes place, any vital information that is lacking as the public service drafts technical laws and regulations will be eagerly accepted. Even at the political level, the group may be able to present data and alternative analyses of policy that will lead ministers to rethink their proposals. Closely associated with information is the professional expertise of the pressure group's staff, and in this connection, the large business groups are able to produce mounds of well-researched and glossy documents. The Canadian Bar Association makes frequent representations to parliamentary committees, royal commissions, and government departments, and because of its expertise both in the substance of many issues and in the drafting of legislation, it is often asked for advice.

The sympathy of the government and the popularity of the cause are also important. If a basic correspondence exists between the demands of the group and the government's stated objectives or the prevailing public opinion, the pressure group will have greater success than if there is a vast gap in ideological perspective between the group and the values of the government or society in general. It is not surprising, for example, that the CLC would be virtually ignored by the business-oriented Mulroney government. Similarly, the minister responsible for the Status of Women in that cabinet repeatedly refused to meet the National Action Committee on the Status of Women because of the group's intense criticism. The government even cut NAC's annual grant and gave the first federal grant to the small, rival, REAL Women (Realistic, Equal, Active for Life). A related point is the sharing of a professional orientation between group leaders and the bureaucracy. Many examples could be given of the success of a group because its officials shared the professional norms of the relevant public servants in their reciprocal relationship.

Since many pressure group demands relate to the spending of public money, the financial position of the government will often influence a group's success. In the prosperous and free-spending 1960s and 1970s, for example, requests for funds were more likely to be fulfilled than in the 1980s and 1990s, an era of government restraint.

Finally, a group will be more influential if it has no organized opposition. One of the reasons for the success of the Canadian Medical Association over the years, for example, was that it had medical politics almost all to itself.[12] Contrast that situation with the abortion issue, where for many years the two vehemently opposing sides were evenly divided.

....

Lobbying in Canada

The tendency of the rich and powerful, including big business, to benefit from pressure group politics and elite accommodation can only be enhanced by recent developments in the practice of lobbying in Canada. If lobbying is the activity of trying to influence the authorities, it is, of course, a perfectly legitimate activity for anyone to undertake in a democracy. Traditionally, individuals, companies, unions, and pressure groups of all kinds have done their own lobbying, but in recent years Canada has seen the mushrooming of professional lobbying—consultant or government relations firms that lobby on behalf of an individual, company, or pressure group in return for a fee.

Those engaged in the new lobbying industry justify their existence largely in terms of the increasing size and complexity of government. The federal government grew enormously in the 1960s and 1970s, and the policymaking process was restructured such that corporations and interest groups could no longer find their way around Ottawa. The early 1980s constituted a period in which new means of influence were being sought, and an expansion of such firms appeared to take place about the time the Mulroney government was elected in 1984. Many of the leading figures in the establishment of first wave of professional lobby firms were old cronies of the prime minister.

Given that the bureaucracy can satisfy many of the corporations' needs, ex-bureaucrats have also joined or formed lobbying firms in order to capitalize on their inside knowledge and connections. Federal conflict-of-interest guidelines preclude senior government employees from dealing with their former departments for one year after their departure from public employment, but these rules are sometimes broken.

The largest consultant lobbying firms and a sample of some of their principal clients are given in Table 10.2.

Registration of Lobbyists

After the emergence of such professional lobbying firms, a consensus developed among politicians that legislation, registration, and regulation were necessary. The registration idea was part of the Mulroney government's ethics package

TABLE 10.2 LARGEST CONSULTANT LOBBYING FIRMS AND A SAMPLE OF THEIR CLIENTS, 2001

Global Public Affairs Inc.: Sun Life, Irving, BP Amoco, Telemedia
Capital Hill Group: Canadian Tire, AOL Canada, Cineplex Odeon
Hill & Knowlton Canada Ltd.: Eurocopter, Amex, Bristol Myers, Monsanto
GPC Government Policy Consultants: Bombardier, Air Canada, Time Warner
Grey, Clark, Shih & Associates Ltd.: Magna, Maple Leaf, Camco, Hong Kong
SAMCI (S.A. Murray Consulting Inc.): Pepsi-Cola, Procter & Gamble, Visa
Earnscliffe Strategy Group: Microsoft, Canadian Pacific, Bombardier

Source: Prepared by author in May 2001 on the basis of the Public Registry available on the Industry Canada Web site http://strategis.ic.gc.ca/cgi-bin/sc_mrks/lobbyist/bin/lrs.e/lrsmain.phtml (Retrieved 15 May 2001). Reproduced with the permission of the Minister of Public Works and Government Services Canada, 2001.

unveiled after its early troubled record of cabinet resignations due to conflicts of interest and numerous legal charges against Tory backbenchers.[13] Parliament consequently passed the Lobbyists Registration Act in 1989. According to that act, a lobbyist is an individual

> *who, for payment, on behalf of any person or organization ... undertakes to arrange a meeting with a public office holder or to communicate with a public office holder in an attempt to influence*
>
> *(a) the development of a legislative proposal ...*
>
> *(b) the introduction, passage, defeat or amendment of any bill or resolution ...*
>
> *(c) the making or amending of any regulation ...*
>
> *(d) the development or amendment of any policy or program ...*
>
> *(e) the awarding of any monetary grant or contribution or other financial benefit ... or*
>
> *(f) the awarding of any contract.*

The law divided lobbyists into two categories: those who work for any client for a fee are classified as "Tier I" lobbyists, while "Tier II" lobbyists include those who engage in traditional pressure group or corporate lobbying—that is, in-house employees of an organization whose duties involve communicating with public officeholders on behalf of that organization.

The legislation acknowledged that lobbying public officeholders is a legitimate activity, but required lobbyists to register because it is desirable that officials and the public know who is attempting to influence government and because paid lobbyists should not impede free and open access to government. With certain exceptions, lobbyists had to file a return including the name and address of the lobbyist and the lobbying firm, the name and address of the client, and the subject matter of the solicitation.

Many critics felt that the 1989 legislation was very weak and contrasted it with the U.S. law on this subject adopted in 1946.[14] Some lobbyists did not register, and even when they did, the disclosure provisions in the Canadian law were minimal. The law did not even require revelation of the specific object of the representations; moreover, the act was almost totally lacking an effective enforcement mechanism.

The whole procedure provided a lucrative living to those who claimed to be intimates of ministers or ministries, and favoured those who could afford to hire such professional lobbyists. In what John Sawatski calls "one of the most odious lobby campaigns in the history of Canada," the fight of the Pharmaceutical Manufacturers Association to extend drug patent protection, "Gerry Doucet handled the PMAC file in GCI's [Government Consultants International's] office; his brother Fred handled the issue in the Prime Minister's Office."[15]

A Parliamentary committee reviewed the Lobbyists Registration Act in 1993 and made many recommendations to strengthen the act. Not surprisingly, the lobbyists lobbied ferociously against greater transparency in their operations, and the amendments that were finally adopted in 1995 were a pale imitation of what had been recommended by the committee and promised by the Liberals during the 1993 election campaign. The new act recognized three categories of lobbyists: Tier I (consultant lobbyists who lobby for clients) and two types of Tier II lobbyists, in-house lobbyists (corporate), and in-house lobbyists (organization)—that is, employees of corporations or interest group organizations for whom lobbying was a significant part of their duties. By December 2000, there were 765, 316, and 360 lobbyists respectively registered in the three categories.

As well, the new legislation required coalitions and grassroots lobbying to be registered, and was slightly more rigorous in what else had to be reported. The specific legislative proposal, bill, resolution, regulation, policy, program, or contract in question now has to be identified, along with the name of each department or other governmental institution lobbied. Contingency fees (fees based on the successfulness of the lobbying effort) are not outlawed, but any such fees must be disclosed to the registrar, as must the source and amount of any government funding of the client. As for enforcement, the registrar may audit information contained in any return or other document submitted and issue interpretation bulletins and advisory opinions. The six-month limitation of proceedings on contraventions was extended to two years. The ethics counsellor previously appointed by the Liberal government to administer the Conflict of Interest Code for cabinet ministers was required to work with interested parties to develop a code of conduct for lobbyists. The code came into effect in 1997, and lobbyists had a legal obligation to comply with it. The ethics counsellor was to investigate and publicly report on breaches of the code, and could report publicly the fees, disbursements, and expenses paid to a lobbyist relating to any lobbying activity. Unfortunately, this official reports only to the prime minister, rather than to Parliament. Perhaps the most positive aspect of the 1995 changes therefore was the electronic registration of required information and public accessibility to the registry through the Internet.

While this revised law was an improvement on the original, it remained highly defective. "By leaving vague the definitions of lobbying, and by excluding any lobbying associated with a consultative exercise, the government ... left much room for those sincerely wishing to avoid disclosing their activities or their aims to do so."[16] In other words, much lobbying is simply not recorded. The law did not require lobbyists to disclose positions currently or recently held in national political parties, ministers' offices, or the federal public service; it did not actually prohibit the use of contingency fees; and it did not require disclosure of the global cost of each lobbying campaign. At the same time, the industry was invaded by associates of the Liberal Party, such as defeated Cabinet Minister Douglas Young.

It was not until 1999 that the RCMP looked into its first potential violation of the act in connection with a Liberal activist close to the prime minister. This activist did not register as a lobbyist but allegedly met civil servants on behalf of a Shawinigan hotel owner who received a $100 000 government cheque to expand his operation. After their investigation, the RCMP found insufficient facts to support filing a criminal charge. Two later cases were reviewed by the Registrar of the Lobbyists Registration (LR) Branch, but not referred to the RCMP for further investigation.

The reports of the LR Branch are not particularly revealing, so it is fortunate that a private company, Advocacy Research Centre (ARC), fills the gap with a biweekly edition of the *Lobby Monitor*. This publication reveals the major lobbying efforts currently in progress, the techniques being used, and the people involved. Since the *Lobby Monitor* is an investigative effort that reveals much more than is required under the law, it helps the public to gain a better understanding of the lobbying process. The organization Democracy Watch also keeps its eye on the minimal efforts by the Ethics Commissioner to police the Lobbyists Registration Act.

DISCUSSION QUESTIONS

1. Why do business groups have more influence than other kinds of groups?
2. Would groups that lack close links with the authorities (the poor, Aboriginal peoples, etc.) be better advised to work through regular political channels or to opt for more confrontational tactics in order to try to influence public policy?
3. How democratic is the sort of lobbying that goes on around Parliament Hill, often behind closed doors? Does the Lobbyists Registration Act provide adequate transparency?

FURTHER READING

Ayers, Jeffrey M. *Defying Conventional Wisdom: Political Movements and Popular Contention against North American Free Trade*. Toronto: University of Toronto Press, 1998.

Coleman, William. *Business and Politics*. Montreal: McGill–Queen's University Press, 1988.

Coleman, William, and Grace Skogstad. *Policy Communities and Public Policy in Canada*. Mississauga: Copp Clark Pitman, 1990.

Pal, Leslie. *Interests of State: The Politics of Language, Multiculturalism, and Feminism in Canada*. Montreal: McGill–Queen's University Press, 1993.

Phillips, Susan. "Competing, Connecting, and Complementing: Parties, Interest Groups, and New Social Movements." In A. Brian Tanguay and Alain-G. Gagnon, eds. *Canadian Parties in Transition*. 2nd ed. Scarborough: Nelson Canada, 1996.

Pross, Paul. *Group Politics and Public Policy*, 2nd ed. Toronto: Oxford University Press, 1992.

Sawatsky, John. *The Insiders: Government, Business, and the Lobbyists*. Toronto: McClelland and Stewart, 1987.

The Lobby Monitor. Ottawa: ARC Publications, biweekly.

Notes

1. Paul Pross, *Group Politics and Public Policy* (Toronto: Oxford University Press, 1986).
2. Ibid., esp. ch. 11.
3. William D. Coleman, *Business and Politics: A Study of Collective Action* (Montreal: McGill–Queen's University Press, 1988); Stephen Brooks and Andrew Stritch, *Business and Government in Canada* (Scarborough: Prentice-Hall Canada, 1991), ch. 7; W.T. Stanbury, *Business–Government Relations in Canada* (Toronto: Methuen, 1986).

4. William D. Coleman, "One Step Ahead: Business in the Policy Process in Canada," in Mark Charlton and Paul Barker, eds., *Crosscurrents: Contemporary Political Issues*, 2nd ed. (Scarborough: Nelson Canada, 1994).

5. Paul Pross, *Group Politics and Public Policy*, ch. 5.

6. Susan Phillips, "Competing, Connecting, and Complementing: Parties, Interest Groups, and New Social Movements," in A. Brian Tanguay and Alain-G. Gagnon, eds., *Canadian Parties in Transition*, 2nd ed. (Scarborough: Nelson Canada, 1996).

7. Jeffrey M. Ayers, *Defying Conventional Wisdom: Political Movements and Popular Contention against North American Free Trade* (Toronto: University of Toronto Press, 1998).

8. Leslie Pal, *Interests of State: The Politics of Language, Multiculturalism, and Feminism in Canada* (Montreal: McGill–Queen's University Press, 1993).

9. Pross, *Group Politics and Public Policy*, ch. 6.

10. Robert Presthus, *Elite Accommodation in Canada* (Toronto: Macmillan, 1973). Presthus calls this phenomenon "elite accommodation."

11. Colin Campbell, *The Canadian Senate: A Lobby from Within* (Toronto: Methuen, 1983); John McMenemy, "The Senate as an Instrument of Business and Party," in Paul Fox and Graham White, eds., *Politics: Canada*, 7th ed. (Toronto: McGraw-Hill Ryerson, 1991).

12. Malcolm Taylor, "The Role of the Medical Profession in the Formulation of Public Policy," *Canadian Journal of Economics and Political Science* (February 1960): 108–27.

13. Ian Greene, "Conflict of Interest and the Canadian Constitution: An Analysis of Conflict of Interest Rules for Canadian Cabinet Ministers," *Canadian Journal of Political Science* (June 1990): 233–56.

14. Brooks and Stritch, *Business and Government in Canada*, 240; John Sawatsky, *The Insiders: Government, Business, and the Lobbyists* (Toronto: McClelland and Stewart, 1987), Epilogue.

15. Sawatsky, *The Insiders*, 315–16.

16. John A. Chenier, ed., *The Federal Lobbyists 1995* (Ottawa: ARC Publications, 1995), ii.

PART 3

The Constitutional Context

If "politics" and "government" can be separated, the first half of this text dealt with politics and the second half considers government. The second part is itself divided between the constitutional context and the process of governing. The Constitution forms the framework of the whole political system, and is analyzed in the following two chapters. Chapter 11 outlines the historical development of the Canadian Constitution, its ingredients and principles, and the addition of the Charter of Rights and Freedoms in 1982. Since one of the most important aspects of the Constitution is the relationship between the federal and provincial governments, Chapter 12 examines all aspects of Canadian federalism.

The Canadian Constitution and the Charter of Rights and Freedoms

This chapter begins with an overview of Canadian constitutional history and the road to Canadian Confederation. It then proceeds to examine the basic ingredients and principles of the Canadian Constitution. The final section of the chapter provides a more detailed treatment of the Charter of Rights and Freedoms, which was added to the Constitution in 1982.

Chapter Objectives

After you have completed this chapter, you should be able to:

Explain the main principles of the pre-Confederation Canadian constitutional documents

Enumerate the reasons for and outline the process leading toward Confederation

List the various ingredients of the Canadian Constitution

Recount the main provisions of the Constitution Act, 1982

Enumerate the six basic principles of the Canadian Constitution

Distinguish among various methods of protecting rights and freedoms

Enumerate the rights and freedoms included in the Charter and provide examples of prominent cases involving judicial interpretation of various clauses in the Charter

Discuss how the reasonable limits and notwithstanding clauses modify the guarantees of the Charter

Discuss how the Charter has judicialized politics and politicized the judiciary, and whether this is a positive change in the political system

Early Political Institutions

The territory that is now called Canada was first occupied by Aboriginal peoples. France and Britain colonized parts of this territory in the 1500s and 1600s, and periodically fought over them for nearly 200 years. After the 1759 Battle of the Plains of Abraham, part of the Seven Years' War between these traditional European rivals, the 1763 Treaty of Paris transferred Quebec, Prince Edward Island, Cape Breton, and New Brunswick to British control. Interaction between the new British power and the Aboriginal peoples is discussed in Chapter 4.

The **Royal Proclamation of 1763,** the first distinctively Canadian constitutional document, created the colony of Quebec.[1] Apart from Aboriginal peoples, Quebec at the time was largely made up of French-speaking farmers, clergy, and seigneurs. The British-appointed government was English-speaking, and the nonagricultural economy increasingly came under British control. On the other hand, British governors resisted the idea of imposing the English language and Protestant religion on such a homogeneous French-Catholic population.

In 1774, the **Quebec Act** provided for a new set of government institutions. The governor appointed a council to advise him, but there would be no elected assembly in the colony. Roman Catholics were allowed freedom of religion and could be appointed to the council, and the colony combined British criminal law with French civil law. Meanwhile, the first elected assembly in the "Canadian" part of British North America had been summoned in Nova Scotia in 1758, followed by Prince Edward Island in 1773.

When the residents of the 13 "American" colonies revolted against British rule in 1776, French Canadians essentially remained neutral. Thousands of ex-Americans loyal to Britain—the United Empire Loyalists—migrated to "Canada." This influx led to the severing of New Brunswick from Nova Scotia in 1784, together with the creation of its own assembly, since the Loyalists were accustomed to operating with such elected offices. Then, in response to pressure from those Loyalists who migrated to what is modern-day Ontario, as well as to reward the loyalty of the French in Quebec, Britain passed the **Constitutional Act of 1791.** It divided the colony into two—Upper and Lower Canada—each with a governor, an appointed executive council, an appointed legislative council, and a locally elected assembly. In Upper Canada (Ontario), almost exclusively English, the Constitutional Act provided for British civil law. The executive council gradually evolved into the cabinet, while the legislative council was the forerunner of the Senate. Thus, by 1791, all the colonies had achieved **representative government,** that is, a set of political institutions including an elected legislative assembly.

Figure 11.1   Evolution of Canadian Pre-Confederation Political Institutions

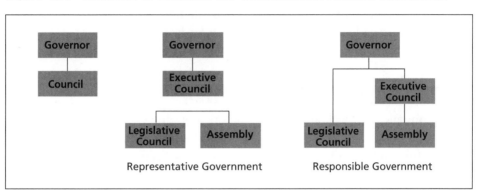

Discord subsequently developed between the local assembly and the executive, composed of the governor and his appointed executive council. The elected assembly represented the people and could articulate their views, but had no real power over the appointed councils. This situation was complicated by the cultural division in Lower Canada—a French assembly and an English executive—with "two nations warring in the bosom of a single state."[2] Reformers demanded **responsible government,** in which the members of the executive council would come from and reflect the views of the elected assembly. This problem eventually erupted into the Rebellions of 1837 in both Upper and Lower Canada, led by William Lyon Mackenzie and Louis-Joseph Papineau respectively. The British government put them down by force and then appointed Lord Durham to investigate the situation.

The 1839 **Durham Report** recommended that the principle of responsible government be implemented, so that the executive branch would govern only as long as it retained the confidence of the assembly. Durham outlined a division of powers between local and imperial authorities such that in local matters the governor would follow the advice of colonial authorities, but in matters of imperial concern he would act as an agent of the British government. Overcoming British resistance, responsible government was adopted in Nova Scotia, New Brunswick, and the colony of Canada in 1848, and three years later in Prince Edward Island. Thus, by 1851, all the pre-Confederation colonies operated on the basis that the cabinet or executive council had to resign if it lost the confidence of the elected legislative assembly.

Durham also recommended that Upper and Lower Canada be united into a single colony of Canada, partly as one last attempt to submerge and assimilate the

French. The colonies were amalgamated by the 1840 **Act of Union,** but when it became clear that this assimilation would not be achieved, French was recognized as the second official language of the legislature. Moreover, most governments of the period had joint English and French leaders.

....

The Road to Confederation

Economic, political, and military factors soon drove the British North American colonies to consider uniting.[3] Because the British had discontinued colonial trading preferences, and because a reciprocity treaty with the United States had expired, the colonies hoped to establish a new, free trade area among themselves. This large internal market would be enhanced by a railway link between the Maritimes and central Canada, also providing the latter with a winter Atlantic port. The future prospect of annexing and developing the West was seen as a further source of economic prosperity.

Meanwhile, the colony of Canada had experienced political deadlock between its two parts, then called Canada East (Quebec) and Canada West (Ontario), as well as between French and English component groups. Public decisions had to be made in one combined set of governmental institutions, yet the needs and demands of the two parts were often quite different. This led to the practice of requiring a "double majority" (a majority of members from each part of the colony) for the passage of bills. Confederation would grant greater autonomy to the two parts because provincial governments would handle distinctive internal matters on their own, while a central government would deal with common problems. Such a two-tier structure also appealed to the Maritime provinces, which did not wish to turn all decisions over to a distant central government.

The individual colonies also felt vulnerable in a military sense. The United States had a powerful army on their doorstep, and the British government no longer seemed interested in providing military protection. By joining together, the colonies would make American aggression more difficult.

In the 1860s, Nova Scotia, New Brunswick, and Prince Edward Island began to consider forming a Maritime union, and called the Charlottetown Conference of 1864 for this purpose. When delegates from the colony of Canada arrived, however, the idea of a larger union was put up for debate. The essentials of the **Confederation** scheme were agreed upon at the Quebec Conference later that year, and the London Conference of 1866 fine-tuned the agreement, leaving Prince Edward Island temporarily on the sidelines. Thus, the four provinces of Nova Scotia, New Brunswick,

Quebec, and Ontario were officially united on July 1, 1867, by the **British North America Act,** later renamed the **Constitution Act, 1867.**

....

Components and Principles of the Canadian Constitution

The Canadian Constitution would be easier to comprehend if it consisted of a single piece of paper by that name. In the absence of such a document, we can define a **constitution** as the whole body of fundamental rules and principles according to which a state is governed. Canada's Constitution provides for the basic institutions of government and relations between them, relations between national and provincial governments, and relations between governments and citizens.[4] Such a comprehensive definition suggests that the final product may not be neat and tidy, and that some of it may not be written down at all.

In the search for the components that fit the definition of a constitution provided above, it will be seen that the Canadian Constitution is a great hodge-podge. It essentially consists of the following:

- Constitution Act, 1867, and its amendments
- British and Canadian statutes
- Constitution Act, 1982, principally the Charter of Rights and Freedoms
- judicial decisions
- constitutional conventions

The Constitution Act, 1867, and its Amendments

We turn first to the formal, legal documents, the most important of which is the Constitution Act, 1867, as mentioned above. That act provided much of the basic machinery and institutions of government and established a federal system.

Part III of the act deals with the executive power, for example, and section 9 declares that the executive authority over Canada is vested in the Queen. Subsequent clauses refer to the governor general and to the Canadian **Privy Council,** which is "to aid and advise in the Government of Canada." Section 13 observes that the "governor general in council" refers to the governor general acting by and with the advice of the Canadian Privy Council. Note that the prime minister and cabinet are not explicitly mentioned.

Part IV establishes the legislative power—the Senate and House of Commons. The act requires that money bills (bills that involve the raising or spending of money) originate in the House of Commons, and within it, from members of the executive branch.

Part V concerns provincial constitutions, including the position of lieutenant governor. Since the 1867 act created the provinces of Ontario and Quebec, it had to establish their legislatures, whereas the legislatures of Nova Scotia and New Brunswick continued in their pre-Confederation form.

Part VI, the "Distribution of Legislative Powers" or **division of powers** between the central and provincial governments, is probably the most important part of the document. The core of Canadian **federalism** in a constitutional sense consists of section 91, the federal powers; section 92, provincial powers; section 93, education; and section 95, concurrent powers.

Part VII is concerned with the judiciary. It is a short section that gives the governor general the power to appoint superior, district, and county judges. It also provides for judges' retirement and removal, and allows Parliament to set up a general court of appeal. Note that the 1867 act does not explicitly establish the Supreme Court of Canada.

Part VIII deals with the division of provincial revenues, debts, and assets at the time of Confederation. It makes clear that the provinces have possession of their own lands, mines, and minerals. Part IX is a miscellaneous collection, including section 132, the treaty power, and section 133, regarding English and French languages. The final section provides for the admission of other colonies.

The Constitution Act, 1867, was thus very brief on the executive and judicial branches of government, and included virtually nothing about limiting the powers of government in relation to the people. The act also lacked any mention of the means to amend it, but since it was a statute of the British Parliament, most formal changes to the act until 1982 were made by that Parliament at Canadian request.

Such formal amendments to the 1867 act are also part of the Canadian Constitution, some more important than others. They were often termed "British North America Acts," of whatever year in which they were passed, but in 1982, they were mostly renamed "Constitution Acts" of the appropriate year. For example, the BNA Act, 1940, which is now called the Constitution Act, 1940, transferred jurisdiction over unemployment insurance from the provincial to the federal level of government.

British and Canadian Statutes

The second major component of the Canadian Constitution is a collection of British statutes and orders-in-council, and Canadian statutes. Chief among acts passed by the British Parliament that are of constitutional status for Canada is the **Statute of Westminster, 1931**, which declared Canada to be totally independent of Britain. Henceforth, no British law would apply to Canada unless (as in the case of constitutional amendments) Canada requested it. The Northwest Territories, British Columbia, and Prince Edward Island were British colonies added to Canada by means of British orders-in-council, that is, decisions of the British cabinet as distinct from acts of Parliament. Therefore, they must be considered another ingredient of the Canadian Constitution.

So are the Canadian statutes that carved provinces out of the Northwest Territories, the Manitoba Act of 1870, and the Saskatchewan and Alberta Acts of 1905. Other Canadian statutes of constitutional significance include the Supreme Court Act, an ordinary law that fleshes out the provisions of the 1867 act with respect to the judicial branch of government, the Federal Court Act, the Parliament of Canada Act, the Bill of Rights, the Canada Elections Act, the Citizenship Act, the Emergencies Act, the Canadian Human Rights Act, the Yukon Act, and the Nunavut Act.

The Constitution Act, 1982

Although the **Constitution Act, 1982,** was in a sense the last amendment to be passed by the British Parliament to the Constitution Act, 1867, it is worthy of separate mention. Although Canada was completely self-governing after 1931, most amendments to the 1867 act still had to be made by the British Parliament, because no formula had been developed to do so in Canada. The Constitution Act, 1982, contained such a domestic constitutional amending formula, and the Canada Act passed by the British Parliament at the same time finally terminated all British authority over Canada. Part V of the act provided five different amending formulas, depending on the subject matter of the amendment:

- unanimous consent of federal and provincial legislatures
- consent of Parliament and seven provincial legislatures representing at least 50 percent of the population
- consent of Parliament and one or more provinces affected
- consent of Parliament alone
- consent of a provincial legislature alone

The second main aspect of the Constitution Act, 1982, was to add the **Charter of Rights and Freedoms** to the Canadian Constitution (discussed in detail later in the chapter). The 1982 act also contained statements on Aboriginal peoples' rights and equalization payments to have-not provinces. As far as the division of powers was concerned, a new section 92A was added to clarify and extend provincial powers over natural resources. The 1982 document did not alter the position of the monarchy in Canada, however; Elizabeth II continues to be recognized as Queen of Canada, having no connection to the British government in this role.

Judicial Decisions

The fourth ingredient of the Canadian Constitution consists of judicial decisions that have clarified or altered provisions of the 1867 act or other parts of the Constitution. The largest body of such decisions are the judgments of the British **Judicial Committee of the Privy Council,** Canada's final court of appeal until 1949. It was John A. Macdonald's intention to create a strong central government, but the Judicial Committee interpreted the 1867 act in such a way as to minimize federal powers and maximize those of the provinces. The court decisions that effected such a wholesale transformation of the federal nature of the country must be considered a part of the Constitution alongside the actual provisions of the original act. The very power of the courts to invalidate legislation in this manner—**judicial review**—is a basic principle of the Constitution.

Constitutional Conventions

Thus far, all the ingredients listed can be found in written form, although not in one place. The final component of the Constitution, on the other hand, has never been committed to paper. It consists of **constitutional conventions,** that is, unwritten rules of constitutional behaviour that are considered to be binding by and upon those who operate the Constitution, but that are not enforceable by the courts.[5] Conventions develop from traditions, and through constant recognition and observance become as established, rigid, and sacrosanct as if they were written down. Many of these informal rules have been inherited from Britain, some have been modified in the Canadian environment, and others are unique to Canada. Many relate to the executive branch of government, given such slight attention in the 1867 act. The dominant position of the prime minister and cabinet, the subordinate place of the governor general, and the principle of responsible government are three of many conventions that are part of the Constitution.

Principles of the Constitution

The preceding discussion has identified three basic principles of the Canadian Constitution: responsible government, federalism, and judicial review. At least three other fundamental principles are also embedded in the Canadian Constitution: constitutional monarchy, the rule of law, and democracy.[6]

In terms of its head of state, Canada is a **constitutional monarchy.** This is not a principle that attracts much attention, largely because the monarch herself lives in another country and because her actual power, as well as that of her Canadian representative, the governor general, is not extensive. Nevertheless, the monarchical system underlies a great deal of the operation of government in Canada, largely in the form of the Crown, as discussed in Chapter 13.

The **rule of law** is another constitutional principle inherited from Great Britain that rests largely on convention and judicial precedent. In essence, it means that all government action must be based on law and that governments and government officials must obey the law. In other words, the law is supreme, and no one, including the lawmakers, is above it. Courts in Canada as well as in Britain have had occasion to overturn government decisions and actions that were not based on law. Democracy was analyzed fully in Chapter 6.

....

The Charter of Rights and Freedoms

In the eyes of some observers, the pre-1982 Canadian Constitution was deficient in lacking a statement of **civil liberties,** that is, the rights and freedoms that individuals enjoy beyond the reach of the government or the state. Such rights and freedoms are an integral part of a democratic political system and represent territory into which the government is not allowed to enter. In typical British manner, however, the fact that they were not written down did not mean that they did not exist.

Political systems that value civil liberties have adopted two principal methods to protect them. The British approach is to make Parliament supreme, but on the presumption that neither the legislature nor the executive would infringe such rights and freedoms because both branches of government are held in check by public opinion, tradition, the political culture, and self-restraint. Civil liberties are so deeply ingrained in the values of the people and politicians alike that they do not need to be written down, and the authorities would never think of infringing them—even though, in theory, Parliament could do so. While the courts cannot overturn legislation in Britain—that is, they do not have the power of judicial review—they have wide **judicial discretion** in the interpretation of laws, and many safeguards of civil liberties have been introduced into the law as canons of interpretation. Thus, even in the British system, judicial precedents accumulated into the **common law** offer some protection against arbitrary government action. So does the basic constitutional principle, the rule of law.

The American approach, derived in reaction to an imperial government that did encroach upon colonial liberties, is to provide for a written statement of civil rights in the constitutional Bill of Rights. Then, if legislation is passed or the executive takes action that is felt to violate a person's rights, such acts can be challenged in the courts. It is up to the courts to determine whether the government has infringed rights and freedoms as defined in the Constitution. The courts thus have the power of judicial review, and can overturn offensive legislation or executive acts.

In Canada, federal and provincial politicians occasionally violated civil liberties, such as in the case of the Quebec Padlock Law and the Alberta Press Bill, which blatantly interfered with such freedoms as speech, press, and assembly. Such actions persuaded Prime Minister Diefenbaker to enact the **Canadian Bill of Rights** in 1960. The bill's apparent aim was to allow the courts to invalidate legislation that they found to conflict with the Bill of Rights, but this aim was not clearly articulated. Other serious gaps in the bill were that it applied only to the federal government, not to the provinces; that it allowed legislation to be passed that overrode the bill, as long as this was acknowledged (that is, a notwithstanding clause); that as an ordinary piece of legislation, the bill could be amended in the routine way; and that it was superseded by the War Measures Act, at the very time when it might be needed most.

Not surprisingly, the courts made very limited use of the Bill of Rights. In only one case, the *Drybones* case of 1970, did they decide that a clause of an act violated the Bill of Rights and was therefore inoperative. The bill was more useful in clarifying legal rights and was referred to in several cases to fill in gaps in such definitions as what was meant by the "right to counsel," the "right to an interpreter," and the "right to a fair hearing."

Prime Minister Trudeau recognized the limitations and ambiguities of the Canadian Bill of Rights and wanted to incorporate new kinds of rights into the Constitution. Finally, in 1982, with the adoption of the Charter of Rights and Freedoms, he accomplished his objective. The Charter was entrenched in the Constitution, and it is increasingly the task of the judiciary to determine if and when governments have encroached upon the following rights and freedoms:

- fundamental freedoms
- democratic rights
- mobility rights
- legal rights
- Aboriginal rights
- equality rights

- language rights
- minority language education rights

Trudeau not only wanted to remedy the deficiencies in the Bill of Rights but was also determined to protect official minority language rights across the country in an effort to undercut Quebec's claim that it alone represented French Canada. Moreover, Trudeau hoped to counter centrifugal forces throughout the land and pressures for decentralization to the provinces by creating an instrument that the courts could use to cut down self-serving provincial laws. As a new national symbol, the Charter would also serve to increase the allegiance of all citizens to the national government.

The Charter is generally a much stronger document than its predecessor. Besides being broader in scope, the Charter applies equally to both federal and provincial governments, and being entrenched into the Constitution, it is difficult to amend. It also states very clearly that the courts are to invalidate any legislation that they find to conflict with the provisions of the Charter. We will briefly examine the provisions of the Charter and note some of the prominent court decisions it has inspired.

Guaranteed Rights and Freedoms

It must first be said that the rights articulated in the Charter are not absolute. Section 1 indicates that these rights are subject to "such reasonable limits, defined by law, as can be demonstrably justified in a free and democratic society." The courts are thus allowed to find that, while a piece of legislation violates certain rights, it is still acceptable according to their definition of **reasonable limits.** In fact, the Supreme Court has made extensive use of section 1, upholding many laws that it considered to be in violation of Charter rights but that were saved by having reasonable limits upon them.

FUNDAMENTAL FREEDOMS

At least from a political point of view, section 2 of the Charter is probably most important. It lists the following **fundamental freedoms**: freedom of conscience and religion; freedom of thought, belief, opinion and expression, including freedom of the press and other media of communication; freedom of peaceful assembly; and freedom of association.

With respect to freedom of religion, in an Alberta case, the Supreme Court threw out the Lord's Day Act as an infringement of freedom of religion because its restrictions on Sunday activities were clearly related to the Christian sabbath and discriminated against other religions. On the other hand, the Court upheld Ontario's Retail Business Holidays Act, an act designed to limit Sunday shopping and preserve Sunday as a day of rest on a secular rather than a religious foundation. The Court also decided that public schools may no longer hold a compulsory and exclusively Christian school prayer. While Ontario's publicly funded Roman Catholic separate school system was upheld as a pre-Charter constitutional right, public funding for other private religious schools is not guaranteed.

Freedom of expression has brought a wide range of issues before the courts. Perhaps most controversial was the Supreme Court's rejection of the French-only sign provision of Quebec's Bill 101, which also violated Quebec's own Charter of Rights. The Court decided that freedom of expression not only included the freedom to express ideas but also the freedom to choose the language in which to express them. Moreover, the concept of freedom of expression incorporated "commercial expression," such as a company's right to erect a sign or engage in advertising. Thus, the federal government's first attempt at prohibiting tobacco advertising was also deemed a violation of tobacco companies' freedom of expression. But a majority of the Court concluded that a partial ban on such advertising as well as prohibiting the dissemination of hate literature were both acceptable as reasonable limits on freedom of expression.

Obscenity also falls into the category of freedom of expression. In the *Butler* case, the Court divided pornography into different categories, saying that portrayal of sex with violence and sex that is degrading or dehumanizing can be restricted by the authorities, but that portrayals of explicit sex that is neither violent nor degrading is generally acceptable unless children are involved. In later cases, an artist's depiction of children in various sexual activities was deemed to be art rather than pornography, and customs officers were instructed not to differentiate in the standards they applied to homosexual and heterosexual materials. In the 2001 *Sharpe* case, the Supreme Court unanimously upheld the provisions of the Criminal Code that prohibit the possession of child pornography as a reasonable limit on freedom of expression. As for prostitution, the Court similarly upheld the prohibition on communicating for the purposes of sidewalk solicitation.

Freedom of expression and freedom of the press in connection with election campaigns have also fostered several constitutional cases. The Supreme Court decided that the blackout period before election day in which newspapers could not publish public opinion polls was too long, and as mentioned in Chapter 8, repeated efforts by Parliament to restrict "third-party" advertising during election campaigns were thwarted by the lower courts in Alberta, at least prior to 2000.[7]

Case Study

The Supreme Court and Parliament of Canada Tangle over Tobacco Advertising

After ad hoc earlier initiatives at restricting tobacco advertising in Canada, Parliament finally prohibited cigarette advertising by means of the Tobacco Products Control Act of 1988. The two largest tobacco companies in Canada, RJR MacDonald and Imperial Tobacco immediately challenged the legislation in the courts as an infringement of their freedom of expression, and the case was decided by the Supreme Court of Canada in September 1995. Everyone agreed that the legislation did violate the companies' freedom of expression, and by this time the Court had extended such Charter rights beyond individuals to corporations. The only question was whether it was a reasonable limit on the companies' freedom. The Court was seriously divided on the issue, but a 5 to 4 majority ruled that this was not a reasonable limit because the prohibition was too comprehensive—it impaired the right too much. The Court added, however, that some lesser measure—a partial prohibition—would be acceptable. Although Parliament could have used the notwithstanding clause to circumvent the Court decision, it chose to bring in a new law that would meet the views of the majority of the Court. Thus, in April 1997, Parliament repealed all previous legislation on this subject and passed the Tobacco Act, which permitted certain kinds of tobacco advertising directed at adults only. Regulations under the act banned all tobacco company sponsorships by 2003. Needless to say, tobacco companies have tried to overturn this act, too, as well as the new warnings required on cigarette packages.

In another controversial decision (with two prominent members dissenting), the Supreme Court ruled that freedom of association does not guarantee the right of trade unions to strike. In other words, freedom of association does not prevent federal or provincial legislatures from passing back-to-work legislation or otherwise interfering in the collective bargaining process.

DEMOCRATIC AND MOBILITY RIGHTS

Under **democratic rights** in sections 3 to 5, the Charter guarantees that every citizen of Canada has the right to vote in federal and provincial elections; that no

Parliament can continue for more than five years, except in time of real or appre-hended war, invasion, or insurrection; and that Parliament must sit at least once every year. Section 3 has been used in several cases dealing with federal and provincial electoral laws that denied the vote to certain categories of people. One of the few restrictions left standing in federal elections relates to prisoners serving jail terms of two years or more. Rather unexpectedly, the democratic rights sec-tion has also been used to assess the validity of electoral maps that determine the size of constituencies.

Under section 6, **mobility rights,** every citizen of Canada has the right to enter, remain in, and leave Canada, and every citizen or permanent resident has the right to take up residence and pursue a livelihood in any province. On the other hand, laws establishing reasonable residency requirements for receiving public services are acceptable, as is giving preference to local residents if the unem-ployment rate in that province is higher than the national rate. Trudeau included mobility rights because of his concern that some provinces were restricting the entry of residents of other provinces, as in the case of cross-border employment, but these clauses have not featured frequently in judicial interpretation.

Legal Rights

Legal rights are contained in sections 7 to 14. In section 7, everyone has the right to life, liberty, and security of the person and the right not to be deprived thereof except in accordance with the principles of fundamental justice. "Security of the person" was used to invalidate the abortion provision of the Criminal Code in the famous *Morgentaler* case in 1988. A majority of the Court ruled that the law, with all its arbitrary and bureaucratic procedures, violated the security of the person of the woman concerned and constituted a "profound interference with a woman's body." Sue Rodriguez, dying of Lou Gehrig's disease, was not so fortunate in arguing that security of the person provided her with the right to assisted sui-cide—only a minority of judges agreed with her.

In the *Singh* case, "security of the person" required that the Immigration Department provide an oral hearing for refugee claimants when their lives could be in danger if deported. "Fundamental justice" also necessitated giving such claimants an opportunity to state their case and to know the case against them. In cases of sexual assault, the Supreme Court has grappled with the right of the accused to use evidence about the victim's previous sexual activity against the right of the victim not to be unnecessarily hounded on the subject on the witness stand. To some extent, the result of several such cases was to tighten up the con-cept of consent in sexual matters: "no means no."

Steve Nease (*Oakville Beaver*). Reproduced with permission.

Section 8 establishes the right to be secure against unreasonable search and seizure. In dismissing the charge of collusion between the Southam and Thomson newspaper chains, the Court extended this right to corporations and decided that the search of their offices by anticombines officials had indeed been unreasonable. The Court has also used this section in cases involving police officers making spot checks, taking blood samples, or entering houses; strip searches by customs officers at border points; and guards frisking prisoners.

Section 9 grants the right not to be arbitrarily detained or imprisoned, and section 10 reads that on arrest or detention, everyone has the right to be informed promptly of the reasons therefor, and the right to contact a lawyer without delay and to be informed of that right. The Court has ruled that random police spot checks are a reasonable limit on the right not to be arbitrarily detained, and that roadside breath tests do not include the right to retain counsel. However, a person who fails that test and is asked to accompany the police officer to a police station has a right to retain counsel before the breathalyzer test is conducted there. Moreover, the Court has ruled that a person has the right to be told of his or her right not only to a lawyer but also to legal aid, and must have a reasonable opportunity to exercise these rights.

Section 11 includes a variety of rights available to a person charged with an offence. "To be tried within a reasonable time" has been extremely controversial after the *Askov* decision found that a delay of almost two years between a preliminary hearing and a trial had been excessive. The lower courts took this to mean that everyone had a right to a trial within six to eight months of being charged, and some 34 500 cases were thrown out in Ontario alone. Persons charged cannot be compelled to testify against themselves, cannot be denied reasonable bail without just cause, and are presumed innocent until proven guilty according to law in a fair and public hearing by an independent and impartial tribunal. The presumption of innocence was addressed in the *Oakes* case. Under the "reverse onus" clause of the Narcotics Control Act, a person proven to be in possession of a narcotic was also presumed to be guilty of trafficking, and it was up to the person charged with possession to prove his or her innocence on the trafficking charge. The *Oakes* case invalidated this clause as an unreasonable limit on the presumption of innocence. Persons charged with an offence are guaranteed a trial by jury where the maximum punishment for the offence is imprisonment for five years or more, and, whether finally acquitted or found guilty and punished, they cannot be tried for the offence again.

Everyone has the right not to be subjected to any cruel and unusual treatment or punishment. In the 2001 Latimer case, the Supreme Court rejected the claim that the minimum mandatory sentence of 10 years in jail constituted cruel and unusual punishment in the case of a father who took the life of his severely disabled daughter because he could not bear to see her in such pain. A party or witness in any proceedings who does not understand or speak the language in which the proceedings are conducted or who is deaf has the right to the assistance of an interpreter.

EQUALITY RIGHTS

Equality rights are contained in section 15, which reads as follows:

> *Every individual is equal before and under the law and has the right to the equal protection and equal benefit of the law without discrimination and, in particular, without discrimination based on race, national or ethnic origin, colour, religion, sex, age or mental or physical disability.*

In the *Andrews* case, the Supreme Court laid down a two-step process for interpreting equality rights. The Court first determines if there has been a violation of the equality rights listed in section 15 (or of others analogous to them), and then whether there has been a harmful or prejudicial effect. In other words, inequalities and distinctions are permitted if no negative discrimination is involved. According to Ian Greene, the Court made it clear that "it intends to interpret section 15 to help clearly disadvantaged groups in society."[8] Moreover, the second part of the section permits **affirmative action** programs that give preference to those who have been discriminated against in the past. Equality rights are, of course, subject to reasonable limits, and on this basis the Supreme Court has allowed several kinds of discrimination to continue. In the case of mandatory retirement at age 65, for example, the Court ruled such laws and policies were a violation of equality rights and did involve discrimination, but could be allowed as reasonable limits.

Perhaps the most innovative use of section 15 has been in connection with sexual orientation and same-sex rights. In 1995, the Supreme Court ruled unanimously that the Charter prohibited discrimination on the basis of sexual orientation, even though this was not explicitly listed in section 15. After "reading in" this addition to the list in section 15, the Court made the same order with respect to the Individual Rights Protection Act in Alberta. Then, in 1999, the Court moved on to same-sex partnerships, finding that in most situations, laws could not discriminate between same-sex and opposite-sex couples.[9]

LANGUAGE RIGHTS

Sections 16 to 22 of the Charter constitutionalize the federal and New Brunswick Official Languages acts. These sections guarantee that certain government agencies will operate on a bilingual basis, as discussed in Chapter 3. Section 23 constitutionalizes **minority language education rights,** and some would argue that this was the only part of the Charter with which Pierre Trudeau was truly concerned. The clause guarantees such access to Canadian citizens who constitute English- and French-language minorities in all provinces in areas "where numbers warrant." The Supreme Court can decide when the number of francophone students warrants a French-language school, and it has also ruled that such a school must have a "distinct physical setting" and that French-language parents must have a say in the "management and control" of it. The Supreme Court struck down the provision in Quebec's Bill 101 that limited access to the English school system in Quebec to the children of parents who were themselves products of that system (the "Quebec clause"). Indeed, section 23 (the "Canada clause") was deliberately drafted so that it would conflict with Bill 101, in order that Canadian citizens who moved to Quebec could also send their children to the English schools.

OTHER PROVISIONS

Section 24 makes clear, where the Bill of Rights did not, that the courts have the power to interpret the Charter and to invalidate laws that conflict with it. The

Pierre Elliott Trudeau, Father of the Charter of Rights and Freedoms (Photographer unknown/Canapress)

Charter does not actually bar illegally obtained evidence, as in the United States; the admission of such evidence is acceptable as long as it does not bring the administration of justice into disrepute.

Sections 25 through 30 relate to specific groups in society. Section 25 reads that the rights and freedoms in the Charter shall not be construed so as to abrogate or derogate from any Aboriginal, treaty, or other rights or freedoms that pertain to the Aboriginal peoples of Canada, including any rights or freedoms that have been recognized by the Royal Proclamation of 1763 and any others that may be acquired by the Aboriginal peoples of Canada by way of land claims settlements.

Section 27 asserts that the Charter shall be interpreted in a manner consistent with the preservation and enhancement of the multicultural heritage of Canadians, and section 28 ensures that notwithstanding anything in the Charter, the rights and freedoms referred to in it are guaranteed equally to male and female persons. The women's movement considered the addition of section 28 to be essential in order that governments would not be able to use the notwithstanding clause (section 33) to override the gender-equality provision of section 15. According to section 29, nothing in the Charter abrogates or derogates from any rights or privileges guaranteed by or under the Constitution of Canada in respect of denominational schools. This section thus protects section 93 of the 1867 Constitution Act, which guaranteed existing Protestant and Roman Catholic separate schools.

Section 32 clarifies that the Charter applies to the Parliament and government of Canada, to the legislature and government of each province, and to the northern territories. By implication, it also applies to the municipal level of government. Thus all legislation in Canada must be consistent with the Charter, as must all actions of government executives, including ministers, public servants, and police officers. The Charter is not intended to apply to the private sector, but certain institutions occupy an ambiguous position. The Charter has been applied to community colleges, for example, but more autonomous semi-public institutions such as hospitals and universities are exempt. Federal and provincial human rights codes are intended to prevent discrimination in the private sector, but since such codes take the form of laws, they must also remain consistent with the Charter.

Limitations on Rights and Freedoms

As mentioned above, the "reasonable limits" clause in section 1 allows the courts to exempt certain laws from the application of the Charter. In order to decide which restrictions can be "demonstrably justified in a free and democratic society," the Court developed guidelines in the *Oakes* case that have come to be called the **Oakes test.** The objective of the government in limiting a Charter right must be pressing and substantial, and the means adopted must be proportional to that objective. The means must be rationally connected to the objective and must impair the right as little as possible, while the benefits of the restriction must exceed its costs.

The second limitation on Charter rights revolves around the **notwithstanding clause** in section 33. In the areas of fundamental freedoms, legal rights, and equality rights, either level of government is allowed to pass legislation contrary to the Charter. On the other hand, the legislation cannot be used to circumvent democratic rights, mobility rights, or linguistic rights. The notwithstanding clause would normally come into play when legislation was introduced to override a judicial decision regarding a Charter right. Such a bill can be exempted from the provisions of the Charter only for a five-year period, however, after which it becomes inoperative if not passed once again for another five years.

Despite the number of times the Supreme Court has invalidated federal or provincial legislation since 1982, governments have rarely re-enacted such provisions under section 33. Over the first 15 years, it was used only in Saskatchewan and Quebec. The government of Grant Devine used section 33 (unnecessarily, as it turned out) to pass back-to-work legislation to end a public-service strike in 1986. The first Parti Québécois government in Quebec (1976–85) routinely applied the notwithstanding clause, as a matter of principle, to all new legislation. The next Liberal government discontinued that practice, but when the Supreme Court ruled that French-only store signs violated their owners' freedom of expression, Premier Bourassa invoked section 33 (and the equivalent clause in the Quebec Charter of Rights) and then passed what he considered to be a compromise law that allowed certain bilingual signs inside the store. While this incident in particular gave the notwithstanding clause a negative reception in most of English Canada, section 33 is often defended as a general principle. It allows democratically elected legislators, if they choose, to have the final say in many areas.

Although they have not yet used the notwithstanding clause, Alberta politicians have occasionally threatened to invoke it. That province probably contains the leading critics of judicial activism in the defence of minority rights,[10] and federal members of the Alberta-based Reform/Canadian Alliance have also advocated the use of section 33 on occasion.

Implications of the Charter for the Political System

The Charter of Rights and Freedoms has attracted both passionate support and opposition. Supporters and opponents alike agree, however, that the adoption of the Charter has significantly changed the operation of the Canadian political system. The courts have become involved in almost all of the most difficult political issues that have arisen over the past 20 years: Aboriginal peoples' rights, abortion, assisted suicide, child pornography, euthanasia, French-only signs, gender equality, impaired driving, mandatory retirement, minority language schools, official bilingualism, political rights of public servants, pornography, prostitution, redistribution of constituency boundaries, the right to strike, same-sex spousal benefits, separate schools, sexual assault, sexual orientation, Sunday shopping, testing the Cruise missile, and tobacco advertising. Such cases have enmeshed the courts in considerable political controversy and, as Peter Russell says, the Charter has "judicialized politics and politicized the judiciary."[11]

While most Canadians seem pleased with this development (some of them ignorant of the fact that most rights and freedoms were equally enjoyed before 1982), a minority have made scathing attacks on the "legalization of politics" in Canada. Michael Mandel, for example, argues that the courts make highly political decisions, but judges disguise this fact through legal interpretations and abstract principles that are unintelligible to the general public. Mandel challenges the generally accepted view that politicians make decisions that are popular, political, and self-serving, while judges' decisions are impartial, objective, technical, rational, and in the public interest. Their invocation of the reasonable limits clause, for example, has been highly discretionary.[12]

Mandel's second argument is that while the Charter has been sold as enhancing democracy and the power of the people, it has really reduced the degree of popular control over government. It has transferred power from representative, accountable legislatures and politicians to unrepresentative, unaccountable, and unrestrained judges, courts, and an elitist legal profession.

Third, legalized politics enhances individual and corporate rights against the collective welfare of the community. The adoption of individualistic American values in the Charter, as opposed to traditional Canadian collectivism, is strengthened by the tendency of the courts to cite American precedents when making their decisions.

Mandel's fourth point is that legalized politics is conservative, class-based politics that defends existing social arrangements and undermines popular movements. For a variety of reasons—including the cost of litigation, the background and attitudes of judges, and the biases in the law and the Charter—the socially disadvantaged and labour unions were better off without it.

Another implication of adopting the Charter is that minority groups increasingly ignore the usual political processes—legislatures, Cabinets, and bureaucracies—and take their demands to the courts instead.[13] To some extent this happened when such groups were unable to accomplish their goals through traditional political activity, in which case this alternative avenue is probably advantageous. However, groups may simply believe it is less trouble to go to court than to engage in the struggle of mobilizing popular support for their cause. Few observers would welcome a general transformation of political activity into legal activity with the attendant loss of political skills and organization that traditionally characterize a democracy. Seymour Martin Lipset fears that the Charter will remove one of the last traits that distinguish Canadians from Americans by increasing the litigious character of citizen–state relations, and bring about a "rights-centred" political culture.[14]

In making these points, Mandel, Russell, Lipset, and other critics at least offer a salutary reminder to question the face value of court decisions, to refrain from glorifying the Charter, judges, lawyers, and courts, and to remember traditional ways of making public decisions and of protecting rights and freedoms. On the other hand, even Britain is moving in the direction of writing down such rights and freedoms and giving the courts more discretion in protecting them.

Although reflecting the fact that it was born of political compromise, the Charter nonetheless retains one main limitation on judicial interpretation, the notwithstanding clause. As long as it says so explicitly, any legislature may pass an act violating certain aspects of the Charter. Canadians are left with a strange system under which the courts can overrule the legislatures but the legislatures can overrule the courts. Canadian political compromise that it is, this system of protecting rights and freedoms may turn out to be superior to either total legislative supremacy or exclusive judicial review. Some observers advocate the abolition of the notwithstanding clause, but others (including the author), not wanting to entrust their fate entirely either to legislatures or to courts, prefer the check and balance that they provide on each other. The truth of the matter, however, is that politicians are now afraid to use the clause because of an anticipated public backlash.

The main nonpolitical effect of the Charter has been to restrict the behaviour of police officers and others engaged in law enforcement. The manner in which they deal with those suspected or accused of committing an offence is subject to rigid Charter rules. Many apparent cases of guilt have been thrown out because according to a judge, police officers' collection of evidence brought the administration of justice into disrepute. This was commonly because the accused gave a confession in unusual circumstances; because the accused was denied the right to retain and instruct counsel without delay; or because police (or anticombines) officers did not comply with a judge's interpretation of Charter restrictions on search and seizure. Thus, law enforcement officers often complain that they are expected to do their job with their hands tied behind their backs.

DISCUSSION QUESTIONS

1. What were the symbolic, legal, and political consequences of adopting the Constitution Act, 1982?
2. Is the increase in judicial power in the Canadian political system as a result of the adoption of the Charter of Rights and Freedoms an asset or a liability?
3. Should the notwithstanding clause in the Charter be removed?

FURTHER READING

Borovoy, Alan. *When Freedoms Collide: The Case for Our Civil Liberties*. Toronto: Lester & Orpen Dennys, 1988.

Favreau, Guy. *The Amendment of the Constitution of Canada*. Ottawa: Queen's Printer, 1965.

Greene, Ian. *The Charter of Rights*. Toronto: Lorimer, 1989.

Heard, Andrew. *Canadian Constitutional Conventions*. Toronto: Oxford University Press, 1991.

Knopff, Rainer, and F. L. Morton. *Charter Politics*. Scarborough: Nelson Canada, 1992.

Mandel, Michael. *The Charter of Rights and the Legalization of Politics in Canada*. Toronto: Wall and Thompson, 1989; rev. ed., 1994.

Morton, F. L. and Rainer Knopff. *The Charter Revolution and the Court Party*. Peterborough: Broadview Press, 2000.

Reesor, Bayard. *The Canadian Constitution in Historical Perspective*. Scarborough: Prentice-Hall Canada, 1992.

Romanow, Roy, J. Whyte, and H. Leeson. *Canada … Notwithstanding: The Making of the Constitution 1976–1982*. Toronto: Methuen, 1984.

Russell, Peter. *Constitutional Odyssey*. 2nd ed. Toronto: University of Toronto Press, 1993.

Notes

1. Bayard Reesor, *The Canadian Constitution in Historical Perspective* (Scarborough: Prentice-Hall Canada, 1992).

2. Lord Durham, *Report of the Affairs of British North America*, ed. Gerald M. Craig (Toronto: McClelland and Stewart, 1963).

3. P. B. Waite, *The Confederation Debates in the Province of Canada/1865* (Toronto: McClelland and Stewart, 1963); Donald Creighton, *The Road to Confederation* (Toronto: Macmillan, 1964).

4. See also Alan C. Cairns, *Constitution, Government, and Society in Canada* (Toronto: McClelland and Stewart, 1988), 31.

5. Andrew Heard, *Canadian Constitutional Conventions* (Toronto: Oxford University Press, 1991). The author's definition is an amalgam of those Heard cites.

6. Reesor, *The Canadian Constitution in Historical Perspective*, ch. 4.

7. The best way to keep track of this endless saga is through the Elections Canada Web site.

8. Ian Greene, *The Charter of Rights* (Toronto: Lorimer, 1989), 172.

9. The leading cases in this respect are *Egan v. Canada*, [1995] 2 S.C.R. 513; *Vriend v. Alberta*, [1998] 1 S.C.R. 493; and *M. v. H.*, [1999] 2 S.C.R. 3.

10. F. L. Morton and Rainer Knopff, *The Charter Revolution and the Court Party* (Peterborough: Broadview Press, 2000).

11. Peter Russell, "The Political Purposes of the Canadian Charter of Rights and Freedoms," *Canadian Bar Review* (March 1983).

12. Michael Mandel, *The Charter of Rights and the Legalization of Politics in Canada* (Toronto: Wall and Thompson, 1989; rev. ed., 1994).

13. Russell, "The Political Purposes of the Canadian Charter."

14. Seymour Martin Lipset, *Continental Divide* (New York: Routledge, 1990).

Chapter 12

The Provinces and the Federal System

The adoption of a federal system was one of the crucial decisions in the creation of Canada, and the shape of the federal–provincial relationship remains at the heart of contemporary Canadian politics. This chapter begins by outlining the federal system in Canada at its creation and then traces the evolution of that system, especially through changes in the division of powers and federal–provincial financial relationships. The chapter concludes with a discussion of Canadian federalism today.

In a formal sense, **federalism** can be defined as a division of powers between national and provincial governments such that neither is subordinate to the other. This definition distinguishes the relationship between provincial and national governments from that between municipal and provincial governments, for in the latter case the municipalities are clearly subordinate entities. This federal–provincial equality of status is provided for in the constitutional division of powers between the two levels of government that is found primarily in sections 91 and 92 of the Constitution Act, 1867. Other aspects of federalism are also important, however, such as federal–provincial financial relations and joint policymaking mechanisms. The recent tendency of federal and provincial governments to download their responsibilities illustrates both the subordinate and the increasingly significant role of municipalities.

Chapter Objectives

After you have completed this chapter, you should be able to:

Define federalism and distinguish it from other forms of intergovernmental relations

Enumerate the ingredients of the Confederation Settlement, and understand the reasons for their inclusion

Comment on the structure of sections 91 and 92 of the Constitution Act, 1867, and distinguish between the intended division of powers between federal and provincial governments and the actual judicial interpretation of these sections

Comment on the intended division of financial powers, and discuss the evolution of federal–provincial finance, including taxation agreements; conditional, unconditional, and block grants; and equalization payments

Explain how the centralized federation of 1867 became the decentralized Canada of today

Identify the characteristics of "cooperative federalism," discuss the concepts of executive and bureaucratic federalism, and outline the major features of Canadian federalism today

....

The Confederation Settlement

The fundamentals of Canadian federalism, often called the **Confederation Settlement,**[1] were incorporated into the **Constitution Act, 1867.** As noted earlier, the principal architect of Confederation was Sir John A. Macdonald, who intended the new country to be a highly centralized federation, with Ottawa retaining most of the power. In fact, the Confederation Settlement was not consistent with the modern definition of federalism because in certain respects the provinces were made subordinate to the central government.

The Confederation Settlement consisted of five principal components:

- division of powers between federal and provincial governments
- division of financial resources
- federal controls over the provinces
- provincial representation in central institutions
- cultural guarantees

The Fathers of Confederation gave the provinces 16 specific **enumerated powers** in section 92 (e.g., hospitals and municipal institutions) and then left everything else—the **residual powers**—to Ottawa in section 91. For greater certainty, however, they also included 29 enumerations of federal powers such as trade and commerce and national defence. Two **concurrent powers**—agriculture and immigration—were listed in section 95, and the treaty power in section 132 gave the federal government the power to implement Empire treaties, regardless of their subject matter.

In the division of financial resources, federal dominance was even more apparent. The settlement gave Ottawa the power to levy any mode or system of taxation, including both **direct** and **indirect taxes.** Since the only tax widely used at the time was the customs duty, an indirect tax, the provincial power over direct

TABLE 12.1 THE CORE OF THE FEDERAL–PROVINCIAL DIVISION OF POWERS

Federal Powers	Provincial Powers
trade and commerce	direct taxation within the province
any form of taxation	public lands
national defence	hospitals and health care
banking	municipal institutions
Indians	education
criminal law	property and civil rights
interprovincial transportation and communication	administration of justice

taxation was not considered to be significant. Instead, the provinces were expected to raise their revenues from the sale of shop, saloon, tavern, and auctioneer licences, as well as to rely on federal subsidies. The federal government was to pay each province an annual per capita grant of 80 cents plus a small subsidy to support its government and legislature. The act also stated that the federal government would assist the provinces by assuming their pre-Confederation debts. It should be added that the provinces were authorized to raise revenues from their natural resources, but this source was not taken seriously at the time because few such resources had yet been discovered.

Third, in a clear departure from what is now regarded as the federal principle, Ottawa was given several means of controlling the provinces. As an alternative to granting royal assent, the lieutenant governor, a federal appointee, was permitted to reserve provincial legislation for the consideration of the federal cabinet, which could then approve or reject it. Even if the lieutenant governor gave assent to a piece of provincial legislation, however, the federal cabinet could subsequently disallow it. In addition, the federal government could declare any local work or undertaking to be for the general advantage of Canada and unilaterally place it within federal jurisdiction. These three controls are respectively referred to as **reservation, disallowance,** and the **declaratory power.**

Given the highly centralized nature of the division of powers, the limited financial resources of the provinces, and the federal controls, it is clear that the Confederation Settlement of 1867 placed the provinces in a subordinate position, somewhat akin to municipalities, rather than giving them the equal or coordinate status provided for in the modern definition of federalism.

In the light of the federal government's dominant position, it is not surprising that the smaller provinces were concerned with their representation in Ottawa. The fourth aspect of the 1867 Settlement, therefore, was agreement on provincial representation in the House of Commons and the Senate, a question of much more concern at the time than the division of powers. The great compromise that allowed Confederation to go forward was agreement that the provinces would be represented according to population in the Commons but that regional equality would prevail in the Senate. Thus, each of the three original regions—the Maritimes, Quebec, and Ontario—was to receive 24 senators, appeasing smaller provinces that could be easily outvoted in the lower chamber.[2]

Confederation was more than just a union of provinces; it was also seen as a union of two cultural groups, English and French. Thus, the fifth aspect of the Confederation Settlement might be called cultural guarantees. Considering the anxiety of French Canadians about the preservation of their language and culture, these guarantees were surprisingly minor. Section 133 of the 1867 act made French and English official languages in the federal Parliament and federal courts as well as in the Quebec legislature and Quebec courts—but nowhere else. At the time, religion was probably of greater concern than language, so existing separate school systems in the provinces (especially Ontario and Quebec) were guaranteed by allowing the federal government to step in to restore them, if necessary. French Canada was also protected by giving power over property and civil rights to the provinces so that Quebec could maintain certain cultural particularisms, including its civil law system.

John A. Macdonald, the architect of a centralized federal system (William Topley/National Archives of Canada/PA-027013)

Of these five components of the Confederation Settlement, only three relate directly to the relationship between federal and provincial governments. This chapter will therefore proceed to track the development of the Settlement in these three aspects: the division of powers, financial resources, and federal controls. In discussing the evolution of Canadian federalism, it is critical to understand how the very centralized federation created in 1867 became the highly decentralized Canada of today. This trend is apparent in all three areas.

Division of Powers

If changes to the **division of powers** between federal and provincial governments have resulted in the provinces being more important today, there are two ways in which this could have happened. First, formal constitutional amendments could have altered the division of powers in the provinces' favour; second, judicial decisions that interpreted sections 91 and 92 of the Constitution Act, 1867, could also have had this effect.

Since 1867, only four formal constitutional amendments have been adopted that directly affected the division of powers. In 1940, unemployment insurance was added to the list of federal powers in section 91 after the courts had earlier declared it to belong to the provinces. In 1951, old age pensions were made a concurrent power, allowing the federal government into this area as well, and in 1964 Ottawa's jurisdiction was enlarged to include widows' and survivors' benefits and disability pensions. In 1982, the new section 92A increased provincial jurisdiction over natural resources, while at the same time, the Charter of Rights and Freedoms generally reduced the powers of both levels of government. Thus, in the first three cases, the net result was a slight increase in federal powers, but this increase was accomplished with the unanimous consent of the provinces. The 1982 amendment was the only formal constitutional amendment that in any way increased provincial powers at the expense of Ottawa. Formal constitutional amendments, therefore, do little to explain the more powerful provinces of today.

Judicial interpretation of the federal and provincial powers in the 1867 act is a much more complicated and significant subject. Before 1949, the **Judicial Committee of the Privy Council (JCPC)** in London was Canada's final court of appeal, and its decisions had a major impact in transforming Canadian federalism from a centralized to a decentralized system. The most important JCPC decisions related to the federal peace, order, and good government clause as opposed to the provincial power over property and civil rights.

The **peace, order, and good government clause (POGG),** one of two parts of Section 91 in the 1867 act, says that all powers not given to the provinces in section 92 are left with the federal government. This clause is also known as the residual clause. The second part of section 91 provides "for greater certainty" a list of 29 examples of federal powers. In the course of its judgments, the Judicial Committee drove a wedge between these two parts of section 91, deciding that the 29 enumerations were the real federal powers rather than just examples, and ignoring the peace, order, and good government clause except in cases of national emergency. But in times of national emergency, as determined by the JCPC, federal powers were almost unlimited. This became known as the **emergency doctrine,** and how the courts managed to transform the residual clause into an emergency power is very difficult to fathom. In normal times, on the other hand, the JCPC gave an extremely broad interpretation to section 92-13, property and civil rights in the province, finding that almost any matter that was the subject of a federal–provincial constitutional dispute could be incorporated within this provincial power.[3] That is why so little was left over for the federal residual clause.

The effect of the judicial interpretation of the peace, order, and good government clause, along with other clauses such as trade and commerce and treaty powers, was to reduce significantly the intended dominance of the federal government. The complementary broad interpretation of property and civil rights increased substantially the scope of provincial powers. This influence has been very controversial in political, judicial, and academic circles because it was clearly contrary to John A. Macdonald's conception of Canadian federalism and because it did not permit Ottawa to take initiatives that centralist advocates often wished.[4]

Other observers contend, however, that the Judicial Committee's line of interpretation was consistent with the increasing size and distances that characterized the country as time went on, as well as with societal forces and public orientations, at least outside Ontario. They argue that the provincial bias pervading so many of the JCPC's decisions was "in fundamental harmony with the regional pluralism" of the federal, decentralized, diversified nature of Canadian society. However desirable centralization may have seemed at the outset, it was inappropriate in the long run "for the regional diversities of a land of vast extent and a large, geographically concentrated, minority culture."[5]

....

Federal–Provincial Finance

In the Confederation Settlement, the federal government was given the power to levy any kind of tax, while the provinces were restricted to direct taxation.[6] The federal government was also committed to pay the provinces small annual grants. While the intention was thus to create a highly centralized federation, the financial factor also ultimately contributed to the increased power of the provinces. This situation came about because the provinces levied direct taxes that they were not expected to use, such as income taxes; because the provinces successfully lobbied for larger federal grants; and because some provincial revenues, such as those from natural resources, turned out to be more significant than anticipated.

Provincial revenues proved to be inadequate from the beginning, and it did not take long for the provinces to begin levying their own direct personal and corporate income taxes and to demand larger sums from Ottawa. With both levels of government taxing the same personal and corporate incomes, but in a totally uncoordinated fashion, and with provinces always lining up for more federal funds, the federal–provincial financial situation became very complicated. This muddied state of affairs worsened with the advent of the Depression, when even fewer funds were available to go around. As a result, Prime Minister Mackenzie King appointed the Rowell-Sirois Commission, officially the Royal Commission on Dominion–Provincial Relations, in 1937. Its only recommendation to be immediately implemented was that the costly responsibility for unemployment insurance be transferred to the federal government.

Before 1940, therefore, the two levels of government were relatively independent on both the taxation and expenditure sides of public finance. Since the Second World War, on the other hand, they have become intimately intertwined, and Ottawa has taken the lead (sometimes with provincial encouragement) in coordinating the various ingredients of the financial relationship. The complicated federal–provincial financial situation since 1940 might be simplified somewhat by taking three aspects separately: taxation agreements; conditional and block grants; and equalization payments.

Between 1942 and 2001, the taxation side was characterized by a series of five-year federal–provincial **taxation agreements.** The name and terms of the agreements changed over the years, but the basic objective was the same: to effect a degree of coordination in the field of federal–provincial taxation. The main taxes in question were personal and corporate income taxes. While the federal personal income tax was standard across the country (except for Quebec), each province was able to determine its own rate as a percentage of the federal tax, so that the provincial portion varied widely. Except for Quebec, all personal income taxes have been collected by Ottawa in the first instance, after which the provincial portion was transferred back, an arrangement that until recently was found to be satisfactory to all concerned. Quebec has always collected its own personal income tax, so that its residents completed two separate income tax forms. By 2001, however, all provinces had separated their provincial income tax from the federal income tax system, so that the provincial tax is no longer necessarily calculated as a percentage of the federal tax.

The second aspect of the federal–provincial financial picture was **shared-cost programs.** These expanded considerably after 1940 in the joint development of a welfare state. The most important shared-cost social programs were postsecondary education (1952), hospital insurance (1957), the Canada Assistance Plan (1966), and medical insurance (1968). Health insurance later replaced the two earlier measures in this field. These programs are termed the "major" federal transfers to the provinces, but a large number of "small" transfer programs also exist.

Federal grants for postsecondary education have always been of a **block grant** variety, that is, a sum of money given to each province for the operating costs of postsecondary educational institutions but without any conditions or strings attached. Such a grant significantly helped to fund universities and colleges and allowed provinces to keep tuition fees relatively low. The other major shared-cost programs originally fell into the **conditional grant** category. The usual pattern here was for the federal government to pay approximately 50 percent of the cost of each program provided that the provinces met Ottawa's conditions. For example, Ottawa would fund half of any provincial health care program that was comprehensive (covering all necessary health services provided by hospitals and medical practitioners), universal (covering the whole population), portable (covering the costs of provincial residents while temporarily absent from the province), accessible (not impeding or precluding reasonable access to services by extra charges), and publicly administered. Under the **Canada Assistance Plan,** Ottawa similarly provided half the funding for almost any provincial or municipal program that provided social assistance and welfare services to persons in need. In this case, the main condition was that anyone in need had to be included, and no one could be forced to work for welfare. Without federal contributions to health and social assistance programs, many provinces would not have been able to finance them.

Most of these programs fell constitutionally within provincial jurisdiction, but Ottawa always maintained that its **spending power** allowed it to make payments to individuals, institutions, and other governments in fields over which parliament did not necessarily have the power to regulate. The federal government even claimed that it could attach conditions to such spending and has often done so. In the exercise of its spending power, Ottawa was able to establish national standards in a number of social programs.

While a combination of provincial pressure and federal political and bureaucratic expansionism inspired most of these programs, the provinces often criticized the federal conditions attached to them as being out of place in areas of provincial jurisdiction. Quebec in particular took this point of view in the early 1960s. In response, the Pearson government allowed the provinces to opt out of certain conditional grant programs and continue to receive federal funding as long as they maintained an equivalent program. Then, in the 1970s, Ottawa became upset at the rapidly escalating costs of many of these programs and its commitment to finance 50 percent of whatever the provinces spent on them.

In 1977, therefore, the federal government passed the **Established Programs Financing Act,** which encompassed postsecondary education and health care. This act had two major implications. First, Ottawa removed the detailed conditions attached to the health insurance programs, as many provinces wished. But in return, the federal government no longer felt obliged to pay 50 percent of the provincial program costs. The federal grants now took the form of tax transfers (giving the provinces more room to levy their own taxes) as well as cash, and henceforth, Ottawa would increase its funding of such programs only by a certain annual percentage. Removing the conditions from health insurance grants, however, led to problems with hospital user fees, doctors double- or extra-billing, and provinces using health care funds for other purposes.

Unhappy with these developments, the federal government consequently passed the **Canada Health Act** in 1984. The act resurrected the five earlier conditions connected to health care and penalized those provinces permitting extra charges. At the same time, especially after 1982, the federal share of such programs fell below 50 percent, and the 1990s saw a progression of freezes and cuts in funding. For a time, the Canada Assistance Plan (CAP) remained a conditional grant program, with Ottawa continuing its 50 percent contribution, but the Mulroney government put a ceiling on its CAP contributions to the three richest provinces in the early 1990s, and the Liberals repealed the plan completely.

Brian Gable (*The Globe and Mail*). Reprinted with permission from *The Globe and Mail*.

The 1994 federal budget brought in by Finance Minister Paul Martin announced a freeze on all major federal transfers except equalization payments, and the 1995 budget inaugurated a significant transformation of federal–provincial transfers. Beginning in 1996–97, Established Program Funding (postsecondary education and health insurance) and the Canada Assistance Plan (social assistance and welfare services) were combined into one block grant called the **Canada Health and Social Transfer (CHST)**.

It would be a combination of cash payments and tax points (federal withdrawal from joint tax fields), but would represent a significant reduction in previous amounts. It was at this time that postsecondary education fees skyrocketed, as provinces in turn reduced university and college funding. As a block grant, the CHST would not contain the conditions of CAP nor would Ottawa's expenditures be driven by provincial costs. The only condition on welfare transfers would be that provinces not impose a minimum residency requirement. As a result, many provinces reduced social assistance programs and/or brought in workfare. Despite the protests of almost all social reformers, who did not trust provincial governments to provide adequate social assistance programs, Ottawa felt that it could not retain such conditions when it was reducing its contributions. On the other hand, the federal Liberal government continued to defend the principles of the Canada Health Act and fought with Alberta over the funding of private health clinics that charged "facility fees." Ottawa later accepted Alberta's Bill 11, which most observers saw as a violation of the federal act, and seemed reluctant to enforce it in a number of instances in other provinces.

The third aspect of federal–provincial finance consists of **equalization payments.** In 1957, the federal government began to pay these unconditional grants to have-not provinces based on provincial need, so that all could offer a relatively equal standard of services. The essence of equalization payments was to bring the have-not provinces up to the national average tax yield per capita. Typically, Ontario, British Columbia, and Alberta have been above the national average and have not received equalization payments, while the other seven provinces receive an annual payment based on the per capita shortfall of tax revenues multiplied by the province's population. Equalization payments were not touched by the federal reforms of 1995.

Combining these major federal contributions to the provinces, Ottawa paid the provinces a total of $37 billion in 1994–95, but due to federal belt-tightening, that total declined by $3.5 billion four years later. Provincial and public complaints, plus a rosier economy that increased federal tax revenues, persuaded the federal government to increase these transfers again at the turn of the new century. As seen in Table 12.2, they reached over $43 billion in 2001–02.

TABLE 12.2 MAJOR FEDERAL TRANSFERS TO PROVINCES, 2000–01*

	($ Millions)		
	CHST	Equalization	Total
Newfoundland	594	1098	1579
P.E.I.	154	251	378
Nova Scotia	1049	1298	2228
New Brunswick	842	1224	1938
Quebec	8245	5152	12 795
Ontario	13 195	—	13 195
Manitoba	1280	1185	2350
Saskatchewan	1132	240	1218
Alberta	3405	—	3405
B.C.	4558	—	4558
Total	34 565	10 448	43 755

Totals may not add due to rounding. Equalization associated with CHST tax transfer is included in both CHST and Equalization. Totals have been adjusted to avoid double counting.

*as estimated in Nov. 2001.

Source: Federal–Provincial Relations Division, Finance Canada. http://www.fin.gc.ca/fedprov/mtpe.html (Retrieved 15 Nov. 2001). Reproduced with the permission of the Minister of Public Works and Government Services Canada, 20001.

In addition to their grants from Ottawa, the provinces have levied over 30 forms of direct taxation that were unanticipated in 1867. The enormous natural resource revenues that some provinces (especially Alberta) receive on top of direct taxation and federal contributions are also significant.[7] A comparison of federal transfers and the provinces' own revenues (taxes plus natural resource and other revenues) is shown in Table 12.3.

Thus, the combination of unanticipated federal grants, direct taxes, and natural resource revenues has contributed significantly to the enhanced status of the provinces in the Canadian federal system. It should also be reiterated that the two levels of government began by operating more or less independently of each other, taxing and spending in different areas, with federal grants being unconditional in nature. Then, for about 60 years, the federal and provincial governments became closely intertwined by taxation agreements on the revenue side and by conditional and block grant programs in terms of expenditures. As they entered the 21st century, however, the degree of integration had declined, especially with the disengagement at federal and provincial personal income systems. Some observers advocated new national programs such as pharmacare or daycare, while others

TABLE 12.3 FEDERAL TRANSFERS, PROVINCES' OWN REVENUES, TOTAL PROVINCIAL
REVENUES, AND PERCENT OF TOTAL PROVINCIAL REVENUES FROM OWN
SOURCES, 2000-01

	Federal Transfers	Provinces' Own Revenues	Total Provincial Revenues	Percent of Total Provincial Revenues from Own Sources
Newfoundland	1 664.0	2 336.0	4 000.0	58.4
P.E.I.	378.8	602.5	981.3	61.4
Nova Scotia	2 206.6	3 631.0	5 837.6	62.2
New Brunswick	1 940.6	2 984.8	4 925.4	60.6
Quebec	12 443.3	69 962.7	82 406.0	84.9
Ontario	11 818.3	110 019.8	121 838.1	90.3
Manitoba	2 255.0	5 261.7	7 516.7	70.0
Saskatchewan	1 383.7	8 029.2	9 412.9	85.3
Alberta	3 030.5	36 844.5	39 875.0	92.4
B.C.	4 186.7	29 041.1	33 227.8	87.4
Total	41 307.5	268 713.3	310 020.8	86.7

Source: Canada Tax Foundation, *Finances of the Nation, 2000*, calculations by author. Used with permission.

warned about the deterioration and/or abandonment of existing national programs and standards.

Federal Controls

As mentioned, the 1867 Constitution Act contained three specific federal controls over the provinces: reservation, disallowance, and the declaratory power. In
the first 30 years after Confederation, all three controls were actively used, and
this had the effect of keeping the provinces subordinate to Ottawa. Their use
gradually declined and then ceased—the reservation and declaratory powers were
last used in 1961, and disallowance in 1943. As these were the federal powers that
originally precluded Canada from being classified as a true federation, their disuse
has meant that the provinces have shrugged off their subordinate status. Canada
is now a genuine federation, and a highly decentralized one at that.

· ·

Canadian Federalism Today

Federal–provincial relations in Canada have gone through many different phases since 1867, depending on shifting attitudes of federal and provincial governments, states of war and peace, and variations in judicial interpretation. In fact, Canadian federalism has experienced pendulum-like swings between centralization and decentralization, and the evolution from a centralized to a decentralized federal system has not been a unilinear process.

Cooperative Federalism

The phase of Canadian federalism that began after the Second World War might be called **cooperative federalism.** The essence of this concept is that while neither level was subordinate to the other, the federal government and the provinces were closely intertwined rather than operating independently. Here the crucial variable was financial relations. As noted in that connection earlier, the post-1945 period has been marked by federal–provincial taxation agreements on the revenue side and a host of shared-cost programs in terms of expenditures.

Cooperative federalism resulted from several developments.[8] First, federal and provincial objectives often had to be harmonized if public policy was to be effective. Second, public pressure forced the federal government to establish minimum national standards throughout the country in certain public services even within provincial jurisdiction such as health care. Third, the two levels of government competed for tax revenues and needed to coordinate these efforts to some extent, at least for the convenience of taxpayers. Fourth, given a generally vague division of powers, federal and provincial ministers and bureaucrats usually sought to maximize their jurisdiction and the programs of the two levels of government eventually overlapped.

Cooperative federalism was made operational by hundreds of **federal–provincial conferences** at all levels—first ministers, departmental ministers, deputy ministers, and even lesser officials—who engaged in almost continuous consultation, coordination, and cooperation. Cooperative federalism can be conducted on a multilateral basis, involving the federal government and several or all provinces, or alternatively, on a bilateral basis in which Ottawa interacts with individual provinces. Since the ministers and bureaucrats involved are all part of the executive branch of government, cooperative federalism is sometimes called **executive federalism.** Two main implications of executive federalism are that legislatures, political parties, and the public at large are not given much role to play in decisions that emerge from the secrecy of such meetings, and that federal–provincial conflicts are worked out in conferences or meetings rather than being referred to the courts.

Executive federalism can therefore be defined as "relations between elected and appointed officials of the two levels of government."[9] When it is practised at the level of first ministers, it is often called "federal–provincial summitry." The **first ministers' conference**—that is, a conference of premiers and the prime minister—is not provided for anywhere in the written Constitution and rests upon a conventional base. Nevertheless, especially since 1945, this institution has made many significant policy decisions with respect to constitutional issues, shared-cost programs, and taxation and fiscal arrangements. Some of these had to be ratified later by federal and provincial legislatures, but except on constitutional matters, legislative ratification was usually a formality. Such agreements could rarely be altered in any legislature because they would then have to be changed in all 11. First ministers' conferences became more elaborate and institutionalized over time. They were usually held in the Government Conference Centre in Ottawa, the refurbished old train station across from Parliament Hill. They could be televised, in whole or in part, but it was generally agreed that any serious negotiation had to take place behind closed doors. The prime minister functioned as chair, in addition to representing the federal government, and individual ministers from either level of government were usually allowed to speak as well. Every delegation brought along a host of advisers. After the collapse of the Charlottetown Accord, however, such first ministers' conferences fell into disrepute, and were replaced by occasional first ministers' dinners at the Prime Minister's residence.

Executive federalism conducted at the level of departmental ministers and leading bureaucrats is sometimes labelled "functional" or "bureaucratic" federalism. This form of executive federalism is usually more successful than federal–provincial summitry, partly because the officials involved often share certain professional norms, and once they reach a consensus, these experts may be able to "sell" it to their departmental ministers.

The Decline of Cooperative Federalism

Canadian federalism between 1945 and 1960 may have been "cooperative" in the sense that the two levels of government were closely intertwined, but it continued to be highly centralized in the immediate postwar period. The ministers and bureaucrats in Ottawa who had almost single-handedly run the country during the Second World War were reluctant to shed their enormous power. Moreover, they had discovered **Keynesian economics,** which prescribed a leading role for the central government in guiding the economy. The Diefenbaker government after 1957 was more sensitive to provincial demands, and the whole picture was increasingly complicated from 1960 onward by the Quiet Revolution in Quebec. This period still manifested an intertwined, nonsubordinate relationship between the two levels of government, but with Quebec regularly rejecting federal initiatives, cooperation was sometimes harder to come by. The concept of opting out was a hallmark of this phase of federalism, which saw a significant degree of decentralization take place.

Between about 1970 and 1984, federal–provincial relations were racked with conflict. Quebec and the other provinces were more aggressive than ever, but the Trudeau government was not prepared for any further decentralization. Thus, taxation agreements were accompanied by more provincial unhappiness, and block funding replaced conditional grants in important areas, leaving the two levels less intertwined than before. Moreover, especially at the level of first ministers, federal–provincial conferences frequently failed to come to any agreement and Ottawa often chose to act unilaterally. In this phase, federal–provincial conflicts were more frequently referred to the courts, resulting in a renewed emphasis on the judicial interpretation of the division of powers.

The Trudeau era was characterized by years of federal–provincial discord over resource and energy policies, especially the National Energy Program, conflict with Newfoundland over offshore oil, and conflict with Saskatchewan over the regulation and taxation of that province's oil and potash industries. When these disputes coincided with Trudeau's attempt to unilaterally amend the Constitution and entrench official bilingualism as a national policy, many Western Canadians began to re-examine their place in the federation. Some of the heat was reduced when Trudeau conceded the new section 92A of the Constitution Act, 1982, which recognized enhanced provincial jurisdiction over natural resources. He made this concession in order to secure federal NDP support for his constitutional package and as a peace offering to the West.

When Brian Mulroney came to power in 1984, he was determined to improve federal–provincial relations and embark on another period of decentralized, genuinely cooperative federalism. In this objective he was somewhat successful, for much of the federal–provincial animosity of the Trudeau years seemed to dissipate. Western and Eastern concerns about energy resources were respectively resolved to a large extent in the 1985 Western and Atlantic Accords. During its second term, however, the Mulroney government increasingly aroused provincial anger, especially as it became obsessed with deficit reduction and cut back on grants to the provinces. The Mulroney government even enforced the Liberals' Canada Health Act, imposing penalties on provinces that allowed doctors to extra-bill or permitted hospitals to charge user fees. The major federal–provincial dispute of the Mulroney years concerned the Goods and Services Tax (GST). To some extent it was just "good politics" for provincial premiers to jump on the anti-GST bandwagon because of widespread popular opposition. Most provinces refused to integrate their sales taxes with the new federal tax, even though many mutual advantages would have accrued from doing so.

The Chrétien Liberals were initially popular with provincial governments in offering funds under the national infrastructure program, and were somewhat successful in negotiating a reduction in provincial barriers to the free movement of people, goods, services, and capital across the country in the **Agreement on Internal Trade.** They had only partial success in implementing their promise to replace the GST (in reality, harmonizing it with the provincial retail sales tax in a handful of provinces), and then angered the provinces with reductions in their transfers, especially after 1995. The provinces' principal complaints included severe reductions in health, postsecondary education, and welfare transfers, although provinces also joined in to protest the cuts to almost every other aspect of federal government operations, such as a wide range of transportation subsidies. On the other hand, Ottawa did not cut equalization payments.

More harmoniously, the Chrétien government transferred responsibility for labour market training to the provinces via bilateral deals rather than constitutional amendment, and replaced the Child Tax Benefit with a new integrated National Child Benefit system developed through federal–provincial cooperation. Most important, perhaps, was the 1999 **Social Union Framework Agreement (SUFA),** a framework on which to construct or modify federal, provincial, or joint social programs. Ottawa agreed to consult with and provide advance notice to provincial governments prior to renewing or significantly changing social transfers; it also agreed not to introduce new social programs involving transfers of money to the provinces without the support of a majority of provinces. On the other hand, Ottawa retained the right to use its spending power to make transfers directly to people, such as in the case of the Millennium Scholarship program. This phase of federalism has thus gained the label of "collaborative" but "disengaging" federalism.[10]

While the two levels of government remain intertwined in a large number of areas (collaborative), both levels of government increasingly desire to extract themselves from joint programs (disengaging). One reason for this development is that provinces wanted to establish their own income tax systems. Another is that integration involves a certain amount of duplication that probably increases program costs. In some cases, when Ottawa is no longer funding programs so generously, it cannot impose national standards on them; in other cases, right-wing provincial governments reject such standards. The net result is that the quality of social programs has declined, with much discussion erupting over the issue of two-tier health care.

DISCUSSION QUESTIONS

1. Are you a centralist or a decentralist? What are the advantages and disadvantages of each approach to Canadian federalism?
2. Should the federal government increase its financial transfers to the provinces, or should it give them increased taxation room instead?
3. Should the federal government be able to spend money for any purpose, even within provincial jurisdiction? Should it be able to set conditions on provincial medicare programs?

FURTHER READING

Canada: The State of the Federation. Kingston: Institute of Intergovernmental Relations, Queen's University, annual.

Canadian Tax Foundation. *Finances of the Nation.* Toronto, biennial.

Hogg, Peter. *Constitutional Law of Canada.* 4th ed. Toronto: Carswell, 1997.

Mallory, J. R. "The Five Faces of Canadian Federalism." In P.-A. Crépeau and C. B. Macpherson, *The Future of Canadian Federalism.* Toronto: University of Toronto Press, 1965.

Mellon, Hugh, and Martin Westmacott, eds. *Challenges to Canadian Federalism.* Scarborough: Prentice-Hall Canada, 1997.

Milne, David. *Tug of War: Ottawa and the Provinces under Trudeau and Mulroney.* Toronto: Lorimer, 1986.

Russell, Peter, et al. *Federalism and the Charter.* Ottawa: Carleton University Press, 1989.

Smiley, D. V. *The Federal Condition in Canada.* Toronto: McGraw-Hill Ryerson, 1987.

Notes

1. Donald Smiley, *The Canadian Political Nationality* (Toronto: Methuen, 1967).
2. Provincial representation within the institutions of the national government is sometimes called "intrastate federalism," as opposed to relations between federal and provincial governments or "interstate federalism."
3. Peter Russell et al., *Federalism and the Charter* (Ottawa: Carleton University Press, 1989); Peter Hogg, *Constitutional Law of Canada*, 4th ed. (Toronto: Carswell, 1997).
4. V. C. MacDonald, "Judicial Interpretation of the Canadian Constitution," *University of Toronto Law Journal* 1 (1935–36): 260–85; *O'Connor Report*, Senate of Canada, 1939. It is ironic that judicial interpretation contributed to decentralizing a centralized Canadian federation but centralized a decentralized federation in the United States. See Roger Gibbins, *Regionalism* (Toronto: Butterworths, 1982), ch. 4.
5. Alan C. Cairns, "The Governments and Societies of Canadian Federalism," *Canadian Journal of Political Science* (December 1977): 695–725; Cairns, "The Judicial Committee and Its Critics," *Canadian Journal of Political Science* (September 1971): 301–45.
6. Direct taxes are derived from the very people who are intended to pay them, while indirect taxes are extracted from one person with the expectation that they will be passed on to someone else.
7. G. V. La Forest, *The Allocation of Taxing Powers under the Canadian Constitution*, 2nd ed. (Toronto: Canadian Tax Foundation, 1981); Canadian Tax Foundation, *Provincial and Municipal Finances* (1989), 12: 1.
8. Donald Smiley, *Canada in Question: Federalism in the Seventies* (Toronto: McGraw-Hill Ryerson, 1972), 56.
9. Ibid.
10. Harvey Lazar, ed., *Canada: The State of the Federation 1997*; Lazar and Tom McIntosh, eds., *Canada: The State of the Federation 1998/99*; and Lazar, ed., *Canada: The State of the Federation 1999/2000*. Kingston: Queen's University Institute of Intergovernmental Relations.

PART 4

Governing

Having examined the societal context of the political system and the means of linking people to government in the "politics" part of this book, and the constitutional context as the first part of the "government" section, we can now focus on governing itself. This section, therefore, examines the individual institutions of government in detail. These institutions comprise the executive, including the Crown, the prime minister and the cabinet; the bureaucracy or public service; Parliament, including the House of Commons and the Senate; and the judiciary. The functions and operations of each branch of government are outlined, as are the kinds of outputs or authoritative decisions each makes. Initially, however, these institutions are put into the context of the "policymaking process," providing an overview of how they interact with each other in order to produce public policies.

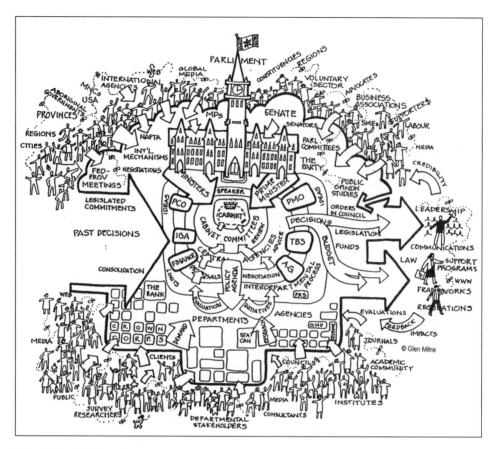

The Policy Marketplace

Reproduced with permission from the publication and seminar *Making Policy: A Guide to the Federal Government's Policy Process* (Ottawa, 2001). Glen Milne, Ottawa, (613) 562-4333, ggdm@istar.ca.

Chapter 13

The Executive

The prime minister and cabinet constitute the political **executive** and are the key players in the Canadian policymaking process. Their decisions are sometimes overturned by the courts and occasionally even by Parliament, and are based to a considerable extent on advice from the bureaucracy and other sources. But in the end, the prime minister and cabinet—often called the **government** of the day— are responsible for making the biggest political decisions in the country. This chapter begins with a brief discussion of the policymaking process and the Crown, and then concentrates on the prime minister and cabinet.

Chapter Objectives

After you have completed this chapter, you should be able to:

Outline the policymaking process in its most comprehensive form

Appreciate the ways in which the monarchy or Crown is engrained in the political system

Understand the ceremonial and symbolic functions of the Crown and assess the use of the discretionary powers of that office

Comprehend the importance of the prime minister and cabinet in the policymaking process and in providing political leadership, and understand the sources of their power

Enumerate the factors that contribute to the preeminence of the prime minister

Discuss the factors that influence the composition of the cabinet

Discuss the principles and processes of cabinet operation

Enumerate the functions of the four main cabinet support agencies

....

The Policymaking Process

The analysis of the individual institutions of government that follows in this and subsequent chapters will be more meaningful if first put in the context of the policymaking process. This section provides an overview of that process, indicating in a general way how the institutions interact with each other in the making of public policy. **Public policy** can be defined as "a course of action or inaction chosen by public authorities to address a given problem or interrelated set of problems."[1]

Chapter 1 contained a model of the whole political system that included such components as demands, authorities, and outputs. When we focus on the "authorities" part of that model, the result would look something like Figure 13.1.

As this model suggests, the actual process can be divided into six phases: initiation, priority-setting, policy formulation, legitimation, implementation, and interpretation. Most policies and decisions do not involve such an elaborate process; indeed, many can be made unilaterally by the prime minister, the cabinet, the bureaucracy, or the courts. But the model shows the policymaking process in its broadest form, that is, a policy that requires the passage of a new law, or an amendment to an existing law, and that is later interpreted by the courts. Think of the evolution of the laws restricting tobacco advertising or possession of guns.

The authorities are bombarded daily with hundreds of demands. These demands emanate from many different sources, and most have no impact. But the policymaking process is set in motion when the prime minister and cabinet are struck by a demand being made and decide to look into it further. On a smaller scale, a single minister may also make such a decision. It is at this point that a demand is sometimes said to become an issue. An issue, therefore, is a demand that has made it onto the public agenda and that is under serious consideration by the authorities.

The second phase of the policymaking process involves the prime minister and cabinet again, this time in their priority-setting capacity. They decide which of the proposals they have previously selected for consideration are worthy of adoption. In other words, the prime minister and cabinet (or, on lesser issues, an individual minister) must decide whether or not to take action on the issue, and if they decide to act, they must determine the general lines of the new initiative. For example, they decide that they will restrict tobacco advertising and they will control guns.

The limited number of projects that have been given the green light by the cabinet in the priority-setting phase then enter the policy formulation phase. Once the cabinet has approved a proposal in principle, it sends a directive to the bureaucracy to work out the details. This is usually a very time-consuming process requiring coordination among many federal government departments. It may also involve consultation with provincial governments, interest groups, and others. Questions may be referred back to the cabinet for further direction, but eventually a Memorandum to Cabinet is submitted, outlining the policy in detail.[2] Assuming the proposal requires legislative action, the policy formulation stage culminates in a bill being drafted on the basis of the Memorandum to Cabinet.

The proposal then enters the legislative arena, as did the two bills in question. The relevant minister may accept technical alterations to the bill as it proceeds through the House of Commons and the Senate, but the main intent or principle of the bill cannot be changed without approval from the cabinet. The legislative stage is referred to as "legitimizing" the bill because it is put under the scrutiny of the democratically elected representatives of the people and made legitimate by their approval. The cabinet and members of Parliament contribute political expertise to the process, but given the shortage of time and limited technical expertise characteristic of the legislative branch, most such bills are passed in "skeletal" form, with details to be added later. The legitimation stage ends with the token approval of the governor general, signifying that the policy has been officially sanctioned.

Royal assent is by no means the end of the policymaking process. Few laws attain any significance just by sitting on the statute books; they must be implemented in order to be made effective. Implementation almost always involves the drafting of detailed **regulations** by the bureaucracy, to add meat to the skeleton of the statute. What wording or pictures will be used on cigarette packages, or how will guns be registered? Even though they have the same legal standing as if they were part of the enabling statute itself, the regulations that a law authorizes the executive to make are given only the scarcest scrutiny by either ministers or Parliament, and thus are almost the exclusive preserve of the bureaucracy. Implementation normally requires the setting up of new administrative machinery—new staff, agencies, field offices, and operational manuals, among other things. It is therefore not surprising that most legislation does not automatically take effect upon royal assent; it is not "proclaimed" or made operational until the government is ready to implement it. It took more time and money than anticipated, for example, to set up the national gun registry.

The policymaking process may well end, at least for the time being, with the implementation phase. But if new legislation is involved, it is often subject to judicial interpretation. Thus, it is appropriate to add a sixth phase to the policymaking process, that of judicial interpretation. Judges always had an impact on a law by means of how they interpreted it, but the law's very constitutionality may

Figure 13.1   The Canadian Policymaking Process

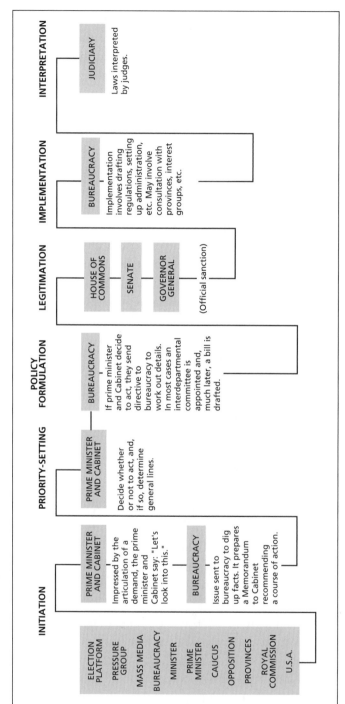

even be challenged in the courts. In such a case, the judiciary must decide whether the provisions of the law are contrary to the Charter of Rights and Freedoms or to the division of powers between federal and provincial governments. The gun control and tobacco advertising laws were both subject to such judicial interpretation.

The Crown

To classify Canada as a **constitutional monarchy** essentially means that it is a democracy headed by a king or queen. In other words, the Queen is the Canadian head of state, but she reigns according to the Constitution. Canada is also said to have a dual executive, meaning that the formal and largely symbolic executive powers are given to the Queen, but the effective executive is made up of the prime minister and cabinet. The prime minister is called the head of government.

The concept of the **Crown** revolves around the head of state and can be defined as the collectivity of executive powers exercised by or in the name of the monarch. Although the Crown is largely irrelevant to the effective functions of government, many government operations are performed in the name of the Queen or governor general.[3] Moreover, the Crown does perform useful functions in the political system that are largely of a symbolic and ceremonial nature.

The Crown is not only the collectivity of executive powers but also represents the entire state and embodies what belongs to the people collectively. This can be

Governor General Adrienne Clarkson reads the Speech from the Throne (Tom Hanson/CP Picture Archive)

seen in **Crown corporations** (state-owned corporations) or Crown lands (state-owned lands). In addition, the Crown is central to the legal system. Crown attorneys prosecute crimes on behalf of society; court cases are initiated in the name of the Queen, for example, R. (for Regina) *v. Canadian Newspapers Co.*, or against the government (*Russell v. The Queen*); branches of the judiciary are called the Court of Queen's Bench; and lawyers are awarded the title of Queen's Counsel (Q.C.). The term "royal" is also widely used in Canada to refer to institutions that function for the advantage of all in the name of the Queen: royal commissions, which investigate problems for the general good, and the Royal Canadian Mounted Police, who are charged with capturing violators of society's laws. In another branch of government, three important aspects of Parliament reflect the existence of the monarchical system: royal assent, the Speech from the Throne, and Her Majesty's Loyal Opposition. "Loyal Opposition" demonstrates that criticism of the government has been legitimized and institutionalized in the name of the Queen.

The Queen of Canada, Elizabeth II, is also Queen of other countries, and normally resides in Britain. That means that she needs a local representative in Canada, the **governor general,** who may, in her absence, perform any of her functions and exercise any of her powers. Until 1926 the governor was a double agent: besides being the representative of the monarch, he was an agent of the British government, and as long as Canada was a British colony, the governor general exercised authority over Canada on behalf of the British cabinet. Today, the governor general has no connection whatsoever to the British government. The Canadian prime minister nominates the governor general, who, upon appointment by the Queen, serves a term of approximately five years.

Some of the powers of the Crown are provided for in the Constitution Act, 1867, while others, the **prerogative powers,** are left over from the era when the monarch really ruled. Despite this impressive theoretical list of powers, there is no doubt that in a democratic age almost all of them must be exercised on the advice of the government—the prime minister and cabinet—of the day. The most important prerogative power of the governor general is the appointment of the prime minister, but this must be performed on the basis of constitutional convention. In ensuring that the office of prime minister is never vacant, the governor general normally relies on the operation of political parties and elections, and does not have far to look. On two occasions in the 1890s, however, the governor had to help find a prime minister, John Abbott in 1891 and Mackenzie Bowell in 1894. Political parties are better organized today, and prefer to choose their own leader. Thus, if the position should suddenly become vacant, such as through the death or unexpected resignation of the prime minister, the cabinet and/or government caucus would name an acting leader pending a leadership convention.

The two most controversial discretionary acts of governors general took place in 1896 and 1926 when the governors not only acted on their own initiative but also refused the advice of the prime minister and cabinet. The first occasion concerned the question of making government appointments. Many appointments, such as those of senators and judges, are announced by the governor general, even though they are decided upon by the cabinet. But the Charles Tupper government chose to retain office after it lost the 1896 election (awaiting defeat in the House of Commons), and during that interim period presented a list of several recommended appointments to the governor general, which he refused to make.

The second famous case of refusing government advice, the **King–Byng dispute,** involved the dissolution of Parliament. The governor general normally dissolves Parliament to precipitate an election on the advice of the prime minister, but in 1926 Lord Byng refused Mackenzie King's request to do so. In this case, the governor general was primarily influenced by the fact that a motion of censure against the government regarding a scandal in the Customs Department was under debate in the House of Commons. The request for a dissolution appeared to be an attempt to avoid defeat in the Commons. In addition, the Opposition Conservatives actually had more seats than the governing Liberals (who had been kept in power with the support of the Progressives), and an election had been held only eight months before. Thus, it seemed logical to Lord Byng to try to avoid an election when an alternative government might be available.

Whether such discretionary action is appropriate today as a check on unconstitutional behaviour by prime ministers and cabinets remains an open question. Everyone is agreed, however, that in normal circumstances governors general must act on the advice of the prime minister and cabinet. Before governors general invoke such emergency powers, "they must be sure they have reached the danger point, and that their actions will stand up to the subsequent judgment of other institutions and the people."[4] The governor general has been called a "constitutional fire extinguisher" whose emergency powers can be used only "when normal controls cannot operate and a crisis gets out of hand."[5] Andrew Heard adds that "governors should intrude into the democratic process only to the minimum extent absolutely required for the basic functioning of Parliamentary government."[6] Since the governor general is intended to function as an impartial symbol of unity, any act that could remotely be interpreted as partisan must be avoided.

The Prime Minister and Cabinet
Powers of the Prime Minister and Cabinet

The prime minister and **cabinet** have the power to make the most significant governmental decisions. Given their importance, it is ironic that they are not provided for in the written parts of the Constitution, their functions and powers resting instead on custom and convention. What is provided for in the 1867

Constitution Act is a **Privy Council** to advise the governor general in the exercise of the powers of that office. In fact, the cabinet acts as a committee of the Privy Council, but rather than merely advising the governor general, it actually makes the decisions in question. With rare exceptions, the prime minister and cabinet exercise whatever powers are given to the Queen or the governor general in the Constitution. Such decisions often take the form of **orders-in-council.**

Thus, after an election, the governor general calls upon the leader of the party with most members elected to the House of Commons to become prime minister and to form a government. The prime minister assumes the title "Right Honourable" and selects the cabinet ministers, all of whom are sworn into the Privy Council, which allows them to use the title "Honourable" for life.

In normal circumstances, then, the prime minister and cabinet exercise the powers of the Crown. These powers include summoning and dissolving Parliament, the pardoning power, and the appointment of senators, judges, other officials, and royal commissions. The prime minister and cabinet recommend **money bills** to Parliament, and all international acts and the general conduct of foreign relations are the prerogative of the cabinet, including declarations of war and peace, signing treaties, appointing ambassadors, and recognizing foreign governments. The cabinet may feel it politically advantageous to have Parliament debate declarations of war and may need to submit legislation to Parliament to make treaties effective, but unlike the system in the United States, such international acts are essentially within the purview of the executive branch of government, not the legislature.

Exercising the powers of the Crown is only a small part of the reason that the prime minister and cabinet are the centre of gravity in the Canadian political system, however. More importantly, and similar to the executive of any organization, they have the responsibility for providing political leadership and determining priorities. That is, the prime minister and cabinet decide which problems to deal with, establish the general thrust and direction of new policies, and determine the spending priorities of the government. In the British and Canadian systems, the responsibility for initiating legislation rests primarily with the cabinet. As seen in Chapter 15, opportunities do exist for other members of Parliament to introduce bills, but most of the time of the House of Commons is set aside for government business. The Speech from the Throne provides the cabinet with an opportunity to outline its legislative program at the beginning of the session. The cabinet's virtual monopoly over the passage of legislation should ensure coordination among government policies, while its total monopoly over financial legislation is designed to guarantee a close relationship between policies adopted and the funds to make them effective. Such strong executive leadership, based on tradition, necessity, and the Constitution Act, and backed up by vast resources and advice, has generally proven itself to be an effective way to run a country.

Beyond the powers of the Crown and this general leadership function, cabinet power is also derived from specific acts of Parliament. Almost every law delegates to a minister or the **Governor-in-Council** (i.e., the cabinet) the power to make decisions of many kinds. Similarly, it is largely on the basis of acts of Parliament that individual ministers are charged with supervising the administration of their departments. Ministers provide direction and leadership, establish priorities, and transmit their personal, party, and cabinet perspectives, all in an effort to ensure that public servants remain accountable to democratically elected leaders and public opinion. As mentioned, ministers are also given quasi-legislative powers to issue regulations under a law, sometimes called delegated or subordinate legislation, which flesh out the bare bones of the statute. In addition, ministers are involved in Parliament, answering questions about the department's operations, defending departmental spending proposals, and piloting bills emanating from the department.

The principle of individual **ministerial responsibility**—each minister being held responsible to Parliament for everything that goes on in his or her department—was once thought to entail a minister's resignation over public servants' errors, even those the minister knew nothing about.[7] In an age of big government, however, the principle has lost most of its meaning. Ministers can still be criticized for departmental failures and are expected to correct them, but they rarely resign except for monumental personal mistakes and **conflicts of interest.** In

HARROP, *Back Bench*. Used with permission.

recent years, the lax administration of the Human Resources Development department attracted much criticism, but the principle of ministerial responsibility required only that the minister, Jane Stewart, clean up the mess, not resign.

The Prime Minister

The system of government that Canada inherited from Britain has traditionally been called **cabinet government,** but such a label does not do justice to the modern preeminence of the prime minister. Most observers agree that cabinet government has been transformed into a system of **prime ministerial government,** and no one doubts that the prime minister has enormous power and should be singled out for special attention.[8] The preeminence of the prime minister over cabinet colleagues can be seen in 10 of the PM's principal powers, rights, or responsibilities. In many cases, these relate to the different arenas in which the prime minister must operate, such as cabinet, Parliament, party, media, federal–provincial relations, international diplomacy, and the economy:[9]

- cabinet maker
- chair of cabinet meetings
- party leader
- chief policymaker
- leading player in the House of Commons
- chief personnel manager
- controller of government organization
- adviser to governor general
- chief diplomat
- public persuader

First, the prime minister is the cabinet-maker. Prime ministers select their own ministers, subject to certain conventions discussed below, and decide what portfolios to assign each of them. Ministers thus owe allegiance to the prime minister, who also issues them "mandate letters" that inform them of the PM's policy expectations in their portfolio.[10] The prime minister also promotes and demotes ministers, asks for their resignation, or, if necessary, dismisses them.

Chairing cabinet meetings is a second main source of the prime minister's power. To start with, the prime minister determines the agenda of such meetings, but in addition to the usual advantages of a chair, the prime minister benefits from the peculiar way in which cabinet decisions are arrived at. Rather than by motions and votes, the decision is reached when the PM summarizes the discussion and articulates the "consensus"--either by extracting a real consensus from the meeting or by imposing his or her own viewpoint. Ministers who do not agree with this interpretation either keep quiet or resign. Even though many decisions are now made by cabinet committees, the prime minister decides which committees will be struck, who will chair them, who will sit on them, and which matters will be sent to them, so that this delegation of power from the full cabinet does not necessarily reduce the PM's control.

Third, the prime minister is the leader of the party, and the PM's preeminence has probably increased over the years as political parties have become more cohesive and as election campaigns have come to focus on party leaders. In fact, many ministers may have been elected on the leader's coattails. As leader, the prime minister can control party organization, personnel, strategy, and policy, and in exceptional circumstances impose or veto party candidates. Jean Chrétien "appointed" a number of Liberal candidates in recent elections, for example, while Brian Mulroney refused to sign the nomination papers of Sinclair Stevens in order to improve his party's reputation for integrity.

Fourth, the prime minister could be called chief policymaker. The PM has the last word on government policy, whether in personal interaction with individual ministers, within the cabinet chamber, in Parliament, or in other forums such as the media. Modern government, of course, is too complex for one person to have an active role in formulating all policies, but the prime minister "can play a critical role in problem definition."[11] A recent example of prime ministerial power is the Clarity Act, which Jean Chrétien bulldozed through despite widespread opposition from cabinet colleagues, the Liberal caucus, and most informed observers.

Fifth, the prime minister is the central player in the House of Commons. Even though control of the parliamentary agenda is now delegated to the government House leader, the PM is still expected to be there and speak for the government in the oral Question Period almost every day.

A sixth source of prime ministerial preeminence is an enormous power of appointment. This includes the appointment of ministers, senators, Supreme Court judges, deputy ministers, and heads of a wide range of government agencies.

Given the extent and power of the bureaucracy today, the prime minister's seventh power, control over government organization, is also significant. Subject to usually routine parliamentary approval, the PM can decide to create new departments and set out their mandates, reorganize government departments, abolish departments or agencies, or privatize Crown corporations.

Eighth, the prime minister personally advises the governor general on such matters as when to call the next election. Chrétien called the November 2000 election, for example, against the virtually unanimous advice of cabinet and caucus.

In an era of summit diplomacy, the prime minister often overshadows the minister of Foreign Affairs on the world stage, functioning as Canada's chief diplomat. This role can be observed in annual bilateral meetings with the U.S. president, annual meetings of the Group of Seven (or Eight) leading industrialized countries, Commonwealth Conferences, meetings of the Francophonie, other summits, and occasional appearances at the United Nations.

The prime minister is also the chief "public relations officer" of the government, or "public persuader."[12] Television has become the main instrument for transmitting the prime minister's message to the party, the government, and the public. Survival in the battleground of media relations "threatens to become the key determinant of prime ministerial success."[13]

Given all these powers as well as a deferential majority in the House of Commons, the PM can usually succeed in controlling the policy and personnel of government. In many respects, in fact, the Canadian prime minister is more powerful than the American president, except of course in international clout. In order to get his agenda adopted, the latter must bargain with Congress in which party discipline is not strong, whereas prime ministers can normally count on a disciplined majority to back their measures. Indeed, the expansion of prime ministerial staff, the holding of prime ministerial news conferences, the making of televised addresses to the nation, luxurious travel arrangements, and other conspicuous trappings of power have led many observers to criticize the "presidentialization" of the office of prime minister.[14]

Others continue to emphasize the restraints on the power of the prime minister. Theoretically including the media, opposition parties, the Constitution, and the party, they more practically involve financial constraints, opposition from the provinces, international influences, and the limits within which government policy of any kind can effect societal change. The prime minister is often at the mercy of events, which may bring about a fall in public support and a loss of much overall influence in turn. On the other hand, there are two potential constraints that prime ministers do not have to worry much about. First, however much ministers may resent the prime minister's dominance, cabinet revolts are rare, only two having occurred in Canadian history (against Mackenzie Bowell and John Diefenbaker). Second, especially in the case of Jean Chrétien, having to conduct himself ethically was not a problem. Chrétien's conflict of interest rules for himself and cabinet ministers were neither clear nor enforceable, and the ethics counsellor was appointed by the prime minister and reported only to him rather than to Parliament. Indeed, the lack of general accountability, transparency, access to information, and ethics in government is an increasing problem.

Table 13.1, which contains a list of prime ministers ranked by length of tenure, reveals the variations in prime ministerial political fortunes.

TABLE 13.1 PRIME MINISTERS OF CANADA, RANKED BY LENGTH OF TENURE

Mackenzie King, 21 yrs., 5 mo.	Lester Pearson 5 yrs.
John A. Macdonald, 19 yrs.	Alexander Mackenzie 4 yrs., 11 mo.
Pierre Elliott Trudeau 15 yrs., 5 mo.	John Thompson 2 yrs.
Wilfrid Laurier 15 yrs., 3 mo.	Arthur Meighen 1 yr., 8 mo.
Brian Mulroney 9 yrs., 9 mo.	John Abbott 1 yr., 5 mo.
Robert L. Borden 9 yrs., 9 mo.	Mackenzie Bowell 1 yr., 4 mo.
Louis St. Laurent 8 yrs., 7 mo.	Joe Clark 9 mo.
Jean Chrétien 8 yrs., 4 mo.*	Kim Campbell 133 days
John Diefenbaker 5 yrs., 10 mo.	John Turner 80 days
R.B. Bennett 5 yrs., 3 mo.	Charles Tupper 69 days

*as of February 2002

Composition of the Cabinet

In theory, all cabinet ministers are equal, although in practice this is far from being the case. All recent PMs, for example, designated one minister as deputy prime minister. In some cases, this title seemed to carry more prestige than any real power, but when Herb Gray was appointed to this position in 1997, it was seen as quite significant.

Below the deputy PM are the regular departmental ministers, each normally in charge of a single department. An informal ranking of these departments may result in variations in influence among this group of ministers, with Finance, Foreign Affairs, Justice, Industry, Health, International Trade, Treasury Board, and Human Resources Development usually being among the key portfolios. The cabinet also contains some ministers who do not have full-fledged departments to administer, especially the government leaders in the House of Commons and the Senate. This category may also include junior ministers, variously called ministers without portfolio, ministers of state, or secretaries of state. They could be in charge of small agencies or assigned to assist a senior minister, and until Jean Chrétien became PM, the Canadian tradition was that all ministers, even these junior ones, were included in the cabinet.

Since the cabinet occupies such a central position in the Canadian policy-making process, every interest in the country would like to be represented in its deliberations. This desire alone creates pressure to expand its size. In general, the cabinet contained about 13 or 14 ministers before 1911, then rose to around 20 until about 1960, increasing to 30 under Trudeau, and to around 40 in the Mulroney period. Chrétien reduced the cabinet's size to 23 in 1993, supplemented by 9 junior ministers, called secretaries of state, who were part of the ministry but not invited to cabinet meetings. The secretaries of state each had a small staff and operating budget, and received 75 percent of a cabinet minister's pay. After the 2000 election, Chrétien's cabinet grew to 29, along with 8 secretaries of state in the ministry.

Several conventions have developed to constrain the PM's prerogatives in the selection of ministers. In the first place, reflecting the fact that Canada is a democracy and that the ministers represent the people, all cabinet ministers must have a seat in Parliament. Ministers sit in the legislative branch of government at the same time as they form the executive. Almost all ministers therefore have a seat in the House of Commons. It is possible for the prime minister to name someone to the cabinet who has not won election to the Commons, but convention dictates that such a person run in a by-election as soon as possible in order to obtain a seat. This sometimes happens when a PM chooses to appoint a person of unusual qualifications from outside parliamentary life, rather than a sitting backbencher, as Jean Chrétien did with Stéphane Dion and Pierre Pettigrew in 1996. The modern tradition is to include only one senator in the cabinet, usually serving as government leader in that chamber and having no departmental responsibilities.

The next constraint on the prime minister is the convention that each province be represented in the cabinet. This flows from the fact that Canada is a federation and that the Senate has never performed its intended role of representing provincial interests in Ottawa. Thus, with the occasional exception of Prince Edward Island, every province that has elected a member to the government side of the Commons has been awarded a cabinet position. This convention usually results in some ministers being appointed only because their province needs cabinet representation, rather than on their merits, leaving worthy MPs from other locations excluded. In both the Trudeau and Clark governments, the prime minister chose to appoint senators to the cabinet to represent provinces that had not elected any or enough government members (the three Western provinces in the former case and Quebec in the latter). That such a practice breaks the modern convention of having only one senator in the cabinet attests to the importance of provincial representation. In 1997, Chrétien responded to the absence of Liberal MPs from Nova Scotia by choosing his one senator from that province.

It is not only that residents of a province feel more secure if one of their number is in the cabinet; it is also very useful for the cabinet itself to have such provincial representation.[15] In fact, ministers essentially wear two hats: they speak for their department as well as for their province. This arrangement is functional for patronage as well as policy purposes: appointments and contracts awarded on a partisan basis in any province will be the responsibility of the resident minister, often called the "political minister" for that province.

Larger provinces are not content with a single minister, of course, and in a cabinet of 30 or 40 members, Ontario and Quebec have sometimes exceeded 10. In such cases the ministers can be distributed so that each region within the province gains its own representative. Prior to 1984, however, Quebec was usually underrepresented in the cabinet when the Conservatives were in power, and the West was inadequately represented in the Pearson and Trudeau cabinets.

The next convention of Canadian cabinet-making is a recognition of the need for a balance of ethnic representatives. A proper balance of anglophone and francophone ministers—that is, about one-third francophone and two-thirds anglophone—may result almost automatically from the carefully constructed provincial representation. French Canadians were underrepresented even in Liberal governments before 1963, however, and often grossly underrepresented in Conservative cabinets. It was only in the Pearson, Trudeau, and Mulroney cabinets that francophone ministers achieved or exceeded the one-third benchmark. Those of other ethnic origins were not proportionately represented in the past, except perhaps in the Clark and Mulroney cabinets, but now expect fairer cabinet representation.

As for other social divisions, religion was much more important in the pre-1900 period than it is today. Prime ministers are now more concerned to appoint women to the cabinet. Since it was difficult to include representatives of all social groups in his 1993 cabinet of only 23, Chrétien tried to appease some of the others in the appointment of the secretaries of state: three women, one member from P.E.I., one Aboriginal person, and one Asian.

The cabinet is therefore a principal locus of elite accommodation, and William Matheson writes of a representative cabinet as follows: "in the Canadian context the cabinet has filled a dual role, for in addition to exercising the usual functions of executive leadership, the cabinet has provided an arena in which the elites may counter the dysfunctional and unstabilizing effects of cultural, regional, and religious fragmentation."[16]

Once the PM has chosen the people who will form the cabinet, they must be assigned portfolios, that is, departmental responsibilities. It is not normally expected that ministers will be expert in the field to which they are appointed, partly because the electorate is not likely to furnish the prime minister with members of Parliament having such credentials. Indeed, an argument can be made that a semi-expert is more dangerous than a total amateur since the latter will have enough sense to listen to the real experts within the department, while the former might try to substitute his or her limited knowledge for theirs. Thus, apart from the minister of Justice's normally being a lawyer, there is no necessary relationship between ministers' training or pre-political occupation and their departmental assignment.

Operation of the Cabinet

CABINET SOLIDARITY AND CABINET SECRECY

The cabinet is usually considered to be a collective decisionmaking body. Exceptions to this notion include the prime minister's penchant to make decisions single-handedly, and decisions taken by cabinet committees or by individual ministers. Regardless of which or how many ministers are involved in the making of such decisions, however, the cabinet operates on the principle of **cabinet solidarity,** meaning that all ministers must publicly defend all cabinet policies or else resign. Ministerial resignations because of policy differences are rare in Canada, perhaps only 28 since 1867,[17] suggesting that the thought of giving up the perks of office engenders considerable flexibility in ministers' principles. The most extreme manifestation of cabinet solidarity can be seen in terms of the annual Budget, which is usually the most important government policy statement of the year. Only the Finance minister and PM know much about it until the budget is delivered in Parliament, yet all ministers must support it.

Cabinet solidarity is related to the principle of collective ministerial responsibility to Parliament. If the government loses the confidence of the legislature, it must collectively resign or call an election.

Cabinet solidarity is also linked to the principle of **cabinet secrecy** or confidentiality. Cabinet operations are shrouded in secrecy, and ministers are not supposed to disclose information about its deliberations. Such confidentiality protects state secrets, protects the cabinet against opposition and media exploitation of ministerial discord, and protects senior civil servants from identification and public criticism. Cabinet documents are not normally made public for 20 years, and, as a result, we do not know as much about how the cabinet operates as about decisionmaking bodies that meet in public. In fact, this exception from the

Access to Information Act, together with the weakness of the ethics counsellor, frustrates everyone who wants to understand why the cabinet makes the decisions it does. On the other hand, clever ministers are conscious that information represents power and that a well-timed "leak" can sometimes be of benefit when involved in a battle within cabinet.

CABINET PROCEDURE

Before 1960 or so, perhaps especially in the Mackenzie King and St. Laurent eras, ministers and departments were largely autonomous. Each developed its own policies and programs with little regard for central coordination and with only minimal prime ministerial interference. Strong ministers could make many decisions and policies without consulting their colleagues, and such ministers tended to remain in charge of a single department for long periods of time. Such autonomous departmental ministers often doubled as strong regional ministers, who were also allowed to handle regional responsibilities on their own. In addition, senior bureaucrats usually served their careers within a single department and became "carriers of the interests, traditions, skills and memories of these particularized bureaucratic organizations."[18]

Despite what has been said above about collective cabinet decisionmaking, the change from autonomous ministers to collegial cabinet decisions is really a product of the post-1960 period and the enormous expansion of government activity in the following 25 years. As society and its problems became more complex, individual ministers and departments could no longer make decisions and policies in isolation; the policies of one department almost inevitably affected those of another. More consultation and coordination were called for, with the result that ministerial collegiality replaced departmental autonomy. To some extent the need for policy coordination coincided with the view that cabinet ministers should have greater control over the bureaucracy; another stimulus was the concern for more rational government decisionmaking. The Pearson era was transitional in this respect, and the major change was adopted in the Trudeau period.

Prime Minister Trudeau attempted to increase the rationality of government policymaking in a variety of ways.[19] First, the PM and cabinet gave more attention to setting the overall priorities of the government. Second, the four central agencies—Prime Minister's Office, Privy Council Office, Finance Department, and Treasury Board Secretariat—were expanded and strengthened so as to provide policy analysis to the prime minister and cabinet independent of other government departments. Third, to avoid cabinet overload and to enhance specialization and policy coordination within it, most of the cabinet's work was done in committees. Fourth, cabinet procedures were rigidly adhered to, including agendas, advance notice of issues, and advance circulation of background documents. All of these measures tended to render cabinet decisions more coordinated, organized, and disciplined, hence the term institutionalized cabinet.[20]

The cabinet as a whole normally meets for about three or four hours once a week. An agenda is prepared by the Privy Council Office under the prime minister's supervision. It is circulated in advance, together with background documents—largely **Memoranda to Cabinet** from individual departments—and cabinet committee decisions and recommendations. The PCO will also have prepared a briefing note for the PM for guidance in getting through the meeting successfully, most PMs preferring that ministers and departments sort out their differences beforehand.[21] Rather than resolving questions by a formal vote, the prime minister sums up the discussion on each item and articulates the consensus arrived at. If this bears little resemblance to the actual tenor of the meeting, ministers who do not agree with this interpretation either keep quiet or resign, as noted above. A handful of senior officials is on hand to take note of the discussion and decisions, and to circulate minutes afterward. They are rarely asked to speak, but may pass notes to the PM. Given the demands on the time of those involved, meetings are conducted in a very businesslike manner.

The first item on the agenda is "General Discussion," which includes whatever is on the PM's mind. The second item is "Presentations," in which ministers may be invited to brief the cabinet on various issues. The third item is a list of "Nominations" or government appointments to be confirmed. The fourth item is cabinet committee decisions, attached to the agenda as appendices. A prime minister usually finds it annoying if any minister challenges a cabinet committee decision at this point.

As mentioned, since the mid-1960s more and more such work has been done by cabinet committees rather than by the full cabinet, each committee also normally meeting once a week. Unlike full cabinet meetings, ministers may bring advisers along to cabinet committees, so they are less reliant on their own personal resources. Between the Pearson and Mulroney regimes, the Priorities and Planning Committee was clearly the most important cabinet committee. Its special functions included setting priorities, allocating budgets, reviewing other committee decisions, making many important decisions itself, and supervising federal–provincial relations. Being chaired by the prime minister and containing the most important ministers (including the chairs of other cabinet committees) also added to its significance.

Jean Chrétien hoped to revert to the St. Laurent model of a cabinet operation in which individual ministers and departments were allowed to look after their own affairs. The maze of cabinet committees was reduced, leaving five after the 2000 election: Economic Union, Social Union, Treasury Board, Government Communications, and the Special Committee of Council.[22] Chrétien curtailed the scope of many other coordinating, central agencies, and departments were allowed more leeway in moving funds from one program to another. Even in an era of government downsizing, however, many observers felt that the complexity of issues required greater coordination and consultation, and that the 40-year-old model was no longer adequate. The Finance Department began to fill the gap, as it dominated the **Expenditure Management System.** This was partly because the Budget and the deficit were the driving forces of the day, but also because some kind of coordinating device was needed. The PCO also remained a significant coordinating mechanism.

Cabinet committees function much like cabinet as a whole. Working with the chair and the PM, the PCO will develop and distribute an agenda that is largely composed of Memoranda to Cabinet from various departments. Much interdepartmental discussion and negotiation will have taken place in advance, but if the committee cannot come to a consensus, the memorandum is returned for further work. If it is approved, it is attached to the agenda of the next meeting of the full cabinet.

Cabinet Support Agencies

As mentioned, the four main **central agencies** that exist to support the prime minister and/or the cabinet as a whole are the

- Prime Minister's Office
- Privy Council Office
- Finance Department
- Treasury Board

The **Prime Minister's Office** handles the prime minister's correspondence, media relations, partisan appointments, public appearances and speeches, and briefs the PM on legislative proceedings. It monitors political developments and offers policy advice from a partisan point of view. Jean Chrétien's PMO of about 90 bodies was headed by chief of staff Jean Pelletier until 2001, when Percy Downe took over; its other principal official was senior policy adviser Eddie Goldenberg. The PM usually meets daily with the head of the PMO to be briefed on developments from a partisan perspective.

The **Privy Council Office** has served several unique purposes since it was recognized as the cabinet secretariat and since cabinet meetings became more businesslike in 1940 due to the pressures of war. First, it provides logistical support for the cabinet—organizing meetings, preparing agendas, writing and distributing background material, taking and circulating minutes, and communicating cabinet decisions. In these ways the PCO is engaged in the coordination of overall government policy. The PCO also performs the same services for cabinet committees. PCO officials brief cabinet committee chairs and the prime minister even on the strategy of conducting their meetings. All these functions help the PCO obtain the kind of decisions that it considers best. Another example of its influence is in its detailed strategy notes for the prime minister when meeting important people or making critical telephone calls.

Other sections of the Privy Council Office have responsibility for the machinery of government, the appointment of senior public service personnel, and federal–provincial relations. The head of the PCO, the **Clerk of the Privy Council and Secretary to the Cabinet,** is regarded as the government's highest-ranking public servant. The Clerk meets daily with the prime minister to review problems and render nonpartisan advice. The PCO under Jean Chrétien was initially headed by Jocelyne Bourgon, the first woman to occupy this prestigious post, and then by Mel Cappe. The Clerk of the Privy Council could be called the lynchpin of the government of Canada. Being the closest adviser to the PM, the Clerk has his or her hands on almost everything that really counts: drafting the Speech from the Throne, working with the Department of Finance on the Budget, organizing the machinery of government, writing mandate letters for ministers and deputy ministers, appointing and evaluating deputy ministers, chairing the coordinating committees of deputy ministers, keeping an eye on Memoranda to Cabinet, helping to strategize cabinet and cabinet committee meetings, and keeping track of federal–provincial relations. The prime minister may be the most important player in the actual making of government decisions, but the Clerk will be advising on almost every one.

The **Department of Finance** and the Treasury Board primarily supply financial information to the cabinet, and have historically exercised a cautioning, restraining influence on new program proposals. The role of the Finance Department is to look at the government's overall revenue and expenditure situation, including its accumulated debt and annual deficit, and to advise on allocations among departments. Under the powerful deputy minister, it is also the chief adviser on taxation policy and on transfer payments to the provinces. While reporting directly to the minister of Finance and in that sense an ordinary department of government, Finance has a special responsibility of advising the cabinet collectively on such matters, being incorporated into the process of developing Memoranda to Cabinet as well as preparing the budget. In an age of government restraint and retrenchment, the influence of Finance necessarily increases, and in the first part of the Chrétien regime, that department basically determined the government's whole agenda.[23]

The **Treasury Board** is a committee of cabinet chaired by the minister called President of the Treasury Board, who is in turn in charge of a full-fledged government department, the **Treasury Board Secretariat.** This secretariat has the overall responsibility for controlling regular departmental spending, being involved in the development of detailed departmental budgets—the Estimates—and overseeing the actual expenditure of funds. The Treasury Board is also in charge of labour relations in the public service and issues policies on personnel, administration, and finance. In particular, Treasury Board approval is required for the hiring of any new personnel. Although its perspective is more detailed than that of Finance, the two agencies usually see things in a similar light, and Treasury Board's influence also increases when a government is obsessed with its deficit.

Figure 13.2 illustrates how these central agencies, as well as other relevant departments, have to be persuaded to support any departmental initiative before it can appear on the agenda of a cabinet committee en route to the cabinet as a whole.

Figure 13.2   Flow of a Departmental Initiative to Cabinet

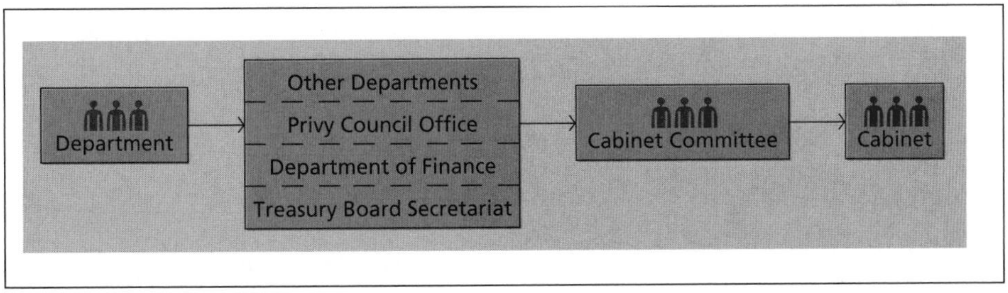

DISCUSSION QUESTIONS

1. What are the advantages and disadvantages of recognizing the Queen as the Canadian head of state?
2. Does the Prime Minister have too much power in the Canadian system of government?

3. Should individual departments and ministers have more power at the expense of collective decisionmaking processes and central agencies?

FURTHER READING

Bakvis, Herman. *Regional Ministers.* Toronto: University of Toronto Press, 1991.

Greenspon, Edward, and Anthony Wilson-Smith. *Double Vision: The Inside Story of the Liberals in Power.* Toronto: Doubleday Canada, 1996.

Heard, Andrew. *Canadian Constitutional Conventions.* Toronto: Oxford University Press, 1991.

Mancuso, Maureen, et al., eds. *Leaders and Leadership in Canada.* Toronto: Oxford University Press, 1994.

Milne, Glen. *Making Policy: A Guide to the Federal Government's Policy Process.* Ottawa: Glen Milne, 2000.

Robertson, Gordon. *Memoirs of a Very Civil Servant: Mackenzie King to Pierre Trudeau.* Toronto: University of Toronto Press, 2000.

Savoie, Donald J. *Governing from the Centre: The Concentration of Power in Canada.* Toronto: University of Toronto Press, 1999.

Smith, David E. *The Invisible Crown.* Toronto: University of Toronto Press, 1996.

Notes

1. Leslie A. Pal, *Public Policy Analysis: An Introduction* (Toronto: Methuen, 1987), 4.
2. Department of Justice, *The Federal Legislative Process in Canada* (Ottawa: Supply and Services, 1987).
3. David E. Smith, *The Invisible Crown* (Toronto: University of Toronto Press, 1996).
4. Frank McKinnon, *The Crown in Canada* (Calgary: McClelland and Stewart West, 1976), 124.
5. Andrew Heard, *Canadian Constitutional Conventions* (Toronto: Oxford University Press, 1991), 123.
6. Ibid., 47.
7. Kenneth Kernaghan and David Siegel, *Public Administration in Canada: A Text,* 2nd ed. (Scarborough: Nelson Canada, 1991), 379–85.
8. Donald J. Savoie, *Governing from the Centre: The Concentration of Power in Canada* (Toronto: University of Toronto Press, 1999); Gordon Robertson, *Memoirs of a Very Civil Servant: Mackenzie King to Pierre Trudeau* (Toronto: University of Toronto Press, 2000).
9. Leslie Pal and David Taras, eds., *Prime Ministers and Premiers: Political Leadership and Public Policy in Canada* (Scarborough: Prentice-Hall Canada, 1988); Peter Aucoin,

"Prime Ministerial Leadership: Position, Power, and Politics," in Maureen Mancuso et al., *Leaders and Leadership in Canada* (Toronto: Oxford University Press, 1994).

10. Savoie, *Governing from the Centre*, pp. 137–39; 343.

11. Leslie Pal, "Hands at the Helm? Leadership and Public Policy," in Pal and Taras, *Prime Ministers and Premiers*, 25.

12. Frederick Fletcher, "The Prime Minister as Public Persuader," in Thomas A. Hockin, ed., *Apex of Power*, 2nd ed. (Scarborough: Prentice-Hall Canada, 1977).

13. David Taras, "Prime Ministers and the Media," in Pal and Taras, *Prime Ministers and Premiers*.

14. Denis Smith, "President and Parliament: The Transformation of Parliamentary Government in Canada," in Hockin, *Apex of Power*, 315.

15. Herman Bakvis, *Regional Ministers* (Toronto: University of Toronto Press, 1991); "Cabinet Ministers: Leaders or Followers," in Maureen Mancuso, *Leaders and Leadership in Canada*.

16. W. A. Matheson, *The Prime Minister and the Cabinet* (Toronto: Methuen, 1976), ix, 22–23.

17. S. L. Sutherland, "Responsible Government and Ministerial Responsibility: Every Reform Is Its Own Problem," *Canadian Journal of Political Science* (March 1991): 101.

18. Donald Smiley, *The Federal Condition in Canada* (Toronto: McGraw-Hill Ryerson, 1987), 88.

19. Bruce Doern and Peter Aucoin, eds., *Public Policy in Canada* (Toronto: Macmillan, 1979).

20. J. Stefan Dupré, "Reflections on the Workability of Executive Federalism," in Richard Simeon, ed., *Intergovernmental Relations* (Toronto: University of Toronto Press, 1985).

21. Glen Milne, *Making Policy: A Guide to the Federal Government's Policy Process* (Ottawa: Glen Milne, 2000), p. 44.

22. On the Chrétien changes, see *The New Face of Government: A Guide to the New Federal Government Structure*, 2nd ed. (Ottawa: Canada Communication Group, 1994). He later appointed a cabinet committee on Antiterrorism.

23. Edward Greenspon and Anthony Wilson-Smith, *Double Vision: The Inside Story of the Liberals in Power* (Toronto: Doubleday Canada, 1996).

Chapter 14

The Bureaucracy

Most citizens encounter public servants as providers of services, but the **bureaucracy is** probably even more significant in its advisory role. Modern government is so pervasive and complex that the prime minister and cabinet ministers hardly make a move without the advice of their permanent, expert staff. In fact, the bureaucracy has become so large and indispensable that many observers wonder whether it can be kept under political control. This chapter begins by examining the functions and powers of the bureaucracy, and then deals in turn with the three main kinds of bureaucratic organization. It concludes with a discussion of controlling the bureaucracy and recent attempts to reform it.

Chapter Objectives

After you have completed this chapter, you should be able to:

Identify the role of the bureaucracy in the phases of the policymaking process

Describe the structure of a government department, distinguish between the roles of the minister and deputy minister, and explain the principle of ministerial responsibility

Indicate which central agencies impinge on the operation of government departments, and discuss the links between departments, their provincial counterparts, and pressure groups

Discuss the merit system and assess the attempts to make the public service more representative of society

Provide examples of Crown corporations, and outline their structure and operations

Provide examples of administrative agencies and regulatory tribunals, and outline their structure and operations

Enumerate the ways in which we attempt to control the bureaucracy

Discuss recent attempts to reform the bureaucracy

Functions and Powers of the Bureaucracy

As a veteran of the federal policy process, Glen Milne observes, "only major decisions require cabinet approval and fewer still require new legislation or amendments. In practice, the vast majority of federal government decisions are made at the bureaucratic level within a hierarchical framework of policies decided by cabinet and individual ministers."[1] But even when the other institutions of government are involved, the bureaucracy is usually there too. Thus, the significance of the bureaucracy can be demonstrated by examining its presence in the model of the policymaking process presented in Chapter 13. First, the bureaucracy plays a crucial part in the initiation phase. The bureaucracy may be a source of demands, since administrators of any program may be among the first to recognize its inadequacies. Even if a demand reaches the cabinet from other sources, once the politicians decide to look into an issue further, the public service will be asked to provide additional information and advice.

If the cabinet decides to take action at the priority-setting stage, the bureaucracy is then centrally involved in the policy formulation phase. With its concentration of technical information and experience, the public service spends a great deal of its time in formulating policies, since the details of such policies are usually beyond the grasp of the politicians. Once the policy, program, or law has received political authorization by cabinet and/or Parliament, implementation is almost exclusively a bureaucratic responsibility. In today's complex society, the politicians are forced to leave wide discretionary powers to the public service to carry out their general, abstract goals.[2] Because of the time and informational constraints on Parliament, most bills are passed in rather general or skeletal form, and the real meat or substance of the law is expressed in the regulations issued under it. These are published under the authority of the minister or cabinet in the *Canada Gazette*. A considerable lag often exists between the political approval of a law and its effective implementation, during which time the public service drafts such regulations, sets up new administrative machinery, and hires new personnel. The implementation phase may involve time-consuming negotiations with the provinces or with relevant interest groups. Once the date arrives for the start of a new program, it is the bureaucracy again that actually provides the service, does the regulating, or performs whatever other functions are involved. Implementation also requires the bureaucracy to disseminate information to the public about new policies or programs, and may even involve exercising quasi-judicial powers.

Given its role in almost all phases of the policymaking process, reference to "bureaucratic power" in political science or contentions that the bureaucracy is more powerful than the legislature or even the prime minister and cabinet should not be surprising. While it is more conventional to say that the prime minister and cabinet make the most important decisions in the political system and that they theoretically control the bureaucracy, this is not to deny the extent of bureaucratic power in the modern state. The most common forms of bureaucratic operations are government departments, Crown corporations, and administrative agencies and regulatory tribunals.

Government Departments

Most of the Government of Canada's operations are organized into government **departments.** Although each is created by an act of Parliament that sets out its responsibilities, the cabinet can determine the internal structure of the department and can even transfer responsibilities from one department to another.

A major consolidation of departments took place in 1993, reducing the overall number from 25 to about 20. As of early 2002, these were as follows:

- Agriculture and Agri-Food
- Canadian Heritage
- Citizenship and Immigration
- Environment
- Finance
- Fisheries and Oceans
- Foreign Affairs and International Trade*
- Health
- Human Resources Development
- Indian and Northern Affairs
- Industry
- Justice
- National Defence
- National Resources
- Public Works and Government Services
- Solicitor General
- Transport
- Treasury Board
- Veterans Affairs

*one department but two separate ministers

The government department assumes a pyramidal shape, with the minister at its apex. Since ministers in this system are chosen from among the politicians elected to Parliament, it is too much to hope that they will be experts in the work of the department. All that is expected is that they have intelligence, ideas, common sense, and an ability to relay government priorities and public opinion to departmental experts as well as to relate expert advice from the department to Parliament and the public. Ministers will naturally develop some expertise if they stay in one cabinet position for any length of time, but they are often shuffled to another department just as they are getting the hang of it. Jean Chrétien reverted to the earlier practice of leaving ministers in place if moves could be avoided.

Ministers are responsible for their department in the sense that they are expected to provide overall direction and to accept criticism for its faults. In other words, ministers take most of the credit or blame for what the department does, whether or not they know what is going on within it. As pointed out in Chapter 13, the principle of **ministerial responsibility** was once thought to mean that ministers had to resign for serious mistakes made by their public servants. But no cases of this occurring have been recorded since 1867, and in this age of big government it is not a realistic proposition.[3] What does ministerial responsibility mean today? First, ministers occasionally resign over their personal mistakes or conflicts of interest. Second, they must take political responsibility and answer to Parliament for all actions of their officials. The minister must explain and defend the actions of the department in Parliament, especially during Question Period, and when a bureaucratic error is made, the minister must apologize and promise to correct the mistake. Third, although ministers may discreetly discipline the offender, they should not violate the traditions of public service anonymity.[4] The lax accounting of job-creation funding at Human Resources Development in 2000 is a recent illustration that this is all that ministerial responsibility means. As a result of that case and others, the Auditor General wrote in 2001 that "Canada has never modernized its doctrine to distinguish between a minister's area of public responsibility and that of his senior public servants. To me, there is a certain lack of realism in holding ministers ultimately accountable for everything."[5]

The more permanent head of the department is the **deputy minister.** Even though appointed by the prime minister (on the advice of the Clerk of the Privy Council and Secretary to the Cabinet), "deputies" or "DMs" are usually career public servants. Deputy ministers have two principal roles: they act as chief policy adviser to the minister and function as manager of the department. Such officials used to spend a lifetime working their way toward the top of a single department and became great experts in its subject matter. Over the past 35 years, however, emphasis in the appointment of deputy ministers has switched to managerial skills that can be applied in any administrative setting. Even though DMs are now frequently shuffled from one department to another, they are still usually there longer than the minister, and are thus likely to develop greater knowledge of the department's work. Deputy ministers also interact regularly with DMs in other federal departments, provincial DMs in corresponding departments, and the heads of pressure groups particularly interested in the department's work.

The relationship between the minister and the deputy minister is of great interest and concern to political science and public administration.[6] Ideally, the minister sets the priorities for the department while the DM provides a number of options among which the minister can choose. The deputy should give the minister advice based on administrative, technical, and financial considerations, but the advice must also be sensitive to the political context. Evidence exists that the reality of the relationship sometimes approaches this theoretical ideal. On the other hand, weak ministers may be mere puppets of their bureaucratic advisers. Even strong ministers may be presented only with alternatives favoured by the department or may encounter bureaucratic resistance to new initiatives, such as in being denied relevant information, having it delayed, or having new policies implemented without enthusiasm. It has been said that the Department of Finance could impose its ideological bias even on a strong minister like Paul Martin.[7]

It is not easy for a single, solitary, temporary, amateur minister to impose his or her will on thousands of expert, permanent public servants who have established departmental attitudes, values, policies, and procedures. Ministers are allowed to appoint a small personal, partisan staff, but they are primarily engaged in promoting the image and reputation of the minister. In the Mulroney regime, ministers set up large offices headed by a powerful chief of staff, and these were, among other things, the target of most lobbying efforts. As in other ways, Chrétien reverted to an earlier era by reducing the size and significance of ministerial offices and eliminating the chief of staff position, replacing it with the Executive Assistant.

Nevertheless, the minister's political staff is significant.[8] They manage the minister's agenda, correspondence, travel, appointments, media liaison, public appearances, and meetings with lobbyists and interest groups. While the staff may also provide partisan policy advice and bargain with their counterparts in other ministers' offices, any effort to interfere in the administration of the department will be strongly resented by the deputy minister.

Under the deputy minister, the department is typically divided into several branches, each headed by an assistant deputy minister (ADM). The hierarchy broadens out below them. Those divisions of a department that actually carry out services and interact with the public are said to be performing "line" functions. Except for the top managerial posts, most of the line positions in any department will be located in the "field"—in local offices in communities across the country. But every department will also have "staff" divisions serving internal needs: policy development and research, personnel, financial, information, and legal divisions. These positions are normally located in Ottawa along with the heads of the line divisions.

Hundreds or thousands of public servants in the department are ranged in descending levels of authority under the deputy minister and share four basic characteristics: they are expert, permanent, impartial, and anonymous. First, they are chosen on their merits—ability, knowledge, training and/or experience—for the duties their position entails. Second, they are career public servants, normally remaining within the public service until retirement. Third, they are nonpartisan and expected to serve whichever party comes to power with equal loyalty and enthusiasm.[9] Fourth, bureaucrats are not normally identified in public; instead, the minister speaks for the department and takes responsibility for its performance. Figure 14.1 illustrates an organizational chart of a hypothetical government department.

The federal public service is divided into six main occupational categories: management or executive; scientific and professional; administrative and foreign service; technical; administrative support; and operational. The first four categories are called "officer" categories, generally requiring postsecondary education,

Figure 14.1   Organizational Chart of a Hypothetical Government Department

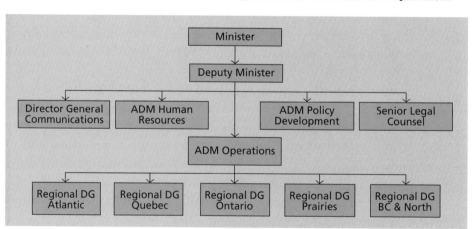

and the last two are called "support." University graduates are normally hired in the administrative and foreign service or scientific and professional groups and work their way up from there. Within each group are many levels or steps that determine one's salary level.

Relations with Other Departments and Central Agencies

The operation of a government department is complicated by the necessity of interacting with other departments as well as by the authority of various central bureaucratic agencies to intervene in its affairs. Since almost any law, policy, or program affects a variety of departments, many interdepartmental committees exist. Among the permanent ones are two Coordinating Committees of Deputy Ministers, one on management and the other on policy. In addition, whenever any new policy is under active consideration, an ad hoc interdepartmental committee is appointed to look into it. The problem must not only be examined from a number of departmental perspectives but also be subject to considerable bureaucratic "politics" and territorial claims.

The central agencies that regularly complicate the life of a department include the Public Service Commission (PSC), the Treasury Board Secretariat (TBS), and the Privy Council Office. The **Public Service Commission** is a three-member board theoretically in charge of all hiring, promotions, and dismissals. It polices the merit system and prevents appointments and promotions from being made on partisan or discriminatory grounds. In practice, however, the PSC delegates much of its authority to individual departments. The **Treasury Board Secretariat's** responsibility for personnel, financial, and expenditure management was outlined in Chapter 13. The TBS determines the terms and conditions of employment for the public service, approves the creation and classification of new positions, and represents the employer in the collective bargaining process. It is responsible for the preparation of the Estimates, and issues all sorts of administrative policies such as those on purchasing, contracts, and travel. The Department of Finance is normally allied with the TBS as an opponent of new departmental spending programs.

Relations between the Privy Council Office and government departments primarily arise in connection with policy development and coordination, reallocation of programs between departments, reorganization of departments, and senior management appointments. The PCO will have drafted the prime minister's mandate letter to the minister of the department and will take a great interest in any new policy proposals emanating from it.

Staffing the Bureaucracy

The Canadian public service originally operated on the spoils system, under which the party that won an election replaced those holding civil service positions with its own friends and supporters. One of the main motives for entering the political arena in that era was to reward family and friends with **political patronage**—government jobs and contracts.[10] Such partisan, amateur personnel proved to be increasingly inadequate as government operations grew more complex after the turn of the century, leading to the creation of the Civil Service Commission, predecessor to the Public Service Commission, in 1908. Henceforth, public servants in Ottawa were supposed to be hired on merit—that is, on the basis of their qualifications, training, and experience, rather than on partisanship or nepotism. And after passage of the 1918 Civil Service Act, field positions were also to be based on merit. Politicians were reluctant to give up their traditional right to reward their supporters with government jobs, however, and the foundations of the modern merit system in Ottawa were not really laid until the 1930s.[11]

Even if patronage was virtually eliminated in the public service, there remained considerable scope for partisan appointments in other areas. Senators, the boards of administrative agencies, regulatory tribunals, Crown corporations, certain diplomatic posts, the PMO and ministers' offices, lieutenant governorships, citizenship judgeships, and some real judgeships were all positions where partisan appointments still prevailed. The Liberals accused Brian Mulroney of excessive patronage, but the Chrétien government was no more restrained.[12]

Almost as soon as the **merit system** was fully effective, people began to demand that the bureaucracy be more representative of the society that it served. Given the power of the public service, many critics argued that the public service could be responsive to all parts of society only if it included a proportional representation of various groups in the population. The senior levels of the public service had always overrepresented males, anglophones, the middle and upper classes, the well educated, and Ontarians. Thus it was claimed that policy recommendations and implementation reflected an insensitivity to women, the working class, the poor, francophones and other ethnic groups, and the peculiarities of hinterland regions.

The first main concerns in this connection were the small number of francophones in the higher reaches of the bureaucracy and the virtual absence of the French language at policymaking levels. The passage of the **Official Languages Act** in 1969 essentially bilingualized the executive branch of government. It gave both English- and French-speaking citizens the right to deal with head offices of government departments in either official language, as well as with local offices where numbers warranted. It also expanded language-training programs, made recruitment and promotion of francophones a higher priority, and designated certain positions as bilingual. It was fortunate that the Quebec educational system had improved by this time so that the new policy involved little or no loss of quality in government appointments and promotions. The policy did, however, ignite a backlash against the preference given to French Canadians and to bilingualism. As of March 31, 1998, 32 percent of public-service positions had been designated as bilingual, 57 percent as English essential, 6 percent as French essential, and 4 percent as requiring either official language. As for the people who occupied these positions, about 71 percent are anglophones and 29 percent francophones, figures that bear a reasonably close approximation to countrywide census statistics.[13]

Women were targeted for increased representation in the higher levels of the public service in the 1960s and 1970s.[14] In addition, the pay equity program of the 1980s and 1990s was designed primarily to ensure that women received equal pay for doing work having the same value as that done by men. It is not easy to compare dissimilar jobs for purposes of compensation, but many occupational groups comprising largely women have argued that their work was undervalued just because they were women. Many have consequently had their salaries increased under the pay equity program; for example, a $3.6 billion pay equity settlement was negotiated in 1999 for some 200 000 secretaries and clerks.

The next stage in creating a more **representative bureaucracy** came in 1983 when an explicit affirmative action program was adopted for women, Aboriginal peoples, and people with disabilities, and two years later visible minorities were added to the list. Once again, this did not necessarily result in a decline in the quality of appointments and promotions, but it sparked opposition from those who did not fall into the designated categories, such as able-bodied, anglophone, white males. A stronger Employment Equity Act in 1995 required the adoption of policies and practices that would ensure that people in the four designated groups achieved a degree of representation in each occupational group proportional to their numbers in the Canadian work force. Table 14.1 provides 1998 figures by equity categories.

The Estimates System

Besides staffing government departments, determining their budgets is a major concern. As noted earlier, the authorities spend a great deal of their time dis-

TABLE 14.1　**Public Service by Employment Equity Categories**

	Women		Aboriginals		People with Disabilities		Visible Minorities		
	Number	%	Number	%	Number	%	Number	%	Total
Executive	803	25.1	58	1.8	93	2.9	91	2.8	3 203
Scientific & Professional	7 174	32.2	366	1.6	508	2.3	2 247	10.1	22 306
Administrative & Foreign Service	37 673	52.2	1 867	2.6	2 995	4.1	3 544	4.9	72 200
Technical	3 846	24.7	285	1.8	411	2.6	527	3.4	15 583
Administrative support	38 328	84.0	1 514	3.3	2 339	5.1	2401	5.3	45 634
Operational	2 977	14.2	680	3.3	597	2.9	450	2.2	20 905
Total	90 801	50.5	4 770	2.7	6 943	3.9	9 260	5.1	179 831

Source: Treasury Board of Canada Secretariat, *Employment Equity in the Public Service, Annual Report 1997–1998.* Reproduced with the permission of the Minister of Public Works and Government Services Canada, 2001.

cussing the expenditure of public funds. Members of Parliament want money allocated to their constituencies, premiers and federal ministers press to get funds allocated to their priorities and provinces, and bureaucrats seek funding for their programs and departments. In addition, much of the pressure from interest groups and corporations consists of demands for federal funds. In earlier eras, such spending was the prerogative of individual politicians or governing parties and was carried out on a patronage basis. Nowadays, the spending process has been highly bureaucratized, and it is the function of the **Estimates** system to decide how such funds will be allocated in any fiscal year. Of course, partisan considerations have not been entirely eliminated.

On the advice on the Finance Department, the Treasury Board, and the Privy Council Office, the cabinet decides what the government's financial priorities and overall levels of government revenue and expenditure will be, as well as approving any new spending initiatives. The preparation of the Estimates involves projections of the cost of new and existing programs at the departmental level within these limits and guidelines. A great deal of interaction takes place between departments and the Treasury Board Secretariat as deputy ministers and ministers try to maximize their departmental allocations while Treasury Board personnel engage in cutting them back. At the end of the process, the Estimates are consolidated for cabinet approval and introduced into Parliament by the President of the Treasury Board before the beginning of the next fiscal year.

Interaction with Provinces and Pressure Groups

Much of the interaction between federal and provincial governments takes place at the bureaucratic level. Because the division of powers is often vague and because both federal and provincial personnel usually try to maximize their jurisdiction, the two levels end up operating programs in the same fields. Limitations on provincial finances have also prompted the provinces to request federal financial assistance, to which Ottawa has usually attached conditions, making the federal government even more intertwined with provincial governments.

At the height of cooperative federalism, federal and provincial program administrators would often interact harmoniously in the design and operation of such integrated programs as the Canada Assistance Plan.[15] In many federal departments, line officials still interact regularly with their provincial counterparts. Nowadays, however, with federal funding in short supply, they are less likely to be engaged in developing new initiatives and are more often trying to "disengage."

The close relationship between pressure groups and the bureaucracy was discussed in Chapter 10. Groups wishing to influence either the formulation or the implementation of policies and programs are active in taking their message to the relevant government department. Sometimes public servants resist the approach of self-seeking groups, but the department will be more receptive if the group has vital, reliable information that will lead to the development of a more effective program or can help muster support for the departmental initiative among other key players in the policymaking process.

These mutually advantageous contacts between a group and a department may result in a symbiotic, **clientele relationship.** It will generally be in the interest of both the department and the group to keep their relationship somewhat confidential so that they can present a united front in case central agencies and cabinet committees become involved.

Crown Corporations

The second-most important form of bureaucratic organization is the **Crown corporation.** These are government-owned operations that assume a structure similar to a private corporation. There are about 50 major Crown corporations at the federal level, including

- Atomic Energy of Canada Ltd. (AECL)
- Bank of Canada
- Business Development Bank of Canada
- Canada Mortgage and Housing Corporation (CMHC)
- Canada Pension Plan Investment Board
- Canada Post Corporation
- Canadian Broadcasting Corporation
- Canadian Wheat Board
- Marine Atlantic Inc.
- St. Lawrence Seaway Authority
- VIA Rail Canada Inc.

The largest in terms of employees in 1999 were Canada Post (43 064), the Canadian Broadcasting Corporation (6 728), AECL (3 675), VIA Rail (2 969), and CMHC (2 366).

One major difference between a Crown corporation and a regular government department can be seen in its structure. A Crown corporation includes a board of directors, president, vice presidents, etc. The cabinet appoints the president as well as the board of directors, who theoretically set the general policy of the corporation.

A second distinguishing feature of the Crown corporation is that it is not subject to day-to-day political direction. The statute that creates it sets out its objectives to some extent, and the cabinet may issue general policy guidelines, but the corporation otherwise operates more or less independently. The cabinet minister to whom the Crown corporation is attached acts largely as a channel of communication between it and Parliament, passing on answers to parliamentary inquiries but not being held responsible for the corporation in the same way as for a regular department. On the other hand, because the government created the Crown corporation, appoints its leading personnel, and usually provides some of its funds, the minister and cabinet cannot avoid complete responsibility for its actions. A government obsessed with its deficit can make deep cuts in a Crown corporation's budget, as the CBC found throughout the Mulroney and Chrétien periods.

Third, Crown corporations are freer of bureaucratic controls relating to personnel or finance than ordinary government departments. As a general rule, the greater the financial self-sufficiency of the corporation, the greater its autonomy. They can therefore operate more flexibly than government departments, especially if in competition with private firms.

The Crown corporation is thus a logical structure for a governmental operation of a commercial or industrial nature. It may also be used in politically sensitive areas such as broadcasting, and/or if the operation has private-sector competition. More specifically, Crown corporations have been created to promote national integration (VIA Rail, Canada Post, and Marine Atlantic), national identity (CBC and Canada Museums), a particular industry (Canadian Wheat Board), and business in general (Business Development Bank).

Like other government operations, then, Crown corporations have a public policy purpose. They are created where, for one reason or another, the private sector has not met public needs. The basic objective of Crown corporations is to provide a public service, not to make a profit, but because most Crown corporations need annual public subsidies, they are often criticized for being inefficient. In fact, however, they may be just as efficient as private companies; the subsidies are necessary because many Crown corporations operate in areas where no profit is feasible.

The 1980s witnessed a worldwide trend toward the **privatization** of public enterprises, led by Margaret Thatcher in Britain, and the Mulroney government happily jumped on the bandwagon. Privatizations were made largely for two ideological reasons: the government had an instinctive preference for the private sector, and the sale of Crown corporation shares helped to reduce the national deficit. Privatizers also argued that such Crown corporations no longer served a public policy purpose and that they would operate more efficiently as private companies. The Chrétien government also did its share of privatization, such that by the turn of the new century, the following major Crown corporations were no longer owned by government: Air Canada, Canadian National Railway, Eldorado Nuclear, Fishery Products International, Petro-Canada, Teleglobe Canada, and Telesat.

Administrative Agencies and Regulatory Tribunals

Administrative agencies and regulatory tribunals are the third basic form of bureaucratic organization. Such agencies regulate many aspects of our daily lives, some of the most important being listed below.

- Canadian Nuclear Safety Commission (formerly Atomic Energy Control Board)
- Canadian Customs and Revenue Agency

- Canadian Food Inspection Agency
- Canadian Human Rights Commission
- Canadian Radio-television and Telecommunications Commission (CRTC)
- Canadian Transportation Agency
- Immigration and Refugee Board
- National Energy Board
- National Parole Board

In structure, administrative agencies and regulatory tribunals bear considerable resemblance to Crown corporations. They comprise a chair and board appointed by the cabinet and are advised by a permanent, expert staff. The incidence of partisanship in appointments to the chair and board is unfortunately quite large; indeed, these remain one of the last refuges of patronage in the political system. Such agencies typically receive policy guidelines from the cabinet, but as with Crown corporations, ministers are kept at arm's length from their day-to-day operations.

Administrative agencies and regulatory tribunals may make **quasi-legislative** rules and regulations, such as in the case of the Canadian-content regulations of the CRTC. A typical regulatory agency also makes **quasi-judicial** decisions based on the cabinet's policy guidelines and its own regulations. Among other things, regulatory agencies decide contentious immigration cases (Immigration and Refugee Board), review transportation rates (Canadian Transportation Agency), approve exports of natural gas and electricity (National Energy Board), and allow prisoners out of jail (National Parole Board).

These functions could presumably be performed by regular government departments, but they are given to semi-independent agencies in order to divorce them from political and partisan considerations. Such adjudicative functions could also be performed by the courts, but these kinds of decisions demand a technical expertise not expected in judges. Moreover, given the backlog in the court system, it is hoped that the decisions of administrative agencies and regulatory tribunals will be made more quickly and more cheaply than those of the courts.

At the same time, however, regulatory agencies are expected to provide an impartial, court-like hearing, and in many cases lawyers are present in the same capacity as in court. Decisions of such agencies are normally appealable to the courts on procedural grounds, but not on the substance of the case, and some are appealable to the cabinet.

Many observers have argued that there are too many regulatory agencies with too much power. Hence, **deregulation** was a companion ingredient to privatization in the neoconservatism of the past 15 or 20 years. The Canadian transportation industry in particular was deregulated to a large extent.

***

Not all government operations fall into the three categories discussed above. Others include central agencies (e.g., PCO), royal commissions, advisory councils (e.g., National Council of Welfare), funding bodies (e.g., Social Sciences and Humanities Research Council), and agents of parliament (Auditor General, Elections Canada, the Information Commissioner, and the Commissioner of Official Languages). One-of-a-kind agencies include Statistics Canada, the RCMP, the Correctional Service, and the Canadian Security Intelligence Service.

Royal commissions are formal, in-depth inquiries set up by the cabinet to investigate some difficult problem for which the resources of the regular public service are considered inadequate. Royal commissions may be headed by up to 10 commissioners, usually people of stature and expertise, and normally involve extensive public hearings and an elaborate research program. They are often regarded somewhat cynically because of their cost and because of the length of time it takes them to produce a report. Cynics also point out that governments have not had a good record of implementing royal commission recommendations, and that such commissions often appear to be appointed to take the heat off a particular issue on which the government has no intention of taking action. Sometimes they are also seen as devices with which to educate the public to the government's way of thinking or to generate support for a policy the government already had in mind. For example, their terms of reference may exclude alternatives that the government has already rejected, such as in the case of the Royal Commission on Electoral Reform and proportional representation. Nevertheless, many royal commissions have served a useful purpose and many public policies such as equalization payments, medicare, official bilingualism, and free trade owe their existence, at least in part, to royal commission reports.

· ·

Controlling the Bureaucracy

Given the enormous influence and considerable power of the bureaucracy in the modern state, democracies are understandably concerned about keeping the public service under control. Means of doing so can be identified in Figure 14.2.

First, individual ministers and the cabinet as a whole are supposed to provide political control of the bureaucracy. The minister gives direction to the public service and has the power to veto any of its proposals. Ministers have provided varied accounts of what happens in practice: some argue that they do control their departments, while others feel that they are manipulated by their public servants. In a more specialized context, civilian control of the military and police is an important principle in a democratic society.

····································· ····

Figure 14.2   Means of Controlling the Bureaucracy

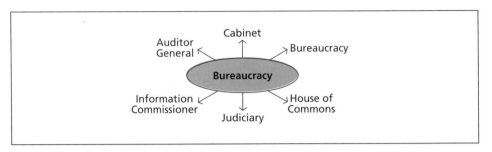

Second, the power of some bureaucrats is controlled by other bureaucrats. This includes the financial control of the Treasury Board Secretariat and the Finance Department, the personnel control of the Public Service Commission, and the policy control of the Privy Council Office.

The third line of defence against bureaucratic power is the House of Commons. One principle of parliamentary government is that the executive (cabinet or bureaucracy) is not allowed either to raise or to spend money without Parliament's approval. In practice, proposals for tax changes as well as spending proposals all originate with the executive, they are rarely altered in the legislative process, and the taxing and spending usually begins before Parliament has given its consent. Examining the Estimates, however, gives the House of Commons an opportunity to question and criticize ministers and deputy ministers about all aspects of their departmental spending, programs, and policies. Furthermore, once the money has been spent, an official of Parliament, the **Auditor General,** inspects the Public Accounts and informs Parliament of instances where funds were spent unlawfully or unwisely.[16] The **Public Accounts Committee** of the House (chaired by an opposition member) goes through the Auditor General's report and calls onto the carpet those ministers or deputy ministers who have committed the worst financial faults.

Considerable controversy raged in the 1980s over the size of the Auditor General's staff, their ability to gain access to cabinet documents, and whether they should function narrowly as auditors or make broader policy recommendations. The Auditor General's staff now perform "legislative audits," which go beyond traditional financial auditing, but the independence of the office needs stronger protection.[17]

The House of Commons has several other means of exercising some control over the bureaucracy, the first being the daily oral Question Period. In this case, the Commons acts through the intermediary minister who is theoretically responsible for everything the department does. Although the minister is expected to take the blame for bureaucratic errors, public servants seek to avoid bringing such embarrassment or disrepute upon their minister and department. In addition, members of Parliament receive requests on a daily basis from their constituents to intervene on their behalf to speed up or correct bureaucratic decisions. MPs and their staff normally handle such problems with a telephone call or a letter to the public servant or minister concerned. Another aspect of parliamentary control of the bureaucracy is exercised by the Standing Joint Committee on the Scrutiny of Regulations, which attempts to review the reams of regulations that the bureaucracy produces annually. On the other hand, as the Auditor General pointed out in 2001, Parliament needs more information about the government's use of resources and about the results of government programs.

A fourth kind of control of the bureaucracy is provided by the judiciary. The power of the courts to overturn decisions of bureaucrats in regular government departments is essentially restricted to cases of breaches of the law or actions taken beyond the public servant's jurisdiction. The Charter of Rights provides more scope for this kind of judicial review than has existed in the past. In the *Singh* case, for example, the Supreme Court ruled that the Immigration Department had to provide an oral hearing for all refugee claimants rather than deport such claimants on the basis of written documents alone, as was previously done. The *Little Sisters* case involved a book store complaining that customs officers routinely rejected books and magazines the store had ordered merely on the basis of the publications' sexual orientation. The Supreme Court told customs officers that they must not discriminate against gay or lesbian material; all sexually oriented material must be judged by the same criteria.

In the Words of the Court

"The Customs treatment was high-handed and dismissive of the appellants' right to receive lawful expressive material which they had every right to import…. [I]t is fundamentally unacceptable that expression which is free within the country can become stigmatized and harassed by government officials simply because it crosses an international boundary…. A large measure of discretion is granted in the administration of the Act, from the level of the Customs official up to the Minister, but it is well established that such discretion must be exercised in accordance with the Charter."

Little Sisters Book and Art Emporium v. Canada (Minister of Justice).

Police officers are a special category of bureaucrats who have also had their professional behaviour severely restricted by judicial interpretation of the legal rights section and/or section 24 of the Charter, as noted in Chapter 10. Regulatory agencies are usually expected to operate in a court-like manner, and their decisions can be overturned by the courts for procedural abuses as well as for exceeding their jurisdiction. The Federal Court of Canada, discussed in Chapter 16, specializes in hearing appeals from such regulatory agencies.

Finally, of several independent watchdog agencies, the most important next to the Auditor General is the **Information Commissioner.** Canadian governments have traditionally functioned under a cloak of secrecy at both the cabinet and bureaucratic levels. This tradition prevented the opposition and the public from knowing what alternative policies were considered, what kind of public opinion polling was done, or what advice was actually offered by the bureaucracy. The 1983 **Access to Information Act** considerably improved the situation, although the many exemptions in the act mean that it is not entirely effective. If a citizen, journalist, company, or pressure group is denied access to a desired piece of government information, they can appeal to the Information Commissioner, who can overrule the department in the matter. The government can, however, appeal to the Federal Court, and in recent years that court has frequently sided with the government, especially the PMO, when the Information Commissioner supported more openness.

· ·

Reform of the Bureaucracy:
The New Public Management

Apart from the problem of keeping the bureaucracy under some kind of democratic control, three other problems or dysfunctions are often identified. First, from the public's perspective, the bureaucracy is accused of being bound up in "red tape." This generally includes a collection of sins that characterize the behaviour of all large organizations, not only governmental ones, including delays, a multitude of forms, excessive rules and regulations, difficulty in finding the appropriate official to solve a problem, and lack of helpful, personal attention. If these dysfunctions are more characteristic of government than of large private firms, it is primarily because governments are required to operate according to the law and the regulations issued under the law. Government must treat everyone in exactly the same way, and unlike private firms, cannot show favouritism or make individual exceptions. Delays are usually the result of public servants wanting to be

Denny Pritchard. Reproduced with permission.

certain that their decision is absolutely right, because mistakes may be criticized in Parliament or in the media.

A second general criticism of bureaucracy is that it is inefficient because it lacks the profit motive of the private sector. Officials in private firms are said to move more quickly because they are in greater danger of losing their jobs and because minimizing costs is a higher priority. To some extent this is true, or at least may once have been. Given that the essential difference between the public and private sectors is that the bureaucracy is charged with providing a public service, however, it should be judged primarily on the adequacy of that service. Nevertheless, the widespread belief that there is much "fat" and inefficiency within the bureaucracy led both the Mulroney and Chrétien governments to impose severe financial restraints on government departments and Crown corporations, leading them to make across-the-board cuts, terminate programs, lay off staff, freeze hiring, charge user fees, and contract out certain services.[18]

From a management point of view, the main dysfunction of the public service is that deputy ministers and other managerial personnel are too hemmed in by rules and regulations and their authority is too limited by central agencies. Several recent reforms have been introduced to provide more autonomy and managerial flexibility to deputy ministers by relaxing some of the detailed rules and reporting requirements.

The reforms mentioned above—giving managers more autonomy, privatizing Crown corporations, deregulation, and the major restructuring of government departments in 1993—were merely part of a major transformation of the Canadian federal public service over the past 15 years that has parallels around the world and that is often called the **New Public Management (NPM).** General factors leading to such public service reform included debt and deficits, changing public and private sector expectations, globalization, new technologies, growing doubts about the capacity of state institutions to fulfill their mandates, and citizen demands for direct political participation.[19]

The 1994 and 1995 federal Budgets inaugurated a process generally labelled Program Review. This involved a fundamental rethinking of what government did and how it did it—or redefining the role of government.[20] Through this process, the federal government determined which activities it could continue to deliver or support within a much reduced budget. It also identified which activities to cease providing, scale back, devolve, or deliver or finance differently. The process involved significant reductions in subsidy programs, increased user fees, and put many government activities on a commercial basis. In the 1995 Budget, the minister of Finance ensured that real Program Review would happen when he declared his intention to eliminate 45 000 public-service jobs by 1998 to help the government reduce its deficit.

Another part of New Public Management was called **Alternative Service Delivery (ASD).** ASD is a generic term covering a variety of innovative means of providing government services that involve reducing the size and expense of government, making government more citizen-oriented, involving users and more flexibility in service delivery, enhancing employee motivation, and incorporating new developments in information technology. ASD consists primarily of Special Operating Agencies and developing partnerships with provinces or commercial or nonprofit organizations outside government.

Special Operating Agencies (SOAs) are units that function with relative autonomy within government departments. In most cases they have the potential to become self-financing, and their objective is to deliver a service along private-sector lines, that is, in a manner that is more sensitive to client requirements, that promotes a more creative entrepreneurial working environment, and that brings savings to government. The Passport Office and the Translation Bureau are examples of the 19 SOAs in existence.

The first kind of "partnership" involves the provinces, and the two main initiatives in this category were the Canadian Food Inspection Agency and the Canada Customs and Revenue Agency. The former combines the food inspection services previously provided by three separate federal departments and opens the way for provincial government involvement. The CCRA is a transformation of the Revenue Canada department into an agency responsible for collecting federal, and if the province wishes, provincial taxes.[21]

The federal government may enter other kinds of partnerships with private firms, nonprofit, noncommercial, or volunteer organizations. The government–private company relationship behind the construction and operation of the Confederation Bridge between Prince Edward Island and New Brunswick and the creation of local authorities to operate Canadian airports are prominent examples. Another is NAV CANADA, the agency created to replace the government's air traffic control system. Its board of directors includes representatives of the airlines, government, and employee unions, and it sets its rates so that it breaks even. In some cases, government employees have been encouraged to deliver services from the private sector that they previously provided as public servants.

It should be said, however, that not everyone thinks the reality of NPM matches its rhetoric, and many observers do not believe it to be a good idea at all. For example, the whole movement stems from a preoccupation to cut government expenditures, which involved the elimination of thousands of government jobs. Beyond the fact that fewer public servants are now delivering fewer public services is a troubling question of democratic accountability. It can certainly be argued that with semi-independent partners of various kinds supplying public services, any semblance of democratic ministerial responsibility has been lost.

Apart from ASD, public service reform at the dawn of the new century primarily centred on both making the public service a better place to work and strengthening its policy capacity. La Relève was an initiative undertaken in 1997 to address "the quiet crisis of downsizing, pay freezes, criticism, insufficient recruitment, and premature departure of experienced public servants." [22] Besides improving the quality of the workplace for those already there, including accelerated executive development, it involved the recruitment of qualified new blood. La Relève evolved into the Leadership Network in 1998, a separate agency reporting to the cabinet secretary to ensure the effective management of ADMs as a valued corporate resource. Ottawa will also have to replace a huge number of retirees in the near future. To help guide these efforts, the PM established a task force on Modernizing Human Resources Management in the Public Sector in April 2001.

The latest innovation in government operations is "e-government," that is, making government "electronic" and putting it on-line. By 2004, Ottawa intends to be more electronically connected to its citizens than any other government in the world, with Canadians able to access all government information and services on the Internet.

DISCUSSION QUESTIONS

1. To what extent should Canada establish a "representative bureaucracy?"
2. Given the necessity of the bureaucracy in the modern state, are the democratic controls on its power sufficient?
3. How do you feel about downsizing the public service, privatizing Crown corporations, deregulation, and the various initiatives involved in the New Public Management?

FURTHER READING

Auditor General. *Reflections on a Decade of Serving Parliament, Report of the Auditor General of Canada.* February 2001.

Clerk of the Privy Council and Secretary to the Cabinet. *Annual Report to the Prime Minister of Canada.*

How Ottawa Spends. Toronto: Oxford University Press annual.

Inwood, Gregory J. *Understanding Canadian Public Administration: An Introduction to Theory and Practice.* Scarborough: Prentice Hall Canada, 1999.

Kernaghan, Kenneth, and David Siegel. *Public Administration in Canada: A Text.* 2nd ed. Scarborough: Nelson Canada, 1991; 3rd ed., 1995; 4th edition, 1999.

Osbaldeston, Gordon. *Keeping Deputy Ministers Accountable.* Toronto: McGraw-Hill Ryerson, 1989.

Pal, Leslie A. *Beyond Policy Analysis: Public Issue Management in Turbulent Times.* Scarborough: ITP Nelson, 1997.

Peters, B. Guy, and Donald Savoie. *Taking Stock.* Montreal: McGill-Queen's University Press, 1998.

Notes

1. Glen Milne, *Making Policy: A Guide to the Federal Government's Policy Process* (Ottawa: Glen Milne, 2000), p. 4.
2. Kenneth Kernaghan and David Siegel, *Public Administration in Canada: A Text,* 2nd ed. (Scarborough: Nelson Canada, 1991), 137.
3. S. L. Sutherland, "Responsible Government and Ministerial Responsibility: Every Reform Is Its Own Problem," *Canadian Journal of Political Science* (March 1991): 91–120.
4. Kernaghan and Siegel, *Public Administration in Canada,* 379–85; S.L. Sutherland, "The Al-Mashat Affair: Administrative Responsibility in Parliamentary Institutions," *Canadian Public Administration* (Winter 1991): 573–603.

5. Auditor General, *Reflections on a Decade of Serving Parliament, Report of the Auditor General of Canada* (February 2001), p. 57.

6. Gordon Osbaldeston, *Keeping Deputy Ministers Accountable* (Toronto: McGraw-Hill Ryerson, 1990).

7. Linda McQuaig. *The Cult of Impotence* (Toronto: Penguin Books, 1998).

8. Milne, *Making Policy*, p. 43.

9. When the government is pursuing a policy not favoured by the bureaucrats, the latter have been known to leak documents to the Opposition!

10. Jeffrey Simpson, *Spoils of Power* (Toronto: Collins, 1988); S.J.R. Noel, "Leadership and Clientelism," in David Bellamy et al., eds., *The Provincial Political Systems* (Toronto: Methuen, 1976).

11. J.L. Granatstein, *The Ottawa Men: The Civil Service Mandarins 1935–1957* (Toronto: Oxford University Press, 1982).

12. See, for example, *The Globe and Mail* (December 10, 1997), p. A4.

13. Treasury Board of Canada Secretariat, *Annual Report to Parliament on Official Languages, 1997–1998.* (Ottawa: Ministry of Public Works and Government Services, 1998) cat. No. BT23-1/1998.

14. Kathleen Archibald, *Sex and the Public Service* (Ottawa: Queen's Printer, 1970); Task Force on Barriers to Women in the Public Service, *Beneath the Veneer*, Vol. 1 (Ottawa: Supply and Services, 1990).

15. Rand Dyck, "The Canada Assistance Plan: The Ultimate in Cooperative Federalism," *Canadian Public Administration* (Winter 1976).

16. S.L. Sutherland, "On the Audit Trail of the Auditor General: Parliament's Servant, 1973–80," *Canadian Public Administration* (Winter 1980): 616–44; S.L. Sutherland, "The Politics of Audit: The Federal Office of the Auditor General in Comparative Perspective," *Canadian Public Administration* (Spring 1986): 118–48.

17. Auditor General, *Reflections on a Decade of Serving Parliament*, 47, 54.

18. Kernaghan and Siegel, *Public Administration in Canada*, 498–502.

19. Leslie A. Pal, *Beyond Policy Analysis: Public Issue Management in Turbulent Times* (Scarborough: ITP Nelson, 1997); Guy B. Peters and Donald Savoie, *Taking Stock* (Montreal: McGill-Queen's University Press, 1998).

20. Jocelyn Bourgon, *Third Annual Report to the Prime Minister of Canada*, 1995; Treasury Board, *Getting Government Right: Governing for Canadians*, February 1997.

21. Kernaghan and Siegel, *Public Administration in Canada*, 4th ed., p. 302.

22. Bourgon, *Fourth Annual Report to the Prime Minister of Canada*, 1997; *Fifth Annual Report*, 1998.

Chapter 15

Parliament

Although the term theoretically includes the Queen and the Senate, the word **"Parliament"** is popularly synonymous with the House of Commons, by far its most important part. Hence, those elected to the House of Commons are called members of Parliament or MPs. The House of Commons is the central link between the public and the government in Canadian democracy; it is where the elected representatives of the people meet in daily, open, verbal combat. This chapter examines the House of Commons from a number of perspectives, and later explores the role of the other branch of the legislature, the Senate.

Chapter Objectives

After you have completed this chapter, you should be able to:

Discuss the functions of the House of Commons and its members within and beyond the policymaking process

Comment on the extent to which MPs are representative of the population

Outline the weekly and yearly parliamentary timetables

Evaluate the advantages and disadvantages of strict party discipline

Identify the different stages and kinds of legislation

Identify the various officers of the House of Commons

Discuss the committee system of the House

Comment on the various roles MPs perform and members' services

Discuss the balance between government and opposition, distinguishing between majority and minority situations

Enumerate the intended functions of the Senate and assess its performance

Discuss possible avenues of Senate reform

Functions and Powers of the House of Commons

The **Westminster model** of government employed by Canada begins with a bicameral **legislature**—an elected lower house, the House of Commons, with primary legislative powers answerable to the people through elections, and an upper house, the Senate, with limited legislative powers. The executive is part of the Commons and, through the cabinet, drives or "energizes" the legislative process. The **government** or cabinet is in charge of and responsible for the conduct of parliamentary business, while an institutionalized opposition has the right and duty to criticize the government. This model therefore promises potent government and political stability through the cabinet, along with political accountability through open debate. MPs can thus be divided into three main groups: those who serve as cabinet ministers, those who support the cabinet (government **backbenchers**), and those who oppose the government (the **opposition**).[1]

Historically, the sovereignty or **supremacy of Parliament** has been a basic principle of Canadian government. Apart from interfering in provincial jurisdiction and with other minor exceptions, Parliament could pass laws that were virtually beyond review by any other organ of government, including the courts. With the adoption of the Charter of Rights and Freedoms in 1982, however, this principle was considerably transformed. The courts have now been given the power of **judicial review,** that is, the right to examine both federal and provincial legislation in terms of the Charter, and to invalidate such legislation to the extent of any contradiction. On the other hand, rather than throw out a law, the courts have often suggested that the legislation be redrafted to fit within the boundaries of the Charter; moreover, the notwithstanding clause allows for the reassertion of Parliamentary sovereignty on many points.

In discussing the functions of the House of Commons it is instructive to examine its role in the chart of the policymaking process illustrated in Figure 13.1 on page 272. First, Parliament may be involved in the initiation phase by raising issues in the daily Question Period and in general debates, in criticizing existing spending programs, or by means of private members' bills. It is then virtually nonexistent in the priority-setting and policy-formulation phases. However, the Commons dominates the legitimation stage. Whether or not bills are refined in the process, cabinet proposals are made legitimate by their passage through the formal, authorized, democratic channels of the Commons. The House may not make many significant changes, but it does subject bills to extended debate and publicizes their advantages and disadvantages before converting them into laws or statutes. The legislative stage serves to inform the public of the content of new policies, and out of this "prolonged warfare," consent or acceptance is eventually obtained. This debate essentially prepares the electorate for its decision on how to vote in the next election.

....

Composition of the House of Commons

The basic principle of representation in the House of Commons is that each province is represented in proportion to its population. Chapter 8 outlined how the 301 seats in the Commons are distributed among the provinces, as shown in the accompanying box.

Seats in the House of Commons

Ontario	103	New Brunswick	10
Quebec	75	Newfoundland	7
British Columbia	34	P.E.I.	4
Alberta	26	N.W.T.	1
Manitoba	14	Yukon	1
Saskatchewan	14	Nunavut	1
Nova Scotia	11	Total	301

Even if members of Parliament other than cabinet ministers have only a limited role in the policymaking process, the social background characteristics of ordinary members merit examination. To the extent that MPs are not representative of the population, certain issues will not likely be addressed.

Since they are elected to represent territorial units and usually live in or near their constituencies, MPs almost automatically become representative of the population in a geographic sense, at least. MPs are also representative in terms of English and French ethnic background. The Constitution Act, 1867, required from the beginning that all House documents be printed in English and French, but the absence of simultaneous interpretation until 1958 and the unilingualism of most MPs served to limit interaction between the two linguistic groups.

On the other hand, members of Parliament do not reflect the population very well in terms of other ethnic origins, education, occupation, class, or gender. Although not as exclusive in these respects as cabinet ministers, MPs have higher educational levels and higher-status occupations than the general population. Historically, the legal profession has furnished the largest single group in the Commons, but the two largest groups since 1984 have been educators and those with a business background. Lawyers and administrators occupy the next two slots, leaving a gross underrepresentation of the working class.[2] Relatively few women are elected to the House of Commons, although the number is increasing, reaching 53 of 295 in 1993 and 62 of 301 in 1997 and 2000 respectively.

What is probably most striking about Canadian MPs, especially compared to members of other legislatures around the world, is their rapid turnover in office. There are relatively few **safe seats** in Canada, so that the proportion of new members after each election averages 40 percent, and the typical MP serves less than 10 years.[3] This is partly a reflection of the low degree of party identification among the electorate and means that few members remain in Parliament long enough to develop an understanding of the institution or to stand up to a long-serving prime minister. The 1993 turnover was over 75 percent, as a result of the decimation of the Conservatives and NDP; in 1997 it was over 30 percent, and in 2000, 15 percent.

....

The Parliamentary Timetable

Perhaps the best way to get an overview of the work of the House of Commons is by examining the parliamentary timetable—the agenda of a typical session and a typical week.

The Typical Session

The normal practice is to have each session of Parliament last about one year. A session begins with the **Speech from the Throne,** prepared by the prime minister and read by the governor general. Its function is to outline the government's legislative plans for the session, and it introduces the Throne Speech debate, a six-day debate in which MPs can talk about anything that comes to mind. Party leaders and cabinet ministers may use the occasion to articulate their priorities, while backbenchers often expound on the wonders or troubles of their constituency.

The second major event of the session is the **Budget** and the Budget debate. The minister of Finance delivers the Budget, a statement chiefly concerned with tax changes (the revenue side of the government's books) but also dealing with government finances in general. Among other things, the Budget usually fleshes out the promises of the Speech from the Throne. The Budget sets the stage for a four-day freewheeling debate and provides the opposition with a second opportunity to try to defeat the government. Legislation incorporating the specific tax changes mentioned in the Budget comes along later, although the changes usually take effect as of Budget night.

A third part of the session consists of the government's spending proposals for the next fiscal year, the **Estimates.** Their presentation is the third major item of business in the session. Once tabled, however, the Estimates are transmitted to standing committees of the House for scrutiny, so that they occupy little time of the Commons as a whole.

A fourth element of the session consists of the 21 **opposition days** when the opposition parties choose the subject of debate and the government in turn responds. These are divided proportionally among the opposition parties and distributed throughout the session.

Other than these four components, the time of the House of Commons is taken up with the discussion of bills, and most of that time with bills introduced by the government. Indeed, it is partly because of the volume of government legislation that some sessions of Parliament exceed a year in length. Since bills that have not passed die at the end of the session, governments are tempted to allow sessions to continue beyond one year until all current legislation is disposed of.

The Commons sits for about 135 days per year. When the government wishes to take a break within a session, it adjourns the House. When it wants to bring a session to an end, it prorogues the Commons, setting the stage for a new Speech from the Throne to initiate a new session. Finally, an election call results in the **dissolution of Parliament.**

The Typical Week

The House begins its sessions at 11:00 a.m. on Monday and meets at 10:00 a.m. on the other four weekdays. The weekly schedule can be seen in Figure 15.1 (see page 322).

The most exciting part of the day is the 45-minute oral **Question Period.** It is this period that offers the opposition its best opportunity to criticize and embarrass the government, as it grills cabinet ministers about their deficiencies and faults. Ministers are not given notice of such questions, but before going into the chamber they are briefed by aides who try to anticipate what questions might be asked. Even greater daily effort goes into the preparation and rehearsal of questions by opposition party leaders and their staff. The **Leader of the Opposition** and the leader of any other recognized parties begin the attack, and the Speaker of the House distributes the opportunity to question to various opposition parties in a rough proportion to their numbers. Since ministers often respond in a deliberately vague manner, several supplementary questions are allowed, but the

Figure 15.1, **Weekly Order of Business**

HOURS	MONDAY	TUESDAY	WEDNESDAY	THURSDAY	FRIDAY	HOURS
10:00–11:00		Routine Proceedings		Routine Proceedings	Government Orders	10:00–11:00
11:00–11:15	Private Members' Business (3)				Members' Statements	11:00–11:15
11:15–12:00					Oral Questions	11:15–12:00
12:00–1:00					Routine Proceedings (1)	12:00–1:00
1:00–1:30	Government Orders	Government Orders (2)	Review of Delegated Legislation (4)	Government Orders (2)	Government Orders (2)	1:00–1:30
1:30–2:00					Private Members' Business	1:30–2:00
2:00–2:15	Members' Statements	Members' Statements	Members' Statements	Members' Statements		2:00–2:15
2:15–2:30	Oral Questions	Oral Questions	Oral Questions	Oral Questions		2:15–2:30
2:30–3:00						2:30–3:00
3:00–5:30	Routine Proceedings (1) Government Orders (2)	(1) Government Orders (2)	Routine Proceedings (1) Notices of Motions for the Production of Papers Government Orders (2)	(1) Government Orders (2)		3:00–5:30
5:30–6:30		Private Members' Business (3)	Private Members' Business (3)	Private Members' Business (3)		5:30–6:30
6:30–7:00	Adjournment Proceedings (2)	Adjournment Proceedings (2)	Adjournment Proceedings (2)	Adjournment Proceedings (2)		6:30–7:00

(1) Possible extension of Routine Proceedings to complete Introduction of Government Bills pursuant to Standing Order 30(4).
(2) Possible extension or delay pursuant to Standing Order 33(2) respecting Ministerial Statements.
*(3) Possible delay or rescheduling pursuant to Standing Order 30(7) to compensate for a delay or an interruption of more
    than 30 minutes, and pursuant to Standing Order 33(2) respecting Ministerial Statements.*
(4) If required, House to sit at 1:00 p.m. for the review of Delegated Legislation pursuant to Standing Order 128(1).

Source: House of Commons. Used with permission.

objective of the opposition is not so much to elicit information as to portray the
government in a negative light. Such exchanges, along with corridor interviews
and hallway "scrums" based on Question Period, find their way onto the television news and form the backbone of media reporting on the House. Government
backbenchers are also allowed to participate, but they usually ask "planted" questions to which relieved ministers give prepared and self-serving replies.

Immediately before Question Period, 15 minutes are set aside for members' statements, during which individual MPs have 60 seconds to get something off their chests. After Question Period, unless the House is involved in one of the special events—the Throne Speech or Budget debates or an opposition day—the regular business is the discussion of government orders, usually **government bills.** Government bills are those introduced by a cabinet minister with the full backing of the cabinet and government caucus, and these debates are the basic routine of Commons life. At this point in the day most of the **parliamentary press gallery** and MPs leave the chamber in search of more pressing or more interesting activity. The speeches in these debates are generally dull and boring; the public and media can hardly be blamed for paying so little attention to them when MPs themselves rarely listen to each other. The few members assigned to make up quorum on any day are more likely to be answering their mail or reading the newspaper.

Only five hours a week are reserved for **private members' bills** and motions, at the normal rate of one hour per bill. These bills and motions, introduced either by government supporters who are not in the cabinet or by opposition members, are usually of little interest to anyone else. They are virtually assured of being dropped to the bottom of the pile when their hour on the stage has elapsed.

Finally, the adjournment proceeding is a half-hour opportunity at the end of the daily sitting (6:30 to 7:00 p.m.) four times a week for opposition MPs to pursue issues that they feel were inadequately answered in the Question Period. Ministers usually send their **parliamentary secretary**—an MP assigned to help them in any way they see fit—to fill in for them when called to account so late in the day.

Given the sharply adversarial nature of Question Period and the dullness of the rest of the parliamentary day, television coverage of the House of Commons does little to enhance the public's support of the government or politicians in general. On the other hand, "the all-consuming ritual of adversarial combat completely dominated by political parties"[4] has its defenders: it serves the functions of keeping government conduct under constant surveillance and presents a clear-cut picture to the electorate of which party is responsible for everything that has been done. In an ideal situation, it also identifies an alternative government.

Party Discipline and the Caucus

The most significant aspect of the operation of the House of Commons is probably that everything is organized along party lines and that **party discipline** is so rigid. Almost all members belong to one party or another, and with rare exceptions, the MPs of each party vote together. Why is it that members of Parliament so consistently toe the party line?

The most obvious reason for party discipline, at least on the government side of the House, is the system of **responsible government.** It is commonly believed that if the cabinet is defeated on a major measure, it must resign or call an election; therefore, its backbenchers must always ensure that cabinet proposals are passed. Until such time as the principle of responsible government is interpreted more flexibly, government supporters will always be pressured to put party loyalty ahead of their own views or those of their constituents. That kind of reform could be accomplished by regarding a limited number of nonconfidence motions as really critical, and then allowing the cabinet to carry on in spite of the occasional defeat of a piece of legislation, a mode of operation that is more characteristic of Britain.

Several other reasons can also be cited to explain why MPs stick together with party colleagues in parliamentary votes. One is the tendency of people who belong to a political party to see things in a similar light—a natural cohesiveness common to most organized groups. Related to this cohesiveness is an equally natural deference to the leadership of the party and a desire to present an image of party unity to the public. In addition, MPs are encouraged to support the party line because of the prospects of promotion. Government backbenchers who are well behaved can become committee chairs, parliamentary secretaries, or cabinet ministers, while even opposition party members can be moved up to more important responsibilities, such as into their party's "shadow cabinet." Members also want to participate in the distribution of perks available in parliamentary life, especially opportunities to travel at public expense, which are generally in the control of the party whips. Another inducement is to receive full support of the party organization in the next election, including campaign funds and a visit by the party leader. Moreover, given the high turnover rate, many MPs depend on the government to provide them with employment if they suffer defeat. The ultimate sanctions for disloyal behaviour are expulsion from the party caucus and denial of the party label in the next election. For all these reasons, parties vote as blocs and a government with a

Jean Chrétien took a hard line on party discipline (Adrian Wyld/CP Picture Archive)

majority of seats in the Commons feels confident that it can get parliamentary approval for almost anything it wants.

In modern times, three Conservative MPs were expelled from the caucus and two were denied the party's candidacy.[5] Despite concessions made to Liberal dissenters and other opponents of the Chrétien government's gun control bill, three backbenchers voted against it due to pressure from their constituents. The PM quickly retaliated by removing them from their committee assignments. When veteran MP Warren Allmand voted against the 1995 Budget because it dismantled historic Liberal social programs, the prime minister removed him as a committee chair. Chrétien even threatened not to sign the nomination papers of Liberal candidates in the next election if they had voted against government measures. When John Nunziata did so, based on the claim that the government had violated its Red Book campaign promise to replace the GST, he was quickly booted out of the party.

The Canadian Alliance caucus experienced much discord after the 2000 election. By September 2001, eight MPs had been expelled from the caucus for calling on Stockwell Day to resign as party leader. Referring to themselves as the Democratic Representative caucus, they joined forces with Joe Clark's Progressive Conservatives in an unusual coalition on the opposition side of the House.

It is fashionable to advocate more **free votes** and greater opportunity for MPs to represent the interests of their constituencies rather than slavishly following the dictates of the party. Rare free votes have been held on such subjects as capital punishment and abortion, and few would argue against a little more autonomy and freedom for the individual MP. On the other hand, free-vote advocates sometimes fail to appreciate the merits of an executive-centred system. Forcing MPs to toe the party line has allowed the executive to pursue a collectivist public interest beyond the narrow interests of constituencies, provinces, and other pressures, and has permitted Canadian governments to be more activist and welfare-oriented than legislature-centred systems such as the United States.[6] Party discipline protects MPs individually and collectively from the blandishments and threats of single-interest pressure groups and lobbyists and promotes the accountability of the government party to the electorate. It also frees the prime minister from time-consuming negotiations with individual MPs. Some observers retort that rather than reflect a collectivist approach, the prime minister and cabinet may already have responded to the interests and lobbying of the business community!

To balance this public display of party discipline, MPs are allowed to speak their mind in the secrecy of the **party caucus.**[7] The caucus consists of all the elected members of each party (and such senators who choose to attend) who meet behind closed doors on Wednesday mornings. In a government caucus meeting of over 150 MPs, the opportunity to make an effective contribution is obviously limited. As in the case of cabinet secrecy, however, members occasionally "leak" caucus information for their own benefit. Provincial and regional caucus meetings of each party are held before the general caucus meeting, and caucus committees are often appointed. In the case of the government party, the prime minister and cabinet ministers attend such meetings, unlike the practice in Britain.

Stages and Kinds of Legislation

The great bulk of legislation introduced takes the form of **public bills.** These are general legislative proposals, such as the Income Tax Act or the Employment Insurance Act, that affect all Canadians. Most public bills (and all **money bills,** that is, those involving the raising or spending of money) are sponsored by the government and introduced by a cabinet minister, thereby being titled government bills. As noted earlier, most of the weekly and yearly agenda is taken up with such government business. However, a certain amount of time (now normally five hours per week) is set aside for members who are not in the cabinet to introduce legislation and motions of their own. Since these MPs (on whichever side of the House) are private members, their proposals are called private members' bills. These bills are still of a general nature, such as those attempting to restore capital punishment, but they almost never reach the statute books. That is because the government arranges to have them "talked out:" it ensures that a backbencher is still talking when the time for consideration of the bill expires and they therefore do not come to a vote. Historically, the most that private members could hope for was that the cabinet might incorporate their ideas into a government bill. Since 1992, however, provision has been made for a more in-depth examination of a random sample of 30 private members' bills and motions per session. A committee decides which ones are "votable," and up to 10 of these get expanded debate and can come to a vote. Then, if successful, they could continue in the regular legislative channels. Lynn McDonald's 1988 private member's bill on nonsmokers' rights was a rare example of one that made it to the statute books; others included the earlier bill to change the name of Trans-Canada Airlines to Air Canada, and the act that recognized the beaver as a symbol of Canadian sovereignty.[8]

    Private bills, on the other hand, refer to a specific person or corporation. Certain divorces used to be effected by act of Parliament and took the form of private bills, although today this category consists mostly of bills incorporating companies or other organizations. Private bills now originate in the Senate, and occupy very little of the Commons' time.

Turning to the stages of the legislative process, the first requirement is for three readings in each chamber. Most government bills originate in the Commons, although with the exception of money bills, they may be first introduced in the Senate. First reading simply means that a bill has been introduced—it is tabled, printed, and made public—and may be briefly explained. Some days later, the bill comes up for second reading. This stage involves a debate on the principle of the bill and may last several days, or even weeks if it is controversial. A favourable vote at the end of the second reading debate means that the bill has been approved in principle.

Even if the opposition has little chance of defeating a bill, it may hope that prolonged exposure of the flaws in the legislation will persuade the government to amend it. Failing that, public opinion can be aroused via media coverage so that the electorate will remember the incident when the next election occurs. Excessive opposition debate is called a **filibuster,** but government and opposition rarely agree on what is excessive. The counterpart of the filibuster is **closure,** a rule allowing a majority government to cut off debate. Although the closure rule has been used quite routinely in recent years, a more civilized procedure is for the government to negotiate with the opposition over the time to be allocated to debating various issues.

After second reading, a bill goes to committee, where it is examined in detail. In the small, informal confines of a Commons committee, the bill is scrutinized and voted on clause by clause, while ministers, public servants, interest groups, and other experts may be called upon for explanations or criticisms. After being approved, sometimes with amendments, the bill is reported back to the House in what is called the Report stage. This gives all members of the House, not just those on the committee, an opportunity to propose amendments. In recent years, one opposition party or another has occasionally moved hundreds of amendments at the Report stage of a bill (such as the B.Q. did with the Clarity Act), in the creation of a new delaying tactic. Once the bill is concurred in, it goes to third reading for a final, overall appraisal.

Assuming that the bill started in the Commons, it must then go through the same procedure in the Senate. In the rare case that the Senate amends a bill already approved by the Commons, the bill will have to go back to that house to see if it is acceptable in its amended form. Once a bill is passed in identical terms by both houses, it is given royal assent by the governor general or a Supreme

Court judge acting as "deputy governor general." It then becomes a law or statute, although it may not be immediately proclaimed.

This may seem like an overly complicated process, but each stage has a distinctive purpose, and most bills must be debated for some time before the media and public begin to pay attention to them. Besides being necessary to engender eventual public knowledge of and consent to the law, reasonably lengthy consideration of the merits and faults of the bill serves to help the electorate gradually make up its mind about whether to re-elect the government that introduced such legislation or to opt for an opposition party that criticized it effectively.

....

Officers and Procedure of the Commons
The Speaker

The leading official of the House of Commons is the presiding officer, the **Speaker,** for whom deputy or acting speakers can substitute in the chair. In addition to ceremonial and administrative functions, the Speaker interprets and enforces the written rules of the Commons, called the **Standing Orders,**[9] plus unwritten traditions, practices, and conventions. The powers of the Speaker include recognizing which member can speak and ruling on whether motions are in order, whether debate is relevant, whether questions are urgent, and whether an unruly MP should be expelled. It is therefore important for the person selected to be competent and impartial. Unfortunately, Speakers used to be chosen by prime ministers from among their party's MPs and thus carried the suspicion of being biased in favour of the government. In seeking eventual reward beyond the Speakership, such as promotion to the cabinet, some also feared displeasing the prime minister. In 1986, a major change was adopted that allowed MPs to choose their own Speaker by secret ballot. In 1988, the Speaker was given new authority to "name" (i.e., suspend) a member for the rest of the day and for a period of five days for a second breach of the rules.

Speakers can vote only in the case of a tie and cannot articulate the needs of their constituency or constituents in the Commons as such. In compensation for this silence, ministers and bureaucrats are especially sensitive to the concerns that the Speaker discusses with them outside the Chamber.

House Leaders, Party Whips, and Clerks

From within their ranks, each party selects a House leader and a party whip. The government **House leader** is a cabinet minister who manages the government's business in the Commons. This minister seeks to work out an agenda for House business with the opposition party House leaders, who function as procedural strategists for their parties and often speak for them if their leaders are absent. It is a credit to the five House leaders that the Commons has functioned as well as it has, seeing that it was occupied by five official parties after 1997.

Party whips are responsible for ensuring that their members are present for important votes and that their MPs vote the right way.[10] Whips must therefore know the whereabouts of all their members at all times. Whips also distribute members' offices, assign members to parliamentary committees, and line up the order of party speakers in Question Period and debates. It is largely through the whips that party leaders impose discipline on their members. Members' opportunities to speak, to serve on the committee of their choice, and to travel as part of parliamentary delegations are influenced largely by their degree of party loyalty. In return, whips seek out backbench opinion on various matters and transmit it to the party leadership. Given the power of the party whips and House leaders to organize the business of the House, independent MPs and those belonging to parties with fewer than 12 members find little opportunity to participate.

The chief permanent official of the Commons is the **Clerk of the House,** a position analogous to a deputy minister in a government department. As chief procedural adviser to the Speaker and manager of the support staff attached to the Commons, the Clerk is also required to act in a totally nonpartisan manner. The Clerk is assisted at the table by the deputy clerk and several principal clerks. Figure 15.2 shows the layout of the Commons chamber.

Procedure in the Commons

Votes in the Commons are in the first instance taken orally when the Speaker invites members to say "aye" or "nay." When either side wants a formal recorded vote it will request a **division.** In this case the division bells ring until the government and Official Opposition party whips agree that all their available members have arrived, at which time a standing vote is conducted. It used to be that if either whip refused to give the go-ahead, the bells could ring indefinitely, but after the two-week "bell-ringing incident" of 1982, a 30-minute limit was adopted in 1986. A new procedure in 1994 allowed for deferred divisions with all-party consent.

The length of MPs' speeches has been severely curtailed over the past 20 years. The 1982 reforms generally shortened them from 40 minutes to 20, but this depends on who is speaking, in what debate, and at what stage of the debate. As a debate drags on, the maximum length is reduced to 10 minutes.

Figure 15.2 The Layout of the House of Commons Chamber

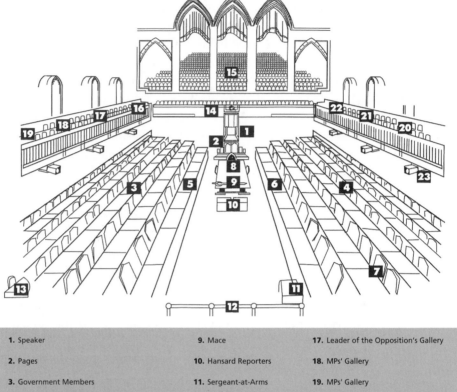

1. Speaker	**9.** Mace	**17.** Leader of the Opposition's Gallery
2. Pages	**10.** Hansard Reporters	**18.** MPs' Gallery
3. Government Members	**11.** Sergeant-at-Arms	**19.** MPs' Gallery
4. Opposition Members	**12.** The Bar	**20.** MPs' Gallery
5. Prime Minister	**13.** Interpreters	**21.** Speaker's Gallery
6. Leader of the Opposition	**14.** Press Gallery	**22.** Senate Gallery
7. Leader of the second-largest party in opposition	**15.** Public Gallery	**23.** T.V. Camera
8. Clerk and Table Officers	**16.** Official Gallery	

Source: Library of Parliament. Used with permission.

The Committee System

Much important legislative work of the House takes place outside the Commons chamber in a variety of committees. Committees allow a small number of people to develop expertise in a particular field and to examine proposals in depth; moreover, if several committees operate simultaneously, a greater volume of business can be accomplished. Committees allow private members to make constructive contributions to the governing of the country and to do so in a consensual rather than adversarial atmosphere. The Canadian Commons committee system did not function well during the first 100 years after Confederation, but repeated reforms since 1968 have made it more significant.

Standing committees are set up more or less permanently in most of the substantive areas of government policy, such as health and finance. They have two principal functions: to peruse the Estimates, that is, the government's spending proposals, and to examine legislation at the committee stage. The Estimates of the Department of Health, for example, are scrutinized by the Standing Committee on Health. In studying bills clause by clause after second reading, committees question ministers, public servants, pressure groups, and other expert witnesses. Largely paralleling government departments, standing committees are also authorized to investigate any aspect of the department with which they are associated, including a review of nonjudicial government appointments. They have a budget to hire a clerk, supporting staff, and researchers, and thus to develop independent expertise. The Standing Committee on Finance is perhaps most important, and now engages in extensive pre-Budget consultations.

Standing committees have varied in size over time, most of them currently being composed of about 16 members. Because they often have a number of different issues on their agenda, they may also set up subcommittees. Representation on all committees is proportional to party standings in the House. Although chairs are elected by committee members, they are usually pre-selected by the PMO, and most retain more loyalty to the PM than to the committee itself. Thus, in a majority situation, the government will have a majority on each committee and its own designated choice as chair. The main exception to this is the **Public Accounts Committee,** which normally has a government majority but has been chaired by the Official Opposition MP since 1958. It has the important function of examining the report of the **Auditor General,** the official of Parliament who audits the government's accounts.

Special committees are set up temporarily for some specific, special purpose. They usually have an investigatory function—to examine an issue before the government has determined how to deal with it.

In addition to the standing and special committees of the House of Commons alone, the Commons and Senate sometimes work together in joint committees. Joint committees avoid duplication and give senators a chance to get involved at an earlier stage of the process than is usually the case. The most important joint standing committee is that on the Scrutiny of Regulations. It has the vital but unenviable responsibility of scrutinizing the mounds of regulations and other sub-ordinate legislation issued by the executive branch each year, and can recommend that offensive delegated legislation be rescinded.

Finally there is the committee of the whole. This is simply the entire Commons membership sitting in the chamber as a committee. In such a case, the Speaker is replaced in the chair by the deputy speaker, and the rules are somewhat relaxed. This committee is used only to debate appropriation bills (once the Estimates have been approved) and certain noncontroversial bills, preference other-wise being given to smaller committees that can meet simultaneously in rooms outside the Commons chamber.

The transformation of the committee system in recent years has enhanced the position of backbench MPs in the legislative process. Committees that are small and stable in their membership become more expert in their field, and as their members develop greater collegiality, they can shed a good deal of their partisan-ship. After 1986, for example, many committees developed a consensus on the issues before them that cut across party lines, becoming newly independent sources of power in the legislative system. This led to the acceptance of an unprecedented number of amendments to government bills. Unfortunately, standing committees have increased in size again in recent years, negating most of these potential strengths; it has also been more difficult to gain a consensus among the five different parties.

....

Members' Roles and Services

The roles that members of Parliament perform can be seen in two different lights. First, in terms of how they vote, MPs can be classified as trustees, constituency delegates, or party delegates. "Trustees" are MPs who feel obliged to vote according to their own conscience, their own understanding of the issue in ques-tion, or their own conception of the national interest. "Constituency delegates," on the other hand, are MPs who vote the way they think a majority of their con-stituents want them to. "Party delegates" are those who vote as directed by the party leader and party whip.

Backbenchers often face the dilemma of opposing the party and risking disci-pline or opposing their constituents and risking electoral defeat. In practice, MPs rarely deviate from the party line: if the party's position conflicts with either their own views or those of their constituents, MPs are almost always obliged to put the party position first. Public pressure for more free votes seems to be increasing, however, and such discipline may also be in decline at the committee stage.

The other way to examine the roles of MPs is in terms of how they spend their time or determine their priorities. The first role in this respect is the "law-maker"—devoting attention to the legislative process by introducing, amending, and debating legislation. MPs are supported in these tasks by the Research Branch of the Library of Parliament.[11] Since this role is usually quite irrelevant to their constituents, MPs are more likely to spend time promoting their constituency to bring it public favours in what could be called a "representational" role. These members lobby ministers and public servants for new public buildings, roads, wharves, and other job-creation facilities so that they will have something "concrete" to show for themselves by the time of the next election. Finally, MPs function as "ombudsmen" or social workers for their individual constituents, intervening with ministers or public servants to hasten administrative decisions, correct bureaucratic errors, and repair governmental injustices. There will always be constituents with passport, immigration, employment insurance, pension, and many other kinds of problems. This "caseload" of MPs is now so heavy that they are provided with considerable administrative assistance in their Ottawa and constituency offices.

In 2001, MPs received a pay raise to $131 400 per year. On top of this basic income, a large number of MPs received additional payments for supplementary responsibilities. Combining the basic two, the leading figures in the House of Commons now receive the following:

- Prime Minister $262 800
- Speaker, Cabinet Ministers, and Leader of the Opposition $194 400
- Secretaries of State $178 700
- Leaders of other recognized parties $176 300

In addition to their basic pay, backbench MPs receive many benefits and services at public expense: they are provided with parliamentary and constituency offices, together with equipment and supplies; they have an annual staff allowance of approximately $190 000; and they have virtually unlimited telephone, mailing, and travel privileges. Recognized parties in the House—that is, groups of at least 12 members—receive substantial annual funding for research purposes, the loss of which was a major blow to the Conservatives and NDP after the 1993 election.

The MPs' pension plan has raised much controversy. Although contributory, many observers felt that it was too generous because it was indexed to the cost of living and because, regardless of age, members became eligible for the pension immediately upon leaving the Commons after at least six years of service. Moreover, those subsequently appointed to a government position continued to receive the pension on top of their new salary. In 1995, some of these provisions for newly elected MPs were removed: they would have to wait until age 55 to collect, they could not "double-dip," and those who thought the plan was too generous could opt out entirely.

The Government–Opposition Balance and Parliamentary Reform

An objective look at Parliament reveals a basic dilemma: the government wants legislation passed expeditiously, but the opposition must have the time to criticize government proposals in order to make the public aware of their defects, as well as to articulate constituency needs.

When the government has a majority of seats in the Commons, the cabinet operates as a virtual dictatorship until it has to face the electorate again some four or five years down the road. About all the opposition can do is criticize and delay government legislation, taking advantage of Question Period, media scrums, and the introduction of amendments. The imbalance of resources between government and opposition is dramatic, and the rules of the Commons are stacked in the government's favour. As the Auditor General reported in 2001, the government does not even provide Parliament with enough information to evaluate the results of public programs.

Many observers who deplore the arrogance of a **majority government** and regret that so much opposition talent and so many opposition ideas ordinarily go to waste prefer a **minority government.** In this situation—where the government is outnumbered by opposition members—it may have to negotiate with opposition parties to some extent, such as to amend its proposals, abandon them, or even accept opposition initiatives. Between 1867 and 2002 there were eight minority governments in Canada; few of these could have been called weak and indecisive. Many were more active and courageous than the majority governments that preceded or followed them. Some were exceptionally bold and decisive, especially the Pearson governments (the Canada Pension Plan, the flag, medicare, and cooperative federalism) and the Trudeau minority, the latter being particularly sensitive to opposition demands with respect to regulating election finance, screening foreign investment, and creating Petro-Canada. Although minority governments admittedly did not last as long as majority governments, not all of them ended in defeat; some ceased when the prime minister decided to call an election with the hope of obtaining a majority.

Because of the imbalance between government and opposition in a majority situation, and because the legislative role of ordinary MPs has been so ineffective, parliamentary reform is never far from the minds of political scientists and politicians alike. Reform proposals are designed to remedy excessive partisanship, cabinet domination, and private members' lack of influence. These proposals commonly take the form of reducing party discipline, allowing more free votes, and giving greater powers to committees.

The question of reforming the House of Commons leads to a discussion of the principle of responsible government, which declares that the cabinet must have the confidence of the Commons or call an election or resign. But it is not always clear whether the cabinet is required to take such drastic action. In a majority situation the problem is most unlikely to arise, but when the government is in a minority position, does it have to resign or call an election over any and every defeat? The Standing Orders are silent on this point, and any doubts about it were probably resolved by the 1968 incident in which the Pearson government was defeated on a piece of financial legislation. Pearson argued that the defeat was a fluke and that his government should be able to carry on. In that case, the matter was decided when the cabinet subsequently survived an explicit **nonconfidence motion.** Any other case of dispute about whether or not a government has been defeated should probably be settled in the same manner.[12] In Britain, a majority government carries on despite the occasional defeat of a piece of its legislation, as long as it retains the confidence of the House on its overall performance.

Other reforms would go further in giving the electorate more direct input. Canada has already experienced a number of **referenda,** including three at the federal level since Confederation, where the public is allowed to vote on a specific matter. The government usually indicates in advance whether it will consider the referendum results to be binding or merely advisory. Another populist device that is sometimes advocated is the **initiative,** whereby a sufficient proportion of the electorate signing a petition would require the government to take some particular action. Finally, the **recall** device would require an MP to resign prior to the next election if a certain proportion of the voters in the constituency signed a petition to this effect.

The Senate
Purposes and Powers

The ideal of democracy was still not enthusiastically accepted in the 1860s. The Fathers of Confederation thus felt it advisable to provide for an appointed body that would exercise "sober second thought" with respect to measures emanating from the popularly elected House of Commons. The Senate was therefore to be the equivalent of the British House of Lords, an older, conservative influence, with a minimum age of 30, appointment for life, and a relatively high property qualification.[13]

Additionally, the smaller provinces would agree to join Confederation and accept representation by population in the House of Commons only if they were overrepresented in the Senate. The Fathers settled on a chamber that would be based on equal regional representation. Such a system gave the Maritimes and Quebec a limited amount of protection against the voting power held by Ontario in the House of Commons. It followed that senators were supposed to represent their regions and provinces within the national policymaking system.

A third function of the Senate, not explicitly provided for in 1867 but that can also be seen as part of the concept of sober second thought, is to improve legislation from a technical point of view. The Senate often acts as a routine revising chamber, picking up on flaws in legislation that have not been noticed during its passage through the busy Commons.

As far as powers were concerned, the Senate was given a veto over all legislation, a power that was not restricted as in the case of the British House of Lords. The only point of Senate inferiority to the Commons was that "money bills"—legislation involving the raising or spending of money—had to be introduced in the lower chamber. Nevertheless, nothing in law prevented the Senate from delaying, amending, or vetoing any bills, whether or not they involved money.[14]

It was not until 1982 that the Senate's power was in any way reduced, and that had to do only with constitutional amendments, not ordinary legislation. According to the Constitution Act, 1982, the Senate can delay a constitutional amendment only for 180 days. If the Senate has defeated the constitutional amendment or not approved it by then, it can be repassed by the Commons, and then will bypass the Senate in the process of ratification.

Composition of the Senate

Ontario, Quebec, and the Maritimes originally received 24 senators each. When Prince Edward Island joined Confederation, it received 4 of the 24 Maritime senators, reducing Nova Scotia and New Brunswick each to 10. In a general reform in 1915 the West was designated as a senatorial region with 24 senators, preserving the principle of equal regional representation. In 1949, Newfoundland was awarded 6 senators in addition to the 96 already allotted, so as to leave the

Maritime contingent intact. Finally, in 1975, the Yukon and Northwest Territories were given 1 senator each, as was Nunavut in 1999, so that the total became 105.

Composition of the Senate

Ontario	24	Newfoundland	6
Quebec	24	Saskatchewan	6
Nova Scotia	10	P.E.I.	4
New Brunswick	10	Nunavut	1
Alberta	6	N.W.T.	1
British Columbia	6	Yukon	1
Manitoba	6	Total	105

The 1867 Constitution Act gives the governor general the power to appoint senators, but by convention this is done on the advice of the prime minister. Prime ministers have almost always chosen partisan supporters, such as sitting MPs seeking a safer haven, defeated MPs or candidates, those who have served the party organization well, retired premiers or other provincial politicians, and federal cabinet ministers who have outlived their usefulness. Hence, almost all of those appointed could be called "party hacks." In addition to rewarding faithful service to the party in the past, many appointments were made on the assumption that the new senator would continue to promote the party in the future. Such senators carried on as party fundraisers, party presidents, organizers, election campaign strategists or managers, or in other partisan capacities. Besides the partisan basis of their appointment, many senators are held in low esteem because of their absenteeism and their corporate connections; occasional convictions for abusing their powers have also occurred.

The Constitution Act, 1867, speaks of "qualified persons" being eligible for appointment to the Senate, language originally understood to include only men. In one of the most famous court cases in Canadian history, however, an enterprising group of women challenged this interpretation of "persons," and in 1929 the Judicial Committee of the Privy Council decided that "persons" did include women![15] Thus, in recent years, increased consideration has been given to the appointment of women, as well as representatives of various ethnic communities.

Senators originally served for life, and many lived to a ripe old age before they died. Lester Pearson had a constitutional amendment passed in 1965 to the effect that incumbent senators could stay until death (all of them gone by 1997) or retire at 75 with a pension; all subsequent appointees have had to retire at 75, but do receive a pension at that point.

Operation of the Senate

Today's senators try to justify their existence primarily in terms of the routine revision of bills, and some observers support the validity of their claim.[16] In addition to this function, the Senate sometimes undertakes protracted examination of complex legislation, such as the Bankruptcy Act or the Criminal Code. Similarly, bills are sometimes introduced simultaneously in both chambers so that the Senate can engage in an unhurried "pre-study" of the bill rather than wait until it has passed three readings in the Commons.

Senators also seek to emphasize other important aspects of their work, such as their consideration of private bills. These concern individuals, companies, churches, professional associations, and other institutions, and are a nuisance to a busy House of Commons. Since 1934, almost all private bills have been introduced in the Senate where the background work can be done so that the Commons can approve them routinely at a later date. This practice does help the Commons, but private bills are not numerous and do not absorb much of anyone's time.

Another kind of work not originally provided for is the study of various public problems by Senate committees in what Colin Campbell calls "social investigations."[17] Senators often have the expertise and certainly the time to conduct inquiries that relieve the pressure on the House of Commons and are cheaper than royal commissions. Among the issues investigated by the Senate over the years were poverty, aging, unemployment, the mass media, science policy, land use, national defence, fisheries, Canadian–American relations, the Canadian Security Intelligence Service, and medical care.

Finally, the Senate reviews regulations issued by various government departments. The Standing Joint Committee on the Scrutiny of Regulations has the responsibility of reviewing the great quantity of subordinate legislation issued every year.

In 2001, senators received a raise to $105 840, a generous salary considering the amount of time involved. The Senate timetable is very lax, and a small group of 15 or 20 senators does most of its work.

The Senate is often considered less partisan than the Commons, but it has occasionally exercised its veto power. In almost all such cases, a Liberal majority in the Senate has obstructed a Conservative majority in the Commons, or vice versa.[18] Brian Mulroney had considerable difficulty with the Senate between 1984 and 1991, when a Liberal majority in that chamber coincided with a Conservative majority in the Commons. The Senate's changes to the Meech Lake Accord, for example, had to be overridden by the Commons after the expiry of the 180-day limit on constitutional amendments. Then, in mid-1988, at John Turner's direction, the Liberal majority in the Senate held up the Canada–U.S. Free Trade Agreement until the electorate had a chance to express its will on this important measure. After the 1988 election, the Senate bowed to the popular will and passed the Free Trade Agreement, but later dug in its heels on other measures, especially the Goods and Services Tax (GST). At this point, Mulroney invoked an obscure clause in the 1867 Constitution Act that allowed him to appoint eight additional senators (two for each of the four senatorial regions) to tip the balance in favour of the Conservatives.[19] After the GST passed in an atmosphere of great bitterness, the Senate defeated the government's compromise abortion bill (on a tie vote). This became the first measure in 30 years that the Senate actually defeated, but some cabinet ministers were probably secretly relieved that the Senate had exercised its rare veto.

By the time the Liberals came to power in 1993, the Conservatives had established a clear majority in the Senate, so positions were reversed, and the Liberals began to pay for their earlier intransigence. The Conservative majority in the Senate was particularly incensed about the Liberal bill cancelling the privatization of Toronto's Pearson Airport, and the bill was defeated (on another tie vote). The PC-controlled Senate then stalled the Liberals' redistribution bill to the point of abandonment. Several other government bills were amended by the Senate, and a number of others were abandoned there when the 1997 election was called. Shortly afterward, a Liberal majority in the chamber was restored, but by then senators of all political persuasions were inclined to play a more active role than previously.

Senate Reform

Given the limited value of the Senate as it currently operates, its reform is always on the political agenda. All sorts of reform proposals have been made, primarily with respect to how senators are chosen and what they should do. The former range from abolition, to election, to having provinces choose some or all of its members. To legitimize its existence in a democratic age, there is an increasing consensus that senators should be elected. With respect to its functions and powers, many reformers have advocated reactivating the Senate's role of representing regional and provincial interests at the federal level.

In the 1980s, Alberta began pushing its **Triple-E Senate** proposal: elected, effective, and equal.[20] The government of Alberta felt so strongly about an elected Senate that it held a "senatorial election" in 1989 when, in the spirit of the Meech Lake Accord, Brian Mulroney asked for a list of provincial nominees to fill a vacancy. The Reform Party candidate won the province-wide contest, and Premier Don Getty forwarded his name to the prime minister, who after some delay reluctantly complied. Alberta held a second senatorial election in 1998, but nobody outside that province paid much attention. Triple-E advocates also want each province rather than each region to have an equal number of senators and want to give it powers to protect smaller, hinterland provinces.

DISCUSSION QUESTIONS

1. If Parliament does not play a significant part in the policymaking process, what are its basic functions?
2. What are the advantages and disadvantages of rigid party discipline in the Commons?
3. Does the Senate do enough to justify its existence; if not, how should it be reformed, or should it be abolished?

FURTHER READING

Bejermi, John. *Canadian Parliamentary Handbook*. Ottawa: Borealis Press, annual.

Campbell, Colin. *The Canadian Senate: A Lobby from Within*. Toronto: Macmillan, 1978.

Docherty, David C. *Mr. Smith Goes to Ottawa: Life in the House of Commons*. Vancouver: UBC Press, 1997.

Franks, C. E. S. *The Parliament of Canada*. Toronto: University of Toronto Press, 1987.

Heard, Andrew. *Canadian Constitutional Conventions*. Toronto: Oxford University Press, 1991.

Normandin, P. G., ed. *The Canadian Parliamentary Guide*. Toronto: INFO GLOBE, annual.

Robertson, James R. *House of Commons Procedure: Its Reform*. Ottawa: Library of Parliament Current Issue Review 82-15E, 2000.

Notes

1. C. E. S. Franks, *The Parliament of Canada* (Toronto: University of Toronto Press, 1987); John B. Stewart, *The Canadian House of Commons: Procedure and Reform* (Montreal: McGill–Queen's University Press, 1977).

2. P. G. Normandin, ed., *Canadian Parliamentary Guide* (Toronto: INFO GLOBE, annual).

3. Franks, *The Parliament of Canada*, 73.

4. Ibid., 142.

5. Andrew Heard, *Canadian Constitutional Conventions* (Toronto: Oxford University Press, 1991), 83–84.

6. Franks, *The Parliament of Canada*, 6, 29, 96, 268.

7. Paul Thomas, "The Role of National Party Caucuses," in Peter Aucoin, ed., *Party Government and Regional Representation in Canada* (Toronto: University of Toronto Press, 1985).

8. Most of the others that passed dealt with changes to the name of an MP's constituency. Heard, *Constitutional Conventions in Canada*, 78.

9. *Standing Orders of the House of Commons* (February 1999), *Précis of Procedure* (5th ed., 1997), and *A Glossary of Parliamentary Procedure: House of Commons Canada* (2nd ed., 1997), all published by the House of Commons and available on its Web site http://www.parl.gc.ca/information/about/process/house/standing orders/toc-e.html

10. Martin Westmacott, "Whips and Party Cohesion," *Canadian Parliamentary Review* (Autumn 1988).

11. The Research Branch of the Library of Parliament regularly publishes excellent summaries of political issues for the benefit of MPs and senators. These summaries are also found in many postsecondary libraries as *Background Papers* and *Current Issue Review* or at http://www.parl.gc.ca/information/library/PRBpubs

12. Other defeats that did not cause much fanfare are noted in Franks, *The Parliament of Canada*, 139.

13. Quoted in R.A. MacKay, *The Unreformed Senate of Canada*, rev. ed. (Toronto: McClelland and Stewart, 1967), 47–48.

14. MacKay, *The Unreformed Senate*, 91–95; F.A. Kunz, *The Modern Senate of Canada 1925–1963: A Re-Appraisal* (Toronto: University of Toronto Press, 1965), 337–47. Andrew Heard argues that a constitutional convention is emerging that the Senate may not insist on altering the financial provisions of money bills. See *Canadian Constitutional Conventions*, 94.

15. Kunz, *The Modern Senate*, 53–56. The case was officially referred to as *Edwards v. Att. Gen. of Can.* [1930] AC 124.

16. MacKay, *The Unreformed Senate*, 110; Kunz, *The Modern Senate*, 186.

17. Colin Campbell, *The Canadian Senate: A Lobby from Within* (Toronto: Macmillan, 1978), 12–19, 147.

18. MacKay, *The Unreformed Senate*, 96–112.

19. In 1873 Alexander Mackenzie had asked the British government to summon additional senators but was refused on the ground that it was not necessary at the time.

20. Peter McCormick, "Canada Needs a Triple E Senate," in Fox and White, *Politics: Canada*; H. McConnell, "The Case for a 'Triple E' Senate," *Queen's Quarterly* (Autumn 1988).

Chapter 16

The Courts and the Administration of Justice

The **judiciary** or court system was traditionally of little interest to political science—usually only in terms of its interpretation of the federal–provincial division of powers. Now that the Charter of Rights and Freedoms has catapulted the courts into the midst of many heated political issues, however, political scientists are giving this fourth branch of government much more attention.

This chapter examines the judiciary as an institution of government, discussing the function of adjudication, categories of laws, the structure of the courts, the operation of the Supreme Court of Canada, and the appointment, removal, and independence of judges. The chapter ends with a brief account of policing and the correctional system in Canada.

Chapter Objectives

After you have completed this chapter, you should be able to:

Discuss the role of adjudication as exercised by the courts

Distinguish between the powers of judicial discretion and judicial review

Assess the equality of access to the judicial system

Distinguish between various categories of laws

Outline the structure of the Canadian court system

Describe the jurisdiction of the Federal Court of Canada

Discuss the powers and operations of the Supreme Court of Canada

Discuss the appointment of federal and provincial judges

Understand the principle of judicial independence and how it relates to the removal of judges

Discuss the function of policing in Canada and the operation of the correctional system

Functions and Powers of the Courts

The judiciary has always been associated with the "adjudication" function in the political system. Adjudication can be defined as interpreting the law in case of dispute, settling disputes by applying the law to them, or making a judgment based on the law. Peter Russell defines the term as "providing authoritative settlements in disputes about the law."[1]

The function of the judiciary therefore is to render formal, impartial, authoritative judgments in the case of legal disputes between two parties that cannot be settled otherwise. The judicial process generally relies on the adversarial system, with lawyers representing each side. The judge, clothed with the authoritative powers of the state, acts as an independent referee and decides which of the disputants is legally right. As a result, the process usually culminates in the designation of a winner and a loser, rather than in the achievement of some acceptable middle ground, which is more characteristic of political conflicts.

Apart from the civil law system in Quebec, the Canadian legal system operates in the tradition of the English **common law.** The basis of that system is the accumulation over the centuries of judicial precedents, both in England and more recently in Canada. Thus, in a typical court case, the two sides seek to find precedents—previous court decisions—favouring their respective points of view. The judge (and sometimes the jury) has to decide which precedents most closely resemble the case currently before the court. The principle that precedents are binding on successive decisions is called **stare decisis.**

If the law were always comprehensive and crystal clear, and if the situations to which it applied were always simple and straightforward, adjudication would be fairly routine, and the potential for **judicial discretion** would be limited. The real world is more complex, however, and the law is unlikely to be clear on all points or to provide for every conceivable situation. Russell refers to the "inescapable generality of the law" such that, while judges theoretically settle disputes according to pre-existing law, they actually shape and develop the law in the very process of settling disputes about it. Judges at least establish priorities among competing legal rules and principles, and in this process they "put flesh on the bare skeleton of the law and shape its substance."[2]

Thus, rather than taking place subsequent to policymaking, the judiciary and the function of judicial interpretation were included in the chart of the policymaking process in Figure 13.1 on page 272. Unlike Americans, Canadian observers have not previously given much recognition to the concept of judicial involvement in this process. Russell argues that this approach "wrongly assumes that all important public policies are expressed in statutes passed by legislatures ... and

Beverley McLachlin, the first woman Chief Justice of Canada (Jonathan Hayward/CP Picture Archive)

overlooks the extent to which [such] policies ... are shaped through the process of being applied in particular cases by judges and administrators."[3] In the course of adjudicating disputes, the courts are inherently involved in policymaking.

Rather than merely interpreting laws with discretion, judicial review is the power of the courts to declare them invalid. The original Constitution Act, 1867, did not contain any such provision, although the courts soon appropriated this power in one respect. Chapter 12 of this book detailed the extent to which the courts invalidated federal and provincial legislation as violations of the division of powers. In rendering federal or provincial legislation void if either encroached on the jurisdiction of the other, the decisions of the courts had a significant effect on the shape of Canadian federalism. The courts' power of judicial review was greatly enhanced with the adoption of the **Charter of Rights and Freedoms** in 1982, and the effects of the first 20 years of that review were discussed in Chapter 11. Peter McCormick writes

> We should recognize that judges have always had power, have always affected our society by the decisions they make ... The Charter has simply made a longstanding reality more immediately visible and directed us belatedly to an assessment of the implications of judicial power.[4]

Thus, especially since 1982, the courts are an active player in the policymaking process. Whether judges leave a law intact or declare it unconstitutional, their interpretation of any law has a major bearing on its effect.

Access to and Costs of Justice

Many people cannot afford to hire a lawyer to defend themselves in a criminal or civil case, yet the objective of the court system must be the search for truth and the obtaining of justice, goals that have traditionally rested on the adversarial system. To ensure that those without the financial resources have a fairer chance to achieve justice, legal aid programs financed jointly by the federal and provincial governments have been established. These go some way to meet the fairness objective, but they vary in detail from one province to another, do not cover every kind of legal work, and have been cut back by governments intent on balancing their budgets. Community legal clinics serve a similar function.

A related means of reducing the costs of the administration of justice are the practices of plea bargaining and pretrial conferences. Plea bargaining involves discussions between defence and Crown attorneys with the aim of achieving agreement on charges to be pursued, typically by having the accused plead guilty to one charge when the Crown drops other charges. This practice is routine at the provincial court level and avoids a lengthy, costly trial. In the higher trial courts it is increasingly common for the judge to hold a pretrial conference with the lawyers for each side. Such conferences can result in a negotiated settlement or at least a time-saving clarification of the issues involved. Pretrial conferences have also proven useful in family and small claims courts. Although plea bargaining and pretrial conferences must not be allowed to subvert justice (as many observers feel was the case with Karla Homolka), they are valuable devices that cut costs for everyone involved (including the public) and reduce the workload of the usually congested court system. Some provinces have tried to save money as well as removing the adversarial nature of small claims or other civil cases by instituting various mediation services, such as Alternative Dispute Resolution (ADR).

······························

Categories of Laws

The law can be defined as "society's system of binding rules."[5] Laws are commonly divided into different categories, one distinction being between "civil" and "criminal." A **civil law** regulates relationships between two private parties such as individuals or corporations, and if private agreement cannot be reached in the case of dispute, one party may take the other to court. Most aspects of civil law in Canada are within provincial jurisdiction, largely based on the provincial power over property and civil rights. Civil cases often involve disputes over commercial contracts or property; such cases are normally resolved by the court's ordering one party to pay damages to the other. Civil cases are decided on the basis of the "balance of probabilities" of the merits of each side.

Criminal law, on the other hand, is primarily a federal responsibility; it is thus more or less uniform throughout the country, and has been consolidated in the **Criminal Code.** In this case, the commission of a crime such as murder, sexual assault, or theft is considered to be a wrong against society as a whole, and the state takes the initiative to bring the suspect to justice by means of the police and Crown attorneys. In criminal cases, judges may impose fines or prison sentences if the accused is found guilty. Such guilt must be proven "beyond a reasonable doubt," which is a considerably higher standard than just a balance of probabilities.

One of the many peculiarities of Canadian federalism is that although criminal law is within federal jurisdiction, it is usually the provincial attorneys general and their agents, the Crown attorneys, who are responsible for initiating proceedings against the person who is charged. This situation has come about because the provinces have jurisdiction over the administration of justice. Sometimes a case contains both civil and criminal elements, such as a drunken driver who does damage to another person's car. The state pursues the violation of the Criminal Code, but the victim's insurance company would have to take the initiative to sue for property damage.

Instead of this basic division between civil and criminal law, a distinction is sometimes made between public and private law.[6] **Private law** is essentially the same as civil law described above, that is, law that primarily involves private interests. Beyond the contracts and property mentioned, private law includes torts, wills, company law, and family law. **Public law,** involving the public interest or the government, goes beyond criminal law to include constitutional, administrative, and taxation law. Constitutional law has traditionally involved questions about federal or provincial jurisdiction, and governments themselves have often been the parties to a constitutional case. With the adoption of the Charter of Rights and Freedoms, a whole new aspect of constitutional law in Canada has emerged. Administrative law concerns the operation of government departments, agencies, and tribunals, and with the expansion of government activity over the years, this branch of law has also increased in significance. Note the later discussion of the Federal Court of Canada.

By giving the provinces jurisdiction over property and civil rights, the Fathers of Confederation allowed the province of Quebec to retain its distinctive private or civil law system, called the **Code Civil du Québec.** The private law system in the other provinces is based on the English common law tradition. The theoretical distinction between the two systems in terms of form is that while the common law consists of a hodge-podge of judicial precedents, the Code Civil is a single comprehensive document. As Gall puts it, "in a common law system, the courts extract existing principles of law from decisions of previous cases, while in the civil law system, the courts look to the civil code to determine a given principle and they then apply the facts of an instant case to that principle."[7]

....

Structure of the Courts

Because the provinces that formed Confederation in 1867 already possessed a court system, and because the Judicial Committee of the Privy Council continued to function as a court of appeal for the whole British Empire, it was not necessary to devote much attention to the judiciary in the Constitution Act, 1867. The provinces were given responsibility for the establishment of a provincial court system, and the federal government was allowed to establish a general court of appeal. McCormick describes the logic of the court structure as follows:

First	Identify the more routine cases and those that involve less serious possible outcomes and assign them to an accessible high-volume, low-delay court, preferably one that sits in many different centres. (Provincial Courts)
Second	Assign the less routine and more serious cases to a lower-volume court that can devote more time and more focused attention to each individual case. (Superior Trial Courts)
Third	Establish a court of appeal to correct simple errors and to promote uniformity in the application of the law within each province. (Provincial Appeal Courts)
Fourth	Establish a "general court of appeal" to promote uniformity in the application of the law within the country as a whole and to provide judicial leadership. (Supreme Court of Canada)
Fifth	Create a system of federal courts for cases directly involving the federal government as a party or raising issues concerning the administrative law applied by federal departments. (Federal Court of Canada)[8]

Source: Peter McCormick, *Canada's Courts.* Used with permission of James Lorimer & Company Ltd. Publishers.

As seen in Figure 16.1, the court systems within each province developed into a reasonably uniform three-level hierarchy. At the top are two "superior" courts—the superior trial court and the court of appeal, although they go by different names from province to province. At the bottom are provincial courts.

Because of the assumption that provinces could not be trusted to make worthy appointments to superior courts, the Fathers of Confederation provided that the judges of these courts would be appointed by the governor general, conventionally meaning the federal cabinet. Such judges were also paid by the federal government. Thus, in another peculiarity of Canadian federalism, each province determines how many superior court judges it needs, but they are appointed and paid by Ottawa. Since these courts and their judges were provided for in section 96 of the 1867 document, they are often called section 96 courts and section 96 judges. Judges of the provincial courts, on the other hand, are appointed by the provincial cabinet.

....

Figure 16.1 The Court Structure in Canada

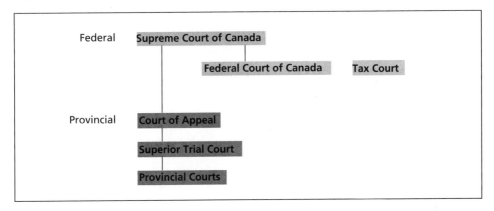

Provincial Courts

Whatever their structure or name, provincial courts generally have the following functions:

- summary offences (less serious crimes and provincial and municipal offences)
- most aspects of indictable offences, some mandatory and others optional
- preliminary hearings for most serious crimes
- bail hearings
- youth criminal offences
- family law, except divorce and proceedings flowing from divorce
- small civil cases

Provincial courts have a monopoly on summary offences except in provinces where this responsibility has been given to lower tribunals such as justices of the peace. Summary offences, as noted, include violations of municipal bylaws, provincial offences, and the least serious Criminal Code offences such as common assault. More serious crimes, called indictable offences, can be subdivided into three categories. Some, such as murder, are reserved for superior courts; others, such as theft, are assigned to provincial courts; and those in an intermediate category can be tried in either section 96 or provincial courts. The federal Youth Criminal Justice Act covers offences committed by those aged 12 to 18, and in some provinces these offences are tried in special youth courts.

Family law is another area of great federal–provincial complexity. Since divorce is a federal responsibility, divorces are dealt with in section 96 courts, and any proceedings flowing from the divorce must also be dealt with there. On the other hand, if divorce is not involved, such matters as custody, access, maintenance, alimony, adoption, guardianship, and protection of children are handled in provincial courts, sometimes called family courts. Several provinces have tried to overcome the problem of the fragmentation of family law with a "unified family court" presided over by a section 96 judge.

Provincial courts, sometimes in a civil division and sometimes called small claims courts, also have jurisdiction over disputes involving small amounts of money. Each province determines the monetary limit for cases that can be considered at that level, with disputes involving larger sums being initiated at the section 96 court level.

The Superior Trial Court

The functions of the superior trial court, whatever its name, are as follows:

- some mandatory and other elective indictable offences
- civil matters over a given monetary amount
- divorces and proceedings flowing therefrom
- appeals from lower courts regarding summary convictions, and juvenile and family cases
- administrative law cases

Provincial Courts of Appeal

Provincial courts of appeal hear criminal, civil, and other appeals. Although some of these courts' judgments can be appealed to the Supreme Court of Canada, decisions of the provincial courts of appeal are usually final, adding to the significance of this level of court.[9] The basic function of an appeal court is to correct errors or injustices that were made in a lower court, so that an appeal court is primarily interested in legal rather than factual issues. The second function of the appeal court is to render an opinion in a **reference case,** that is, on a constitutional issue referred to it by the provincial cabinet. Russell thus speaks of the "law-making" role of appeal courts because their legal interpretations have a "creative legislative dimension."[10] Decisions of the court of appeal are binding on all courts below it in the same province and are "strongly persuasive" for trial courts in other provinces. Courts of appeal normally sit in banks of three judges, but these panels can be increased to five for very important cases. Each side of a case submits a brief or "factum" in advance that summarizes its arguments, and lawyers then engage in oral argument.

The Federal Court of Canada

The **Federal Court of Canada** was established in 1971 with trial and appeal divisions. It was intended to relieve the Supreme Court of Canada of routine appeals from certain federal administrative tribunals and to strengthen judicial review of federal administration by developing a more unified and cohesive body of federal administrative law.[11] The main functions of the Federal Court are as follows:

- citizenship, immigration, and refugee appeals
- intellectual property cases including copyright, trademark, and patent disputes
- appeals from other federal administrative tribunals
- civil cases involving the federal government
- cases involving bills of exchange, promissory notes, admiralty law, aeronautics, and interprovincial works and undertakings
- prerogative writs (e.g., injunctions) applying to agencies of the federal government
- appeals re Access to Information and Privacy Acts
- issuance of Canadian Security Intelligence Service warrants
- Aboriginal law

Although the Federal Court deals with cases in all the above categories every year, it is dominated by those involving the Immigration Act and the Immigration and Refugee Board. It has recently seen a growth in Aboriginal cases dealing with monetary and constitutional issues, land entitlements, and natural resources. The Federal Court also hears appeals regarding the Access to Information Act and the Privacy Act and decides on requests for warrants from the Canadian Security Intelligence Service in order to plant bugs, open mail, and engage in other surreptitious activities.

The Federal Court consists of a chief justice and 10 other judges on its appeal division and the associate chief justice and 19 other full-time and assorted part-time judges on its trial division. The appeal division judges sit in panels of at least three members, and the individual judges of the trial division sit in cases all across the country.

The Supreme Court of Canada

The **Supreme Court of Canada** sits at the apex of the Canadian court system. The Supreme Court hears appeals from the provincial courts of appeal in civil and criminal cases and from the appeals division of the Federal Court of Canada in administrative law matters. The part of its work of most interest to political science involves constitutional law, whether in terms of the division of powers or the Charter of Rights and Freedoms. Besides hearing appeal cases from lower courts, the Supreme Court can be asked by the federal cabinet to give opinions, usually on constitutional matters, in what are called reference cases. A recent example was the case regarding Quebec's right to make a unilateral declaration of independence. Although the Supreme Court hears fewer cases per year than any lower court, it is interested almost exclusively in questions of law. Thus, of all courts, it is the most heavily engaged in a "law-making" role, and its decisions are binding on all lower courts.

Until 1949, the Supreme Court was a seriously deficient institution. First, its decisions could be appealed to Canada's pre-1949 final court of appeal, the **Judicial Committee of the Privy Council (JCPC)** located in London, and it was bound by JCPC precedents. But even more humiliating, appeals could go directly to that Empire court from provincial appeal courts, completely bypassing the Supreme Court of Canada. This weakness in authority was exacerbated by the generally poor quality of judges appointed to it in that earlier period, with some notable exceptions.[12]

Canada could have cut off appeals to the Judicial Committee after obtaining complete independence in 1931, but it was unclear whether the provinces would have to agree to this measure, since their appeals could already go directly to the JCPC. By the late 1940s it was determined that Ottawa could unilaterally curtail all such appeals, and it promptly did so. The Supreme Court of Canada has not been formally bound by Judicial Committee decisions since 1949 and has explicitly overruled them on occasion.

The Supreme Court used to have little discretion in deciding which cases it heard, but since 1974 it has basically controlled its own agenda. Such discretion considerably enhances the stature of the institution. Today, only two categories of cases have an automatic right of appeal to the Supreme Court: provincial reference cases, and murder cases in which the provincial court of appeal was split on a question of law. Applications for leave to appeal discretionary cases are normally handled in writing by a panel of three judges, but sometimes the panel hears them live. Public law cases, especially criminal and constitutional, now clearly predominate over private law disputes on the Supreme Court docket.

Although an increasingly important institution of government, the Supreme Court rests primarily on the **Supreme Court Act** rather than being embedded in any constitutional act as such. That act provides for a nine-member court, three of whom must come from Quebec with its distinctive civil law system. Convention dictates that of the other six, three normally come from Ontario, two from the West, and one from Atlantic Canada. The act requires that at least five judges constitute a quorum, with the result that civil law cases from Quebec can be heard by a five-member panel including a majority from the civil law system. The position of chief justice normally alternates between francophone and anglophone members, simultaneous interpretation is available, and Supreme Court judges are now expected to be at least functionally bilingual. The judges hold office during good behaviour until the age of 75.

The Court holds three sessions of about two months' duration each per year, and then adjourns to write up its decisions. As much as possible, the Court tries to hear cases with a full complement of nine. Judges study the lower court proceedings and judgments in advance, along with the written arguments of the lawyers for each side. Oral arguments normally last only two hours, during which time the judges often ask trenchant questions. In some instances the Court also grants "intervenor status" to provincial governments and interest groups that are concerned about a case but not directly party to it. Once the arguments are completed, the judges usually "reserve judgment" and meet in private conference to discuss the case. Each gives his or her tentative conclusion, and one or more draft opinions are prepared. These are later circulated and evoke comments before being revised. Each Supreme Court judge is assisted by a number of outstanding new law school graduates called law clerks. They help the busy judges search for and sift through precedents and other relevant material on the issues involved. So much effort is put into the process of preparing their opinions that a decision is typically not issued until about six months after the Court hears the case, and it has occasionally taken over a year for all members of the Court to make up their mind. The Court tries to come to a unanimous decision, but if this is not possible, majority and minority opinions will be issued. Membership of the Supreme Court of Canada as of 2001 can be seen in Table 16.1 (see page 354).

The Appointment of Judges

As has already been established, Supreme and Federal Court of Canada judges as well as judges of provincial superior courts are appointed by the federal cabinet, and provincial court judges are appointed by provincial cabinets. There are

TABLE 16.1 MEMBERSHIP IN THE SUPREME COURT OF CANADA, 2001

Appointment	Name
1987	Claire L'Heureux-Dubé
1989	Charles Gonthier
1989	Beverley McLachlin (Chief Justice)
1991	Frank Iacobucci
1992	John C. Major
1997	Michel Bastarache
1998	Ian Binnie
1999	Louise Arbour
2000	Louis LeBel

approximately 1000 judges in each category. All of the first group must be qualified lawyers of at least 10 years' standing, as must provincial court judges in Ontario and Quebec. Elsewhere, provincial court judges have to be members of the bar for a minimum of five years.

In a high proportion of cases over the years, Canadian cabinets at both federal and provincial levels have used judicial appointments to reward faithful party supporters, often defeated candidates.[13] Such **political patronage** raises three main problems: unsuitable individuals are appointed because of their partisan connections; well-qualified candidates are overlooked because of their lack of service to the party in power; and partisan judges may favour their former political colleagues.[14] This patronage system of appointing judges is still alive, although it is not as blatant as it once was.

At the federal level, Pierre Trudeau as minister of Justice instituted an informal practice of submitting names of potential judicial appointments to the National Committee on the Judiciary of the Canadian Bar Association (CBA). Trudeau sullied his own government's record in this field, however, with the appointment of six high-profile Liberal partisans, several to the Federal Court of Canada, in 1984. After an even more partisan record of judicial appointments during its first term,[15] the Mulroney government established a somewhat more satisfactory appointment system in 1988 for all "federal" judges except those on the Supreme Court of Canada, and modified it slightly in 1991. An independent **Commissioner for Federal Judicial Affairs** now maintains a record of those interested in federal judicial appointments. This official then submits such names to a seven-member committee set up in each province, including a section 96 judge;

one nominee of each of the provincial law society, the provincial branch of the CBA, and the provincial attorney general; and three nominees of the federal minister of Justice. This committee ranks each candidate as "highly recommended," "recommended," or "not able to recommend," and the minister makes the final decision, even being entitled to choose from those not recommended.[16] While it is regrettable that partisanship still plays a role in this process, party service or legislative experience should not automatically disqualify a worthy candidate from a judicial appointment.[17]

The prime minister chooses the chief justice in each province, almost always from the existing bench, as well as new members of the Supreme Court of Canada. Prime ministers consult widely before making such appointments, and have managed to overcome their penchant for partisanship in this one area. Patronage has therefore not been much of a problem on the Supreme Court for nearly 50 years.

Given the significant law-making potential of higher-level judges, especially those of the Supreme Court of Canada, many observers have proposed that nominees be subject to public hearings, such as appearing before a parliamentary committee, before being appointed. In this forum, they could be grilled about their views on a wide variety of issues. This is despite the fact that, without a formal consultation process, Supreme Court appointments have rarely generated great controversy. Jacob Ziegel has proposed an alternative to public confirmation hearings: a Supreme Court nominating commission. It would consist of nine people representing a variety of constituencies who would, after interviewing or studying the record of prospective candidates, present the prime minister with a shortlist from which one would be chosen.[18]

At the provincial court level, the attorney general now usually consults with the provincial judicial council or equivalent in making such appointments. A central nonpartisan nominating commission consisting largely of nonlawyers was established in Ontario in 1988, originally headed by political scientist Peter Russell. It screens judicial applicants on their merits and ranks the candidates from which the attorney general chooses. Few Canadians support the concept of elected judges.

Another controversial aspect of judicial appointments concerns the Supreme Court of Canada alone. Because this court must adjudicate federal–provincial disputes, concern has been expressed that all of its members are federally appointed. In theory, once appointed, judges act with total impartiality and their independence is protected in various ways. Nevertheless, it may not appear as if justice has been done in such a situation. The ill-fated Meech Lake and Charlottetown Accords provided for Ottawa to make Supreme Court of Canada appointments from lists provided by the provinces. The 1992 Accord also proposed federal and provincial consultation with Aboriginal peoples in the appointment process.

Even though judges are expected to perform their duties in an unbiased manner, they naturally bring their personal predilections and prejudices to the post. This realization leads us to investigate whether they are representative of Canadian society. Partly as a consequence of equitable geographic representation, judicial appointments have balanced francophone and anglophone origins at both federal and provincial court levels, especially in recent years as provinces have made more French-language court services available. Those of other origins have generally been excluded, but judges such as Laskin (Jewish), Sopinka (Ukrainian), and Iacobucci (Italian) are now appointed to the Supreme Court of Canada and increasingly to lower courts as well. Thus the most serious aspects of judicial underrepresentation relate to women and the working class.[19]

Just as in the case of other ethnic groups, however, more female and working-class law school graduates are becoming available for judicial appointments, and governments have at least begun to recognize the necessity of appointing greater numbers of female judges. The Supreme Court finally saw its first woman member in 1982, and now has a total of three women out of nine, including Beverley McLachlin, the first female Chief Justice. Such female judges have sometimes used their position to point out the male bias in legislatures, judiciaries, and laws.

As noted in Chapter 4, Aboriginal peoples have even more serious reservations about the Canadian judicial system, feeling that it discriminates against them at every turn. Many argue that an increase in the number of Aboriginal judges would not substantially improve this situation, and therefore advocate the establishment of a parallel justice system to deal with Aboriginal defendants (at least where they did no harm to non-Aboriginals), reflecting their own distinctive concepts of guilt and of healing and rehabilitation rather than punishment. While it seems unlikely that such a separate system will be created in the near future, the regular courts are increasingly recognizing such traditional Aboriginal concepts in cases involving Aboriginal peoples: sentencing circles (involving a judge, police, elders, peers, family, and victims), elder sentencing panels, and community mediation processes.

....

Retirement, Removal, and the Independence of Judges

Whatever the process involved in making judicial appointments, judges are expected to abide by the principle of **judicial independence** or impartiality once they are on the bench. They are supposed to adjudicate without fear or favour with respect to private or political interests, and without any incentive to give preference to the government side where it is involved.

The independence of judges is based primarily on security of tenure, and it is difficult for the government to remove judges before their scheduled date of retirement. Judges on the Supreme and Federal Courts of Canada and provincial superior courts have a mandatory retirement age of 75 years, and provincial court judges must retire at 65 or 70. The general rule is that they serve on "good behaviour"—that is, they cannot be removed unless they have been guilty of misbehaviour. Although the meaning of these terms has never been definitively established, judges are certainly removable for serious criminal acts and possibly for reasons of infirmity or incapacity, failure to execute their duties, or bringing the judicial system into disrepute.[20] On the other hand, they cannot be removed merely because the government regards their decisions as erroneous or contrary to government policy, nor because they ruled against the Crown.

The process of removing a judge varies with the level of the position, the degree of difficulty increasing with the court's ranking in the hierarchy. Except in Ontario, where legislation is required, provincial court judges can be removed by an order-in-council of the provincial cabinet but only after an inquiry has been conducted by one of the judge's peers or by the provincial judicial council. It is even more difficult to remove judges of the provincial superior courts and the federal courts. In that situation, the Canadian Judicial Council conducts an inquiry and reports to the minister of Justice, after which the passage of a joint address of both houses of Parliament is required.

The **Canadian Judicial Council** was created in 1971 and consists of all the chief justices and associate chief justices of courts staffed by federally appointed judges. It is chaired by the Chief Justice of the Supreme Court of Canada. Like the provincial judicial councils, its primary purpose is to deal with complaints raised against individual judges, but it also has a role in the continuing education of judges, provides a forum for developing consensus among its members, and makes representations to government with respect to judicial salaries and benefits.

While a number of judges have been reprimanded by judicial councils, the issue of judicial removal has rarely arisen. Several provincial court judges have been removed over the years, a practice that is increasingly common as the public becomes less tolerant of their faults. But only four judges of the old county and district courts met this fate, and not a single superior court judge has been removed from office. Such proceedings were initiated in five cases, but the judges either died or resigned during the removal process.

Besides security of tenure, judicial independence involves financial, administrative, and political independence.[21] Salaries and pensions are fixed in such a way that neither individually nor collectively can judges be intimidated by government threats to reduce them. Some judges did go to court, however, to challenge freezes or reductions in their salaries as part of provincial government restraint programs in the 1990s. In addition, judges are increasingly in control of the administration of the court system. Judges must also be able to function without political pressure—from cabinet ministers, legislators, bureaucrats, or other judges—whether in public or in private. At both federal and provincial levels, many cases have occurred of cabinet ministers contacting judges, but however innocent their questions might seem, this must not be done. Canadian Alliance leader Stockwell Day's public criticism of judges and lawyers on more than one occasion seriously detracted from his reputation and cost Alberta taxpayers thousands of dollars in a libel suit.

It is sometimes thought that the prospect of promotion from one court to another might bias a judge's decisions, but no evidence has been found to justify this fear. On the other hand, judges are not supposed to make public speeches that could compromise their impartiality. For example, when Tom Berger of the B.C. Supreme Court publicly criticized the 1982 Constitution Act for its omission of Quebec and virtual neglect of Aboriginal peoples, certain highly placed opponents of his views brought him before the Canadian Judicial Council. Although its recommendation was not to dismiss him, he resigned to protest the process employed.[22]

Policing and the Correctional System In Canada
Policing in Canada

In Chapter 14, police officers were categorized as a special kind of public servant. Police can be employed by the federal, provincial, or municipal governments. The Royal Canadian Mounted Police (RCMP) is the national police force with many appropriate central functions, such as operating a criminal information system and a forensic laboratory and maintaining international policing linkages. Ontario and Quebec possess their own provincial police forces, and Newfoundland and Labrador retain the Royal Newfoundland Constabulary for certain purposes. Finally, larger municipal governments have local police services, while provinces and municipalities without their own police forces usually sign contracts with the RCMP to provide such functions. But even where provincial and municipal police forces exist, and where they enforce the Criminal Code, the RCMP enforces federal non–Criminal Code statutes such as the Narcotics Control Act.

The basic functions of police officers of any kind are to prevent crime, maintain order in the community, and detect and apprehend offenders. In order to perform these important functions, police officers are given special powers, such as to question suspects, conduct searches, make arrests, and carry guns. On the highway alone, where the bulk of Canadians are most tempted to break the law, police officers can use concealed or unmarked patrol cars, photo radar or radar traps, and spot checks and breathalyzer tests for impaired driving. As mentioned at the end of Chapter 10, however, judicial interpretation of the Charter of Rights and Freedoms has served to restrict such police powers in many circumstances, and to augment the rights of a person suspected of or charged with committing a crime.

Besides being subject to Charter restrictions, police forces must obey civilian authorities. While deliberately designed to operate at arm's length from politicians, police officers are subject to the general supervision of provincial or municipal civilian police commissions, or in the case of the RCMP, of the federal Solicitor General.

The Canadian Correctional System

Since it is judges and the courts that put people into correctional institutions, it is appropriate to add a final word about the Canadian correctional system. As in many other aspects of the judicial system in Canada, there is an important federal–provincial dimension to this subject. Those adult offenders sentenced to two years or more are sent to federal penitentiaries, while those serving less than two years find themselves in provincial prisons or reformatories. In other words, both levels of government maintain correctional institutions, and the distinction between the two is based on the length of the sentence, not on whether the offender broke a federal or provincial law.

Federal legislation also requires the provinces to establish facilities such that young offenders are kept separate and apart from adult offenders. Youth crime is yet another complicated issue of federal–provincial relations, leading the provinces to make frequent criticisms of federal policy.

The Corrections and Conditional Release Act provides that an individual who has served a portion of his or her sentence may be released early (and conditionally) on parole. Three provinces have set up parole boards to review inmates of their own prisons or reformatories for this purpose, while the National Parole

Board performs this function for federal institutions as well as for the other provinces.

DISCUSSION QUESTIONS

1. Is judicial discretion in the interpretation of laws just as important as the power of judicial review?
2. How can fairness in the judicial system be guaranteed for Aboriginal peoples, the poor, women, and minorities?
3. If the current procedure for appointing judges is less than ideal, how should we reform it?

FURTHER READING

Canadian Bar Foundation. *The Independence of the Judiciary in Canada*. Ottawa: Canadian Bar Association, 1985.

Gall, Gerald. *The Canadian Legal System*. 3rd ed. Toronto: Carswell, 1990; 4th ed., 1995.

Green, Ian, et al. *Final Appeal: Decision-Making in Canadian Courts of Appeal*. Toronto: James Lorimer & Co., 1998.

McCormick, Peter. *Canada's Courts*. Toronto: Lorimer, 1994.

McCormick, Peter. *Supreme at Last: The Evolution of the Supreme Court of Canada, 1949–1999*. Toronto: Lorimer, 2000.

McCormick, Peter, and Ian Greene. *Judges and Judging: Inside the Canadian Judicial System*. Toronto: Lorimer, 1990.

Russell, Peter. *The Judiciary in Canada: The Third Branch of Government*. Toronto: McGraw-Hill Ryerson, 1987.

Ziegel, Jacob S. *Merit Selection and Democratization of Appointments to the Supreme Court of Canada*. Montreal: Institute for Research on Public Policy, 1999.

Notes

1. Peter Russell, *The Judiciary in Canada: The Third Branch of Government* (Toronto: McGraw-Hill Ryerson, 1987), 5.
2. Ibid., 14.
3. Peter Russell, "The Effect of a Charter of Rights on the Policy-Making Role of the Canadian Courts," *Canadian Public Administration* (Spring 1982): 2.
4. Peter McCormick, *Canada's Courts* (Toronto: James Lorimer and Company Limited, 1994), 3.

5. Russell, *The Judiciary in Canada*, 6.

6. Gerald L. Gall, *The Canadian Legal System*, 3rd ed. (Toronto: Carswell, 1990), 23–28.

7. Ibid., 30.

8. McCormick, *Canada's Courts*, 23.

9. Ibid., 56,

10. Russell, *The Judiciary in Canada*, 290.

11. Ibid., 313, 319–27; Peter Hogg, *Constitutional Law of Canada*, 2nd ed. (Toronto: Carswell, 1985), 142–48.

12. James G. Snell and Frederick Vaughan, *The Supreme Court of Canada: History of the Institution* (Toronto: The Osgoode Society, 1985); Russell, *The Judiciary in Canada*, 337.

13. Carl Baar quotes an oft-repeated maxim that "to become a judge in the United States, you must be elected; to become a judge in Canada, you must be defeated," in "The Structure and Personnel of the Canadian Judiciary," in Paul Fox and Graham White, eds., *Politics: Canada*, 7th ed. (Toronto: McGraw-Hill Ryerson, 1991), 513.

14. Andrew Heard, *Canadian Constitutional Conventions* (Toronto: Oxford University Press, 1991), 135.

15. During the Mulroney government's first term, 48 percent of all judges appointed were known Conservative supporters compared to 7 percent who supported opposition parties. Peter Russell and Jacob Ziegel, "Federal Judicial Appointments: An Appraisal of the First Mulroney Government's Appointments and the New Judiciary Advisory Committees," *University of Toronto Law Journal* 41 (1991).

16. Commissioner for Federal Judicial Affairs, *Judicial Appointments: Information Guide and a New Judicial Appointments Process* (Ottawa: Supply and Services, 1988).

17. McCormick, *Canada's Courts*, 112.

18. Jacob S. Ziegel, *Merit Selection and Democratization of Appointments to the Supreme Court of Canada* (Montreal: Institute for Research on Public Policy, 1999).

19. Dennis Olsen, *The State Elite* (Toronto: McClelland and Stewart, 1980), ch. 3; Russell, *The Judiciary in Canada*, 164–65.

20. Heard, *Canadian Constitutional Conventions*, 124; Russell, *The Judiciary in Canada*, 176; Gall, *The Canadian Legal System*, 227–39.

21. *Valente v. the Queen*, [1985] 2 SCR 673; Perry S. Millar and Carl Baar, *Judicial Administration in Canada* (Montreal: McGill–Queen's University Press, 1981).

22. Heard, *Canadian Constitutional Conventions*, 131; Russell, *The Canadian Judiciary*, 85–89; Gall, *The Canadian Legal System*, 236–38; McCormick, *Canada's Courts*, 130–31.

Glossary[1]

(Numbers in parentheses refer to the chapter(s) containing the main discussion of the term.)

Aboriginal self-government. A demand by Aboriginal groups that they be able to govern themselves, including recognition that the right is inherent (in their having been here first), and not a gift of the current occupants of their land. (4)

Aboriginal title. The Aboriginal claim to land on the basis of traditional occupancy and use rather than treaty, as recognized in the 1973 Calder case. (4)

Access to Information Act. The 1983 act that gave citizens, journalists, and others the right to gain access to government documents, with certain exceptions, and established the office of Information Commissioner. (14)

Act of Union. The 1840 act that united the colonies of Upper and Lower Canada into the colony of Canada; partly designed to assimilate the French. (3, 11)

Advocacy advertising. Advertising that advocates a political point of view, rather than trying to sell a good or service. (6, 10)

Affirmative action. A law or program that provides preference to individuals with certain characteristics in the hiring or promotion process. (11)

Agreement on Internal Trade. A federal–provincial agreement signed in 1995 in which provinces promised to remove preferences for local individuals and companies and other barriers to the free movement of goods, services, and people across provincial borders. (12)

Alternative Service Delivery (ASD). Part of the New Public Management movement, which embodies a variety of innovative means of providing government services distinct from the traditional departmental model. (14)

Assembly of First Nations. The largest interest group representing status Indians, who now prefer to be called First Nation peoples. (4, 10)

Auditor General. The official of Parliament whose staff audit the expenditures of government departments and who provides an annual report on instances of funds being unlawfully or unwisely spent. (14, 15)

Backbenchers. Members of Parliament on the government side who sit on the backbenches and are not in the cabinet, or those similarly distant from important posts in Opposition parties. (15)

Bandwagon effect. The notion that if and when they know which party or candidate is going to win the election, voters will move en masse in that direction. (7)

Bill 101. The 1977 Quebec language law that sought to make French the official language of Quebec and put

---

[1] A fuller definition of many of these terms can be found in John McMenemy, *The Language of Canadian Politics: A Guide to Important Terms and Concepts*, 3rd ed. (Waterloo: Wilfrid Laurier University Press, 2001).

restrictions on the use of English in the courts, schools, and private sector, such as that all commercial signs had to be in French only. (3)

Block grant. A federal–provincial grant that is given for a specific purpose such as postsecondary education or health but does not contain rigid conditions or standards. (12)

British North America Act. The 1867 Act of the British Parliament that created Canada by uniting the four original provinces, that also provided some of the essential elements of the new country's Constitution, and that was renamed the Constitution Act, 1867, in 1982. (11)

Broker Party. A kind of political party that tries to appeal to many different interests and "broker" compromises among them, rather than having any distinct ideology. (9)

Budget. The annual financial statement of the government issued by the minister of Finance that introduces tax changes and gives an overview of government spending for the next fiscal year. (15)

Bureaucracy. The permanent officials employed by the government, also known as the public service. (1, 14)

Business Council on National Issues. The most powerful peak (general) business interest group in Canada, representing the 150 largest firms in the country. (2, 10)

By-election. An election held between general elections in a specific electoral district due to the death or resignation of the MP or a tie on election night. (8)

Cabinet. The group of ministers selected by the prime minister to function collectively as the political executive. (13)

Cabinet government. A system of government in which the major political decisions are made by the cabinet as a whole, as opposed to one in which the prime minister acts with considerable autonomy or dominance. (13)

Cabinet secrecy. A convention that cabinet and cabinet committee meetings are held behind closed doors and that all documents and discussions relating thereto are strictly confidential. (13)

Cabinet solidarity. A convention that all cabinet ministers publicly support whatever decisions the cabinet has taken, whatever their personal views. (13)

Calgary Declaration. A document drawn up by nine premiers (excluding Quebec) in 1997 that proposed to appeal to Quebec with a recognition of its unique character but at the same time not offend those who believed in the equality of all the provinces. (3)

Canada Assistance Plan. The 1966 act, the last of the major conditional grant programs, under which Ottawa shared the cost of provincial and municipal social assistance and welfare service programs; repealed in 1995. (12)

Canada clause. The clause in the 1992 Charlottetown Accord that attempted to define the fundamental characteristics of Canada. (3)

Canada Health Act. The 1984 act that reimposed conditions on federal grants to the provinces for health programs, especially to prevent extra-billing or other moves toward a two-tier health system. (12)

Canada Health and Social Transfer. The annual federal block grant to the provinces that replaced the Canada Assistance Plan and Established Program Funding (Health Insurance and Postsecondary Education) after 1996–97. (12)

Canada–U.S. Free Trade Agreement. The agreement signed by Canada and the United States that came into effect in 1989 and that gradually eliminated tariffs between the two countries and otherwise prohibited governments from interfering in the private marketplace. (5)

Canadian Bill of Rights. An act of the Canadian Parliament passed in 1960 that outlined the basic civil liberties of Canadians but whose defects caused judicial confusion and limited the bill's effectiveness. (11)

Canadian Broadcasting Corporation (CBC). The large national Crown corporation (including its French equivalent, Radio-Canada) with radio and television divisions whose mandate is to promote meaningful communication among all parts of the country. (5, 7)

Canadian Judicial Council. An agency composed of the federal and provincial chief justices that disciplines federally appointed judges and otherwise provides leadership and coordination among federal and provincial judicial systems. (16)

Canadian Labour Congress. The largest labour interest group in Canada; the political voice of over two million members. (2, 10)

Canadian Radio-television and Telecommunications Commission (CRTC). The regulatory agency established to police the communications industry, including radio, television, telephones, and telecommunications. (5, 7)

Central agencies. Government agencies such as the PMO, the PCO, the Treasury Board, and the Finance Department that have certain coordinating functions across the whole federal public service and that prevent individual departments from acting with too much autonomy. (13)

Charlottetown Accord. The constitutional agreement of 1992 that responded to Quebec's demands for distinct society status, Aboriginal demands for self-government, the West's demand for a Triple-E Senate, and other issues; approved by federal, provincial, territorial, and Aboriginal leaders, but then was turned down in a national referendum. (3)

Charter of Rights and Freedoms. The 1982 document added to the Canadian Constitution that guaranteed fundamental freedoms and rights (legal democratic, linguistic, mobility, egalitarian, limited Aboriginal) to individual Canadian citizens. (1, 11, 16)

Chief Electoral Officer. The independent and impartial official who is in charge of the operation of the whole electoral system. (8)

Civil law. A branch of the law dealing with relations between private parties, such as individuals and corporations, and that do not involve government. (16)

Civil liberties. Liberties or freedoms, including the fundamental freedoms of speech, press, religion, and assembly, that citizens enjoy and that cannot be infringed or encroached on by government. (11)

Clarity Act. The act passed in 2000 that specified the conditions under which the federal government would recognize a referendum result in Quebec on the issue of independence. (3)

Class consciousness. An awareness of the social class to which one belongs, which is notoriously lacking in the case of most working-class Canadians. (2, 8)

Class-based party. A political party that primarily appeals to one socioeconomic class or another. (9)

Clerk of the House. The chief procedural and administrative advisor to the Speaker and to members of the House of Commons who is responsible for a wide range of administrative and procedural duties relating to the work of the House. (15)

Clerk of the Privy Council and Secretary to the Cabinet. The head of the Privy Council Office and head of the federal public service; the chief non-partisan adviser to the prime minister and cabinet. (13)

Clientele relationship. The intimate and mutually advantageous relationship that sometimes develops between a government department or agency and the interest group with which it most frequently interacts. (10, 14)

Closure. A rule in the House of Commons in which a cabinet minister introduces a motion to cut off debate. (15)

Code Civil du Québec. The unique system of civil law used in Quebec and based on the Napoleonic Code. (16)

Coercion. Power based on authorized physical force (including police, armed forces, jails, etc.) on which government has a near monopoly. A term also used by class analysts for what government does (at the behest of the corporate elite) when the state cannot otherwise get the public to accept its decisions. (1)

Collectivism. An ideology holding that the public interest is enhanced by substantial collective action, normally via government, as opposed to individualism. (6, 9)

Commissioner for Federal Judicial Affairs. The official in charge of coordinating the process for the appointment of those judges who fall under the appointing power of the federal minister of Justice. (16)

Common law. The basis of the British and Canadian legal systems, apart from the civil law system in Quebec, that consists of the accumulation of judicial precedents and seeks out the previous decisions in cases most closely resembling the one at hand. (11, 16)

Concurrent powers. Powers officially shared by the federal and provincial governments, which in the Constitution Act, 1867, were agriculture, immigration, and, later, old age pensions. (12)

Conditional grant. A federal grant to the provinces, usually in support of a subject within provincial jurisdiction, to which Ottawa attaches conditions or standards before the province receives the money. (12)

Confederation. The foundation of Canada with the union of four provinces in 1867. (11)

Confederation Settlement. The deal made among the Fathers of Confederation that entailed setting up a new federal system of government with a division of financial powers, federal controls over the provinces, provincial representation in federal institutions, and certain cultural guarantees. (12)

Conflict of Interest. A situation in which any public office holder places personal benefit before the public interest. (13)

Conscription crises. Two political crises in Canada, one in each World War, in which the population and government were divided, largely on ethnic lines, over the necessity of compulsory military service. (3)

Conservatism. A political ideology generally characterized by a belief in individualism and a minimum of government intervention in the economy and society, as well as by tradition, elitism, and opposition to change. (9)

Constituency. An electoral district that sends one member to the House of Commons. (8)

Constitution. The whole body of rules and principles according to which the state is governed that, in the Canadian case, consists of a conglomeration of documents and conventions. (11)

Constitution Act, 1867. The new name (changed in 1982) for the British North America Act, 1867. (3, 5, 11, 12)

Constitution Act, 1982. The act sponsored by Prime Minister Trudeau that primarily contained a made-in-Canada constitutional amending formula and a Charter of Rights and Freedoms. (3, 11)

Constitutional Act of 1791. The British law that divided Canada into two sep-

arate colonies, Upper and Lower Canada, each with a governor, executive and legislative councils, and an assembly. (3, 11)

Constitutional amending formula. The process for amending the Constitution. (11)

Constitutional conventions. Unwritten rules of constitutional behaviour that are considered to be binding by and upon those who operate the Constitution, but that are not enforceable by the courts. (11)

Constitutional monarchy. The official designation of the Canadian form of government, characterized by a monarch who is head of state but who rules according to the Constitution, which confides almost all governmental power into other hands. (11, 13)

Cooperative federalism. A variant of Canadian federalism, in place in the post-1945 and especially post-1960 period, in which neither level of government is subordinate to the other and in which there is an extensive degree of interaction between them. (12)

Criminal Code. A federal document that codifies most of the criminal law in the country. (16)

Criminal law. That branch of the law dealing with wrongs committed against others that are considered to be offensive to society as a whole, for which the state takes the initiative to investigate, and for which perpetrators can be fined or jailed. (16)

Crown. The collectivity of executive powers exercised by or in the name of the monarch. (13)

Crown corporations. Corporations owned by the government that assume a structure similar to a private company and that operate semi-independently of the cabinet. (13, 14)

Declaratory power. The power in section 92(10c) of the Constitution Act, 1867, under which Ottawa can declare any local work or undertaking to be for the general advantage of Canada and thereby place it under federal jurisdiction. (12)

Deference to authority. A value considered to be part of the Canadian political culture in which citizens are respectful of government authority and accept its word and orders with little question. (6)

Democracy. A political system characterized by popular sovereignty, political equality, political freedom, and majority rule. (6)

Democratic Rights. A section of the Charter of Rights and Freedoms that, among other things, guarantees the vote to every Canadian citizen. (11)

Democratic socialism. A leftist political ideology that emphasizes the principle of equality and usually prescribes a large role for government to intervene in society and the economy via taxation, regulation, redistribution, and public ownership. (9)

Department of Finance. The government department that has overall responsibility for the government's finances and its role in the economy and that has a powerful influence on all government policy. (13)

Department. A kind of government organization headed by a minister who is politically accountable for its operations and a deputy minister who is in charge of its hierarchical administrative apparatus. (14)

Deputy minister. The public servant who heads each government department, manages the department, and advises the minister. (14)

Deregulation. A government policy that removes previous regulations, especially those affecting the corporate sector. (14)

Direct tax. A category of taxation that can be used by either level of government to extract money from the very person or corporation that is intended to pay it. (12)

Disallowance. A power given to the federal government in the Constitution Act, 1867, but long since dormant, under which the cabinet can disallow any provincial law. (12)

Dissolution of Parliament. The ending of a Parliament, usually after four or more years, by calling an election, an act normally in the hands of the prime minister but that formally requires the approval of the governor general. (8, 15)

Distinct society clause. A controversial clause in the Meech Lake Accord, and slightly modified in the Charlottetown Accord, claiming that Quebec constituted, within Canada, a distinct society. (3)

Division. A formal standing, roll call vote in the House of Commons in which members' names are recorded in Hansard. (15)

Division of powers. The distribution of legislative powers between the federal and provincial governments, largely contained in sections 91 and 92 of the Constitution Act, 1867. (11, 12)

Durham Report. The 1839 report by Lord Durham that recommended the union of Upper and Lower Canada and the granting of responsible government to the colony of Canada. (11)

Egalitarianism. As opposed to elitism, the philosophy or practice of providing everyone with an equal amount of power and/or of treating everyone more or less equally. (6)

Emergency doctrine. A constitutional doctrine invented by the Judicial Committee of the Privy Council that in times of national emergency, the Peace, Order and Good Government clause of the 1867 Constitution Act became an emergency clause and increased the powers of the federal government. (12)

Employment equity (act). A policy (or act) that seeks to guarantee complete fairness in hiring, promotion, or remuneration, regardless of gender, ethnicity, etc. (4)

Enumerated powers. The powers of the federal and provincial governments explicitly listed in sections 91 and 92 of the Constitution Act, 1867. (12)

Equality rights. A section of the Charter of Rights and Freedoms that prohibits governments from discriminating against certain categories of people. (4, 11)

Equalization payments. A large annual cash payment made by the federal government to have-not provinces to help them provide a satisfactory level of public services. (2, 12)

Established Programs Financing Act. An act passed in 1977 that altered the basis for federal–provincial grants, making health insurance a block grant rather than a conditional grant program. (12)

Estimates. The annual spending plans of government departments and agencies for the following fiscal year, arrived at after gruelling negotiation with the Treasury Board Secretariat. (14, 15)

Executive. That branch of government that provides leadership and makes the major decisions. (1, 13)

Executive federalism. A variant of cooperative federalism characterized by extensive federal–provincial interaction at the level of first ministers, departmental ministers, and deputy ministers, such as the process that produced the Meech Lake Accord. (12)

Expenditure Management System. The current process for determining government financial priorities and the annual distribution of funds. (13)

Extra-parliamentary party. That part of a political party beyond its members of Parliament, that is, party members, local and national executives, and party headquarters. (9)

Federal Court of Canada. A court established by the federal government dealing with cases involving that level of government and other specialized subjects within federal jurisdiction. (16)

Federalism (federation). A system of government characterized by two levels of authority (federal and provincial) and a division of powers such that neither is subordinate to the other. (1, 11, 12)

Federal–provincial conferences. Periodic meetings of federal and provincial officials, especially first ministers or departmental ministers, characteristic of cooperative federalism, often making decisions that legislatures are not allowed to change. (12)

Filibuster.   An organized attempt by the opposition in the House of Commons to prolong debate and delay adoption of government measures. (15)

First Ministers' Conference.   A federal–provincial conference consisting of the prime minister and provincial premiers (and sometimes territorial and Aboriginal leaders). (12)

First past the post.   The kind of single-member electoral system used in Canada in which the candidate with the most votes wins the constituency, regardless of whether it is over 50 percent. (8)

Free vote.   A rare vote in the House of Commons (or Senate) in which members are not required to abide by the party line. (15)

Front de Libération du Québec (FLQ).   The terrorist wing of the Quebec separatist movement in the 1960s and 1970s. (3)

Fundamental freedoms.   Political freedoms—of speech, religion, press, assembly, association, etc.—that governments are not supposed to encroach on and that are guaranteed by the Charter of Rights and Freedoms. (11)

Globalization.   The modern phenomenon of nation states declining in stature and power characterized by giving way to the demands of transnational corporations via comprehensive free trade agreements, by massive diffusion of technological change, and by worldwide corporate competition or mega-mergers. (1, 5)

Government.   (a) The set of institutions that make and enforce collective, public decisions for a society. (1) (b) The set of authorities, centred around a prime minister, cabinet, and party, that currently occupy such institutions. (13, 15)

Government bills.   Bills introduced by a cabinet minister on behalf of the whole government; the kind of bills dominating discussion in the House of Commons. (15)

Governor general.   The representative of the Queen who normally performs her head-of-state functions. (13)

Governor-in-Council.   The prime minister and cabinet (but *not* the governor general) exercising powers of the Privy Council normally derived from legislation. (13)

Horse-race effect.   The notion that election campaigns have degenerated into a "horse race" where everyone, especially the media, is concerned with which party is ahead, not with how parties would tackle serious public issues. (7)

House leader.   The person appointed by each party in the House of Commons to deal with counterparts in other parties with respect to scheduling Commons business. (15)

Indian Act.   The act that governed almost all aspects of Aboriginal life in Canada since the 1870s, giving extensive authority to government bureaucrats and minimal discretion to Aboriginal peoples themselves. (4)

Indirect tax.   A category of taxation, especially a tariff or customs duty, restricted to the federal government, in which the party that pays the tax is assumed to pass it along to some other customer. (12)

Individualism. An ideology that individuals should have maximum freedom or liberty to do as they please, especially in economic terms, and that governments should not get involved in taxation, regulation, redistribution, or ownership. (6, 9)

Information Commissioner. The official of Parliament who encourages government to operate on a more open basis and makes judgments in cases where departments withhold information under the Access to Information Act. (14)

Initiative. A populist device that would require the legislature to respond to a policy initiative endorsed by a certain proportion of the electorate on a petition. (15)

Institutionalized pressure group. A kind of pressure group characterized by permanence, resources, governmental recognition and acceptance, and well-developed links with the authorities. (10)

Interest group/pressure group. Any group seeking to influence government policy without contesting elections; organizations whose members act together to influence public policy in order to promote their common interest. (1, 10)

Issue-oriented group. A kind of pressure group that springs up around an issue and disappears once that issue has been resolved. (10)

James Bay Agreement. The deal signed in 1975 by the government of Quebec and its northern Aboriginal residents that gave the latter land, cash, and hunting rights in return for surrendering land for the James Bay hydroelectric project. (4)

Judicial Committee of the Privy Council (JCPC). A committee of the British Parliament that functioned as Canada's final court of appeal until 1949. (11, 12, 16)

Judicial discretion. The leeway inevitably bestowed on the courts when they interpret laws, even when they do not, or have no power to, overturn them. (11, 16)

Judicial independence. The constitutional principle that the courts should function independently of the rest of the government apparatus, especially the politicians, with implications for security of tenure and remuneration. (1, 16)

Judicial review. The power of the courts to overturn legislation. (1, 11, 15, 16)

Judiciary. The court system. (1, 16)

Keynesian economics. An economic theory first enunciated by John Maynard Keynes that to promote general economic stability, government should counterbalance the private sector, spending (running deficit budgets) in periods of unemployment when the private sector doesn't spend, and taxing in periods of inflation when the private sector is spending too much. (12)

King–Byng dispute. The dispute in 1926 between Prime Minister Mackenzie King and Governor General Lord Byng over King's request for a dissolution of Parliament, which Byng denied. (13)

Leader of the Opposition. The leader of the main opposition party in the House of Commons, normally the party with the second-largest number of seats. (15)

Leadership review. A clause in the constitutions of political parties that allows party members to review the leader's performance and to vote on whether they want a leadership convention. (9)

Left. That part of the ideological spectrum that believes in equality in society and the intervention of government via such collectivist measures as taxation, regulation, redistribution, and public ownership to effect such equality. (9)

Legal rights. The rights of a person suspected or accused of committing a crime, now listed in the Charter of Rights and Freedoms. (11)

Legislature. That branch of government whose function is to represent the people and pass laws. (1, 15)

Liberalism. An ideology based on a belief in the rationality of the individual and on maximizing individual freedom, liberty, and self-fulfillment. Before 1900 this was assumed to entail a minimal role for government, but post-1900 liberalism usually advocated a larger role for the state and therefore was placed on the left of the spectrum. (9)

Lobbying. Any organized attempt to influence the authorities, now often performed by professional lobbyist firms. (10)

Majority government. A situation in which the party in power has over 50 percent of the seats in the House of Commons. (1, 8, 15)

Majority rule. An element in the definition of democracy that in any decisionmaking setting involving a difference of opinion, the larger number should carry the day. (6)

Mandate. The concept that the winning party has an obligation to enact policies it promoted during the election campaign. (8)

Mass media. Principally radio, television, and newspapers, sources of information for the mass public. (1, 6, 7)

Meech Lake Accord. The 1987 package of constitutional amendments intended to bring Quebec back into the constitutional fold. (3)

Memorandum to Cabinet. The formal written document that a minister submits to the cabinet seeking to initiate or change a government policy. (13)

Merit system. A system of hiring or promoting public servants on the basis of their merits (education, experience, etc.) rather than on party preference or other considerations. (14)

Ministerial responsibility. The principle that cabinet ministers are individually responsible to the House of Commons to answer for everything that happens in their department. (13, 14)

Minority government. A situation in which the government party has fewer than 50 percent of the seats in the House of Commons. (8, 15)

Minority language education rights. Rights established by the 1982 Charter of Rights and Freedoms whereby French-speaking Canadians can send their children to French-language schools, wherever their numbers warrant, a principle also extended to English-speaking Canadians where they are a minority. (3, 11)

Mobility rights. A category of rights in the Charter of Rights and Freedoms guaranteeing the freedom to move from one province to another and seek employment there. (11)

Money bills. Bills to raise money for government purposes or to spend public funds. (13, 15)

Multi-party system. Typically European in nature, a party system characterized by many parties, usually without any one having a majority in the legislature. (9)

Multiculturalism. A policy of encouraging ethnic and cultural groups to maintain their customs and traditions, often with public financial assistance. (4)

National Action Committee on the Status of Women. The largest and most vocal women's pressure group. (4, 10)

National Energy Program. A 1980 initiative associated with Pierre Trudeau designed to skim off more petroleum tax revenue for Ottawa, keep the price of petroleum below world levels, encourage conservation, and Canadianize the industry, which met with great opposition in Western Canada. (2, 5)

National Policy. A broad nation-building policy of John A. Macdonald unveiled in 1879 that included tariff protection for central Canadian manufacturing, massive immigration, and the construction of a national transportation system. (2, 5)

Neoconservative. An ideological term characterizing parties or politicians in the 1980s who not only advocated an end to government expansion but also believed in reducing its role via privatization, deregulation, deficit-cutting, and elimination of social programs. (9)

New middle class. A term from class analysis describing salaried professionals such as teachers, public servants, nurses, and so on. (2)

New Public Management. A movement within public administration since about 1990 that involved downsizing government, technological change, finding new ways to provide public services, and forming partnerships with private sector agencies. (14)

News management. A variety of techniques used by politicians and governments to ensure positive media coverage. (7)

Nomination. The act of becoming a candidate in an election, normally entailing being selected to represent a party at a nomination meeting and then completing official nomination forms. (8)

Nonconfidence motion. A periodic motion in the House of Commons, moved by the opposition, inviting the House to demonstrate its lack of confidence in the government, and which, if successful, would require the cabinet's resignation or the calling of an election. (15)

North American Free Trade Agreement (NAFTA). The 1994 extension of the Canada–U.S. Free Trade Agreement to Mexico. (5)

Notwithstanding clause. Section 33 of the Charter of Rights and Freedoms, which allows federal or provincial governments to pass laws that violate certain sections of the Charter. (11)

Nunavut. The eastern half of the Northwest Territories, which was established as a separate, Inuit territory in 1999. (4)

Oakes test. The strategy outlined in the Oakes case for interpreting the reasonable limits clause of the Charter of Rights and Freedoms. (11)

Official Languages Act. The 1969 federal act that established official bilingualism and gave citizens the right to deal with head offices as well as certain local offices of the federal government in English or French. (3, 14)

One-party dominance. A party system characterized by the dominance of a single party, usually related to Conservative Party dominance before 1900 and Liberal Party dominance since. (9)

Opposition. Those members of Parliament who do not support the government of the day. (15)

Opposition days. Twenty-one days per session of Parliament set aside for the opposition to determine the topic of debate and for the government to respond. (15)

Order-in-Council. A formal, legal decision made by the prime minister and cabinet (Governor-in-Council) including regulations and appointments. (13)

Parliament. Theoretically, the Queen, the House of Commons, and the Senate functioning collectively, such as in the approval of legislation, but often used to refer to the Commons alone or sometimes the Commons and Senate. (15)

Parliamentary government. A form of government, distinct from the U.S. Congressional system, characterized by parliamentary supremacy. (1)

Parliamentary party. That wing of a political party made up of its elected members, that is, its MPs or its parliamentary caucus. (9)

Parliamentary press gallery. Those members of the media who are registered to sit in the press gallery in the House of Commons and who report on its proceedings or on government in general. (7, 15)

Parliamentary secretary. A government MP who has been given additional responsibilities to assist a cabinet minister. (15)

Party caucus. The whole body of MPs of any party, who hold a regular weekly meeting, together with such senators as choose to attend, to discuss parliamentary strategy, party policy, and so on. (9, 15)

Party discipline. The convention that all MPs within any party vote together on every occasion, as predetermined by the leader or in the party caucus meeting and as enforced by the party whip. (15)

Party identification. The tendency of a voter to feel attached to a particular political party over an extended period of time. (8)

Party whip. An official of each party in the House of Commons whose function is to enforce party discipline and ensure members are present for all votes. (15)

Pay equity. An element of employment equity programs designed to ensure that all employees are paid equally for work of equal value and are not discriminated against on the basis of gender or other factors. (4)

Peace, Order, and Good Government clause (POGG). The opening words of section 91 of the Constitution Act,

1867, describing the residual powers of the federal government (as well as the essence of the Canadian political culture), but often misinterpreted by the courts as an emergency power only. (12)

Policy communities. The notion that government policy is made in a series of discrete and specialized clusters of government departments and agencies, interest groups, politicians, corporations, and interested individuals. (10)

Political culture. The sum total of the politically relevant values, attitudes, beliefs, and orientations in any political system. (6)

Political efficacy. The feeling that one has political influence, and that one's political participation can make an impact. (6)

Political equality. An element in the definition of democracy that entails the principle of "one person–one vote," that is, every citizen has a vote and each counts equally. (6)

Political freedom. An element in the definition of democracy that entails freedom of speech, press, assembly, association, etc., such that people can organize and advocate in order to influence election results and public policy. (6)

Political party. An organized group that makes nominations and contests elections in the hope of influencing the policy and personnel of government. (1, 9)

Political patronage. Making appointments to public offices or awarding government contracts on a partisan basis. (14, 16)

Political socialization. The process whereby individuals acquire their political values, attitudes, beliefs, and orientations. (6)

Politics. The activity in which conflicting interests struggle for advantage or domination in the making and execution of public policies. (1)

Popular sovereignty. An element in the definition of democracy that entails periodically allowing the public at large to exert its will—to have the final say—normally through general elections. (6)

Popular vote. The percent of all votes cast won by a candidate or party, regardless of who was elected. (8)

Poverty line. An amount of income such that anyone who received less would be living in poverty. (2)

Power. The ability of one actor to impose its will on another, usually considered to be the essence of politics and government. (1)

Prerogative powers. Those residual powers of the Crown—the Queen or governor general—that remain from the era of an all-powerful monarch and that the Crown can still exercise at its own discretion. (13)

Pressure group/Interest group. Any group seeking to influence government policy without contesting elections; organizations whose members act together to influence public policy in order to promote their common interest. (1, 10)

Prime ministerial government. The notion that the prime minister is now so preeminent that the label "cabinet government" no longer accurately describes how decisions are made in the political executive. (13)

Prime Minister's Office (PMO). The office that supports and advises the prime minister in partisan terms. (13)

Private bills. Bills introduced in Parliament that affect only a specific individual, company, organization, or group. (15)

Private law. A branch of law dealing with relationships between such private parties as individuals and corporations, including contracts, property, and personal injury. (16)

Private members' bills. Public bills introduced in the House of Commons or Senate by members who are not in the cabinet. (15)

Private sector. That part of the economy operated by individuals, corporations, and other nongovernmental groups. (1)

Privatization. Transferring a government program, agency, or Crown corporation to the private sector, such as by selling shares in a Crown corporation to individual members of the public. (14)

Privy Council. A body established by the Constitution Act, 1867, to advise the governor general in the exercise of the powers of that office, but effectively taken over by the prime minister and cabinet. (11, 13)

Privy Council Office. The office that supports and advises the prime minister, cabinet, and cabinet committees in nonpartisan terms on such matters as overall government policy, the machinery of government, and senior bureaucratic appointments. (13)

Public Accounts Committee. The House of Commons committee that examines the Public Accounts and the Auditor General's Report and criticizes government officials for illegal or unwise expenditures. (14, 15)

Public bills. Those bills introduced in Parliament that affect society in general. (15)

Public law. A branch of law involving governments or public authorities, including constitutional, administrative, and criminal law. (16)

Public opinion. The sum total of opinions held by members of the public on any subject. (7)

Public opinion polls. Surveys conducted to ascertain the opinions of the public on assorted matters. (7)

Public policy. A course of action or inaction chosen by public authorities to address a given problem or interrelated set of problems. (13)

Public sector. That part of the economy operated or financed by government. (1)

Public Service Commission. The central personnel agency of government designed to police the merit system and ensure that partisanship is kept out of the regular public service. (14)

Quasi-judicial. Court-like functions, powers, and procedures often possessed by regulatory agencies. (14)

Quasi-legislative. Functions and powers of regulatory agencies to make law-like regulations. (14)

Quebec Act. The British law passed in 1774 that provided for a system of government for the colony of Quebec (Canada) and that provided certain privileges to the French-speaking majority. (3, 11)

Question Period. The daily 45-minute period in the House of Commons in which opposition members spar with the prime minister and cabinet ministers. (15)

Quiet Revolution. The dramatic change of values and attitudes, especially toward the state, the new collective self-confidence, and the new brand of nationalism characterizing Quebec in the 1960s. (3)

Reasonable limits clause. Section 1 of the Charter of Rights and Freedoms, which allows the courts to find that even though a law violates a Charter right, it is a reasonable limit on such and is therefore allowed to stand. (11)

Recall. A populist device in which a certain proportion of the electorate signing a petition could cause an elected member of a legislature to resign. (15)

Red tories. A minority faction within the Canadian Progressive Conservative Party that has collectivist leanings akin to many British and European conservatives, stressing order, tradition, stability, and a paternalistic concern for the condition of the working class. (9)

Redistribution. The process of reallocating seats in the House of Commons among the provinces after each decennial census and then redrawing constituency boundaries within each province. (8)

Reference cases. Cases referred to the courts by provincial or federal cabinets in order to obtain a ruling on their constitutionality. (16)

Referendum. A populist device in which certain public policy proposals are submitted directly to the electorate. (3, 6, 15)

Regionalism. Strong feelings of attachment to the region (or province) where one lives that often generate political activity. (2)

Regulations. The detailed rules drafted by the bureaucracy under the authority of laws passed by Parliament that are too voluminous and technical to put into the legislation itself. (10, 13, 14)

Representative bureaucracy. A public service that reflects the composition of the population, with the most usual concerns being gender, ethnicity, or region. (14)

Representative democracy. A system of government based on periodic election of representatives to Parliament, as opposed to more frequent direct participation by voters in making public decisions. (6, 9)

Representative government. A form of government including an assembly elected by the citizens, but one that does not necessarily incorporate the principle of responsible government. (11)

Reservation. An obsolete power of the federally appointed lieutenant governor of each province to refrain from giving royal assent to provincial legislation and to send it instead to the federal cabinet for its consideration. (12)

Residual powers. Those powers not given to the provinces in the Constitution Act, 1867, that were assigned to the federal government under the opening words of section 91. (12)

Responsible government. A form of government in which the political executive must retain the confidence of the elected legislature or assembly and that must resign or call an election if and when it is defeated on a vote of nonconfidence. (1, 11, 15)

Returning Officer. The official in charge of running the election in each electoral district. (8)

Right. That part of the ideological spectrum that cherishes individualism and believes in leaving the private sector to operate with minimal government intervention. (9)

Royal commission. An elaborate investigation set up by the cabinet to research significant policy problems, to listen to and educate the public, and to make recommendations to the government. (10, 14)

Royal Proclamation of 1763. The British policy enunciated after Britain won Quebec from France that in a large area called Indian Territory the purchase or settlement of land was forbidden without a treaty between the Crown and the Indian people concerned. (4, 11)

Rule of law. The constitutional principle that all government action must be based on law and that governments and government officials must obey the law. (11)

Safe seats. Constituencies that a single party can be assured of winning election after election. (15)

Shared-cost programs. Government programs whose cost is shared by the federal and provincial governments. (12)

Social movements. An informal network of organizations and individuals who, on the basis of a collective identity and shared values, engage in political struggle intended to expand the boundaries of the existing system, such as the women's and environmental movements. (10)

Social Union Framework Agreement. An overall framework of federal–provincial relations agreed to in 1999 by the federal government and all provinces except Quebec that sought to end long-standing irritants on both sides and clarify where and how either level of government could act unilaterally or engage in joint programs. (12)

Sovereignty. Ultimate control or independence, whether in terms of Canadian national sovereignty vis à vis other countries or of Quebec sovereignty vis à vis the federal government. (1, 5)

Sovereignty-association. The Parti Québécois proposal in which Quebec would be sovereign while maintaining an economic association with the rest of Canada. (3)

Speaker. The presiding officer of the House of Commons whose additional administrative responsibility includes the operation of the staff of the chamber. (15)

Speech from the Throne. The document prepared by the prime minister and cabinet and read by the governor general at the opening of each session of Parliament that outlines the government's legislative proposals for the session to follow. (15)

Spending power. The unofficial power of the federal government to spend money on any subject, including those within provincial jurisdiction. (12)

Spin doctors. Party officials and ministerial aides who talk to the media and try to influence media coverage by putting the best face on an event from their party's point of view. (7, 8)

Standing committees. Those committees of the House of Commons that are set up semi-permanently and parallel government departments. (15)

Standing Orders. The written rules of the House of Commons. (15)

Staples theory. The notion that Canadian economic development has gone through a series of stages based on the exploitation of one natural resource or another and the export of such resources without the development of a secondary or tertiary sector. (2)

Stare decisis. The legal principle that precedents are binding on similar subsequent cases; it forms the basis of the common-law system. (16)

Statute of Westminster, 1931. The 1931 British law that declared Canada and the other Dominions to be fully independent. (5, 11)

Supremacy of Parliament. The principle that no other organ of government can overrule Parliament or its laws. (15)

Supreme Court of Canada. The highest court in Canada, and the final court of appeal since 1949. (16)

Supreme Court Act. The 1875 law of the Canadian Parliament that provided for the Supreme Court of Canada and that serves as a legal base for the institution in the absence of further constitutional entrenchment. (16)

Taxation agreements. Federal–provincial agreements, especially with respect to personal and corporate income taxes since 1945, under which Ottawa collects the taxes if provinces use a sim-

ilar base for calculating their portion of the tax. (12)

Third-party advertising. Advertising by advocacy groups, as opposed to political parties, during an election campaign. (8, 10)

Transnational corporations. Corporations operating simultaneously in many countries throughout the world that often take orders from company headquarters and that individual states find difficult to control. (5)

Treasury Board. A cabinet committee whose primary responsibility is to restrain government spending. (13)

Treasury Board Secretariat. The government department that advises the Treasury Board in its deliberations and that functions as a restraining influence on departmental spending. (13, 14)

Treaty Rights. Aboriginal rights based on treaties signed with the Crown. (4)

Triple-E Senate. A proposal for Senate reform in which each province would have an equal number of senators, who would be elected, and who would be given effective powers. (15)

Two-party system. A type of party system in which two main parties are of approximately equal strength and alternate in office, as in Canada between 1896 and 1921. (9)

Two-plus, or two-and-a-half, party system. A type of party system in which two main parties are of approximately equal strength and alternate in office, but that are accompanied by one or more minor parties of significant strength, as in Canada between 1921 and 1993. (9)

Visible minorities. Members of ethnic groups, other than Aboriginal peoples, whose skin colour is not white. (4)

War Measures Act. The law invoked during both world wars and during the 1970 FLQ crisis under which the federal cabinet is given emergency powers to deal with a crisis, and that was later replaced by the Emergencies Act. (3)

Western alienation. The feeling shared by many Western Canadians that their interests are not taken seriously in the national policymaking process. (2)

Westminster model. The model of government developed in Britain in which the political executive is given extensive power to provide effective leadership. (15)

White Paper on Indians. The 1969 Trudeau–Chrétien policy proposal to do away with the Indian Act and fully integrate Aboriginal peoples into Canadian society. (4)

Women's movement. The collection of women's groups that mushroomed across the country, starting around 1970, demanding complete equality for women. (4)

World Trade Organization (WTO). Successor to the General Agreement on Tariffs and Trade, an organization to which Canada and most other countries belong and that has the power to disallow national policies and practices that it deems discriminatory against companies from other states. (5)

Index

Aberhart, William, 183
Aboriginal Canadians, 22, 56, 59, 63–74, 78, 101, 108, 161, 186, 194, 207–8, 214–15, 226, 242, 244, 283, 301, 302, 351, 356, 358
Aboriginal land claims, 22, 64–65, 67–70, 73, 242
Aboriginal self-government, 56–57, 64, 70–73
Abortion, 85–86, 198, 218, 238, 244, 325, 339
Access to Information Act, 147, 285, 310, 351
Accountability, 181, 277, 280, 313, 318, 323, 325
Act of Union, 42, 286
Administrative agencies, 305–6, 347, 351
Advocacy advertising, 129, 149, 172, 215
Affirmative action, 77, 85, 240
Agents of political socialization, 126–30
Agreement on Internal Trade, 264
Agriculture, 20–22, 24, 107, 110, 250
Air Canada, airlines, and airports, 17, 111, 305, 313, 326, 339
Alaska Boundary Dispute, 92
Alberta, 22–26, 28, 57, 87, 122, 130, 147, 183, 195, 198, 231, 241, 244, 258–59, 319, 337, 340, 358
Alberta Press Bill, 147, 234
Alternative Service Delivery, 312
Anti-combines legislation, 32, 239
Appointments, contracts, and grants (including political patronage), 6, 33, 158, 204, 219–20, 274–76, 279, 283, 286, 288, 300, 302, 306, 331, 354–55
Armed forces and defence, 2, 84, 94–95, 228, 307, 338
Asper, Izzy, 32, 138–40
Assembly of First Nations (AFN), 67, 206
Atlantic provinces, 12, 19–21, 26–29, 36, 176, 228, 252, 336, 353
Atomic Energy of Canada Ltd. (AECL), 98, 304
Auditor General and Public Accounts Committee, 296, 307–8, 331
Autonomy, Canadian, 92–93, 231, 352
Auto Pact, 108, 110

BCE (Bell Canada Enterprises, including Bell Globemedia), 138, 140, 142
Ballot, 159–60

Banks and banking, 24–25, 32, 109, 183, 214
Bank of Canada, 304
Bennett, R.B., 182, 197, 281
Berger, Thomas, 67, 358
Bilingualism, 7, 23, 42–45, 47–51, 54, 77, 163, 228, 230, 241, 244, 252, 263, 300–301, 307, 319, 353, 356. See also Minority language education rights; Quebec language legislation
Bill of Rights, 231, 234–35
Bills, 213, 219–20, 271–73, 294–95, 318, 321, 323, 326–28, 331–32, 336, 338
Black, Conrad, 138–39, 146
Bloc Québécois (BQ), 55, 58–59, 165, 167, 169, 171, 176, 185–86, 189, 199, 327
Bombardier, 31
Borden, R.L., 44, 80, 92, 182, 281
Bouchard, Lucien, 55, 58–60, 185
Bourassa, Robert, 49, 52–53, 60, 243
Bowell, Mackenzie, 280–81
British Columbia, 22, 26, 28, 57, 65, 67–68, 92, 125, 183, 195, 231, 319, 337
British North America Act (BNA Act). See Constitution Act, 1867
British parliamentary system. See Westminster model
Brokerage, 186–87, 190
Budget, 212, 284, 288, 320–21, 331
Bureaucracy, 6, 10, 66, 70–71, 84, 145, 147, 151, 189–90, 198, 207–8, 210–13, 217–18, 242, 244, 256, 261–62, 269–72, 277, 279, 284–85, 288, 293–313, 327–28, 331, 333, 351, 358
Business Council on National Issues (including business influence), 32–33, 125, 139, 204, 206, 211, 215, 217, 325. See also Corporations

CF-18 contract, 27
Cabinet, 9–10, 82–83, 168, 170, 180–81, 199, 210–13, 226–27, 229, 232, 269–89, 293–95, 302–4, 306–8, 310, 318, 324, 326, 334–35, 348, 350, 353–54. See also Ministers; Prime minister(s)
Cabinet committees, 279, 284, 286–88, 303
Calgary Declaration, 58
Campbell, Kim, 84, 281
Canada Assistance Plan (CAP), 256, 258, 303
Canada Clause, 56

Canada Customs and Revenue Agency, 305, 312–13
Canada Health Act, 257–58, 264. See also Health care
Canada Health and Social Transfer, 258
Canada Pension Plan, 46, 184, 334. See also Pensions
Canada–U.S. Free Trade, 24, 109–10, 125, 129, 172, 175, 184, 206, 215, 307, 339
Canadian Alliance, 26, 32, 79, 146, 162, 165, 167, 169, 172, 175–76, 185–86, 189, 192–96, 198–99, 244, 325. See also Reform Party
Canadian Association of Manufacturers and Exporters, 204, 217
Canadian Auto Workers (CAW), 35, 102
Canadian Bar Association, 206, 212, 217, 354
Canadian Broadcasting Corporation (CBC), 17, 104–5, 139–42, 145, 147, 197, 304–5
Canadian Chamber of Commerce, 204, 209, 213, 216–17
Canadian Conference of Catholic Bishops, 206
Canadian Council for the Arts, 106
Canadian Council on Social Development, 37, 207
Canadian culture, 17–18, 102–6, 110, 125
Canadian Federation of Agriculture, 205, 211–12
Canadian Federation of Independent Business, 204–6
Canadian Federation of Students, 206, 209–10
Canadian Food Inspection Agency, 306, 312
Canadian Labour Congress (CLC), 36, 129, 183, 205–6, 209, 215–17
Canadian Medical Association, 129, 206, 208–9, 211–12, 217–18
Canadian national identity, 78–79, 102, 127
Canadian National Railway (CNR). See Railways
Canadian Pacific Railway (CPR). See Railways
Canadian Radio-television and Telecommunications Commission (CRTC), 17, 105–6, 139–42, 306
Canadian Security Intelligence Service (CSIS), 307, 338, 351
Canadian Television Network (CTV), 138, 140, 142

Canadian Union of Public
    Employees (CUPE), 35
Candidates, 81, 83, 132, 149, 159,
    161–62, 164–65, 170, 172–74,
    180, 192, 279, 325, 337, 354. *See
    also* Nominations
CanWest Global, 138, 140, 142, 146
Capital punishment, 151, 325–26
Central agencies, 285–89, 299, 303,
    307
Charlottetown Accord, 56–57, 72,
    119, 262, 355–56
Charter groups, 54, 245
Charter of Rights and Freedoms, 10,
    52, 71, 77–78, 85, 87, 118, 120,
    123, 125, 184, 191, 214, 231,
    234–46, 253, 273, 309–10, 318,
    343, 345, 347, 352, 359
    section 1 (reasonable limits),
        172–73, 235–36, 239, 241,
        243–44
    section 2 (fundamental
        freedoms), 52, 119, 150,
        172, 214, 235–37
    section 3 (democratic rights),
        161, 237–38
    section 6 (mobility rights), 238
    sections 7–14 (legal rights),
        238–40, 310
    section 15 (equality rights), 77,
        85, 87, 240–41
    sections 16–23 (language
        rights) (*see* Language laws
        and rights; Minority
        language education rights)
    sections 25 and 35 (Aboriginal
        rights), 70–71, 231, 242
    section 33 (notwithstanding
        clause), 52, 85, 237,
        242–46, 318
Chief Electoral Officer, 158, 160
Children, 37, 66, 80, 82, 86, 129,
    236, 264, 349–50
Chrétien, Jean and government, 24,
    36, 50, 58–59, 66, 72–73, 79,
    105–6, 110–11, 140, 162,
    167–68, 199, 221, 257, 264,
    279–83, 287–89, 296–97, 300,
    304–5, 311, 325
Civil law, 12, 42, 74, 81, 226, 252,
    343, 347, 353
Clarity Act, 59, 279, 327
Clark, Joe, 55–56, 184, 281–83, 325
Class analysis, 15, 30–38, 175–76,
    186–90, 245, 319
Class consciousness, 30–31, 176,
    188–89
Cleavages, 8, 15–16, 30, 41–42,
    175–76, 186
Clerk of the Privy Council and
    Secretary to the Cabinet, 84,
    288, 296
Clientele relationship, 211, 303

Closure, 327
Collectivism, 121, 123, 125, 195–98,
    245, 325
Common law, 233, 344, 347
Commonwealth, 92–93, 280
Confederation, 12, 228, 250–52. *See
    also* Constitution Act (1867)
Conflicts of interest, 218–19, 221,
    277, 280, 296, 337
Conscription, 44–45, 119, 133,
    182–83
Conservatism (including
    neoconservatism), 109, 195–99,
    306
Conservative Party. *See* Progressive
    Conservative Party
Constitution, 229–33, 280, 347
Constitution Act (1867), 43, 64, 82,
    92–93, 120, 156, 229–30,
    249–50, 253, 260, 274–76, 319,
    337, 339, 345, 348
Constitution Act (1982), 50–52, 93,
    184, 231–32, 263, 336, 358. *See
    also* Charter of Rights and
    Freedoms
Constitutional Act (1791), 42, 226
Constitutional amending formula,
    53, 58, 93, 125, 231, 336
Constitutional amendments, 230,
    253, 337
Constitutional conventions, 232,
    262, 274–75, 353
Cooperative Commonwealth
    Federation (CCF), 165, 170, 183,
    188
Cooperative federalism, 261–65, 303,
    334
Corporations, 4, 16–17, 29, 32–35,
    49, 66–67, 85, 96–97, 102,
    106–7, 109–12, 127, 129, 165,
    170–72, 191, 204, 206, 210–15,
    218, 220, 236–37, 239, 244, 302,
    326–27, 337–38, 346. *See also*
    Business Council on National
    Issues
Corrections (including jails), 74, 207,
    307, 347, 359–60
Council of Canadians, 209
Courts. *See* Judges; Judiciary;
    Supreme Court of Canada
Criminal law and Criminal Code, 74,
    86, 226, 236, 238, 346–47, 359
Crown, 8–9, 64, 67, 93, 229, 232–33,
    269, 273–74, 276, 317, 346–47
Crown corporations, 16–17, 85,
    98–99, 104, 121, 125, 196–98,
    273, 279, 295, 300, 303–5, 311
Crow Rate. *See* Freight rates
Cuba, 94–95, 98

Day, Stockwell, 129, 185–86, 193,
    199, 325, 358
Debt, deficits, and cutbacks, 32, 125,

197–98, 206, 264, 288, 305, 312,
    346
Defence. *See* Armed forces and
    defence
Deference to authority, 122–23, 125
Demands, 2–8, 16, 19, 22, 32, 87,
    104, 179, 270, 294, 302
Democracy, 118–20, 124–25, 233,
    244–45, 307, 310, 317, 339
Democracy Watch, 221
Democratic socialism, 195–96
Demonstrations. *See* Political protest
Depression, 182–83,188, 255
Deputy minister, 84, 211–12, 261,
    279, 288, 296–98, 302, 308, 311
Desmarais, Paul, 32, 138
Diefenbaker, John, and government,
    47, 94, 175, 183, 234, 263,
    280–81
Disabled, 78, 240, 301–2
Disallowance. *See* Reservation,
    disallowance, and declaratory
    power
Discrimination, 3, 66, 74, 77–79,
    84–85, 87, 214, 240–42, 356. *See
    also* Racism and racial tensions
Dismantling the state, 193, 198, 206
Dissolution of Parliament, 275, 321
Distinct society (Quebec), 48, 50,
    53–54, 56, 58, 60
Division of powers, 10–12, 53, 56,
    58, 208–9, 214, 230, 232,
    249–65, 273, 303, 343, 345, 352
Divorce, 326, 349–50
Douglas, T.C., 183
Duplessis, Maurice, 46, 147, 234
Durham Report, 42, 227

Egalitarianism and inequality, 30,
    123, 125, 195–98, 345–46
Election campaign, 131–32, 145,
    149–51, 161–64, 179, 236, 279
Elections (and electoral system), 119,
    155–76, 237–38, 324, 334–35
Election finance. *See* Party and
    election finance
Electoral behaviour. *See* Voters
Electricity, 20–22, 46, 68, 101, 109
Elite accommodation, 32, 231, 218,
    283
Emergency doctrine, 253–54
Employment and pay equity, 78–79,
    82, 84–85, 301–2. *See also*
    Affirmative action; Women
Energy. *See* Electricity; Petroleum
Environment, 3, 100–1, 110, 207–8,
    215
Equalization payments, 28–29, 123,
    231, 255, 258, 307
Estimates, 289, 299, 301–3, 308, 321,
    331–32
Ethics and Ethics Commissioner,
    218–19, 221, 280, 285

Ethnic origin and ethnicity, 50–51, 63, 74–79, 93, 121, 161, 175, 186, 190, 192, 194, 206, 208, 240, 283, 337, 356
European Union, 100, 107, 109
Evidence (admissibility of), 242, 246
Executive, 6, 9–11, 13, 242, 261–62, 269–89, 318, 325
Executive federalism, 261–62
Expenditure Management System, 213, 287
Extraterritoriality, 98

Farmers, 24, 34, 80, 107, 182, 188, 211
Federal controls. *See* Reservation, disallowance, and declaratory power
Federal Court of Canada, 209, 310, 347, 351–52, 354, 357
Federalism, 11–13, 43, 45, 194–95, 208, 230, 232, 249–65, 345–49, 355, 359
Federal–provincial relations, 46–47, 53–54, 56, 191, 261–63, 286, 288, 355, 359
Federal–provincial finance, 29, 46–47, 53–54, 56, 249–51, 254–61, 263–64, 288, 303
Feminism. *See* Women's movement
Filibuster, 327
Film, 103–6
Finance department, 211, 284–85, 287–89, 297, 299, 302, 308
First past the post, 160, 165
First World War, 44, 80, 92, 160–61, 182
Fishing and fishing rights, 20, 27, 68, 101, 107, 338
Focus groups, 148, 151–52
Foreign investment, 96–99, 334
Foreign Investment Review Agency (FIRA), 98–99, 109
Foreign policy, 8, 95, 276, 278, 280
Forestry. *See* Natural resources
France, 47, 226
Franchise, 66, 80, 119, 160–61, 188, 238
Francophonie, 52, 280
Free trade. *See* Canada–U.S. Free Trade; North American Free Trade Agreement
Free votes, 325, 332, 336
Freight rates, 24, 27
French Canada, 41–60, 181–82, 226, 252
French language. *See* Bilingualism; Minority language education rights; Quebec language legislation
Front de Libération du Québec (FLQ), 48, 134
Fundamental freedoms. *See* Charter of Rights and Freedoms

G7/G8, 108–9, 215, 280
Gay and lesbian issues, 86–87, 198, 207–8, 236, 241, 309
Gender, 63, 162, 186, 242, 244, 319. *See also* Women
General Agreement on Tariffs and Trade (GATT). *See* World Trade Organization
George, Dudley, 69–70
Gerrymandering, 156
Globalization, 8, 91, 99, 106–12, 131, 209, 215, 312
Globe and Mail, 138, 142, 145–46
Goods and Services Tax (GST), 129, 264, 325, 339
Government department, 211, 271, 277, 279, 281, 283–87, 295–303, 307–8, 311, 331, 347
Government advertising, information, and secrecy, 129–30, 145–47, 158, 212, 280, 284, 294, 309–10, 334. *See also* Access to Information Act; Information Commissioner
Governor general, 9, 47, 84, 93, 158, 229, 232–33, 271–76, 278–79, 320, 337, 348
Governor-in-Council, 229, 277. *See also* Cabinet; Privy Council
Gray, Herb, 281. *See also* Foreign investment
Great Britain, 42–43, 64, 75, 91–93, 96, 131, 187, 197–98, 226–28, 231, 233, 245, 274, 305, 324, 326, 335–36, 344
Gun control, 7, 123, 270–71, 273, 325

Harper, Elijah, 55, 72
Harris, Mike, 27, 35, 70, 85, 198–99
Health care, 3, 70, 72, 121, 123, 184, 196, 256–58, 265, 334, 338. *See also* Canada Health Act; Social programs
House of Commons, 8–10, 80–81, 143, 156–67, 167, 180, 213, 229–30, 252, 271–72, 275–76, 278–82, 308, 317–36, 355
committees, 213, 308, 321, 324–25, 327, 329–32, 335
Human rights codes and commissions, 77, 87, 231, 241–42, 306
Human Resources Development Canada (HRDC), 278, 296

Immigration, 22, 48, 53, 64–65, 74–79, 122, 175, 198, 238, 250, 306, 309, 333, 351
Income, 30–38, 84–85, 134. *See also* Class analysis; Egalitarianism and inequality
Indian Act, 64, 66, 70–71

Indians. *See* Aboriginal Canadians
Individualism, 26, 121, 195, 197–98, 244
Information Commissioner, 307, 310. *See also* Access to Information Act; Government advertising, information, and secrecy
Initiative, 335
Interest groups. *See* Pressure groups
International Monetary Fund and World Bank, 108
Internet, 142–43, 209, 313
Inuit. *See* Aboriginal Canadians
Ipperwash. *See* George, Dudley
Irving family, 31, 138–39
Issue-oriented groups, 207. *See also* Social programs
Issues, 5, 63, 66–71, 74, 80, 143, 145, 147, 149, 173–74, 180, 212, 270

James Bay Hydro-electric Project, 21, 68, 71
Japanese-Canadians, 78–79
Judges, 10, 74, 84, 161, 230, 244–45, 274, 276, 279, 300, 306, 343–59. *See also* Judiciary; Supreme Court of Canada
Judicial Committee of the Privy Council, 82, 93, 232, 253–54, 337, 348, 352
Judicial councils, 355, 357–58
Judicial discretion, interpretation, and review, 10, 232–35, 253–54, 271–73, 318, 343, 345
Judicial independence, 10, 240, 355–58
Judiciary, 6, 10, 49–51, 73–74, 87, 119, 161, 191, 214, 230, 232, 234, 240–41, 243–45, 252, 262–63, 269–73, 306, 309, 318, 343–59. *See also* Supreme Court of Canada; Judges

Keynesian economics, 263
King–Byng Dispute, 158, 275
King, Mackenzie, 45, 82, 182–83, 255, 275, 281, 285
Klein, Ralph, 198
Korean War, 94

Labour and labour legislation, 34–36, 86, 108, 205, 216, 243, 299
Landry, Bernard, 60
Language laws and rights, 7, 43, 47, 50–51, 241, 252. *See also* Bilingualism; Minority language education rights; Quebec language legislation
Laurier, Wilfrid, 44, 181–82, 281
Laws, 276–77, 346
Leaders' debate, 144–45, 163
Leaders' tour, 144, 162
Le Devoir, 145

Legal aid, 239, 345
Legislature(s), 6, 8, 11, 243, 245, 248, 261, 271–72, 294, 317–40. *See also* House of Commons; Parliament
Legitimacy, 5, 7, 57, 59, 122, 210, 271–72, 318
Lesage, Jean, 46
Lévesque, René, 49
Liberalism, 195–97
Liberal Party, 32, 151, 162–63, 167–73, 175–76, 181–85, 188–89, 192–99, 216, 220–21, 283, 325, 339
Lieutenant Governor, 230, 251, 300
Lobbying and lobbyists, 32, 151, 203–4, 213–14, 218–21, 297, 325

Macdonald, John A., 12–13, 24, 181, 232, 250, 254, 281
McDonough, Alexa, 83
Mackenzie, Alexander, 181, 281
McLachlin, Beverley, 84, 354, 356
McLaughlin, Audrey, 83
Macphail, Agnes, 80–81
Magazines, 103–4, 106, 108, 142
Majority government, 10, 165, 167, 213, 331, 334–35
Majority rule, 119–20
Mandate, 174
Manitoba, 22–23, 28–29, 43–44, 50–51, 55, 65, 72, 74, 172, 231, 319, 337
Manning, Preston, 60, 183, 185, 195, 199
Manufacturing, 20–22, 24, 96–97, 110
Maritime provinces. *See* Atlantic provinces
Marshall, Donald, 68, 74
Martin, Paul, 32, 199, 258, 297
Marx, Karl, 30–31, 34
Mass media, 4–5, 17, 32, 128, 137–47, 149–50, 162–63, 191–92, 207, 280, 284, 287, 297, 311, 322–23, 327–28, 338. *See also* Newspapers; Television and radio
Meech Lake Accord, 52–55, 57, 71–72, 184–85, 339–40, 355
Members of Parliament (MPs), 10, 213–14, 271, 302, 309, 317–20, 323, 325–26, 328–29, 332–35, 337. *See also* House of Commons; Parliament
Memorandum to Cabinet, 271–72, 286–89
Merit system, 298–300
Métis, 43, 64–65. *See also* Aboriginal Canadians
Mexico, 110–11
Middle class, 30–31, 33–34, 175, 188
Mining. *See* Natural resources

Ministerial responsibility, 277, 284, 296, 313
Ministers, 212–13, 242, 261–62, 270–71, 277–79, 284–88, 294, 296–98, 302, 304, 307–9, 320–22, 324, 326–28, 331, 333, 337, 355, 358. *See also* Cabinet
Minority government, 167, 170, 183, 334–35
Minority language education rights, 50, 208, 214, 234, 241, 244
Minority rights, 120, 151, 244. *See also specific minorities*
Minor parties, 165, 189–90
Missiles, 94–95, 244
Monarchy. *See* Crown
Money bills, 9, 229–30, 276, 326, 332, 336
Morgentaler, Henry, 86, 238
Mulroney, Brian, and government, 23, 26, 32, 52–53, 55, 57, 60, 78–79, 83, 86, 95, 98–99, 101, 105, 109–10, 129, 140, 172, 184–85, 197, 199, 208, 217–18, 257, 263–64, 279, 281–83, 297, 300, 304–5, 311, 338–40, 354
Multiculturalism, 74, 77–79, 122, 242
Multinational corporations, 96–98, 102, 104, 107–8, 111–12, 215. *See also* Corporations
Municipalities, 13, 242, 249, 358–59

National Action Committee on the Status of Women (NAC), 83, 208, 216–17
National Citizens' Coalition, 172–73, 215
National Council of Welfare, 37–38, 307
National Energy Board, 99, 101, 197, 306
National Energy Program (NEP), 23, 25, 99, 101, 109, 184, 263
National Parole Board, 306, 359–60
National Policy (1879), 24, 96
National Post, 138, 145–46
National symbols, 93, 118, 124, 184, 235, 273, 275, 326, 334
NATO and NORAD, 94
Natural resources, 20–23, 97, 99, 211, 230, 232, 251, 253–54, 259, 263
New Brunswick, 20–21, 26–29, 31, 50–51, 55, 138–39, 165, 226–30, 241, 313, 319, 337
New Democratic Party (NDP), 36, 83, 131, 151–52, 162, 165, 167, 170, 176, 183, 186, 188–89, 191–99, 206, 215–16, 263
New Public Management, 312–13
Newfoundland and Labrador, 20–21, 28–29, 35, 55, 130, 263, 319, 333, 337, 358

News management, 145–47. *See also* Government advertising, information, and secrecy
Newspapers, 99, 106, 128, 131, 138–39, 142–46, 150. *See also* Mass media; *specific newspapers*
Nisga'a treaty, 67–68, 73
Nominations, 81, 83, 132, 159, 164, 191–92. *See also* Candidates
Nonconfidence motion, 9, 94, 158, 324, 335
North, 22, 54, 65, 67, 73, 101, 130, 156–57, 231, 242, 319, 337
North American Free Trade Agreement (NAFTA), 110–11. *See also* Canada–U.S. Free Trade
Northwest Territories. *See* North
Notwithstanding clause. *See* Charter of Rights and Freedoms
Nova Scotia, 20–21, 26–29, 74, 226–30, 319, 337
Nunavut, 73. *See also* North

Oakes test, 240, 243
Official Opposition, 167, 191, 274, 318, 320–21, 327, 329, 331, 333–34
Oka standoff, 69, 72, 134, 215
Ontario, 17, 21, 23, 27–28, 44–45, 50–51, 64, 70, 82, 85, 87, 97, 169, 175, 186, 195, 198–99, 226, 228–30, 236, 240, 252, 283, 319, 336–37, 353–55, 357–58
Order in Council, 230–31, 276, 357
Organization of Petroleum Exporting Countries (OPEC), 23, 108

Parizeau, Jacques, 58, 60
Parliament, 8–10, 43, 47, 213, 231, 252, 269, 271, 274, 276, 282, 294, 296, 303–4, 308, 311, 317–40, 357. *See also* House of Commons; Legislature(s); Senate
Parliamentary Secretary, 323–24
Parliamentary sovereignty (supremacy), 233, 318
Parliamentary system. *See* Westminster model
Parliamentary timetable, 320–23
Parti Québécois, 49–50, 58, 184, 189, 192, 198–99, 243
Partisanship and nonpartisanship, 156–57, 179, 215, 283, 287–88, 297–300, 306, 323, 332, 335, 337–38, 354–65. *See also* Appointments, contracts, and grants; Party discipline
Party and election finance, 32, 132, 170–73, 179, 191, 334
Party caucus, 191, 214, 272, 279, 323–26
Party discipline, 10–11, 181, 280, 323–25, 329, 332, 335. *See also*

Partisanship and nonpartisanship
Party identification, 131, 157,
173–74, 189, 320
Party ideology, 131, 187–90, 195–99
Party whips, 324, 329
Peace, order, good government, 120,
122, 253
Peacekeeping, 95, 107, 124
Pearson, Lester, 47, 94, 123, 170, 183,
256, 281, 283, 285, 334–35, 337
Peers, 127–28
Péladeau family (including
Quebecor), 138, 140, 142
Pensions, 35, 197, 207, 250, 253,
333–34
Petro-Canada, 98, 101, 305
Petroleum, 21–23, 27, 101, 109, 183,
211
Pharmaceuticals, 27, 108, 215, 220
Pipelines, 17, 101, 183
Police, 2, 5, 48, 69, 74, 123, 239,
242, 246, 307, 310, 347, 358–59.
See also Royal Canadian
Mounted Police
Policy communities, 210–11
Policymaking process, 191, 218, 267,
268, 269–73, 281, 294, 318,
344–45
Political communication, 17–18,
133–34, 137–52
Political culture, 118–26, 173, 233,
245
Political equality, 119, 157
Political freedom, 119. *See also*
Charter of Rights and Freedoms
Political participation, 36–37,
130–34, 145, 216
Political parties, 4, 128–29, 143–45,
149–50, 160–76, 179–99, 204,
208, 261, 274, 280, 323–24, 337
advertising, 144–45, 162–63,
171, 187
conventions, 144, 191–94
headquarters, 161–63
leaders and leadership, 83, 145,
159, 162–63, 173–74, 180,
187, 190–94, 278–79, 320,
324, 333
membership, 132–33, 191–92
platform, 174, 180, 187 (*see*
also Red Book)
policy-making, 168, 193–94
structures, 191–95
support, 175–76 (*see also*
Voters)
systems, 181–82, 185–90
See also specific parties
Political patronage. *See*
Appointments, contracts, and
grants; Partisanship and
nonpartisanship
Political protest, 33, 67, 111, 133–34,
144, 207, 215. *See also* Violence

Political socialization, 125–30, 174
Politicians, 32, 57, 70–71, 81, 86–87,
118, 144–47, 156, 180, 190, 208,
212, 215, 233, 244, 246, 294,
296, 300, 302, 323, 359
Poor and poverty, 36–38, 65–66, 86,
131, 176, 208, 245, 300, 338
Popular sovereignty, 118–19
Popular vote, 165–70
Population, 17–18, 157
Pornography, 3, 86, 236, 244
Post-secondary education, 2–3, 37,
255–58, 264, 298–99, 319
Prairies, 22–25, 64–65. *See also* West
Premiers, 50, 53, 56–58, 72, 84, 131,
262, 264, 302, 337. *See also*
Provinces; *individual premiers*
Prerogative powers, 274
Press gallery, 143, 323
Pressure groups, 4, 32, 37–38, 67, 83,
129, 133, 151, 187, 190, 203–18,
220, 271–72, 294, 297, 302–3,
325, 327, 331, 353
Primary industry. *See* Natural
resources
Prime minister(s), 6, 9–10, 157–58,
191, 229, 232, 262, 269–70,
272–89, 293, 295–96, 320, 326,
328, 331, 333–34, 337, 355. *See*
also individual prime ministers
Prime Minister's Office (PMO), 147,
220, 285, 287, 300, 310, 331
Prince Edward Island, 28–29, 130,
226–28, 231, 283, 313, 319, 337
Privatization, private sector, 2, 17,
35, 46, 49, 121, 125, 197–98,
242, 305, 311–13, 339
Privy Council, 229, 276
Privy Council Office (PCO),
285–89, 299, 302, 308
Program Review, 312
Progressive Conservative Party, 32,
43–44, 151, 163, 167–68,
170–72, 175–76, 181–85,
188–89, 192–99, 216, 283, 325,
333–34, 339
Progressive Party, 24, 182, 275
Property and civil rights, 252–54, 346
Proportional representation, 169, 307
Prostitution, 86, 236, 244
Provinces, 10–13, 18–30, 51, 53,
55–56, 58, 67–68, 72, 74, 80, 99,
101, 118, 122, 125–26, 156–57,
209, 228, 230, 232, 235, 242,
249–65, 271–72, 280, 282–83,
294, 297, 303, 312, 326, 336–37,
339–40, 346–48, 350, 352–54,
357–59. *See also individual*
provinces
Public opinion and public opinion
polls, 137, 147–52, 157, 161,
163, 187, 189, 191, 217, 233,
236, 327

Public sector, 2, 35, 46, 121, 242,
305, 312–13. *See also*
Dismantling the state
Public Service Alliance of Canada,
35
Public Service Commission,
299–300, 308
Publishing, 99, 103–4

Quebec, 12, 17, 19, 21, 25, 27–30,
35, 37, 42–60, 68–69, 81, 87,
122, 125, 138, 147, 167–69, 172,
175–76, 184–86, 195, 226,
228–30, 234–35, 243, 252,
255–56, 263, 283, 319, 336–37,
344, 347, 352–53, 358
Quebec language legislation, 7, 49,
52, 108, 236, 241, 243–44
Quebec nationalism, 21, 45–46, 49,
145, 184, 263
Quebec separatism, 45, 48–50, 147,
168, 199
Queen. *See* Crown
Question Period, 143, 279, 296, 308,
318, 321–23, 329, 334
Quiet Revolution (Quebec), 46–47,
263

Racism and racial tensions, 64–67,
69–70, 73–76, 78–79, 162. *See*
also Discrimination
Rae, Bob, 56–57, 83
Railways, 17, 24, 75, 197, 228, 305
Recall, 125, 335
Red Book, 162, 175, 193, 325
Red Tories, 197–98
Redistribution (of seats), 156–57,
238, 244
Reference cases, 350, 352
Referendums, 45, 50, 57–59, 119,
125, 152, 199, 335
Reform Party, 26, 79, 146, 163–63,
165, 167, 185, 189, 193–96,
198–99, 244, 340. *See also*
Canadian Alliance
Regional economic disparities and
development programs, 28–30
Regional ministers, 282–83, 285
Regions and regionalism, 15, 18,
23–30, 186, 190, 254, 283, 300,
326, 336, 339, 356
Regulation and deregulation, 16–17,
32–33, 109, 111, 125, 196–98,
209, 212, 306, 311
Regulations, 211–12, 219–20, 271,
277, 294, 306, 309, 331–32, 338
Regulatory tribunals, 16–17, 98, 105,
140, 305–6, 310, 347, 351
Religion, 30, 129, 175–76, 206, 226,
235–36, 242, 244, 252, 283
Representation by population, 12,
156–57, 252, 319, 336
Representative bureaucracy, 300–301

Representative democracy, 8, 119, 124–25, 199. *See also* Westminster model

Research and development (R & D), 98

Reservation, disallowance, and declaratory power, 57, 251, 260

Reserves (Indian), 64–65, 67

Responsible government, 9, 227, 232, 324, 335

Returning officer, 158–59

Riel, Louis, 43–44, 65, 133, 181

Rogers, Ted, 32, 142

Roman Catholic Church in Quebec, 42, 46, 122, 129, 226

Royal Canadian Mounted Police (RCMP), 84, 123, 197, 221, 274, 307, 358–59

Royal commissions, 85–86, 215, 276, 278, 307, 338
  Aboriginal peoples, 72–73
  bilingualism and biculturalism, 47, 77
  dominion–provincial relations, 255
  electoral reform and party finance, 150, 172–73, 307
  newspapers, 139
  status of women, 83

Royal Proclamation of 1763, 64, 70, 226, 242

Rule of Law, 233

Safe seats, 162, 320

St. Laurent, Louis, 183, 281, 285, 287

Same-sex rights, 87, 241, 244

Saskatchewan, 22–23, 28–29, 43, 65, 183, 196, 198, 231, 243, 263, 319, 337

Sauvé, Jeanne, 84

Scandal and corruption, 170, 181, 275. *See also* Conflicts of interest

Schools, 44–45, 47, 49–51, 66, 73, 126–27, 236, 241–42, 252

Second World War, 45, 78, 93, 183, 261, 263, 288

Senate, 8, 10, 12, 53–54, 56–57, 81–82, 86, 156, 170, 214, 226, 229, 252, 271–72, 274, 276, 279, 281–82, 300, 317–18, 326–27, 331, 335–40

Service sector, 20

Shared-cost programs, 54–56, 255–58, 261

Social Credit Party, 25, 147, 165, 183

Social programs, 33, 37, 54, 70, 72, 86, 108, 121, 123, 125, 183–84, 188, 196–98, 255–58, 265, 325

Social Union Framework Agreement, 264

Softwood lumber, 100, 109–10

Sovereignty, 8, 45, 58, 108, 125

Sovereignty-association, 50, 58

Speaker of the House, 84, 129, 157, 321, 328, 332

Special Operating Agencies, 312

Speech from the Throne, 274, 276, 288, 320

Spending power, 54–55, 256–60

Spin doctors, 146–47, 163

Stanfield, Robert, 197

Staples Theory, 20

Statute of Westminster, 93, 231

Strikes, 34–35, 133, 237, 244

Summit of the Americas, 33, 108, 111, 215

Supreme Court of Canada, 51–54, 56, 59, 69, 82, 84, 150, 173, 230–31, 235–46, 279, 309, 350–58. *See also* Judges; Judiciary

Tariffs, 23–24, 27, 92, 96, 100, 109, 228

Task Force on Canadian Unity, 19

Taxation, 3, 30–34, 37, 99, 106, 121, 171–72, 196, 206, 250–51, 254–55, 257, 265, 288, 308, 313, 320

Taxation agreements (federal–provincial), 46–47, 255, 259, 261

Telesat and Teleglobe, 17, 305

Television and radio, 99, 102–6, 128, 131, 139–44, 162–63, 187, 193, 262, 280, 322–23. *See also* Mass media

Terrorism, 8, 48, 91, 95, 109

Third-party advertising, 172–73, 215, 236

Thomson, Ken, 31, 138

Tobacco, 3, 6, 236–37, 244, 270–71, 273, 326

Toronto Star, 138, 146

Trade, 23–24, 99–100, 107–12, 228, 254. *See also* Canada–U.S. Free Trade

Transportation, 16–17, 19, 24, 306. *See also* Air Canada, airlines, and airports; Railways

Treasury Board and Treasury Board Secretariat, 285, 288–89, 299, 302, 308

Treaties, 64–65, 67–69, 92, 230, 242, 250, 254, 276

Trudeau, Pierre, and government, 23–24, 47–51, 53, 60, 66, 94–95, 139, 147, 184, 208, 212, 234–35, 238, 241, 263, 281–83, 334, 354

Tupper, Charles, 274, 281

Turner, John, 144, 281, 339

Unemployment and employment insurance, 27–28, 35–36, 79, 85, 230, 238, 253, 255, 333, 338

Union Government, 44, 182

Union Nationale. *See* Duplessis, Maurice

Unions, 34–36, 86, 102, 165, 170, 188, 191, 194, 205–6, 218, 237, 245

United Empire Loyalists, 42, 121, 197–98, 226

United Farmers. *See* Progressive Party

United Nations and League of Nations, 92, 94–95, 107–8, 124, 280

United States, 11–13, 17, 21, 42, 91–92, 94–112, 120–25, 140–41, 158, 197–99, 220, 226, 228, 234, 242, 244–45, 276, 280, 325

Upper class (including economic elite), 30–33, 45, 60, 99, 175, 188

Values, Canadian, 56, 79, 102, 118–25, 130, 217, 233

Violence, 33–34, 44, 48, 66, 68, 86, 111, 124, 133–34, 144, 215, 227, 236, 238. *See also* Political protest

Visible minorities, 75–79, 162, 301–2

Voter turnout, 37, 130

Voters, 128, 130, 149, 163, 173–76, 180–81, 319, 327–28, 333–34

Voters' list, 159

Wage and price controls, 197

War Measures Act and Emergencies Act, 48, 231, 234

Wells, Clyde, 55

West, 22–26, 57, 159, 167–69, 175–76, 182–86, 199, 228, 263, 283, 336, 353

Western alienation, 25–27, 185, 263

Westminster model, 9–10, 210, 318

White Paper on Indians, 66, 70

Wilson, Bertha, 84

Wilson, Michael, 207, 213

Women, 35, 37, 53, 63–64, 71, 78, 80–87, 108, 123, 161–62, 186, 194, 207–8, 217, 238, 242, 283, 301–2, 320, 337, 356

Women's movement, 80, 82–83, 85, 242

Working class, 30–31, 34–36, 131, 176, 187–90, 300, 320, 356

World Trade Organization (WTO), 106, 108, 215

Yukon. *See* North